# Contributions to Economics

The series *Contributions to Economics* provides an outlet for innovative research in all areas of economics. Books published in the series are primarily monographs and multiple author works that present new research results on a clearly defined topic, but contributed volumes and conference proceedings are also considered. All books are published in print and ebook and disseminated and promoted globally. The series and the volumes published in it are indexed by Scopus and ISI (selected volumes).

More information about this series at https://link.springer.com/bookseries/1262

Goran Karanovic · Persefoni Polychronidou · Anastasios Karasavvoglou
Editors

# The Changing Financial Landscape

## Financial Performance Analysis of Real and Banking Sectors in Europe

Springer

*Editors*
Goran Karanovic
Faculty of Tourism and Hospitality Management
University of Rijeka
Opatija, Croatia

Persefoni Polychronidou
Department of Economics
International Hellenic University
Serres, Greece

Anastasios Karasavvoglou
Department of Accounting and Finance
International Hellenic University
Kavala, Greece

ISSN 1431-1933 ISSN 2197-7178 (electronic)
Contributions to Economics
ISBN 978-3-030-82777-9 ISBN 978-3-030-82778-6 (eBook)
https://doi.org/10.1007/978-3-030-82778-6



This Springer imprint is published by the registered company Springer Nature Switzerland AG
The registered company address is: Gewerbestrasse 11, 6330 Cham, Switzerland

# Preface

This volume is the outcome of the 12th International Conference "The Economies of the Balkan and Eastern European Countries" (EBEEC)—Opatija, Croatia, 29–31 May 2020 organised by the International Hellenic University, Department for Finance and Accounting and University of Rijeka, Faculty of Tourism and Hospitality Management. Due to the epidemic situation with SARS-CoV-2 and numerous restrictions regarding travelling, the conference was held online for the first time. There were 101 manuscripts proposed of which 95 were presented online using Zoom platform. The Board of Editors arranged a meticulous selection process for the submissions based on their quality and originality. In the end, 14 manuscripts were selected to be published as part of Springer volume (book) "Contributions to Economics". The entire manuscript selection process was managed by the Board of Editors in compliance with the highest standards and best practice guidelines on publishing ethics, paying special attention to issues regarding plagiarism, peer review, objectivity, funding, privacy and conflict of interest.

The Easychair system was used for both the manuscript submission and the peer review process. The system ensures the confidentiality and the transparency of all submission and evaluation procedures. Moreover, authors were asked after the conference to submit camera-ready versions of their papers that have been uploaded in the same Easychair system. All of the uploaded papers were included in the blind peer review process, and reviewers prepared their evaluation reports online. The evaluation was formed of an overall assessment of the paper, reviewer's recommendations for paper improvement and a recommended decision, on a scale from "strong reject" to "strong accept" (specifically, reviewers had to choose the following decisions: reject, weak reject, borderline paper, weak accept, accept, strong accept). The overall evaluation provided a detailed review of the paper, including the reasoning behind the scores. Reviewers were required to provide both a score and a review text, as well as their level of expertise regarding the topic of the paper being reviewed: expert, high, average, low and non-expert. All reviewers had at least an average level of expertise in the reviewed fields.

The number of papers evaluated with "weak reject" or "strong reject" are very small. The remaining papers were evaluated with "accept" and "strong accept". The latter reviews were sent to the authors; the final decision of paper acceptance of a paper being taken only after all concerns raised by reviewers was considered by authors. In the end, the authors were asked by the volume's editors to apply to their manuscripts Springer editorial standards to be found at the following links:

https://www.springer.com/cda/content/document/cda_downloaddocument/manuscript-guidelines-1.0.pdf and
https://www.springer.com/cda/content/document/cda_downloaddocument/Manuscript+Key+Style+Points?SGWID=0-0-45-1410203-p175157688

We hope that the above description meets your expectations.

*Editors*

Opatija, Croatia — Goran Karanovic
Serres, Greece — Persefoni Polychronidou
Kavala, Greece — Anastasios Karasavvoglou

# Contents

# Introduction

**Goran Karanovic, Persefoni Polychronidou, and Anastasios Karasavvoglou**

Due to endogenous and exogenous forces, the only constant in the complex world of business and finance is continuous change and development. New ideas, novelty in products, technology development, new regulations, changes in environment, behaviour changes and other novelties in everyday life alter the economy on daily basis. Perpetual growth and evolvement of all participants has been modelling business and finance sector to today's level of the systems. The few past decades' have been highly turbulent, and it could be expressed by two phenomena's; first one is crisis, and other one is changing economic environment due to the digital transformation. Business performance analysis in these day is more complex and demanding than ever before. Risk management and performance analysis because of pace of changes require new knowledge's and implementations of new economics models. Global-level changes, tensions and issues like political, health, environmental, technological are influencing shift of paradigms in world economy. Europe is not an island, and changes are influencing to its financial landscape. Some changes are endogenous, like Brexit, and some are exogenous like "America First" politics, SARS-COV-2, etc. Financial landscape of the Europe is inevitable changing. All these changes are unquestionably being changing financial landscape of the Europe and equally real and banking sectors affected.

This volume encompasses manuscripts with focus on assessments of the financial performance analysis of the real and the banking sectors in Europe, with the particulate interest to the Central and Southeastern European countries. The original perspective of the authors, researchers and practitioners, on the issue and utilised

G. Karanovic (✉)
Faculty of Tourism and Hospitality Management, University of Rijeka, Opatija, Croatia

P. Polychronidou
Department of Economics, International Hellenic University, Serres, Greece

A. Karasavvoglou
Department of Accounting and Finance, International Hellenic University, Kavala, Greece



G. Karanovic et al. (eds.), *The Changing Financial Landscape*, Contributions to Economics, https://doi.org/10.1007/978-3-030-82778-6_15

complex quantities and qualitative models, delivers firm ground for quality scientific conclusions and recommendations for further discussions. The majority of the researchers that this volume gathers have affiliation of higher education and research institutions from Central and Southeastern Europe.

The international conference "**Economies of the Balkan and Eastern European Countries** (EBEEC)", through its twelve previous editions, has become a recognised forum where the knowledge, and experiences gained by academics specialized in economics and business in the region of Central and Southeastern Europe are exchanged, debated and validated. Besides that, the results of the EBEEC conference are numerous publications disseminated to the scientific public and practitioners all over the world. In this effort, substantial assistance and contribution comes from renowned publishers such as Springer.

The 12th International conference "**Economies of the Balkan and Eastern European Countries**" was organised jointly in Opatija, Croatia, by the International Hellenic University, Department of Accounting and Finance and University of Rijeka, Faculty of Tourism and Hospitality Management, in 29–31 May 2020. The aim of the conference was to gather scientists and practitioners' that will present academic papers and to exchange theoretical and empirical results on contemporary issues in economy with specific focus in real and banking sectors in Central and Southeastern European countries. Due to the epidemic situation with SARS-CoV-2 and numerous restrictions regarding travelling, the conference was held for the first time online. The conference brought together more than 101 manuscripts and by more than 150 authors from 20 countries from Europe and all over the world. A broad range of issues—Finance and Banking; Sustainable Tourism Development; International Political Economy; Macroeconomic and Economic Policy; Management and Marketing; Knowledge Economics; Business Information Systems; Entrepreneurship; Labour Markets; Corporate Governance and Corporate Performance; Regional Integration with special reference to the EU, etc.—have been discussed at the conference and in the resulting published manuscripts.

This volume as one of the publications resulting from the **12th International Conference "Economies of the Balkan and Eastern European Countries" (EBEEC)—Opatija, Croatia, May 2020** has goal to present to the worldwide audience new and original research and conclusions in a specific field of financial performance analysis of real and banking sector in Europe. The volume includes 14 selected manuscripts based on their quality and originality from the field of economy real and banking sectors, arranged and presented at 12th EBEEC conference in Opatija, Croatia. The entire manuscript selection process was managed by the Board of Editors in compliance with the highest standards and best practice guidelines on publishing ethics, paying special attention to issues regarding plagiarism, peer review, objectivity, funding, privacy, and conflict of interest. All selected manuscripts have gone through the peer review process and carefully edited are certainly making a significant contribution to the broader field of economy. Research ideas and applied quantitative methods indicate that scientists emerging from Central and Southeastern Europe are developing new worthy of attention knowledge' and conclusions in this field. This is result of changing nature of the economy thus in Central and Southeastern European countries and merits attention increase of the scientific quality work. The manuscript included in this volume covers a wide range of financial performance analysis of real and banking sectors. Selected papers are independent and do not constitute joint research their appearance in the volume is aimed to present analogues topics in the field of economy and finance and to attract the attention of scientific public and also practitioners. The manuscripts in this volume are presented in two parts, as follows:

Part I—Financial Development and Performance of the Real Sector
Part II—Evolvement of the Bank Sector

## 1 Part I—Financial Development and Performance of the Real Sector

The book opens with the paper written by **Chris Grose** (International Hellenic University, Greece), **Maria Argyropoulou** (International Hellenic University, Greece), **Dimitrios Koufopoulos** (University of London, UK), **Dionisia Tzavara** (University of Liverpool and Laureate online Education, UK), **Maria Efraimidou** (International Hellenic University, Greece) and **Stamatia Theodorakoglou** (International Hellenic University, Greece) who investigate the link between gender diversity in the board and firm financial performance by focusing on the non-financial firms listed on the main market in UK. The importance of effective corporate governance is an ever-important topic, but in the last few decades, the questions of the board of directors' structure have emerged as hot topic. Despite the advances achieved, the female representation in boards remains far from the desired levels, especially in the countries with non-mandatory gender quotas. Therefore, the main goal of this paper was to investigate the impact of gender diversity in corporate boards to the financial performance. The authors used the panel data analysis to examine the relationship between female boardroom participation, measured by several variables and firm value (measured by a proxy for Tobin's Q). The authors findings demonstrate that the presence of women on the board of directors does not affect firm value. However, the diversity of the board (measured by the percentage of women and by the Blau and Shannon indexes) has a positive impact on firm value. Additionally, results indicated that firm value has no influence on women's presence and on gender diversity.

The second paper of the volume, authored by **Valerija Botrić** (The Institute of Economics, Croatia) aims to empirically assess the role of financial constraints for exporting propensity of Croatian firms. The specific contribution of this paper displays in the examination of the role of financial crisis, by analysing separately period before the crisis (1999–2007) and after the crisis (2008–2017), thereby acknowledging the effects of the changes on the global and local financial markets. Considering fact that Croatian Economy is highly dependable on the tourism and its export. In the paper, the author has separately performed an empirical analysis for the manufacturing and service sector, the latter specifically entailing tourism and ICT.

Results did not indicate that there are any systematic differences between pre- and post-crisis financial constraints' effect. The authors argue that, in the case of manufacturing sector, leverage indicator is systematically significant in the period since the crisis for all firm sizes which suggests that previous indebtness of the firms in manufacturing sector creates important obstacle for active participation in international market. For firms in the service sector, significant obstacles have been found only for micro-firms, who probably due to their size are also having difficulties in finding adequate sources of financing in general, not just related to enhance their export endeavours. The author implies, Croatian underdeveloped financial systems is overly dependent on the banks and that relative unwillingness of the banking sector to provide additional finances could contribute to the financial constraint impediment to exporting.

The next paper, prepared by **Georgiana Vrinceanu** (The Bucharest University of Economic Studies, Romaina), **Alexandra Horobet** (The Bucharest University of Economic Studies, Romaina), **Consuela Popescu** (The Bucharest University of Economic Studies, Romaina) and **Lucian Belascu** ("Lucian Blaga" University of Sibiu, Romaina), studies relationship of financial industry (banks, investment funds, insurance companies and stock exchange) to the oil price volatility. The finding brought by this paper may have significant implications for political and economic decisions as shocks of either sign affecting a market can be transmitted quickly to other markets, a phenomenon called contagion. The authors have analysed 43 listed financial companies on stock exchanges in seven Central and Eastern European countries countries—Bulgaria, Croatia, Czech Republic, Hungary, Poland, Romania and Slovenia—and daily Brent oil price changes during the period from 18.01.2010 to 30.12.2019. The two-stage GARCH (1,1) model is used to explore the relationship between stock and oil prices. Results have indicated that the relationship between stock prices and oil price volatility is significant in the CEE region. In that light, the authors summarise that the financial industry has the fundamental role of transmitter of economic shocks towards the real economy.

The Initial Public Offering (IPO) and the influence on the financial soundness of the company in short-, medium- and long-term period is the topic of the manuscript prepared by **Dominika Kordela** (The University of Szczecin, Poland). The author has investigated multilateral trading facilities (MTF) at the Warsaw Stock Exchange the NewConnect as the source of the increase in equity for young and innovative firms, which have very limited earnings and low credibility. In Poland, companies listed on alternative market differ from companies from main markets; essentially, they have much lower equity value, much lower capitalisation, and lower assets value, shorter business history. The author has analysed financial soundness of the IPOs carried at the NewConnect at the year of offering, first, fifth and tenth years. As the general result of this study, the authors suggest that it cannot be stated as well that IPO improves liquidity and performance of the company. In spite of the fact that in majority of studied cases liquidity was on the safe level (even excess liquidity occurred), performance did not improve.

The following paper arranged by **Laurențiu Droj** (University of Oradea, Faculty of Economic Sciences, Romania), **Olimpia I. Ban** (University of Oradea, Faculty of

Economic Sciences, Romania) and **Gabriela Droj** (University of Oradea, Faculty of Economic Sciences, Romania) explores financial performance of the tourism and hospitality companies in five Central and Eastern European counties. The issue of firm performance is one of the most popular concepts and most important part of business process. Due to highly idiosyncratic nature of tourism, issues are being raised on measuring performance in tourism. The performance in the tourism has gone beyond plain financial indicators and has taken into account relationship to the carbon reduction; green practices, consumer satisfaction, etc. The authors have used IMIS database and chosen 15 companies from five Central and Eastern European countries—Slovenia, Croatia, Hungary, Romania and Serbia. They have investigated financial performance in the five-year period 2014–2018, and for that, they have implemented and tested composite index PERF. The results suggested the differences in financial performance and the specifics of the differences, reflected in the values of the financial indicators, specific for each country. The PERF composite indicator provided a particularly attention-grabbing overview of the private tourism sector from all the five private countries analysed.

Authors **Fatbardha Morina**, **Uğur Ergün** and **Chrysanthi Balomenou** (all from Department of Banking and Finance, Epoka University, Albania) examine the impact of renewable energy policies and financial development on $CO_2$ emissions and economic growth. Last few decades, the importance of environmental protection as well as significance of the renewable energy has become widely accepted from scientists, policymakers to the common people. Efforts to reduce $CO_2$ emissions are widely accepted on the world level. To examine link between impact of renewable energy policies and financial development on $CO_2$ emissions and economic growth, the authors have done study in which they have examined state in EU countries for period 2000–2017. The authors have employed panel VAR model. The finding of this study brings new perspective on incentives for renewable energy and their impact to the economic growth as well as productivity.

The first part of the volume closes with the paper written by **Agnieszka Kwarcińska** (University of Szczecin, Institute of Management, Department of Human Capital Management, Poland) who has analysed corporate social responsibility and perception towards the benefit of the company. Corporate social responsibility can be observed through the prism of the responsibility towards the employees. The author of this study investigated human resource initiatives for employees on 300 Polish companies and employers' perception of these incentives towards the company benefit. Mutual interactions of employers and employees repeatedly decide about the reciprocal respect, engagement, loyalty and shape of cooperation as well as the future of the organisation. This awareness probably induces employers to take a number of diverse initiatives that constitute the carriers of the dual nature of benefits, both for employers and for employees. Employee involvement should be integrated into the process or the human resource management strategy. The funding of this study points towards that companies focus on preparation for work including initial training and support from experienced colleagues, as well as professional development through participation in training. Additionally, from the employers' perspective and benefit to company, all initiatives towards employees have had been expressed as significant.

## 2 Part II—Evolvement of the Bank Sector

The second part of the volume, dedicated to evolvement of the bank sector, opens with the paper of **Anita Peša**, **Martina Maté** and **Marijana Jerić** (all from University of Zadar, Department of Economics, Croatia). The authors have investigated efficiency of the banking industry in the European Union using traditional and DEA approach for the period 2016–2018. Banks have crucial role in the entrepreneurship development, and the effective banking sector is requirement for economic growth. Measuring banks efficiency is trending topic; however, this study brings new perspectives and findings on European bank industry because authors have compared and calculated share of total banking sector assets in country's GDP. Besides DEA approach, the authors have introduced Malmquist index in calculation to express the change in efficiency in the observed period. DEA and Malmquist index results show improvement of efficiency in countries as Italy, Portugal, Spain and France. Decrease in efficiency, compared with other sectors, is shown in Croatia, Cyprus and Greece. Although significant indicator for these countries, these results are not significant for overall EU-28 banking sector due to amount of total banking assets of these countries.

**Ana Kundid Novokmet** (Faculty of Economics, Business and Tourism, University of Split, Croatia) has exercised dynamic panel data analysis of South-Eastern European (SEE) banks over 10-year period, and this paper explores risk-taking implications of changes in capital buffers. This papers suggest new and original empirical analysis estimations of capital buffers' implications on the banks' risk exposure for South-Eastern European (SEE) economies in the post-transitional era. This study is novel and contributes and advances the literature on capital buffers because it moves forward from the empirical work obtained mainly for developed countries. Before this analysis, this topic had an issue because—how do banks react to changes in capital buffers—remained partly an empirical issue with modest proof of applicability of the capital buffer theory for the commercial banks' behaviour in the SEE countries. The author has investigated pre-Basel III period (2000–2010) and has used annual data set for active commercial banks from Croatia, Bosnia and Herzegovina, Serbia, Macedonia, Romania, Bulgaria, Albania and Greece. The author concludes that the capital buffer theory is confirmed as banks adjust risk-taking behaviour in dependence with their capital buffers. Also, it is highlighted capital buffers add to bank's asset riskiness they reduce its overall riskiness and are irrelevant for an increase in the credit price.

The next paper, written by **Grazia Dicuonzo**, **Francesca Donofrio**, **Grazia Onorato** (all from Department of Economics, Management and Business Law, University of Bari, Italy) and **Mario Turco** (Department of Economic Sciences, University of Salento, Italy), aims to imply enterprise risk management for the main European banking groups, designated by the European Banking Authority. For this purpose, the authors have used global systemically important institutions (G-SIIs) and chosen 30 banks. The authors have built a quantitative score to summarise the banks' level of performance integrating ERM in their systems, and they have named it—bank's ERM index. Findings have several important implications for both practitioners and scholars. The research model represents an analysis tool to understand how and if banks integrate the ERM framework in their corporate and decision-making processes. In this way, investors and practitioners could make their decisions and assessments more consciously. Second, the research model also assumes an important internal functionality because it can be adopted by banks as a diagnostic tool to perform a self-assessment process.

A multinational team of authors—**Chris Grose** (International Hellenic University, Greece), **Aglaia Kanella**, (International Hellenic University, Greece), **Theodoros Kargidis** (International Hellenic University, Greece), **Mihaela Mocanu** (Bucharest University of Economic Studies, Romania) and **Theodoros Spyridis** (Customs Officer Independent Authority for Public Revenue, Greece) analyses bank profitability in a sample of UK commercial banks during the period 2007–2018. Due to the importance of the banking sector and spillover effect that has on the economy, this manuscript has significant significance. Position of the banks and banking sector as core force that has immense impact to the overall economy has emerged in the global financial crisis. The authors have examined the determinants of bank's profitability and the analysis they performed with the use of variables Return on Average Assets (ROAA), Return on Average Equity (ROAE) and Net Interest Margin (NIM). The finding of this study implies that the size of the banks has a negative role in the profitability due to the existence of economies of scale for the smaller banks and diseconomies for the larger ones. With respect to liquidity, the impact is not clear and depends on the measure of profitability. The derived results could prove useful in the formation of strategic policies on the part of financial institutions and regulators.

Efficiency and productivity of Islamic banking industry by using DEA method is the topic of the manuscript prepared by **Dario Maradin, Stella Suljić Nikolaj** and **Bojana Olgić Draženović** (all from University of Rijeka, Faculty of Economics and Business, Croatia). This manuscript presents the most important studies of performance management of banking sector in Islamic countries. The interesting and original ideas provided in this manuscript may provide the basis for further empirical research of the relative efficiency or productivity growth of the Islamic banking sector. Despite its humble beginning, the Islamic banking system has today become worth attention, and it is competitive compared to the conventional banking system. It is noticeable rapid development of the Islamic banking sector, and it is reasonable to expect that the performance of Islamic banks becomes the centre of research interest. Double regulation of Islamic banks is noticeable. In the most countries, the operations of Islamic banks are based on the rules of national central banks, and banks have to follow the fundamental law of Islam—Sheria. The paper analyses two concepts of performance evaluation of Islamic banking industry applying data envelopment analysis.

Authors **Zoe Papadopoulou, Stavros Valsamidis, Ioannis Petasakis, Athanasios Mandilas** (all from Department of Accounting and Finance, International Hellenic University, Greece) addresses the issue of radical changes and improvements in the banking industry with specific focus on online and offline banking. The authors have investigated factors that effect on costumers to use online banking than offline banking. The last decade digital transformation of economy is changing habits, way of doing business in all sectors and especially in the bank sector. In the process of transition from offline to online, banking emerges an issue of security and trustworthiness. To investigate intrinsic and acquired behaviours, the authors have done survey analysis of 200 bank customers in Greece. The authors suggest main reasons for avoiding using online banking are the fear for the security of transactions, the low familiarity with technology and the fear of making a mistake when individuals do online banking on their own. The originality derives from the updated identified factors that influence the attitude of customers towards the services offered by online banking versus offline banking. The contribution of the study is the valuable information for banks so that improve online banking services and develop new products and programmes.

The last paper included in the volume, authored by **Radulescu Magdalena** (University of Pitesti), **Belascu Lucian** and **Dita Sandra Maria** (both of them from University "Lucian Blaga" Sibiu, Romania) investigated correlation of profitability of the banking system in Central and Eastern European counties towards macroeconomic environment. In the past decades, most countries in Central and Eastern Europe (CEE) have adopted structural reforms in view of increasing the size, stability and efficiency of financial systems. During the global financial crisis, the CEE banking sectors performed better than other developed European countries. The macroeconomic variables have direct or indirect implications to all sectors. For that reason, emerges the significance of this study and conclusions. The authors pin pointed that low unemployment rate and low interest rate bonds yields are associated with the increase of the banking profitability ratios in the CEE region. A low taxation level supports net interest margin (NIM). An increase of the GDP per capita and high concentration level of the banking systems are associated with a decrease of NIM but are associated with the increase of ROE. The high inflation rates and large public deficits in some CEE countries significantly supported the increase of the banking profitability ratios in this region, but that cannot represent a solution in the long-run for the banking managers in the CEE countries.

Hoping that the paper selection included in the volume confirms the research quality standards needed for addressing the Financial Performance Analysis of Real and Banking Sectors in Europe and offers insightful look at the changing financial landscape; we leave to the readers the final assessment of their quality, as well as of their ability to disseminate new approaches and ideas that may be further used by academics, practitioners and public decision-makers alike.

# Financial Development and Performance of the Real Sector

# Female Members in Corporate Board of Directors and Financial Performance

**Chris Grose, Maria Argyropoulou, Dimitrios Koufopoulos, Dionisia Tzavara, Maria Efraimidou, and Stamatia Theodorakoglou**

**Abstract** The supervisory role the board of directors is an essential corporate governance control mechanism, particularly in countries where external mechanisms are not well developed. The composition of the board based on gender can affect the quality of this supervisory role and thus the financial performance of the firm. While some national capital market regulators, such as UK, Germany and Australia, have introduced recommendations and disclosure requirements, other countries, such as Norway, Spain and France, have by legislation a minimum requirement of women's participation in a company's board of directors. While the matter of board gender diversity has captured researchers' attention in recent years, most empirical results use US data. The present paper attempts to contribute to the growing literature of non-US studies investigating the link between gender diversity in the board and firm financial performance by focusing on the UK. We use panel data analysis and find that gender diversity—as measured by the percentage of women on the board and according to two indices—has a positive effect on firm value. That means that it is the balance between women and men that UK companies should focus on instead of merely the presence of women since the latter alone does not have any impact on firm performance. Our study also suggests that investors in the UK do not penalize firms which increase their female board membership and that greater gender diversity can generate economic gains.

C. Grose (✉) · M. Argyropoulou · M. Efraimidou · S. Theodorakoglou
International Hellenic University, Thessaloniki, Greece
e-mail: cgrose@af.ihu.gr

M. Efraimidou
e-mail: m.efraimidou@ihu.edu.gr

S. Theodorakoglou
e-mail: s.theodorakoglou@ihu.edu.gr

D. Koufopoulos
University of London, London, UK
e-mail: dimitrios.koufopoulos@london.ac.uk

D. Tzavara
University of Liverpool and Laureate Online Education, Liverpool, UK
e-mail: dionisia.tzavara@online.liverpool.ac.uk

 
G. Karanovic et al. (eds.), *The Changing Financial Landscape*, Contributions to Economics, https://doi.org/10.1007/978-3-030-82778-6_1

**Keywords** Corporate governance · Board of directors · Gender diversity · Financial performance

**JEL Classification Codes** G32 · G35

# 1 Introduction

The importance of effective corporate governance is an ever-important topic, especially following the scandals of the early 2000s. Within this context, the board of directors structure remains a topic central to corporate governance measures. Despite the actions of some countries to enact guidelines or impose mandatory laws with the aim of increasing the presence of women on the boards of the listed companies, the vast majority of boardrooms are still made up of primarily male directors (Terjesen et al. 2016). The concerns raised about board profiles stems from the increased belief that diverse groups are likely to be more effective since different perspectives will improve discussion, creativity and decision making (Reguera-Alvarado et al. 2017). These organizational aspects that diversity bolsters ultimately make up the foundation for organizations that perform better financially. Some national capital market regulators (e.g., the UK, Germany and Australia) have passed recommendations and disclosure requirements. In contrast, other countries (such as Norway, Spain, France, the Netherlands and Italy) have by legislation required that 40% of a company's directors be women (Adams and Ferreira 2009; Rose 2007).

Despite the advances achieved, the female representation in boards remains far from the desired levels (less than 10% of women on German supervisory boards in the 30 largest listed companies), especially in the countries with non-mandatory gender quotas. It is therefore imperative to investigate the impact of gender diversity on corporate boards from both economic and ethical points of view. This is important for a number of reasons. First, experts believe that workplace diversity increases employee satisfaction and fosters positive attitudes and behaviors and creates better decision making through combining diverse groups of thinkers. Also, an organization with a reputation for being a good place to work for diverse groups finds it easier when recruiting talent from today's diverse hiring pool a fact that can save money and time. Moreover, according to women's nature there is a general belief that companies with women directors deal more effectively with risk (Shrader et al. 1997). Not only do they better address the concerns of customers, employees, shareholders and the local community, but also, they tend to focus on long-term priorities. Finally, women directors are likely to be more in tune with women's needs than men, which helps develop successful products and services.

Nonetheless, results on the impact of women presence in boards on company performance are mixed (Adams and Ferreira 2009; Rose 2007). Carter et al. (2003) consider the link between board diversity and firm value in the context of agency theory and conclude that a firm with gender diversity would more efficiently monitor managers and workforce in general. These empirical evidence may be explained in many ways. First, the studies relate to different countries and to differing time periods, and the effect of board gender diversity may be dependent on the timing and on the legal and institutional context. Second, the conflicting results may be due to the different estimation methods employed by various researchers. For example, in some studies no controls are made for factors such as firm size and leverage, which usually affect firm performance. Further, there may be other unobserved factors which affect firm performance. Therefore, the use of panel data in our study facilitates a more reliable picture than that arising from purely cross-sectional studies.

The UK is a great laboratory for research regarding the impact of women on boards. In March 2015, the UK Department for Business, Innovation and Skills issued a report that showed that 263, or 23.5% of FTSE 100 board seats, belong to women, reflecting an increase of 11% from 2011. This breaks down as 8.6% of FTSE 100 executive directors and 28.5% of non-executive directors. Within the FTSE 100, 41 have boards with at least 25% female presence, up from just 12 in 2011. All the FTSE 100 companies have at least one female board member, in contrast to 21% all-male boards in 2011. There remain 23 all-male boards among the FTSE 250, although there are now eight female board chairs in this group. Therefore, exploring women presence on boards and attempting to relate this to performance represents an ever-important research question especially given the fact that the pertinent literature has focused on the US market. We find that women presence in boards has a positive effect on performance. In this respect, companies should gradually focus on the balance between men and women on the boards rather than simply the inclusion of women.

## 2 Literature Review

Despite the growing numbers of educated women entering the workforce, their increasing buying power and influence, women continue to hold only a small proportion of leadership positions in business. It is often advocated that women do not lack the experience, credentials or skills to sit on boards, but they do lack the demographic similarities that boardroom gate keepers assume will minimize social uncertainty in governance. The literature indicates how governance is connected to the gender diversity on the board of directors, focusing on the fact that poor governance means lower diversity (Adams and Ferreira 2009; Hermalin and Weisbach 2001).

There are three major theories that indicate the effect of gender diversity on the corporation's performance, agency theory, the theory of resource dependency and the stakeholder theory (Kang et al. 2010). Firstly, the agency theory focuses on the relation between the agency and the principal. To the point, it puts emphasis on the conflicts that occur between owners and managers, because of the asymmetry of information. These conflicts can lead to agency costs. An heterogeneous board can provide a wider range of views, thus decreasing the possibilities for agency costs through the gender diversity and so increasing the possibilities for higher value of the firm. However, there is a great dilemma as agency theory does not provide a clear prediction concerning the link between board diversity and firm value. Hermalin and Weisbach (2001) state that although such principal-agent modeling provides many insights, it is not particularly useful for explaining board-specific phenomena. Nevertheless, most of the empirical research and literature publications state that corporate diversity promotes a better understanding of the marketplace, diversity increases creativity and innovation, produces more effective problem-solving, enhances the effectiveness of corporate leadership and promotes more effective global relationships.

The second theory, that of resource dependency, is one among those that should be considered as it associates the gender diversity with the firm's performance. To be more specific, the resource dependence theory states that diversity can be a powerful weapon for accessing resources that are critical to the firm's success and can enhance its overall problem-solving capacity (Reguera-Alvarado et al. 2017). Resources help reduce dependency between the organization and external contingencies, diminish uncertainty for the firm, lower transaction costs and ultimately aid in the survival of the firm. This fact puts emphasis on the board's ability to extend its independency, as the members establish external links and resources to gather crucial information for the company. Thereafter, the theory of resource dependency, as well as the agency theory, suggests the gender diversity drives to more effective organizational performance.

The third theory, stakeholder theory, is a perspective that emphasizes the interest of other stakeholders besides the shareholders (employees, investors, competitors, government regulation, customers, suppliers, education and financial institutions and so on), something that creates value for the firm. Consequently, it is a factor that should be considered for the decision-making process as the firm has to reflect the stakeholders' interests. Toward this direction, and with the target of maximizing the firm's value, the existence of gender diversity on the board and other managerial and crucial positions is a sign of a stakeholder-oriented firm.

The essence of good corporate governance is ensuring trustworthy relations between the corporation and its stakeholders such as employees, customers, suppliers and the community of which it is a part. Trust is the foundation of sustainable development. As the world continues to get smaller, our mutual interdependence increases and we all need to be able to accumulate the resources and benevolence of others to succeed. That can only be achieved through gaining their trust. Therefore, the ability of gaining the trust of global financial markets and of all the stakeholders in the value chain is becoming the key to success. Good corporate governance is a culture and a climate of consistency, responsibility, accountability, fairness, transparency and effectiveness that is expanded throughout the organization. Boards are responsible to ensure sustainable improvements in corporate valuations by providing strategic guidance and oversight regarding management decisions, as well as selecting and changing the management whenever necessary.

The board of directors is the most essential element of the governance mechanism, although the nature of the alignment between different interest groups is also partly determined by the legal environment. Four countries (Australia, Ireland, the UK and the USA) are generally characterized as having predominantly "dispersed" ownership structures. The aggregate share of these countries global market capitalization decreased from 58% in the period of 1998–2002 to 49% in the most recent period of 2013–2015, according to OECD calculations based on World Bank data. Yet, these figures may underestimate the tendency of companies throughout the world to make use of concentrated ownership structures. For example, despite the classification of the USA as a country with predominantly dispersed company ownership structures, many of its largest listed companies have controlling owners (e.g., Amazon, Berkshire Hathaway, Facebook). Five countries (Canada, Germany, Japan, the Netherlands and Switzerland) have been classified as having a "mixed" ownership structure.

A diverse board of directors brings a range of perspectives and talent that synergizes the board as a whole entity (Hillman and Dalziel 2003). Many important discussions take place on boards. It is the differing perspectives of board members that lessen the potential for group thinking and lead to well-rounded decisions. Arguments for greater female boardroom representation can be split into two broad categories: ethical and economic. The former argues that it is unethical for women to be excluded from corporate boards on the sense of gender and that firms should increase gender diversity to achieve a fairer outcome for society. Accordingly, these arguments suggest that firms should regard greater female representation not as an obligation but as a desirable end in itself. On the other hand, economic arguments are based on the statement that firms which fail to select the most able and qualified candidates for the board of directors damage their financial performance. We now consider the theory that lies behind this "business case" about how board diversity increases a firm's competitive advantage compared to firms with less diversity (Liu et al. 2014). Therefore, one would expect board composition to systematically vary across industry sectors according to the cross-sector variation in the demographic composition of customers and employees. In this context, Brammer et al. (2007) in their study of UK corporate boards find that the highest rates of female directors are associated with retailing, banking, the media and utilities—all sectors such as resources, engineering and business services. Second, it is argued that diversity increases creativity and innovation as these characteristics are not randomly distributed in the population, but tend to vary systematically with demographic variables such as gender (Nicholson and Kiel 2004). Third, it is argued that diversity can enhance problem-solving as the variety of perspectives that emerges from a more diverse board means that more alternatives are evaluated. By taking a broader view, the board will have a better understanding of the complexities of the business environment and thus improve decision making.

A more gender diverse board may also improve a firm's competitive advantage if it improves the image of the firm and if this has a positive effect on customer's behavior and thus on a firm's performance (Smith et al. 2006). They suggest a more diverse board may increase the independence of the board as women are more inclined to ask questions that would not be asked by male directors. However, they also point out that a fresh perspective may not necessarily result in more effective monitoring if female board members are marginalized and conclude that there is no prior reason to expect greater gender diversity to enhance board monitoring (Prado Lorenzo et al. 2009). Another argument for a more diverse board is that it may improve the quality of the directors if they are selected without prejudice from both genders (Roberson and Park 2007).

In the UK, in 2004, women accounted for 10% of FTSE 100 board positions and 4% of executive and 13% of non-executive directors. It is found that there are many reasons for scarcity of women in leadership positions and they interact in subtle and complex ways. Some of them are historical, some stem from the nature of organizations themselves, some are to do with deep-rooted differences in the male and female mind (and the differences in outlooks, attitudes and appetites these generate) and childbearing and child-rearing roles assigned to women by nature (and society) contribute to their rarity at the top of companies. This study will therefore attempt to delve deeper on the issue of women representation on boards today and their role in company performance.

## 3 Research Methodology

The UK institutional framework is a great laboratory for this research since it represents the largest market capitalization market in Europe. The sample for the panel data analysis comprises non-financial firms listed on the main market in UK during the period from January 2012 to December 2016. The sample comprises of 139 companies. A selection procedure was applied using several filters to obtain our final sample. Below, we are describing them step by step. Initially, financial firms were decided to be excluded. Secondly, we decided to include in our sample those entities that have positive current market value as we apply a Tobin's Q regression. Third, we eliminated those observations with outliers for any variables considered through the time under our empirical study. We also chose those firms that were headquartered in UK and had female presence percentage (on Board of Directors) information published for at least one year of the period under investigation. Finally, we decided to focus on a specific country (UK) as we use country information (as GDP) for the regression to take into consideration law and economic crisis effects on firms' financial performance.

The financial information of the companies was obtained from Amadeus and Thomson Eikon Reuters databases. Moreover, data on the composition of the board of directors regarding the gender characteristics, were derived from the corporate governance report of each company analyzed.

**Table 1** Firms with published percentage of female presence in BOD

| | 2012 | 2013 | 2014 | 2015 | 2016 |
|---|---|---|---|---|---|
| Number of firms | 121 | 124 | 123 | 135 | 138 |
| Mean female percentage (%) | 12.90 | 15.15 | 19.55 | 19.73 | 21.30 |

Since our research is related to the gender diversity and the presence of females in the Board of Directors, Table 1 provides information about the percentage of women representation in BOD annually for the years between 2012 and 2016.

We decided to use as a measure of firm value an approximation of Tobin's Q (Q), defined as the sum of the market value of stock and the book value of debt divided by the book value of total assets. We use Tobin's Q as a measure of firm value in our study rather than accounting-based measures because it reflects the market's expectations of future earnings and is thus a good proxy for a firm's competitive advantage. The unity value of the Tobin's Q ratio provides a clear yardstick for the measurement of firm performance: firms with a Tobin's Q ratio greater than 1.0 are expected by investors to be able to create more value by using available resources effectively, while those with a Tobin's Q ratio of less than 1.0 are associated with poor utilization of available resources.

To compare the presence of women in the board to the total number of members, we created the TAMCAD variable. TAMCAD measures the board size (total number of members), and to continue our study, we examine how this is relativized to the women's percentage in the BOD. Following Reguera-Alvarado et al. (2017), we created three variables as proxies for the description of gender diversity in the board. The first one is the PWOMEN variable, which measures the women's presence in the board of directors in a percentage form. We calculate two further variables that take into consideration the distribution evenness of the board's members between the two gender categories (male and female). We try to combine the two categories of gender diversity and their distribution in the boar to examine the variety or the balance in it. The first variable is the Blau Index, which is calculated by the following equation:

$$\text{Blau Index} = 1 - \sum_{i=1}^{n} * P_i^2$$

where $P_i$ is the percentage of board members in each one of the two categories (male and female) and $n$ is the total number of board members.

Blau Index takes values between 0 and 0.5 (maximum), with 0.5 meaning that the number of women and men is the same.

The second variable is the Shannon Index, which is calculated as follows:

$$\text{Shannon Index} = -\sum_{i=1}^{n} P_i \ln P_i$$

where $P_i$ and $n$ have the same meaning as in Blau Index.

Shannon Index ranges between 0 and 0.69, with 0.69 as maximum value, meaning equal presence of men and women in the boardroom. In addition to these, we decided to include eight more variables in our research. In line with Reguera-Alvarado et al. (2017), we calculate the LNTAB variable which is used as a proxy for the firm's size and is calculated as the natural logarithm of total assets for each one of the firms of our sample. Secondly, we decided to turn our interest to operating revenue (sales). Consequently, the next variable used is LNOPR which is calculated as the natural logarithm of operating revenue. Operating revenue is revenue (sales) generated from a company's daily business activities, which means revenue coming from sales of company's products or services. Our next step combines two ratios, so we decided not to include EPS (earnings per share) as a variable, which is a key ratio for evaluating a firm's stock price, but operating revenue as it is a primary source for EPS calculation. The two ratios mentioned above are ROA and ROE. Higher ROA means higher profitability and gives an idea about how efficient management is at using the firm's assets to generate earnings. Combining it with percentage of women in boardroom and the previous variables we examine its contribution to Tobin's Q configuration. Similarly, ROE is used as a profitability index which explains the relation between the capital provided by the shareholders of the firm and the profit derived from the effective exploitation of this capital. Consequently, it is a proxy of the effective management. Furthermore, to take into consideration, the effect of the economic crisis on a UK firm's financial performance, we decided to include a variable named GDP, obviously representing the country's annual GDP and one more named UNERATE representing the annual unemployment rate of UK. Finally, we define two more variables: the lagged variable named LAG_TOBINSQ, which is used in order to examine the endogeneity as well, and the dummy variable RECOMVDUMMY. The last one, is designated according to the mean of the women' percentage of presence in the board of directors. The benchmark is 0.25. UK FTSE 100 firms' presence of women had reached 25% since 2015, a target that set by Lord Davies in 2011. So, we decided to use it as milestone, taking into consideration the UK law.

As previously mentioned, and according to literature sources (Adams and Ferreira 2009), there are problems related to endogeneity, existing between a firm's financial performance and the presence of women in positions of major importance. This leads us to examine how gender diversity affects the financial 2.

According to Reguera-Alvarado et al. (2017), an instrumental variable is considered as valid if it is not correlated with the error term of the main performance equation, except through control variables included in the regression and if it is correlated with the endogenous variables (PWOMEN, BLAU, SHANNON)'. Under these conditions, we decided to set as instrumental variable the LAG_TOBINSQ, standing up for the hypothesis stating that if the endogenous variables affect the LAG_TOBINSQ, it is expected to act in this way in a future level of several years.

As far as the methodology is concerned in order to examine the influence of the board's gender diversity on the financial performance of the firm, we implemented a two-stage instrumental variable regression. Regarding the first stage of this methodology, the instrumental variable regression (IV) is based on a generalized method of moments (GMM) and the two-stage least squares analysis (2SLS) which will be analyzed in a subsequent stage. The target is to examine the possibility of endogeneity and causality existence related to relations between the women percentage of presence in the boardroom and the financial position of the firm. To address this concern, GMM test is applied for examining the endogenously determined factors. Throughout the implementation of the two-stage instrumental variable analysis, we conclude to the following equation which includes all the selected variables, considered as determinants for a firm's financial performance:

$$
\begin{aligned}
\mathrm{TOBINSQ} = {} & \beta_o + \beta_1 * \mathrm{PWOMEN}_{it} + \beta_2 * \mathrm{BLAU}_{it} + \beta_3 \mathrm{X} * \mathrm{SHANNON}_{it} \\
& + \beta_4 * \mathrm{LNTAB}_{it} + \beta_5 \mathrm{LNOPR}_{it} + \beta_6 \mathrm{ROA}_{it} + \beta_7 X * \mathrm{ROE}_{it} + \beta_8 * \mathrm{GDP}_{it} \\
& + \beta_9 * \mathrm{UNERATE}_{it} + \beta_{10} \mathrm{LAG\_TOBINS} Q_{it} \\
& + \beta_{11} X * \mathrm{RECOMVDUMMY}_{it} + \varepsilon_{it}
\end{aligned}
$$

where $i$ represents each one of our sample's firms and $t$ means time (each one of the years under investigation), TOBINSQ measures the firm's performance, PWOMEN, BLAU and SHANNON are used as proxies for the description of women' presence in the boardroom, LNTAB is the company size, LNOPR is the company's operating revenue, ROA is the company's return on assets ratio, ROE is the firm's return on equity ratio, GDP is the variation of UK gross domestic product through the 5 years (it is the same for all the firms), UNERATE is the variation of UK unemployment rate through the 5 years, LAG_TOBINSQ is the lagged of the variable TOBINSQ and RECOMVDUMMY is the dummy variable relevant to the 25% percentage proposed by Lord Davies.

Adding the lagged value of the dependent variable to a panel data regression can give rise to problems with autocorrelation. Moreover, the other control variables associated with firm policies may also be endogenous. Arellano and Bond (1991) propose a dynamic panel generalized method of moments estimator to account for these issues.

The panel data approach allows controlling for the unobservable constant heterogeneity or fixed effects term. It allows us to eliminate any unobservable heterogeneity that may be present among the companies in our sample. If unobservable heterogeneity is correlated with the explanatory variables, thereby biasing the coefficients obtained, we undertake a conditional inference (estimation by fixed effects). This term is intended to reflect the firm-level characteristics, and it thereby avoids the omission bias and renders more efficient estimates. The fixed effects term is unobservable and, consequently, is subsumed in the random disturbance. A key element in panel data is the relation between the fixed effects term and the other explanatory variables. This correlation is analyzed by using the Hausman test, which tests the null hypothesis of the lack of correlation between the independent variables and the fixed effects term.

The methods implemented and performed for examining the endogeneity and causality existence under this analysis are GMM, and 2SLS. The results of these two methods are addressed according to three tests: the Durbin, Hausman and GMM statistic (tests of endogeneity and orthogonality conditions). Following that a panel data approach allows for the analysis of the constant term. This term is relative to the firm's characteristics and aims to more efficient estimates.

# 4 Results and Discussion

The panel of Table 2 presents the descriptive statistics of our sample (139 firms). Women underrepresentation in the board of directors in the firms under investigation is evident. The average board size is 9 directors in the boardroom with a range between 3 and 17. This measurement includes the number of women. The average firm size is 14.5% with a range between 11 and 19.

As we can see from the information provided through the above table for the operating revenue (LNOPR), the mean is calculated to 14.25% while it is really close to the median (14.73%) which is calculated for comparison reasons, but not presented in this panel. Consequently, the firm's financial performance is expected to be most positively affected by the percentage of women in the board of directors (PWOMEN) and the Shannon Index (SHANNON), both of which were used as proxies for the gender diversity. On the other hand, Tobin's Q seems to be negatively affected mainly by Blau Index (BLAU) and the size of the firm (LNTAB). It is reasonable, if we keep in mind that Tobin's Q ratio is calculated if we divide the total market value of the firm with the total asset value. Tobin's Q and total assets are inversely proportional amounts.

In order to analyze the statistic relationship existing between the variables used, we provide, in Table 3, results coming from the Pearson correlation coefficient analysis (PCC). The most relevant relations appear between the variables used as proxies for the gender diversity and between TOBINSQ and LNTAB, LNOPR, ROA, ROE and LAG_TOBINSQ. The correlation between the proxies for gender diversity is being justified through the following analysis, where we examine the endogeneity and causality problems.

**Table 2** Descriptive statistics of the empirical study variables

| Variable | Obs | Mean | Std. dev | Min | Max |
|---|---|---|---|---|---|
| tobinsq | 693 | 1.341273 | 1.150146 | 0.018000 | 9.440000 |
| tamcad | 684 | 8.785088 | 2.047535 | 3.000000 | 17.000000 |
| pwomen | 640 | 0.178703 | 0.106834 | 0.000000 | 0.500000 |
| blau | 642 | 0.273079 | 0.141378 | 0.000000 | 1.000000 |
| shannon | 555 | 0.486528 | 0.105940 | 0.287000 | 0.693000 |
| lntab | 694 | 14.501730 | 1.442230 | 11.370000 | 18.950000 |
| lnopr | 694 | 14.254620 | 1.560110 | 10.438570 | 19.027150 |
| roa | 694 | 7.530927 | 9.367902 | −55.930000 | 39.450000 |
| roe | 694 | 15.383530 | 34.645770 | −355.430000 | 208.900000 |
| gdp | 694 | 2.058357 | 0.581188 | 1.310000 | 3.070000 |
| unerate | 694 | 6.410173 | 1.201939 | 4.900000 | 7.980000 |
| lag_tobinsq | 694 | 1.328696 | 1.169680 | 0.018000 | 9.440000 |
| recomvdummy | 694 | 0.344380 | 0.475509 | 0.000000 | 1.000000 |

**Table 3** Pearson analysis

| | 1 | 2 | 3 | 4 | 5 | 6 | 7 | 8 | 9 | 10 | 11 | 12 |
|---|---|---|---|---|---|---|---|---|---|---|---|---|
| tobinsq | 1.0000 | | | | | | | | | | | |
| pwomen | −0.0070 | 1.0000 | | | | | | | | | | |
| | 0.8593 | | | | | | | | | | | |
| blau | −0.0176 | 0.9725* | 1.0000 | | | | | | | | | |
| | 0.6571 | 0.0000 | | | | | | | | | | |
| shannon | 0.0153 | 0.9691* | 0.9991* | 1.0000 | | | | | | | | |
| | 0.7199 | 0.0000 | 0.0000 | | | | | | | | | |
| lntab | −0.3694* | 0.3277* | 0.2992* | 0.2369* | 1.0000 | | | | | | | |
| | 0.0000 | 0.0000 | 0.0000 | 0.0000 | | | | | | | | |
| lnopr | −0.2434* | 0.3582* | 0.3420* | 0.2600* | 0.8770* | 1.0000 | | | | | | |
| | 0.0000 | 0.0000 | 0.0000 | 0.0000 | 0.0000 | | | | | | | |
| roa | 0.6174* | 0.0410 | 0.0258 | 0.0594 | −0.2540* | −0.1217* | 1.0000 | | | | | |
| | 0.0000 | 0.3005 | 0.5141 | 0.1624 | 0.0000 | 0.0013 | | | | | | |
| roe | 0.3431* | 0.0822* | 0.0695 | 0.0765 | −0.1144* | −0.0163 | 0.6870* | 1.0000 | | | | |
| | 0.0000 | 0.0376 | 0.0784 | 0.0717 | 0.0025 | 0.6690 | 0.0000 | | | | | |

(continued)

**Table 3** (continued)

| | 1 | 2 | 3 | 4 | 5 | 6 | 7 | 8 | 9 | 10 | 11 | 12 |
|---|---|---|---|---|---|---|---|---|---|---|---|---|
| gdp | 0.0000 | 0.1601* | 0.1556* | 0.0772 | 0.0389 | 0.0382 | −0.0199 | −0.0304 | 1.0000 | | | |
| | 0.9995 | 0.0000 | 0.0001 | 0.0691 | 0.3067 | 0.3155 | 0.6001 | 0.4235 | | | | |
| unerate | 0.0386 | −0.2879* | −0.2657* | −0.1880* | −0.0867 | −0.0592 | 0.1049* | 0.1155* | −0.3802* | 1.0000 | | |
| | 0.3100 | 0.0000 | 0.0000 | 0.0000 | 0.0223 | 0.1193 | 0.0057 | 0.0023 | 0.0000 | | | |
| lag_tobinsq | 0.8787* | 0.0056 | −0.0104 | 0.0481 | −0.3316* | −0.2257* | 0.5598* | 0.2989* | 0.0532 | −0.0240 | 1.0000 | |
| | 0.0000 | 0.8882 | 0.7919 | 0.2581 | 0.0000 | 0.0000 | 0.0000 | 0.0000 | 0.1612 | 0.5281 | | |
| recomdummy | 0.0285 | 0.7702* | 0.6888* | 0.8175* | 0.1299* | 0.1434* | 0.0888* | 0.1200* | 0.0805* | −0.1029* | 0.0396 | 1.0000 |
| | 0.4541 | 0.0000 | 0.0000 | 0.0000 | 0.0006 | 0.0002 | 0.0193 | 0.0015 | 0.0339 | 0.0066 | 0.2977 | |

Notes: * denotes significance at the 5% level

Since we mentioned that there are endogeneity and causality problems that have to be examined as in the previous literature, we decided to evaluate the results according to three endogeneity and orthogonality tests. Both of the analysis are based on the hypothesis that the lagged tobinsq was so far affected by the three proxy variables related to the gender diversity in boardrooms. So, the null hypothesis that corroborates the presence of endogeneity is that if the lagged tobinsq (LAG_TOBINSQ) is affected by PWOMEN, SHANNON and BLAU (the three proxies), then there is endogeneity.

The first analysis is 2SLS (two-stage least squares regression analysis), and the results are depicted in the following panel.

We can observe from Table 4 that the *R*-squared is calculated as 72.38%, meaning that the model is well-structured and defined. We set LAG_TOBINSQ as instrumented and PWOMEN, SHANNON and BLAU as instrumental variables. Through the Durbin and Hausman tests, we concluded to the following *p*-values.

The results confirm the theoretical argument and suggest that the three variables of gender diversity influence the financial performance of the firms for the years under investigation. This conclusion is derived from the low *p*-values as appear in Table 5. Durbin and Hausman test for endogeneity by using the null hypothesis that the instrumental variables are exogenous. Because of small enough *p*-value, this hypothesis is being rejected. On the other hand, we accept the null hypothesis set in our research (Ho).

The second analysis is GMM (generalized method of moments), and the results are as shown in Table 6.

**Table 4** Instrumental variables (2SLS) regression

| Instrumental variables (2SLS) regression | | | | Wald chi2(8) = 962.49 | | |
|---|---|---|---|---|---|---|
| | | | | Prob > chi2 = 0.0000 | | |
| | | | | *R*-squared = 0.7238 | | |
| tobinsq | Coef | Std. err | *z* | *P* > \|*z*\| | [95% conf. interval] | |
| lag_tobinsq | 0.37658 | 0.53458 | 0.7 | 0.481 | −0.6712 | 1.42433 |
| lntab | −0.1815 | 0.12824 | −1.42 | 0.157 | −0.4328 | 0.06986 |
| lnopr | 0.06407 | 0.04737 | 1.35 | 0.176 | −0.0288 | 0.15691 |
| roa | 0.05126 | 0.04272 | 1.2 | 0.23 | −0.0325 | 0.13499 |
| roe | −0.0029 | 0.00343 | −0.85 | 0.393 | −0.0097 | 0.00379 |
| gdp | 0.02313 | 0.06873 | 0.34 | 0.736 | −0.1116 | 0.15784 |
| unerate | 0.00817 | 0.03429 | 0.24 | 0.812 | −0.059 | 0.07537 |
| recomvdummy | 0.04305 | 0.1204 | 0.36 | 0.721 | 0.19293 | 0.27903 |
| _cons | 2.12866 | 1.87088 | 1.14 | 0.255 | −1.4382 | 5.79551 |

**Table 5** Results of Durbin and Hausman tests

| | | |
|---|---|---|
| Durbin score | =0.794223 | *p*-value: 0.3728 |
| Wu-Hausman | =0.781007 | *p*-value: 0.3772 |

**Table 6** GMM regression

| Instrumental variables (GMM) regression | | | | Wald chi2(8) = 410.78 | | |
|---|---|---|---|---|---|---|
| | | | | Prob > chi2 = 0.0000 | | |
| | | | | $R$-squared = 0.7264 | | |
| \| | Robust | | | | | |
| Tobinsq | Coef | Std. err | $z$ | $P > \|z\|$ | [95% conf. interval] | |
| lag_tobinsq | 0.31824912 | 0.36502940 | 1.05000000 | 0.29500000 | −0.33295330 | 1.09793600 |
| lntab | −0.18043850 | 0.08990560 | −2.01000000 | 0.04500000 | −0.35665020 | −0.00422680 |
| lnopr | 0.06372370 | 0.04173710 | 1.53000000 | 0.12700000 | −0.01807950 | 0.14552680 |
| roa | 0.05139000 | 0.02974390 | 1.73000000 | 0.08400000 | −0.00690710 | 0.10968700 |
| roe | -0.00299650 | 0.00249010 | −1.20000000 | 0.22900000 | −0.00787710 | 0.00188410 |
| gdp | 0.02182270 | 0.05477770 | 0.40000000 | 0.69000000 | −0.08553960 | 0.12918500 |
| unerate | 0.00807520 | 0.02773570 | 0.29000000 | 0.77100000 | −0.04628570 | 0.06243610 |
| recomvdummy | 0.04030230 | 0.08638380 | 0.47000000 | 0.64100000 | −0.12900680 | 0.20961140 |
| _cons | 2.11583100 | 1.28981400 | 1.64000000 | 0.10100000 | −0.41215740 | 4.64382000 |

Table 6 appears a representative $R$-squared of 72.64%. The results are being evaluated by using the GMM statistic $p$-value ($p$-value = 0.0781), which offers better results than the Hausman's and Durbin Score. Regression analysis in this study suggests that there is a linear relationship between diversity and performance. Therefore, we conclude that women presence in BOD affects the corporation's financial performance.

These results have interesting implications. In line with Farrell and Hersch (2005), we find a positive relationship between the presence of the women on the board and firm value. Therefore, Lord Davies' call for more diverse boards appears to have solid foundations. More gender diverse boards may encourage stronger identification by directors with the opinions expressed by other directors of the same gender, thus increasing the likelihood of conflict. These results offer room for policy recommendations toward more diverse boards with an increasing inclusion of women.

Carter et al. (2003) also find a positive and a significant relationship between Tobin's Q and the proportion of women on the boards of Fortune 1000 firms, after controlling for size, industry and other corporate governance measures. Erhardt et al. (2003) report that the percentage of women on the boards of large US firms is positively associated with two accounting measures of performance, return on assets and the return on investment.

## 5 Conclusion

In 2011, Lord Davies launched an independent review of women on boards, commissioned by the UK government. He recommended that FTSE 100 companies should aim for a minimum of 25% female board member representation by 2015. This is a target which he believed should be achieved, and marked progress has been seen since his initial report was released. His report recommended that FTSE 350 companies should be setting their own challenging targets and stated the expectation that many will achieve a figure much higher than this minimum. This paper contributes to the literature on board diversity and firm financial performance. It offers new insights into the relationship between board gender diversity and firm value by using data from firms listed in the UK, a country with a highly liquid capital market with dispersed ownership.

We use a panel data methodology to examine the relationship between female boardroom participation, measured by several variables, and firm value (measured by a proxy for Tobin's Q). Our findings demonstrate that the presence of women on the board of directors does not affect firm value. However, we find that the diversity of the board (measured by the percentage of women and by the Blau and Shannon Indexes) has a positive impact on firm value. This implies that the most important focus for UK companies should be the balance between women and men rather than simply the presence of women in boards. We also show that firm value has no influence on women's presence and on gender diversity. Overall, our results suggest, at a minimum, that increased gender diversity can be achieved without destroying shareholder value. UK investors may in fact value the contribution made by female directors.

Board gender diversity adds indirectly value to firms since it broadens the skills and views available set in a board. For this reason, boards should undoubtedly be encouraged to incorporate more women. We suggest though that companies must adopt a more efficient view through incorporating more women on the board. This increased representation during a period that this issue is revisited globally may offer firms greater exposure toward ESG-related policies beyond pure economic benefits. Most certainly regulatory authorities' interventions may help toward promoting the various benefits of including more women in boards and keeping and balance on gender representation. Shareholders, managers, governments and regulators all collectively should consider adopting policies toward this end. The results of this study may also prove useful for countries still considering the adoption of similar policies and the magnitude of the potential female involvement in boards they should suggest given existence data.

An important topic for future research would be to identify the impact on firm performance of female board members who have family ties to the owners and whether the qualifications of female board members are related to performance. Obtaining data on board member qualifications would also enable a distinction to be drawn between economically and socially motivated reasons for boardroom appointments and thus permit to form views as to whether the recent changes in support of positive discrimination are likely to be detrimental to performance in the longer term.

There are important limitations in this study that need to be addressed. First, the sample is drawn from large UK corporations and the results may not be applicable to all companies. Future research is needed to address diversity at board of director levels and its impact on organizational performance for smaller companies. Second, given the research approach used in the present study it is impossible to determine whether the diverse members actually do significantly differ in their behavior compared to non-diverse members. The results only suggest that diversity is positively related to organizational performance. To understand behavioral differences, other approaches such as participant observation and ethnography of executive boards of directors and corporate officers are needed.

## References

Adams RB, Ferreira D (2009) Women in the boardroom and their impact on governance and performance. J Financ Econ 94(2):291–309

Arellano M, Bond S (1991) Some tests of specification for panel data: Monte Carlo evidence and an application to employment equations. Rev Econ Stud 58(2):277–297

Brammer S, Millington A, Rayton B (2007) The contribution of corporate social responsibility to organizational commitment. The Int J Hum Resour Manag 18(10):1701–1719

Carter DA, Simkins BJ, Simpson WG (2003) Corporate governance, board diversity, and firm value. Financ Rev 38(1):33–53

Erhardt NL, Werbel JD, Shrader CB (2003) Board of director diversity and firm financial performance. Corp Gov: an Int Rev 11(2):102–111
Farrell KA, Hersch PL (2005) Additions to corporate boards: the effect of gender. J Corp Finan 11(1–2):85–106
Hermalin BE, Weisbach MS (2001) Boards of directors as an endogenously determined institution: a survey of the economic literature (No. w8161). National Bureau of Economic Research
Hillman AJ, Dalziel T (2003) Boards of directors and firm performance: integrating agency and resource dependence perspectives. Acad Manag Rev 28(3):383–396
Kang E, Ding DK, Charoenwong C (2010) Investor reaction to women directors. J Bus Res 63(8):888–894
Liu Y, Wei Z, Xie F (2014) Do women directors improve firm performance in China? J Corp Finan 28:169–184
Nicholson GJ, Kiel GC (2004) Breakthrough board performance: how to harness your board's intellectual capital. Corp Gov: the Int J Bus Soc 4(1):5–23
Prado-Lorenzo JM, Gallego-Alvarez I, Garcia-Sanchez IM (2009) Stakeholder engagement and corporate social responsibility reporting: the ownership structure effect. Corp Soc Responsib Environ Manag 16(2):94–107
Reguera-Alvarado N, de Fuentes P, Laffarga J (2017) Does board gender diversity influence financial performance? Evidence from Spain. J Bus Ethics 141(2):337–350
Roberson QM, Park HJ (2007) Examining the link between diversity and firm performance: the effects of diversity reputation and leader racial diversity. Group Org Manag 32(5):548–568
Rose C (2007) Does female board representation influence firm performance? The Danish evidence. Corp Gov: an Int Rev 15(2):404–413
Shrader CB, Blackburn VB, Iles P (1997) Women in management and firm financial performance: an exploratory study. J Manag Issues 355–372
Smith N, Smith V, Verner M (2006) Do women in top management affect firm performance? A panel study of 2500 Danish firms. Int J Prod Perform Manag 55(7)
Terjesen S, Couto EB, Francisco PM (2016) Does the presence of independent and female directors impact firm performance? A multi-country study of board diversity. J Manage Gov 20(3):447–483

# The Different Impact of Financial Constraints on Firm-Level Exports in Manufacturing and Service Sector: Evidence from Croatia

**Valerija Botrić**

**Abstract** Extant studies examine the role of financial constraints on the international activity of the firms. However, they are mostly focused on the manufacturing sector, traditionally perceived as tradable. The literature recently recognized the growing role of service sector in international trade, but the analysis of financial constraint on exporting behaviour of this segment of the economy has seldom been performed. This is of particular importance for economies with pronounced de-industrialization and high share of tourism sector, such as Croatia. The analysis in this paper rests on a balance sheet data of Croatian firms during the 1999–2017 period, divided into pre- and post-global financial crisis period. The second novelty of the paper is that assessment of financial constraint is based on the firm-level data. The results suggest an increase in the importance of financial constraints in the period since the crisis, in particular for manufacturing sector. In the case of service sector, financial constraints are significant only for microfirms.

**Keywords** Firm-level exports · Financial constraints · Service versus manufacturing sector · Croatia

**JEL Classification Codes** L25 · F14

## 1 Introduction

When making decision to participate in international markets, firms from countries with relatively underdeveloped financial systems are facing additional adversities. Firms' ability to successfully compete on international markets has been questioned by many scholars since the beginning of transition in European economies. Croatian case was no different. The market liberalization implied increased competition on the domestic market as well as the imperative to successfully compete internationally. During early periods of transition, still predominant soft budget constraint alleviated

V. Botrić (✉)
The Institute of Economics, Trg J. F. Kennedy 7, 10000 Zagreb, Croatia
e-mail: vbotric@eizg.hr



G. Karanovic et al. (eds.), *The Changing Financial Landscape*, Contributions to Economics, https://doi.org/10.1007/978-3-030-82778-6_2

part of the problem, at least for large enterprises with well-established business–government networks. However, global financial crisis starting from 2008 invoked a widespread credit crunch that put internationally operating firms through additional trial related to relatively high costs of maintaining business in declining and uncertain markets. Due to these reasons, financial constraints were put forward as the most important deterring factor for starting to export and maintaining international operations. This was especially important for post-transition economies, whose overall financial position was considered weak and their financial sector vulnerable during the global turmoil.

International trade literature has established that there are important differences between internationally active and home-market-oriented firms when it comes to productivity, wages, size, markups (Melitz 2003; Bernard et al. 2007; Melitz and Ottaviano 2008). Financial constraints might not be as important for exporting in periods when money markets are not tight, simply because not all firms need external funding even though empirical studies suggest that it is frequently the case (Carpenter and Petersen 2002; Greenaway et al. 2007). Although some empirical studies suggest that external sources are essential for removing financial barriers to exporting (Westhead et al. 2001), the literature has not yet reached a univocal conclusion.

The main aim of the paper is to empirically assess the role of financial constraints for exporting propensity of Croatian firms. The specific contribution of this paper is that it explicitly tackles the role of financial crisis, by analysing separately period before the crisis (1999–2007) and after the crisis (2008–2017), thereby acknowledging the effects of the changes on the global and local financial markets. Another important contribution is that empirical analysis is separately performed for the manufacturing and service sector, the latter specifically entailing tourism and ICT. This is of extreme importance for Croatian economy, due to the fact that tourism consumes a large share of its total exports in goods and services, while ICT industry showed significant resilience during the crisis.

The structure of the paper is following. The next section provides brief literature review. Section 3 provides information on the data and methodology used in the empirical analysis. Section 4 presents the results, while the last section offers conclusions and possible extensions for further research.

## 2 Literature Review

Exporting is usually associated with the need for additional funding due to increased costs for entering and sustaining operations on foreign markets. Theoretical models have shown that only financially unrestricted firms are able to participate in international markets (Chaney 2016). Empirical studies found that financial constraints reduce the probability to become an exporter (Bellone et al. 2010, Wagner 2014a; Berman and Hericourt 2010; Minetti and Zhu 2011).

Measuring financial constraints is not straightforward. Although there is some agreement that a firm can be considered financially constrained when faced with inelastic credit supply (Secchi et al. 2016), a researcher does not observe this condition in practice. To overcome this problem, several options have been suggested in the literature, generally divided into direct and indirect approach.

The advantage of direct approach is that it also enables getting insight into decision-making process within a firm and prior to actual exporting. The studies relying directly on managers' opinions, i.e. by asking managers whether they believe that their firm is financially constrained, are relatively scarce (Campello et al. 2010; Kaplan and Zingales 1997).

Indirect approaches have developed in several directions. Some researchers rely on cash flow data (Hutchinson and Xavier 2006). However, Campello et al. (2010) show that during the latest economic crisis financially unconstrained firms were able to maintain the desired level of cash balances, while constrained firms built cash reserves as a buffer against potential credit supply shock (Almeida et al. 2004). So, the cash flow indicator might not be interpreted equally for financially constrained and unconstrained firms. Researchers have also developed a set of indicators relying on the firms' financial accounts that include: poor liquidity, high leverage, low collateral (Greenaway et al. 2007; Forte and Moreira 2018). The rationale for using these indicators comes from mimicking the financial institutions' processes of making decisions whether to extend a loan to an enterprise (Bellone et al. 2010).

Two individual indicators are frequently used in that context: liquidity ratio (Greenaway et al. 2007; Berman and Hericourt 2010; Fauceglia 2015; Miravitlles et al. 2018) and leverage ratio (Forte and Moreira 2018; Greenaway et al. 2007; Miravitlles et al. 2018). It is assumed that the greater the liquidity ratio (indicating the availability of financial resources), the greater the propensity to export. Contrary to that, the higher the leverage ratio (indicating previous indebtness of the firm), the smaller the propensity to export (Greenaway et al. 2007).

Previous research has established that financial constraints in transition economies are more pronounced (Hutchinson and Xavier 2006), particularly after the soft budget constrained period has expired (Konings et al. 2003). The latest economic crisis by itself brought widespread credit crunch that was particularly severe in transition economies (Nguyen and Qian 2014). Studies have also established that during the latest economic crises, the sales of export-oriented firms deteriorated more than the sales of domestic-oriented ones (Coulibaly et al. 2013). Furthermore, the share of exports in total sales declined as well.

In addition to financial constraints, previous empirical studies have established that certain firms' characteristics are related to export propensity (summary provided in Table 1). Size is important both in the context of financial constraints and exporting. Small firms are more likely to face financial constraints (Carreira and Silva 2010; Beck and Demirguc-Kunt 2006; Carpenter and Petersen 2002), because the size of the firm is correlated to their perception of trade barriers (Kahiya and Dean 2016). Small firms face additional challenges when approaching financial institutions due to their perceived low economic merit (Cziraky et al. 2005) and inadequate financial characteristics (Griffith 2011). Larger firms have more internal resources that enable them to deal with trade barriers (Wolff and Pett 2000), including managerial know-how.

**Table 1** Export propensity and firm characteristics

| Variable | References | Operationalization in empirical section | Expected sign |
|---|---|---|---|
| Size | Egger and Kesina (2013), Wagner (2014b) | Separate estimates for: micro (up to 10 employees); small (11–50 employees), medium (51–250), large (>250) | + (it is expected that larger firms will have higher propensity to export) |
| Wage | Greenaway et al. (2007), Stiebale (2011), Schank et al. (2010), Macis and Schivardi (2016) | Relative average wage = average wage (wages/employees) in firm relative to average wage in the NACE 2-digit industry | − (it is expected that firms with higher average labour cost will have lower propensity to export) + (exporting firms pay higher wages) |
| Productivity | Bellone et al. (2010), Wagner (2014b) | Turnover per employee | + (it is expected that more productive firms will have higher propensity to export) |

Two hypotheses offer explanation for positive correlation between productivity and exporting (Bernard and Jensen 1999; Bernard and Wagner 1997): self-selection and learning by exporting. According to self-selection hypothesis, additional costs associated with maintaining operations on foreign markets create too high an obstacle for less productive firms. Learning by exporting hypothesis suggests that by participating in foreign markets firms are exposed to fiercer competition and subsequently must increase their productivity in order to survive.

Studies on firms' exporting behaviour in Croatian economy are relatively scarce, while those on the effects of financial constraints are virtually non-existent. The literature has established that exporters in Croatian manufacturing sector have better firm performance characteristics compared to non-exporters (Valdec and Zrnc 2015) and there is a positive link between productivity and exporting (Valdec and Zrnc 2019). However, little evidence is available on potential effect of financial constraints on exporting. According to the Business Environment and Enterprise Performance Survey,[1] access to finance is (by 16.11% of respondents) still considered as the second most important business obstacle by Croatian firms, after tax rates (23.61% of respondents). Thus, the aim of this paper is to shed the light on this aspect of Croatian firms exporting behaviour.

[1] More information on the Survey can be found at https://ebrd-beeps.com/.

## 3 Data and Methodology

The data rely on financial statements from Croatian firms during the period 1999–2017. The dataset contains variables taken from firms' profit and loss accounts and balance sheet statements, such as: assets (fixed and total), liabilities (short and long term), costs (material, wage bill and total), operating revenue and the number of employees. The data presented in Fig. 1 show that the share of exporters in total economy is relatively low. Figure 1 also reveals that during the economic crisis the share of exporters has decreased, i.e. there is a certain pro-cyclical pattern also identified in manufacturing sector by Valdec and Zrnc (2019). In order to investigate whether financial constraints had important implications for this decrease, we break the overall sample in empirical analysis into two subsamples: (a) period 1999–2007 and (b) period 2008–2017.

Since Croatia is a country with a high share of tourism in GDP (WTTC 2018), the empirical analysis is not restricted to the manufacturing sector, as has been standard practice in similar studies in other countries. Indeed, traditional focus on the manufacturing sector is not being able to account for increasing role of the service sector (such as ICT) in the international trade. The empirical strategy thus distinguishes between manufacturing sector (NACE classification C-manufacturing) and service sector (NACE classification I—accommodation and food service activities and J—information and communication). We focus on the effect of financial constraints on the probability to become an exporter (extensive margin), i.e. a firm is considered an exporter if the share of revenues from exports in total revenues is larger than zero.

As the data in Fig. 2 show, the share of exporters is higher in manufacturing. However, the patterns before the crisis and after the crisis are very similar. Exporting activity decreased with the crisis and it took a while before it reached the pre-crisis levels. The question we want to address in this paper is whether financial constraints played important role in such developments. We use standard indicators of financial constraints based on the firms' financial statement data: (a) liquidity ratio (financial

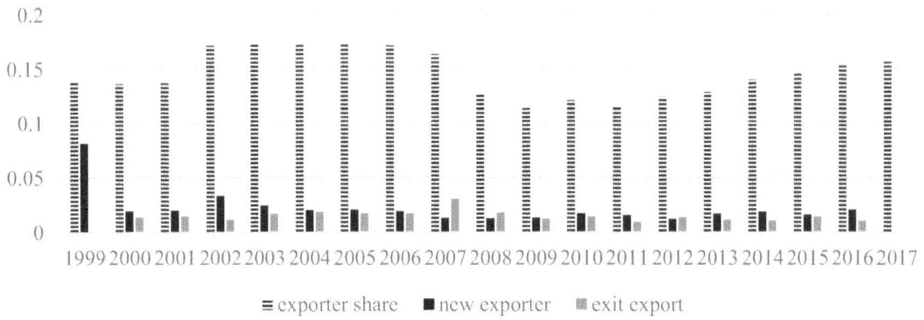


**Fig. 1** Share of exporters, new exporters and firms exiting export in 1999–2017 period. *Notes* new exporters are those exporting in period $t$ and $t+1$, but not in $t-1$; firms exiting export market are those exporting in period $t-1$ and $t$, but not in $t+1$. *Source* Author's calculations based on FINA database

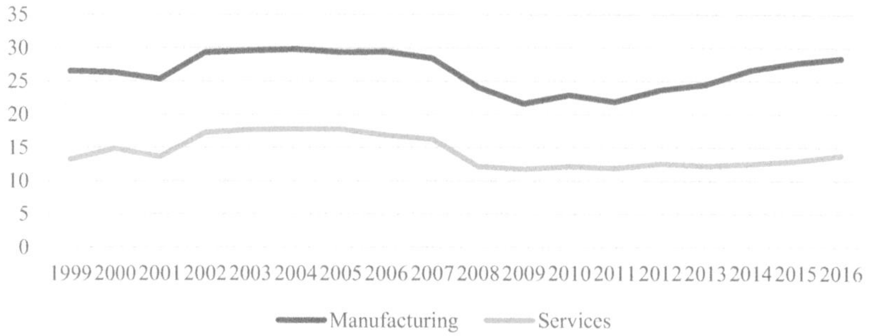


**Fig. 2** Share of exporters in manufacturing and service sector 1999–2016. *Source* Author's calculations based on FINA database

and business receivables over financial and business liabilities) and (b) leverage ratio (short term debt over current assets).

As a first step in the analysis, we explore whether the distribution of the financial constraints variables is similar for exporters and non-exporters by applying Kolmogorov–Smirnov test. If the distribution is similar, financial constraints would not have any effect on the firm's propensity to become an exporter. The results in Table 2 confirm that there are statistically significant differences in distributions, implying that the exporting status is related to the financial constraints indicators.

Next, we empirically assess whether financial constraints have significant impact on propensity to export for Croatian firms. We follow the previous literature (see Table 1) and include additional control variables—productivity, wages, industry dummy variables, regional (county) and time dummy variables—in estimating equation.

Productivity has been estimated as annual turnover over the number of employees. Since Valdec and Zrnc (2019) have established that there is a positive correlation between productivity and exporting, we condition productivity for the sector the firm operates in. Thus, we assume that in order to be an exporter, an enterprise must be more productive than other firms in the same 2-digit NACE industry.

Average wages, estimated as total wage bill over the number of employees, were included to control for the labour cost. The literature is not consistent on the expected sign of this factor—whether wages should be viewed solely through the lens of the costs or the stylized fact of exporter wage premium should be taken into consideration. Regardless of the underlying concept, we assume that relative wages in

**Table 2** Kolmogorov–Smirnov test for equality of distribution functions between exporting and non-exporting firms

| Variable | D: combined test | *p*-value |
|---|---|---|
| Liquidity ratio | 0.1473 | 0.0000 |
| Leverage ratio | 0.1389 | 0.0000 |
| Productivity (relative to sector) | 0.2298 | 0.0000 |
| Wage (relative to sector) | 0.2300 | 0.0000 |

*Source* Author's calculations based on FINA database

comparison with other firms in the same sector are important. Thus, average wages of an enterprise were corrected for the average wage of the 2-digit NACE industry.

Industry dummy variables were included to account for specific demand conditions that could have affected firms' operations. The literature has previously established that the intensity of exporting activities varies considerably across industries (Porter 1980). Also, firms from different industries face different demands for external financing (Rajan and Zingales 1998), while financial institutions might be additionally restricted to spread their credit portfolio by limiting exposure to specific industries by the national regulating agencies.

Regional dummy variables were included to account for specific regional conditions (such as local taxes, local labour supply[2]). Time dummy variable were included to control for general macroeconomic conditions.

We produce separate estimates for different firm sizes: large enterprises (more than 250 employees), medium-size enterprises (50–249 employees), small-size enterprises (11–49 employees) and microenterprises. While studies frequently include size as additional dummy variable in the estimating equation, we opted for separate estimates because the ability to gain resources during the crisis was related to the size of the firm.

The sample is unbalanced and it could be the case that there is unobserved heterogeneity in the sample. One of the potential sources of heterogeneity is related to the internal motivation of the firms' management to be engaged in global competition (Acedo and Galán 2011). We do not assume that the source of unobserved heterogeneity can be linked to the selection into the sample. As all firms in Croatia have legal obligation to submit their financial reports to Financial Agency, those who fail to comply are relatively few. Furthermore, it is very unlikely that unobserved heterogeneity will be linked to our relatively short lists of covariates, which leads us to the random effects with fully robust inference as the most convenient estimation strategy.

All independent variables are included with two lags, in order to allow for certain time for effects to take place. The final specification takes following form:

$$\begin{aligned}\text{Exp}_{i,t} &= \beta_0 + \beta_1\text{Fin}_{i,t-1} + \beta_2\text{Fin}_{i,t-2} + \beta_3\text{Prod}_{i,t-1} \\ &\quad + \beta_4\text{Prod}_{i,t-2} + \beta_5\text{Wage}_{i,t-1} + \beta_6\text{Wage}_{i,t-2} + \alpha_t\text{Time}_i \\ &\quad + \alpha_j\text{Region}_i + \alpha_k\text{Industry}_i + u_{i,t} \qquad (1)\end{aligned}$$

We are not interested in estimated coefficients for all variables, but average partial effects of the selected financial variables on export propensity. Thus, average partial effects of the financial constraints variables on the propensity for firm to export are presented in the following section.

[2] For example, expectations regarding future employment security in trade-related industries may differentially affect regional labour supply responses to trade-based employment shocks compared with domestic shocks (Partridge et al., 2017).

**Table 3** Average partial effects of financial constraints on extensive export margin in Croatian manufacturing

| Firm size | Indicator | 1999–2007 | 2008–2017 |
|---|---|---|---|
| Large enterprises | Liquidity | −0.0047515<br>0.0129657 | 0.0171732<br>(0.0224733) |
| | Leverage | −0.0038422<br>(0.0075228) | −0.0213169***<br>(0.0062963) |
| Medium enterprises | Liquidity | −0.0021265<br>(0.0044939) | 0.0096433<br>(0.0058598) |
| | Leverage | 0.0001703**<br>(0.0000779) | −0.0117682*<br>(0.0070306) |
| Small enterprises | Liquidity | 0.0031575<br>(0.0019804) | 0.0021376<br>(0.0016471) |
| | Leverage | −0.0110312**<br>(0.0047763) | −0.0081133*<br>(0.0042837) |
| Microenterprises | Liquidity | −0.0000814<br>(0.0000972) | 0.0000117<br>(0.0000132) |
| | Leverage | −0.0007267<br>(0.0005008) | −0.0016012*<br>(0.0008598) |

*Source* Author's calculations based on FINA database

# 4 Results and Discussion

The summary[3] of the estimates for each manufacturing sample and each financial indicator in two analysed periods is given in Table 3.

The estimates reveal that leverage indicator is significant only in the period since the crisis. This implies that previous indebtness (probably connected to firms' survival strategy during the crisis) is negatively associated with the probability to export. The same indicator has been significant in the period before the crisis in the case of small enterprises and medium enterprises. This suggests that financial constraints are probably the most important for this group of enterprises. Studies usually find that financial constraints are significant for small- and medium-size enterprises' export propensity (for example, Forte and Moreira 2018), implying a plausible assumption that the smaller the enterprise, the more financially constrained it is.

Table 4 repeats the results of similar exercise for the services sector.

The data in Table 4 reveal that in the case of service sector, only microenterprises are financially constrained in the period after the crises, as revealed by both used indicators. This shows that, as opposed to manufacturing sector in which previous indebtness created restraint for export propensity of firms of all sizes, in service sector this is significant only in the case of microfirms. Furthermore, in case of microenterprises also the liquidity indicator is significant in the period after the

[3] The full set of each of the 31 estimates can be obtained from the author upon request.

**Table 4** Average partial effects of financial constraints on extensive export margin in Croatian services

| Firm size | Indicator | 1999–2007 | 2008–2017 |
|---|---|---|---|
| Large enterprises | Liquidity | −0.0225625 (0.1588107) | 0.000781 (0.1130981) |
| | Leverage | 0.0103921 (0.0145251) | |
| Medium enterprises | Liquidity | 0.00501 (0.0057449) | 0.0004995 (0.019219) |
| | Leverage | 0.0070428 (0.0047816) | −0.0012286 (0.0347466) |
| Small enterprises | Liquidity | 0.0011862 (0.0023105) | 0.000955 (0.000872) |
| | Leverage | −0.0032169 (0.0023873) | −0.000009 (0.0000903) |
| Microenterprises | Liquidity | −0.0003563 (0.0003468) | 0.000003*** (0.0000008) |
| | Leverage | −0.0002362 (0.0001694) | −0.000651*** (0.0002089) |

*Notes* Estimates for large enterprises in case of leverage indicators in the period after crisis did not converge. *Source* Author's calculations based on FINA database

crisis, so the conclusion is that financial conditions since the crisis are not favourable for export propensity of microenterprises in the service sector.

Results in this paper are in line with the findings of previous studies in other countries that are focused on manufacturing sector. Forte and Moreira (2018) analyse small enterprises in Portugal during the 2008–2012 period and find that financial constraints negatively affect the export propensity of SMEs, although the effect is relatively small. Wagner (2014b) finds for German manufacturing industry a positive link between a better credit-rating score of a firm and both the probability that the firm is an exporter and a higher share of exports in total sales. Similarly, Muûls (2008) for a sample of Belgian manufacturing firms during the period 1999–2005 finds that firms are more likely to export if they enjoy higher productivity levels and lower credit constraints. Askenazy et al. (2015) based on a sample of French manufacturing firms during the period 1995–2007 confirm that financial constraints hamper firms' ability to cover fixed foreign market entry costs as well as recurrent costs associated with maintaining the presence in a foreign market, thereby reducing the probability of entering international markets.

Even though we are not able to reveal decision-making process within the firms with the dataset used in the empirical analysis, from the managerial point of view it could be inferred that in order to attempt conquering international markets, a deleveraging process should be considered first. This is specifically important for manufacturing sector, where estimates consistently show that for all sizes of enterprises financial constraints are significant in the period since the crisis.

## 5 Conclusion

The focus in this paper is on financial constraints as an obstacle for exporting in Croatia. Although the size of the effect is not high, it does provide enough support for several previously undocumented problems related to the Croatian firms struggles to increase competitiveness and more actively participate in international market competition.

First, we have established that, not only for manufacturing sector, but for the economy as a whole, exporters systematically differ from non-exporters in terms of productivity and wages (which has been addressed by the previous literature), but also in terms of our selected financial constraints indicators. When focusing on financial constraints, we have found support for the claim that financial constraint is more important in manufacturing sector than for the service sector.

The empirical analysis did not find any systematic differences between pre- and post-crisis financial constraints' effect. However, it seems that in the case of manufacturing sector, leverage indicator is systematically significant in the period since the crisis for all firm sizes. This suggests that previous indebtness of the firms in manufacturing sector creates important obstacle for active participation in international market. For firms in the service sector, significant obstacles have been found only for microfirms, who probably due to their size are also having difficulties in finding adequate sources of financing in general, not just related to enhance their export endeavours.

Although in Croatia there are some government finances financial support measures directed towards exporters, their financial strength is negligible. For the most part, enterprises still rely on banks to provide external finances for their international business endeavours. Since the results have implied that precisely previous indebtness is important financial constraint in the post-crisis period, relative reluctance of the banking sector to provide additional finances could contribute to the financial constraint impediment to exporting. Designing new and better targeted government support for specific activities would be probably warmly welcomed by the business sector in Croatia.

Propensity to export certainly does not depend only on the financial conditions within a firm or within a country. Many aspects not covered by current analysis influence the decision-making process at the firm level. Future research endeavours should address this issue by direct survey methods that have the ability to investigate motivational aspects in more depth. Another aspect that also deserves attention is the intensive exporting margin. Although initial estimates in this paper did not give much evidence that there are important differences on the crude level of analysis, identifying certain threshold levels in intensive margins are certainly worth future research endeavours.

## References

Acedo FJ, Galán JL (2011) Export stimuli revisited: the influence of the characteristics of managerial decision makers on international behaviour. Int Small Bus J 29(6):648–670
Almeida H et al (2004) The cash flow sensitivity of cash. J Finance 59(4):1777–1804
Askenazy P et al (2015) Financial constraints and foreign market entries or exits: firm-level evidence from France. Rev World Econ 151(2):231–253
Beck T, Demirguc-Kunt A (2006) Small and medium-size enterprises: access to finance as a growth constraint. J Bank Finance 30(11):2931–2943
Bellone F et al (2010) Financial constraints and firm export behaviour. The World Econ 33(3):347–373
Berman N, Hericourt J (2010) Financial factors and the margins of trade: evidence from cross-country firm-level data. J Dev Econ 93(2):206–217
Bernard AB, Jensen JB (1999) Exceptional exporter performance: cause, effect, or both? J Int Econ 47(1):1–25
Bernard AB, Wagner J (1997) Exports and success in German manufacturing. Weltwirtschaftliches Archiv/rev World Econ 133(1):134–157
Bernard AB et al (2007) Firms in international trade. J Econ Perspect 21(3):105–130
Campello M et al (2010) The real effects of financial constraints: evidence from a financial crisis. J Financ Econ 97(3):470–487
Carpenter RE, Petersen BC (2002) Is the growth of small firms constrained by internal finance? Rev Econ Stat 82(2):298–309
Carreira C, Silva F (2010) No deep pockets: some stylized empirical results on firms' financial constraints. J Econ Surv 24(4):731–753
Chaney T (2016) Liquidity constrained exporters. J Econ Dyn Control 72:141–154
Coulibaly B et al (2013) Financial frictions, trade credit, and the 2008–09 global financial crisis. Int Rev Econ Financ 26(1):25–38
Cziraky D et al (2005) Determinants of the low SME loan approval rate in Croatia. Small Bus Econ 25(4):347–372
Egger P, Kesina M (2013) Financial constraints and exports: evidence from Chinese firms. Cesifo Econ Stud 59(4):676–706
Fauceglia D (2015) Credit constraints, firm exports and financial development: evidence from developing countries. Q Rev Econ Finance 55:53–66
Forte R, Moreira AS (2018) Financial constraints and small and medium-sized firms' export propensity: evidence from Portuguese manufacturing firms. Int J Econ Bus 25(2):223–241
Greenaway D et al (2007) Financial factors and exporting decisions. J Int Econ 73(2):377–395
Griffith DA (2011) Insights into gaining access to export financing: understanding export lenders ideal exporter profile. J World Bus 46(1):84–92
Hutchinson J, Xavier A (2006) Comparing the impact of credit constraint on the growth of SMEs in a transition country with an established market economy. Small Bus Econ 27(2–3):169–179
Kahiya ET, Dean DL (2016) Export stages and export barriers: revisiting traditional export development. Thunderbird Int Bus Rev 58(1):75–89
Kaplan S, Zingales L (1997) Do financing constraints explain why investment is correlated with cash flow? Quart J Econ 112(1):169–215
Konings J et al (2003) Investment and financial constraints in transition economies: micro evidence from Poland, the Czech Republic Bulgaria and Romania. Econ Lett 78(2):253–258
Macis M, Schivardi F (2016) Exports and wages: rent sharing, workforce composition, or returns to skills? J Law Econ 34(4):945–978
Melitz MJ (2003) The impact of trade on intra-industry reallocations and aggregate industry productivity. Econometrica 71(6):1695–1725
Melitz MJ, Ottaviano G (2008) Market size, trade, and productivity. Rev Econ Stud 75(1):295–316
Minetti R, Zhu SC (2011) Credit constraints and firm export: microeconomic evidence from Italy. J Int Econ 83(2):109–125

Miravitlles P et al (2018) Corporate financial structure and firm's decision to export. Manag Decis 56(7):1526–1540
Muûls M (2008) Exporters and credit constraints: a firm level approach. National Bank of Belgium Working Paper no 139
Nguyen H, Qian R (2014) Demand collapse or credit crunch to firms? Evidence from the World Bank's financial crisis survey in Eastern Europe. J Int Money Financ 47:125–144
Partridge MD et al (2017) International trade and local labor markets: do foreign and domestic shocks affect regions differently? J Econ Geogr 17(2):375–409
Porter MJ (1980) Competitive strategy: techniques for analysing industries and competitors. Free Press, New York
Rajan RG, Zingales L (1998) Financial development and growth. Am Econ Rev 88(3):559–586
Schank T et al (2010) Higher wages in exporting firms: self-selection, export effect, or both? First evidence from linked employer-employee data. Rev World Econ 146(2):303–322
Secchi A et al (2016) Financial constraints and firm exports: accounting for heterogeneity, self-selection, and endogeneity. Ind Corp Chang 25(5):813–827
Stiebale J (2011) Do financial constraints matter for foreign market entry? A firm-level examination. The World Econ 34(1):123–153
Valdec M, Zrnc J (2019) Karakteristike hrvatskih izvoznika iz prerađivačkog sektora I oporavak izvoza tijekom velike recesije – rezultati istraživanja modula za trgovinu Istraživačke mreže za konkurentnost (CompNet), Hrvatska narodna banka, Pregledi P-42
Valdec M, Zrnc J (2015) The direction of causality between exports and firm performance: microeconomic evidence from Croatia using the matching approach. Finan Theory Pract 39(1):1–30
Wagner J (2014b) Credit constraints and exports: a survey of empirical studies using firm level data. Ind Corp Chang 23(6):1477–1492
Wagner J (2014a) Credit constraints and export: evidence from German manufacturing enterprises. Appl Econ 46(3):294–302
Westhead P et al (2001) The internationalization of new and small firms: a resource-based view. J Bus Ventur 16(4):333–358
Wolff JA, Pett TL (2000) Internationalization of small firms: an examination of export competitive patterns, firm size, and export performance. J Small Bus Manage 38(2):34–47
WTTC (2018) Travel & tourism economic impact 2018: Croatia. Available at https://www.wttc.org/economic-impact/country-analysis/country-reports/

# Financial Industry and Oil Price Volatility: An Analysis on Central and Eastern Europe

**Georgiana Vrinceanu, Alexandra Horobet, Consuela Popescu, and Lucian Belascu**

**Abstract** The global economy is considerably dependent on fossil fuels, of which oil is by far the most important, and concerns about the impact of oil price volatility on the real economy have been recently fuelled by the positive correlation between oil and stock prices. This positive correlation might be explained by a joint response of both oil and stock prices to underlying shifts in global demand. In other words, a possible explanation for this positive correlation might be the tendency of stock prices and crude oil prices to react in the same way to common factors, such as changes in aggregate demand or in overall uncertainty and risk aversion. The financial industry seems to be a transmitter channel of macroeconomic and even global risks towards the remaining industries, as indicated by the existing literature and the recent global financial crisis, which raises the interest towards a thorough investigation of the financial industry exposure to risk factors. Our paper proposes an empirical research on the exposure to oil price risk of companies from the financial industry listed on stock exchanges from seven Central and Eastern European countries: Bulgaria, Croatia, the Czech Republic, Hungary, Poland, Romania and Slovenia. The Central and Eastern Europe countries are interesting for research on our topic given their high levels of energy intensity, their significant share of petroleum products in total final energy consumption and their high oil imports dependency rates—i.e. the percentage of oil imports in net available energy. We use daily prices and returns of listed companies from the financial industry, as well as Brent crude oil prices, to estimate a two-stage GARCH (1,1) to capture the effects of temporal dependence in oil prices volatility on financial industry firms' returns. The GARCH model is complemented

G. Vrinceanu (✉) · A. Horobet · C. Popescu
Bucharest University of Economic Studies, Piata Romana 6, 010374 Bucharest, Romania
e-mail: vrinceanugeorgiana16@stud.ase.ro

A. Horobet
e-mail: alexandra.horobet@rei.ase.ro

C. Popescu
e-mail: consuela.popescu@rei.ase.ro

L. Belascu
"Lucian Blaga" University of Sibiu, Victoriei Street 10, 550024 Sibiu, Romania
e-mail: lucian.belascu@ulbsibiu.ro



G. Karanovic et al. (eds.), *The Changing Financial Landscape*, Contributions to Economics, https://doi.org/10.1007/978-3-030-82778-6_3

by Granger causality tests to further explore the relationship between stock and oil prices. The time span of our research is January 2010–December 2019. Our results show that the relationship between stock prices and oil price volatility is significant in the CEE region, which reinforces the fundamental role of the financial industry as transmitter of economic shocks towards the real economy.

**Keywords** Oil price · Stock prices · Volatility · Financial industry · Central and Eastern Europe · GARCH

## 1 Introduction

Modelling volatility and in particular oil price volatility has gained much importance in the past years as it was proved that there is a strong relationship between oil price volatility and stock returns. This finding has significant implications for political and economic decisions as shocks of either sign affecting a market can be transmitted quickly to other markets, a phenomenon called contagion. Unfortunately, there is no clear response whether there is a best choice of models to explain the complexity of the relationship.

Crude oil and petroleum products have the highest share of energy consumption in the EU countries. These countries depended on net imports for 86.7% of the oil products consumed in 2017, and in the last 20 years, EU countries have become increasingly dependent on crude oil imports (Eurostat 2019). Historically, the dependence on crude oil in EU countries during periods of high oil price shocks has led to economic instability (Cambridge Econometrics 2016). Table 1 shows oil and petroleum products final consumption for energy use in seven CEE countries from 2010 to 2017. Poland was the largest consumer of oil and petroleum products for energy use; its final consumption volume measured 24.9 million tons of oil and petroleum products in 2017. Although an improvement has been seen in the past years, CEE economies are more energy intensive than their western counterparts. An explanation for this might be that an improvement in the consumption of

**Table 1** Oil and petroleum products final consumption—energy use (million tons)

| Country | 2010 | 2011 | 2012 | 2013 | 2014 | 2015 | 2016 | 2017 |
|---|---|---|---|---|---|---|---|---|
| Bulgaria | 3.121 | 3.001 | 3.149 | 2.862 | 3.138 | 3.479 | 3.572 | 3.771 |
| Czechia | 6.660 | 6.636 | 6.487 | 6.315 | 6.627 | 6.870 | 6.943 | 7.141 |
| Croatia | 2.837 | 2.749 | 2.620 | 2.654 | 2.583 | 2.718 | 2.771 | 2.954 |
| Hungary | 4.737 | 4.795 | 4.488 | 4.413 | 4.874 | 5.271 | 5.374 | 5.591 |
| Poland | 20.518 | 20.500 | 19.735 | 18.553 | 18.591 | 19.420 | 21.465 | 24.898 |
| Romania | 6.079 | 6.674 | 6.899 | 6.593 | 6.800 | 7.050 | 7.500 | 8.065 |
| Slovakia | 2.366 | 2.310 | 2.339 | 2.244 | 2.247 | 2.299 | 2.501 | 2.839 |

*Source* Eurostat (2019)

energy has been experienced in the last years due a shift from industry to service based economies all over Europe, but also a shift to less energy-intensive production coupled with the closure of inefficient units (Statistics Explained 2020). According to the latest European Commission report on renewable energy, most CEE countries successfully reached their targets of moving from nonrenewable energy to renewable energy in gross final energy consumption (IRENA 2018).

Nowadays, because of the worldwide coronavirus pandemic and governments' strict rules of confinement at home, US consumption of crude oil has fallen to its lowest in the past 30 years, while demand in India has plunged as much as 70%. China, India and the USA account for approximately 40% of the global oil demand. Even after the highly uncertain end of the pandemic, there are voices stating that it will probably take decades for the oil demand to reach the levels of 2019 as new ways of working might be put in place which will require less travelling either by car or by plane (Sell 2020). Thus, lower demand leads to structural overcapacity which puts a cap on oil prices, like the 1990s period. As a period of uncertainty and turbulence is expected in the upcoming months, the price of oil is expected to become very volatile (Lee 2020). Figure 1 shows the OPEC's spare production capacity between 1990 and 2020. This capacity has recently risen more than it has been in over the past three decades, but the OPEC producers are now reducing their production by more than 20% (Sell 2020).

Moving forward, our research hypothesis is built on the economy-wide impact of Brent crude oil price changes, specifically for small open economies, such as the countries from Central and Eastern Europe (CEE). Therefore, our main goal consists in analysing the exposure to oil price movements of a set of listed financial companies from seven CEE countries, all members of the European Union: Bulgaria, Croatia, the Czech Republic, Hungary, Poland, Romania and Slovenia. These companies' exposure to oil price risk is understood as a measure of systemic risk. Our paper contributes to the existing literature by analysing the CEE region countries using a two-stage generalized autoregressive conditional heteroscedasticity—GARCH(1,1)—model. To the best of our knowledge, we are the first authors who use this methodology in this framework. The utility of the GARCH model resides in its ability to capture the effects of temporal dependence in oil prices volatility on financial industry firms' returns.

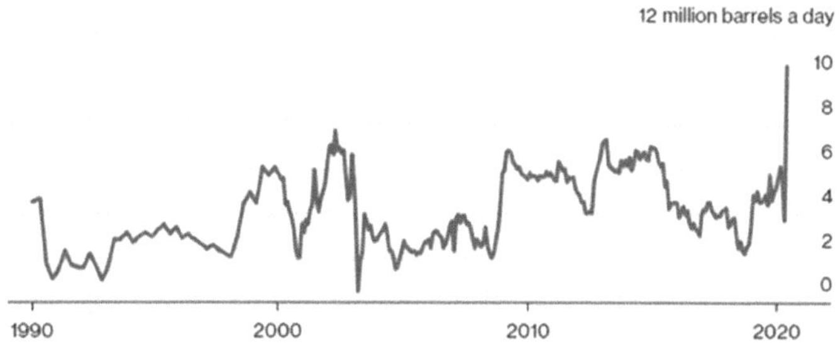


**Fig. 1** OPEC's spare production capacity (1990–2020). *Source* Bloomberg (2020b)

This paper is structured as follows. Section 2 shows the main research directions and results from the existing literature. Section 3 presents the data and the methodological specifications. Our findings are presented and discussed in Sect. 4. Section 5 concludes, discusses the limits of our research and outlines a few directions for future research.

## 2 Literature Review

The academic literature on this subject is currently amplifying. The existing empirical evidence demonstrates that oil price movements correspond to stock prices returns even if the results proved to be rather diverse. Some authors—Cong et al. (2008), Jammazi and Aloui (2010) or Mohanty et al. (2010)—found no significant relationship between oil price fluctuations and stock market returns while others—Ciner (2001) or Tuna et al. (2017)—identified a well-defined relationship between these two variables.

Cong et al. (2008) use multivariate vector auto-regression to investigate the relationship between oil price shocks and Chinese stock market. They find that apart from the manufacturing sector and some oil companies, there is no significant relationship between oil price shocks and stock returns for Chinese companies. Jammazi et al. (2010) also highlight that crude oil shocks do not affect the recession stock market phases in the case of UK and France but do so for Japan. However, they reduce significantly the moderate and/or expansion phases of the stock market, although temporarily.

Ciner (2001) uses nonlinear causality tests and shows that there is a nonlinear relationship between oil price shocks and the S&P 500 stock index returns. The author also documents a feedback relation from the stock index to oil futures markets in the USA, which shows a powerful interdependence between financial markets and the economy in the 1990s. In the same vein, Tuna et al. (2017) analyzed for the first time the cointegration and causality between share price and oil price in two groups of developed versus developing countries. They find a long-term relationship between stock exchange indices and oil price for both categories of countries. In the case of developing countries, there is bilateral causality, while for developed countries, the causality is unilateral, from oil prices to stock prices.

Similarly, Çevik et al. (2018) use time-varying causality tests in mean and in variance and split the sample into developing and developed countries in order to analyze the relationship between oil price innovations and global stock returns. Their results show that during phases of economic turmoil, there is volatility spillover from stock markets to crude oil—valid for both developed and developing countries—and from crude oil to stock markets—valid only for developed countries—as a result of the uncertainty in the market. An interesting outcome is that before the 2008 financial crisis, there was a volatility spillover from developed to emerging markets which disappeared in the immediate period after the crisis and became very weak in time. When it comes to the financial sector, the findings show the presence of negative effects of oil price changes on oil-related sectors, positive effects of the former on oil-related and oil-substitute sector but also insignificant effects on nonoil-related sectors. Horobet et al. (2019) found that EU financial sector is largely exposed to oil price movements over the long run and argue that this exposure should be comprehended in the context of financial companies' exposure to real economy risk factors. The authors consider that this reveals the major role of the financial sector in the EU economy in transmitting systemic shocks. Moreover, the authors identified signs of different behaviours of market investors over the short run versus the long run regarding the valuation of financial companies' stock prices in relation to oil price and other macroeconomic variables, which raises serious challenges for financial authorities.

Several papers use GARCH models to analyse the relationship between oil price and equity returns or oil return volatility and volatility of specific sectors. Falzon et al. (2013) base their study on US and UK markets and find that apart from Oil and Gas, all the other sectors' equity returns (Basic materials, Industrials, Consumer goods, Healthcare, Consumer services, Telecommunications, Utilities) respond negatively to oil price changes. Ratti et al. (2013) use GARCH-M methodology to model the risk and returns of ten Australian sectors. They find that apart from the Energy and Materials sectors, oil price and stock price returns move in opposite directions but also that an increase in oil price return volatility reduces stock return volatility for half of the sectors analysed (including Energy and Materials sectors) and increases stock return volatility for the other half (including Financial sector). Furthermore, Caporale et al. (2015) investigate the time-varying impact of oil price uncertainty on Chinese stock prices in ten sectors using a bivariate VAR-GARCH-in-mean model. The estimation suggests that oil price uncertainty impacts stock returns negatively during periods of aggregate supply-side shocks in Consumer services, Financials, Oil and Gas and positively during periods of aggregate demand-side shocks in Healthcare, Telecommunications, Basic Materials, Consumer Goods, Industrials, Utilities and Technology. Finally, Singhal et al. (2018) investigate the dynamic comovements between oil and Indian stock market returns both at aggregate and sector level. The paper deploys a VAR-DCC-GARCH framework and encompasses data from January 2006 to February 2015 of Brent crude oil and seven sector indices of Bombay stock exchange: Automotive, Energy, Financial, Industrial, Metal, Oil and Gas and Power. Their main findings indicate no significant long-term spillover effect from oil market to stock market at aggregate level, but significant in the case of Automotive, Power and Financial sectors.

Concerning the investigation of the relationship between oil prices and stock prices of companies from CEE countries, we notice that the empirical literature on this subject is poor. Some examples of authors who concentrate their attention on CEE region in their study are Mohanty et al. (2010), Asteriou et al. (2013) or Drachal (2018). For instance, Mohanty et al. (2010) investigated the relationship between oil price changes and stock prices of oil and gas companies from CEE countries between 1998 and 2010 and discovered no significant exposure. On the other hand, Asteriou et al. (2013) investigated the link between oil price shocks and stock prices returns from CEE and found a negative exposure of stock prices returns to changes in oil prices that becomes more significant when oil prices are low. Another research on this subject which refers to CEE countries belongs to Drachal (2018) who examined the causal dynamics between spot oil price, exchange rates and stock prices in five CEE countries: Poland, Czech Republic, Hungary, Romania and Serbia. The author used the Granger causality test and the nonlinear Diks–Panchenko test and the causality in variance was checked with the Hafner–Herwartz test. His results show that there is a strong connection between oil prices, stock prices and exchange rates. The strongest relationships were found for Czech Republic, Hungary and Romania.

Our paper studies for the first time the exposure of a sample of financial companies headquartered in CEE region to oil price risk using a two-stage GARCH (1,1) model, thus filling the gap in the literature combining the framework and the region.

## 3 Methodology

The data set of this study comprises daily returns of 43 listed financial companies on stock exchanges in seven CEE countries, all members of the European Union (Bulgaria, Croatia, Czech Republic, Hungary, Poland, Romania and Slovenia) and daily Brent oil price changes during the period from 18 January 2010 to 30 December 2019. We have selected this time span to avoid the interval of the global financial crisis (2008–2009) and the recent global economic crisis caused by the coronavirus pandemic. The CEE financial companies were included in our analysis based on the maximum data availability for the period chosen in our study. In these seven CEE countries, there were 119 listed financial companies, and we have selected only those that had data available for the period chosen in our analysis. These selected financial companies are banks, investment funds, insurance companies and stock exchanges. The data were obtained from Bloomberg. Table 2 contains the description of the data used for this analysis, the number of listed financial companies from each country and the sample period for each. Moreover, Table 3 presents the selected

**Table 2** Data description

| Country | Total no. of listed companies | No. of listed financial companies | No. of selected financial companies | Sample period |
|---|---|---|---|---|
| Bulgaria | 80 | 16 | 5 | 27.09.2011–30.12.2019 |
| Croatia | 34 | 1 | 1 | 23.01.2012–30.12.2019 |
| Czech Republic | 18 | 4 | 3 | 18.01.2010–30.12.2019 |
| Hungary | 38 | 7 | 3 | 21.02.2011–30.12.2019 |
| Poland | 594 | 71 | 18 | 23.01.2012–30.12.2019 |
| Romania | 119 | 16 | 11 | 05.01.2012–30.12.2019 |
| Slovenia | 13 | 4 | 2 | 25.01.2012–30.12.2019 |

*Source* Authors' own work

**Table 3** Listed financial companies in our sample and their market capitalization (EUR millions, 2020)

| Country | Market capitalization for countries (€m) | Listed financial companies in our sample | Companies' market capitalization (€m) | Share of countries' market capitalization (%) |
|---|---|---|---|---|
| Hungary | 61,469,166.46 | OTP Bank | 2,710,000.00 | 4.49 |
| | | Takarek Mortgage Bank | 34,290.00 | |
| | | CIG Pannonia Life Insurance PLC | 14,480.00 | |
| Czech Republic | 1,004,096.08 | Erste Group Bank AG | 201,300.00 | 36.23 |
| | | Komercni Banka | 98,490.00 | |
| | | Vienna Insurance Group AG | 64,020.00 | |
| Croatia | 92,357.66 | Zagrebacka Banka | 15,630.00 | 16.92 |
| Slovenia | 6,750.53 | Zavarovalnica | 645.68 | 13.44 |
| | | Sava Reinsurance Plc | 261.74 | |
| Bulgaria | 7,192.92 | CB First Investment Bank | 291.84 | 12.42 |
| | | Eurohold Bulgaria | 243.25 | |
| | | CB Central Cooperative Bank | 133.49 | |
| | | Advance Terrafund | 160.86 | |
| | | Bulgarian Real Estate Fund | 63.74 | |
| Romania | 1,670,404.49 | Erste Group Bank AG | 39,260.00 | 4.28 |
| | | Banca Transilvania | 9,960.00 | |
| | | BRD Groupe Societe Generale | 7,830.00 | |
| | | Fondul Proprietatea | 8,830.00 | |
| | | SIF Moldova | 1,430.00 | |
| | | SIF Oltenia | 1,230.00 | |
| | | SIF Banat Crisana | 1,220.00 | |
| | | SIF Transilvania | 679.01 | |
| | | SIF Muntenia | 539.10 | |

(continued)

**Table 3** (continued)

| Country | Market capitalization for countries (€m) | Listed financial companies in our sample | Companies' market capitalization (€m) | Share of countries' market capitalization (%) |
|---|---|---|---|---|
| | | Patria Bank | 262.31 | |
| | | Bursa de Valori Bucuresti | 198.82 | |
| Poland | 776,253.41 | Santander Bank Polska | 16,640.00 | 3.25 |
| | | Bank Handlowy w Warszawie | 4,870.00 | |
| | | Warsaw Stock Exchange | 1,680.00 | |
| | | Bank Ochrony Środowiska | 501.71 | |
| | | MCI Management | 478.93 | |
| | | Getin Noble Bank SA | 258.53 | |
| | | Getin Holding | 217.66 | |
| | | Quercus TFI | 166.09 | |
| | | Votum | 150.00 | |
| | | Vindexus | 59.99 | |
| | | Ipopema Securities | 89.81 | |
| | | Europejskie Centrum Odszkodowań | 22.68 | |
| | | Impera Capital | 7.83 | |
| | | INC | 22.50 | |
| | | Open Finance | 9.29 | |
| | | Capital Partners | 21.59 | |
| | | M.W. Trade | 38.57 | |
| | | Pragma Faktoring | 25.87 | |

*Source* Bloomberg

financial companies and shows their market capitalization at the beginning of 2020 and the percentage of all selected financial companies in total stock exchange market capitalization of the country.

The logarithmic transformation of the daily stock prices returns of the investigated listed financial companies and daily oil prices returns was calculated based on the general formula:

**Table 4** Descriptive statistics of stocks and oil returns (annualized data)

| Stocks/oil returns | Mean | | Standard deviation |
|---|---|---|---|
| | Minimum | Maximum | |
| Bulgaria | 0.000 | 0.166 | 0.396 |
| Croatia | 0.042 | | 0.276 |
| Czech Republic | −0.067 | 0.000 | 0.308 |
| Hungary | −0.239 | 0.074 | 0.385 |
| Poland | −0.330 | 0.150 | 0.503 |
| Romania | −0.046 | 0.135 | 0.416 |
| Slovenia | 0.118 | 0.140 | 0.274 |
| Oil returns | 0.000 | | 0.308 |

*Source* Authors' own work

$$R_{i,t} = Ln\left(\frac{P_{i,t}}{P_{i,t-1}}\right) \tag{1}$$

where $R_{i,t}$ denotes the logarithmic return of the listed financial company's stock price/oil price $i$ in period $t$, $P_{i,t}$ denotes the closing price of the listed financial company's stock price/oil price $i$ in period $t$ and $P_{i,t-1}$ denotes the closing price of the listed financial company's stock price/oil price $i$ in period $t - 1$.

Table 4 presents the common descriptive statistics of the annualized financial companies' stocks and oil returns. The mean represents the average of all observation values, and the standard deviation shows how tightly our data values are clustered around the mean. Furthermore, in order to display the distribution of our data, we have created boxplots of annualized companies' stock returns and standard deviations that indicate how the values in the data are spread out. Figure 2 shows the corresponding boxplots for the annualized companies' stock returns and standard deviations of returns, based on "minimum", first quartile (Q1), median, third quartile (Q3) and "maximum" values. Returns' standard deviations have a higher spread compared to mean returns; outliers are also indicated by both boxplots.

ARCH (autoregressive conditional heteroscedasticity) models, which were proposed by Engle (1982), were the first models that considered a conditional variance process with an autoregressive structure and log returns modelled as a white noise multiplied by the volatility. Several years later, in order to correct the weaknesses of the ARCH models, Bollerslev (1986) further developed them. For the purpose to make it possible for the variance ($\sigma_t^2$) to have a supplementary autoregressive structure within itself, he proposed the GARCH (generalized autoregressive conditional heteroscedasticity) model. This extension of the ARCH models is widely used in the academic literature and in financial time-series modelling. GARCH(1,1) model is conducted on the basis of two principal equations. The first equation is for the mean and the other one is for the variance of the time series:

$$R_t = \theta X' + \epsilon_t \tag{2}$$

$$\sigma_t^2 = \omega + \alpha\, \epsilon_{t-1}^2 + \beta \sigma_{t-1}^2 \tag{3}$$

where the first equation incorporates exogenous variables ($X'$) and an error term ($\ni$), i.i.d. with an expectation of 0 and variance of 1. The conditional variance $\sigma_t^2$ given in the equation for the variance of time series denotes the one-period ahead forecast variance on the basis of the information from the past ($\sigma_{t-1}^2$), news about the volatility of the previous period—i.e. the one-period lag of the squared residuals in Eq. 2, or the ARCH term—and the constant $\omega$. The GARCH(1,1) means that a first-order autoregressive GARCH term (the first 1 in parentheses) and a first-order moving average ARCH term (the second 1 in parentheses) are present in the estimation. The coefficients $\alpha$ and $\beta$ are the parameters of this model.

We employ a model used in the study of Omran et al. (2010), which is a two-stage GARCH (1,1). The authors examine whether GARCH modelling prospers in capturing the effects of temporal dependence in trading volume for individual stocks in the UK market. A reasonable justification for the success of GARCH models in modelling stock returns is expressed by the information flow hypothesis. If it is assumed that the mixing variable, the number of information arrival designs a serially dependent sequence, then it is believable that GARCH model is competent to capture the temporal dependence in this variable.

Firstly, we estimate a GARCH (1,1) for each stock in our sample. This represents the first stage of the model, and it is based on the following formulas:

$$R_{i,t} = a_{i,0} + b_1 R_{i,t-1} + \varepsilon_{i,t} \tag{4}$$

$$\sigma_{i,t}^2 = \alpha_{i,0} + \alpha_{i,1}\varepsilon_{i,t-1}^2 + \beta_{i,1}\sigma_{i,t-1}^2 \tag{5}$$

where $R_{i,t}$ denotes the logarithmic return of stock prices of selected financial companies and $\varepsilon_{i,t} \sim N\left(0, \sigma_{i,t}^2\right)$. We incorporate in Eq. 4 an autoregressive term of order 1 beneficial to correct the small but significant first-order autocorrelation in mean stock returns. The next equation implies the variance of unexpected stock return as a GARCH (1,1) process, where the sum of parameters $\alpha_{i,1}$ and $\beta_{i,1}$, which lies between values 0 and 1, determines the volatility persistence in stock returns.

The next step in our analysis is to estimate the second stage of the model. In this regard, we add a term for oil price change in the conditional variance equation, and it becomes as follows:

$$\sigma_{i,t}^2 = \alpha_{i,0} + \alpha_{i,1}\varepsilon_{i,t-1}^2 + \beta_{i,1}\sigma_{i,t-1}^2 + \omega_{i,1} V_{i,t}. \tag{6}$$

Thereby, if the oil price change constitutes a proxy for new information that appears in the market, then the coefficient $\omega_{i,1}$ is higher than zero and the sum of $\alpha_{i,1}$ and $\beta_{i,1}$ turns to be inconsiderable.

Following the same methodology as Omran et al. (2010), in both stages of the model, the parameters are estimated jointly employing the Berndt–Hall–Hall–Hausman (BHHH) optimization algorithm and the $Q$-statistic is used for the purpose of testing the hypothesis of the lack of GARCH effects in the residuals. We estimate the models in Eviews.

The GARCH (1,1) model is supplemented by a Granger causality test on the relationship between stock returns' unconditional volatility and oil price changes. The Granger causality tests were created by Granger (1969) and imply a statistical concept of causality between two variables in time-series data based on prediction power. Therefore, in terms of Granger causality, a variable $X$ causes (more concretely, Granger causes) another variable $Y$ if past values of $X$ help predicting $Y$ above and beyond the past values of $Y$ alone.

Other studies that employ the GARCH methodology for the purpose of investigating the link between oil price changes and stock prices belong to Narayan et al. (2011) and Chen et al. (2018). Moreover, other studies that employ the Granger causality tests to examine the link between oil price changes and stock prices belong to Çevik et al. (2018) and Drachal (2018).

## 4 Results and Discussion

Firstly, we have checked the assumption of normality by determining whether the residuals have a normal distribution. The results of the Jarque–Bera tests indicated that errors were conditionally normally distributed; therefore, we implemented the GARCH model using this assumption. The results of the first-stage GARCH (1,1) model estimations, the second-stage GARCH (1,1) model estimations and the results of the causal relationships between stock price changes and oil price changes are presented in Tables 5, 6, 7, 8, 9, 10 and 11. We have decided to analyse our research results separately for each country in order to obtain a detailed view at country level regarding the relationships between stock prices volatility and oil price changes.

The first-stage GARCH (1,1) model represents the restricted model where $\omega$ was set equal to zero, while the second-stage GARCH (1,1) model is the unrestricted model. At the same time, the causal relationship between stock prices volatility and oil price changes was tested using the F-statistic test, by applying the Granger causality approach. The first null hypothesis assumes that stock prices volatility does not Granger cause the oil price, and the second null hypothesis supposes that oil price does not Granger cause stock prices volatility.

Table 5 displays the results obtained for the Bulgarian companies. $Q$-statistics at the lag 10 for the squared returns ($Q_{10}^2 R$) show statistical significance for two out of five financial companies. This demonstrates the existence of GARCH effects for two Bulgarian companies' returns.

The persistence in volatility as measured by the sum of $\alpha_1$ and $\beta_1$ is remarkably high: more specifically, it is higher than 0.85 in the case of three out of five companies. On the other hand, $Q_{10}^2 U$ indicate that the squared standardized residuals do not show

**Table 5** Results for financial companies from Bulgaria

| Company | First-stage GARCH(1,1) model estimations | | | Second-stage GARCH(1,1) model estimations | | | Causal relationships | |
|---|---|---|---|---|---|---|---|---|
| | $\alpha_1 + \beta_1$ | $Q_{10}^2 R$ | $Q_{10}^2 U$ | $\omega_1$ | $\alpha_1 + \beta_1$ | $Q_{10}^2$ | $VOL_t \Rightarrow OIL_t$ | $OIL_t \Rightarrow VOL_t$ |
| Advance Terrafund | 0.789 | 4.676 | 1.249 | 0.000 | 0.787 | 1.177 | 0.876 | 0.465 |
| Bulgarian Real Estate Fund | −0.270 | 3.855 | 0.642 | 0.008* | 0.351 | 1.328 | 3.494* | 2.789* |
| CB Central Cooperative Bank | 0.884 | 7.282 | 4.290 | −0.001* | 0.878 | 3.884 | 0.402 | 0.402 |
| CB First Investment Bank | 0.911 | 22.267* | 7.409 | −0.002* | 0.892 | 6.139 | 0.079 | 0.277 |
| Eurohold Bulgaria | 1.001 | 63.846* | 2.840 | 0.001 | 0.997 | 3.468 | 1.050 | 1.833** |

*Note* $Q_{10}^2 R$ denotes $Q$-statistics at the lag 10 for the squared returns, $Q_{10}^2 U$ and $Q_{10}^2$ denote $Q$-statistics at the lag 10 for the squared standardized residuals, $VOL_t$ denotes return volatility, $OIL_t$ denotes oil prices changes, and * and ** indicate statistical significance at least at 1% and 5% level, respectively
*Source* Authors' research results

any significant GARCH effects. The results of estimating the unrestricted model show a statistically significant coefficient of oil price for three out of five companies. Similar to the results obtained in the first-stage GARCH(1,1) model estimations, the persistence in volatility measured by the sum of $\alpha_1$ and $\beta_1$ turned out to be very high in almost all situations, i.e. higher than 0.85 in the case of three out of five companies. The $Q$-statistics at the lag 10 for the standardized residuals do not show significant GARCH effects. Applying the Granger causality approach, in the case of only one out of five financial companies (Bulgarian Real Estate Fund) stock prices volatility causes oil price changes and for two out of five financial companies oil price changes cause stock prices volatility.

Table 6 shows the results obtained for the only listed financial company from Croatia, namely Zagrebacka Banka. We notice that the persistence in volatility as measured by the sum of $\alpha 1$ and $\beta 1$ is very high both in the first-stage and in the second-stage GARCH (1,1) model estimations results (higher than 0.85 in both cases). The $Q$-statistics at lag 10 for the squared returns ($Q_{10}^2R$) show statistical significance for this company and demonstrates the existence of GARCH effects in the returns. Concerning the results of estimating the unrestricted model, the coefficient of oil price does not display statistical significance. Also, by applying the Granger causality approach, we discover that stock prices volatility causes oil price changes in the case of this listed financial corporation from Croatia.

The results obtained for the listed financial companies from Czech Republic are presented in Table 7. We observe that the persistence in volatility is surprisingly high in all situations in both the restricted and unrestricted model estimations. More specifically, it is higher than 0.9 in all the cases. Considering the second-stage GARCH (1,1) model estimations, the coefficient of oil price presents statistical significance for one out of three companies (Erste Group Bank AG). For the same financial company, we find that oil price changes cause stock prices volatility.

Table 8 includes the results for the Hungarian listed financial companies. The coefficient of oil price displays statistical significance for all but one company (OTP Bank). Moreover, the persistence in volatility is surprisingly high in the case of all but one company (Takarek Mortgage Bank) in the restricted model estimations. It is higher than 0.9 in these cases.

The results obtained for the listed financial companies from Poland are presented in Table 9. Regarding the results of the first-stage GARCH(1,1) model estimations, we remark that the $Q$-statistics at the lag 10 for the squared returns ($Q_{10}^2R$) show statistical significance for seven out of 18 financial companies. This statistical significance demonstrates the existence of GARCH effects in seven companies' returns. Moreover, the persistence in volatility as measured by the sum of $\alpha_1$ and $\beta_1$ is higher than 0.85 in the case of ten out of 18 companies. On the other hand, $Q_{10}^2U$ indicate that the squared standardized residuals do not show any significant GARCH effects, except for two companies (Bank Ochrony Środowiska and Santander Bank Polska). Concerning the results of estimating the unrestricted model, the coefficient of oil price displays statistical significance for eight out of 18 companies. Similar to the results obtained in the first-stage GARCH(1,1) model estimations, the persistence in volatility as measured by the sum of $\alpha_1$ and $\beta_1$ turned out to be very high in

**Table 6** Results for the financial company from Croatia

| Company | First-stage GARCH(1,1) model estimations | | | Second-stage GARCH(1,1) model estimations | | | Causal relationships | |
|---|---|---|---|---|---|---|---|---|
| | $\alpha_1 + \beta_1$ | $Q_{10}^2 R$ | $Q_{10}^2 U$ | $\omega_1$ | $\alpha_1 + \beta_1$ | $Q_{10}^2$ | $VOL_t \Rightarrow OIL_t$ | $OIL_t \Rightarrow VOL_t$ |
| Zagrebacka Banka | 0.894 | 24.650* | 2.875 | 0.000 | 0.895 | 2.900 | 1.953* | 0.575 |

*Note* $Q_{10}^2 R$ denotes $Q$-statistics at the lag 10 for the squared returns, $Q_{10}^2 U$ and $Q_{10}^2$ denote $Q$-statistics at the lag 10 for the squared standardized residuals, $VOL_t$ denotes return volatility, $OIL_t$ denotes oil prices changes, and * and ** indicate statistical significance at least at 1% and 5% level, respectively
*Source* Authors' own research results

**Table 7** Results for the financial company from Czech Republic

| Company | First-stage GARCH(1,1) model estimations | | | Second-stage GARCH(1,1) model estimations | | | Causal relationships | |
|---|---|---|---|---|---|---|---|---|
| | $\alpha_1 + \beta_1$ | $Q_{10}^2 R$ | $Q_{10}^2 U$ | $\omega_1$ | $\alpha_1 + \beta_1$ | $Q_{10}^2$ | $VOL_t \Rightarrow OIL_t$ | $OIL_t \Rightarrow VOL_t$ |
| Erste Group Bank AG | 0.966 | 15.333 | 7.418 | −0.004* | 0.922 | 11.974 | 0.570 | 1.619** |
| Komercni Banka | 0.995 | 21.722* | 20.711* | 0.000 | 0.994 | 20.999* | 0.943 | 1.100 |
| Vienna Insurance Group AG | 0.993 | 4.783 | 9.128 | 0.000 | 0.994 | 8.512 | 1.391 | 0.810 |

*Note* $Q_{10}^2 R$ denotes $Q$-statistics at the lag 10 for the squared returns, $Q_{10}^2 U$ and $Q_{10}^2$ denote $Q$-statistics at the lag 10 for the squared standardized residuals, $VOL_t$ denotes return volatility, $OIL_t$ denotes oil prices changes, and * and ** indicate statistical significance at least at 1% and 5% level, respectively
*Source* Authors' own research results

**Table 8** Results for the financial company from Hungary

| Company | First-stage GARCH(1,1) model estimations | | | Second-stage GARCH(1,1) model estimations | | | Causal relationships | |
|---|---|---|---|---|---|---|---|---|
| | $\alpha_1 + \beta_1$ | $Q^2_{10}R$ | $Q^2_{10}U$ | $\omega_1$ | $\alpha_1 + \beta_1$ | $Q^2_{10}$ | $VOL_t \Rightarrow OIL_t$ | $OIL_t \Rightarrow VOL_t$ |
| CIG Pannonia Life Insurance | 0.900 | 15.190 | 6.366 | 0.002* | 0.804 | 5.834 | 0.267 | 0.395 |
| OTP Bank | 0.988 | 15.952 | 4.438 | −0.001 | 0.979 | 4.005 | 0.412 | 0.640 |
| Takarek Mortgage Bank | 0.698 | 9.684 | 0.143 | −0.004* | 0.813 | 0.775 | 1.803** | 0.848 |

*Note* $Q^2_{10}R$ denotes $Q$-statistics at the lag 10 for the squared returns, $Q^2_{10}U$ and $Q^2_{10}$ denote $Q$-statistics at the lag 10 for the squared standardized residuals, $VOL_t$ denotes return volatility, $OIL_t$ denotes oil prices changes, and * and ** indicate statistical significance at least at 1% and 5% level, respectively

*Source* Authors' own research results

**Table 9** Results for the financial company from Poland

| Company | First-stage GARCH(1,1) model estimations | | | Second-stage GARCH(1,1) model estimations | | | Causal relationships | |
|---|---|---|---|---|---|---|---|---|
| | $\alpha_1 + \beta_1$ | $Q_{10}^2 R$ | $Q_{10}^2 U$ | $\omega_1$ | $\alpha_1 + \beta_1$ | $Q_{10}^2$ | $VOL_t \Rightarrow OIL_t$ | $OIL_t \Rightarrow VOL_t$ |
| Bank Handlowy w Warszawie | 0.984 | 31.269* | 7.371 | −0.001* | 0.971 | 6.897 | 0.49 | 1.078 |
| Bank Ochrony Środowiska | 0.774 | 5.528 | 17.952** | −0.001 | 0.772 | 18.121** | 0.961 | 0.989 |
| Capital Partners | 0.971 | 46.260* | 12.422 | 0.001 | 0.97 | 12.514 | 0.555 | 0.653 |
| Europejskie Centrum Odszkodowań | 0.936 | 12.775 | 12.159 | 0.001 | 0.934 | 12.126 | 0.487 | 0.891 |
| Getin Holding | 0.182 | 11.836 | 0.037 | 0.054* | 0.735 | 0.012 | 0.798 | 0.681 |
| Getin Noble Bank SA | 0.811 | 5.463 | 0.04 | −0.034* | 0.742 | 0.039 | 0.362 | 0.193 |
| Impera Capital | 0.977 | 23.334* | 0.076 | −0.041* | 0.607 | 0.015 | 0.129 | 0.374 |
| INC | 1.146 | 17.416** | 5.247 | −0.001 | 1.143 | 5.257 | 0.062 | 0.158 |
| Ipopema Securities | 0.519 | 34.146* | 6.283 | 0.001 | 0.522 | 6.238 | 1.136 | 0.852 |
| M.W. Trade | 0.73 | 20.613* | 0.901 | −0.001 | 0.936 | 42.920* | 1.739** | 0.693 |
| MCI Management | 0.955 | 8.097 | 8.721 | −0.001* | 0.932 | 8.693 | 0.812 | 0.748 |
| Open Finance | 1.408 | 2.719 | 0.387 | 0.046* | 1.187 | 0.06 | 0.593 | 0.247 |
| Pragma Faktoring | 0.636 | 21.551* | 3.336 | 0 | 0.625 | 3.623 | 1.928* | 0.963 |
| Quercus TFI | 0.877 | 13.081 | 14.34 | −0.006* | 0.749 | 30.736* | 0.92 | 0.469 |
| Santander Bank Polska | 0.993 | 10.534 | 20.773* | 0 | 0.993 | 22.401* | 0.404 | 3.118* |
| Vindexus | 0.997 | 8.661 | 4.742 | 0 | 0.997 | 4.744 | 0.189 | 0.837 |
| Votum | 0.823 | 8.177 | 1.167 | −0.001 | 0.829 | 1.363 | 2.401** | 0.887 |

(continued)

**Table 9** (continued)

| Company | First-stage GARCH(1,1) model estimations | | | Second-stage GARCH(1,1) model estimations | | | Causal relationships | |
|---|---|---|---|---|---|---|---|---|
| | $\alpha_1 + \beta_1$ | $Q^2_{10}R$ | $Q^2_{10}U$ | $\omega_1$ | $\alpha_1 + \beta_1$ | $Q^2_{10}$ | $VOL_t \Rightarrow OIL_t$ | $OIL_t \Rightarrow VOL_t$ |
| Warsaw Stock Exchange | 0.715 | 15.448 | 4.179 | −0.001** | 0.861 | 3.776 | 0.744 | 0.77 |

*Note* $Q^2_{10}R$ denotes $Q$-statistics at the lag 10 for the squared returns, $Q^2_{10}U$ and $Q^2_{10}$ denote $Q$-statistics at the lag 10 for the squared standardized residuals, $VOL_t$ denotes return volatility, $OIL_t$ denotes oil prices changes, and * and ** indicate statistical significance at least at 1% and 5% level, respectively
*Source* Authors' own research results

many situations; more explicitly, it was higher than 0.85 in the case of ten out of 18 companies. Also, the $Q$-statistics at the lag 10 for the standardized residuals do not show significant GARCH effects, except only four companies (Bank Ochrony Środowiska, M.W. Trade, Quercus TFI and Santander Bank Polska). By applying the Granger causality approach, in the case of one out of 18 financial companies oil price changes cause stock prices volatility.

Table 10 presents the results for financial companies from Romania. In the restricted model estimations, $Q$-statistics at the lag 10 for the squared returns ($Q_{10}^2R$) present statistical significance for more than half of the Romanian listed financial companies. This points towards the existence of GARCH effects in six out of 11 financial companies' returns. The persistence in volatility is surprisingly high in the case of more than half of the companies. It is higher than 0.85 in the case of eight out of 11 companies. On the other hand, $Q_{10}^2U$ indicate that the squared standardized residuals do not show any significant GARCH effects. For the unrestricted model, the coefficient of oil price presents statistical significance for six out of 11 Romanian companies. As in the restricted model estimations, the persistence in volatility is high in almost all cases and higher than 0.85 for eight out of 11 companies. Moreover, the 10-lag $Q$-statistics for the standardized residuals do not show significant GARCH effects, except for one company (SIF Moldova). Also, by applying the Granger causality approach, we discover that in the case of four Romanian listed financial companies (Banca Transilvania, BRD Groupe Societe Generale, Fondul Proprietatea SIF Oltenia), oil price fluctuations cause stock prices volatility.

Table 11 shows the results for financial companies from Slovenia. The persistence in volatility as measured by the sum of $\alpha_1$ and $\beta_1$ turned out to be surprisingly high for both companies and in both stages of GARCH(1,1) model estimations (higher than 0.9). Moreover, concerning the restricted model, we remark that the $Q$-statistics at the lag 10 for the squared returns ($Q_{10}^2R$) present statistical significance for one company (Sava Reinsurance Plc), and it demonstrates the existence of GARCH effects in the returns. Regarding the results of estimating the other GARCH (1,1) model, the coefficient of oil price does not display statistical significance at all. For both companies, this coefficient is not different than zero, which demonstrates that oil price is not an explanatory variable for the conditional volatility of returns of listed financial companies from Slovenia.

## 5 Conclusion

Our paper's main purpose was to analyse the exposure to oil price risk of companies from the financial industry listed on stock exchanges from seven CEE countries: Bulgaria, Croatia, the Czech Republic, Hungary, Poland, Romania and Slovenia. The countries from CEE region are interesting for investigation given their high levels of energy intensity, their significant share of petroleum products in total final energy consumption and their high oil imports dependency rates—i.e. the percentage of oil imports in net available energy.

**Table 10** Results for the financial company from Romania

| Company | First-stage GARCH(1,1) model estimations | | | Second-stage GARCH(1,1) model estimations | | | Causal relationships | |
|---|---|---|---|---|---|---|---|---|
| | $\alpha_1 + \beta_1$ | $Q^2_{10}R$ | $Q^2_{10}U$ | $\omega_1$ | $\alpha_1 + \beta_1$ | $Q^2_{10}$ | $VOL_t \Rightarrow OIL_t$ | $OIL_t \Rightarrow VOL_t$ |
| Banca Transilvania | 0.929 | 30.523* | 1.613 | −0.002* | 0.929 | 1.492 | 1.087 | 2.550* |
| BRD Groupe Societe Generale | 0.546 | 18.095** | 2.827 | −0.001** | 0.934 | 1.541 | 1.584 | 2.126* |
| Bursa de Valori Bucuresti | 0.724 | 8.732 | 4.22 | 0.000 | 0.733 | 4.298 | 0.627 | 1.004 |
| Erste Group Bank AG | 0.934 | 11.881 | 5.081 | −0.001* | 0.943 | 5.252 | 0.588 | 1.432 |
| Fondul Proprietatea | 0.872 | 7.032 | 4.056 | 0.000 | 0.897 | 4.556 | 1.343 | 2.088* |
| Patria Bank | 1.207 | 6.591 | 0.462 | 0.000 | 1.204 | 0.457 | 0.637 | 1.432 |
| SIF Banat Crisana | 0.922 | 18.731* | 1.798 | −0.002* | 0.879 | 4.302 | 1.13 | 1.014 |
| SIF Moldova | 3.806 | 18.470* | 10.262 | −0.062* | 5.369 | 475.970* | 0.164 | 0.283 |
| SIF Muntenia | 0.911 | 27.973* | 5.962 | 0.000 | 0.915 | 5.655 | 1.377 | 1.316 |
| SIF Oltenia | 0.777 | 7.998 | 4.664 | −0.001 | 0.786 | 4.917 | 1.54 | 2.349* |
| SIF Transilvania | 0.959 | 22.718* | 1.562 | −0.001* | 0.96 | 1.479 | 1.096 | 0.281 |

*Note* $Q^2_{10}R$ denotes $Q$-statistics at the lag 10 for the squared returns, $Q^2_{10}U$ and $Q^2_{10}$ denote $Q$-statistics at the lag 10 for the squared standardized residuals, $VOL_t$ denotes return volatility, $OIL_t$ denotes oil prices changes, and * and ** indicate statistical significance at least at 1% and 5% level, respectively
*Source* Authors' own research results

**Table 11** Results for the financial company from Slovenia

| Company | | | | First-stage GARCH(1,1) model estimation | | Second-stage GARCH(1,1) model estimation | | Causal relationships |
|---|---|---|---|---|---|---|---|---|
| | $\alpha_1 + \beta_1$ | $Q_{10}^2 R$ | $Q_{10}^2 U$ | $\omega_1$ | $\alpha_1 + \beta_1$ | $Q_{10}^2$ | $VOL_t \Rightarrow OIL_t$ | $OIL_t \Rightarrow VOL_t$ |
| Sava Reinsurance Plc | 0.999 | 31.433* | 23.461* | 0.000 | 0.998 | 22.885* | 0.433 | 1.546 |
| Zavarovalnica | 0.920 | 13.500 | 2.799 | 0.000 | 0.925 | 2.706 | 0.394 | 1.018 |

*Notes* $Q_{10}^2 R$ denotes $Q$-statistics at the lag 10 for the squared returns, $Q_{10}^2 U$ and $Q_{10}^2$ denote $Q$-statistics at the lag 10 for the squared standardized residuals, $VOL_t$ denotes return volatility, $OIL_t$ denotes oil prices changes, and * and ** indicate statistical significance at least at 1% and 5% level, respectively
*Source* Authors' own research results

Our research results show that the link between stock prices returns and oil price volatility is significant in this region of Europe, which supports the essential role of the financial industry as transmitter of economic shocks towards the real economy. Consequently, this raises difficult challenges for macroeconomic policy authorities due to the fact that shocks in oil prices may have the capacity to influence the foreign currency reserve policy of the central banks and also to determine higher trade balance deficits and cost-push inflation. Besides, the awareness of the existence of this significant relationship between oil price fluctuations and financial companies' stocks' returns could encourage financial investors to improve their portfolio diversification and execute more proficient investment strategies.

Undoubtedly, our analysis has limits. One of them is the relatively small number of selected financial companies in our sample (from some countries such as Poland), given the lack of data on companies' stock prices. This means that it is not possible to generalize the conclusions for individual companies at the country-wide level. Including more listed financial companies in the sample would offer better insights into the exposure of financial companies to oil shocks. In this context, we believe that an attractive future research direction would consist of examining in detail the channels that drive the financial sector's exposure to movements in oil prices. Also, the utilization of other advanced quantitative methods could be considered for a future research direction of this analysis.

**Acknowledgements** This project was financed by Lucian Blaga University of Sibiu and Hasso Plattner Foundation research grants LBUS-IRG-2019-05.

## References

Asteriou D et al (2013) Assessing the impact of oil returns on emerging stock markets: a panel data approach for ten Central and Eastern European Countries. Energy Economics 38:204–211

Bollerslev T (1986) Generalized autoregressive conditional heteroskedasticity. J Econometrics 31(3):307–327

Cambridge Econometrics (2016) A study on oil dependency in the EU. [online]. Available at: https://www.camecon.com/wp-content/uploads/2016/11/Study-on-EU-oil-dependency-v1.4_Final.pdf. [Accessed 30 Mar. 2020]

Caporale G et al (2015) Oil price uncertainty and sectoral stock returns in China: a time-varying approach. China Econ Rev 34:311–321

Çevik EI et al (2018) Oil prices and global stock markets: a time-varying causality-in-mean and causality-in-variance analysis. Energies 11(10):2848

Chen Y et al (2018) Volatility spillovers between crude oil prices and new energy stock price in China. Rom J Econ Forecast 21(2):43–62

Ciner C (2001) Energy shocks and financial markets: nonlinear linkages. Stud Nonlinear Dyn Econom 5(3):1079–1079

Cong RG et al (2008) Relationships between oil price shocks and stock market: an empirical analysis from China. Energy Policy 36(9):3544–3553

Drachal K (2018) Exchange rate and oil price in selected CEE countries. Economies 6:31

Ec.europa.eu (2019) Oil and petroleum products—a statistical overview. [online]. Available at: https://ec.europa.eu/eurostat/statistics-explained/pdfscache/43212.pdf

Engle R (1982) Autoregressive conditional heteroscedasticity with estimates of the variance of United Kingdom inflation. Econometrica 50(4):987–1007

Falzon J et al (2013) The impact of oil prices on sectoral equity returns: evidence from UK and US stock market data. J Financ Manag 1(2):247–268

Gogineni S (2010) Oil and the stock market: an industry level analysis. Financ Rev 45(4):995–1010

Granger CWJ (1969) Investigating causal relations by econometric models and cross spectral methods. Econometrica 37:424–438

Horobet A et al (2019) Oil price and stock prices of EU financial companies: evidence from panel data modeling. Energies 12:4072

International Renewable Energy Agency (2018) Renewable energy prospects for the European Union. [online]. Available at: https://www.irena.org/-/media/Files/IRENA/Agency/Publication/2018/Feb/IRENA_REmap_EU_2018.pdf. [Accessed 25 Apr. 2020]

Jammazi R et al (2010) Wavelet decomposition and regime shifts: assessing the effects of crude oil shocks on stock market returns. Energy Policy 38(3):1415–1435

Khandelwal P et al (2016) The impact of oil prices on the banking system in the GCC, IMF Working Paper WP16/161, International Monetary Fund

Lee J (2020) Oil's recovery could take decades, not years. [online]. Bloomberg. Available at: https://www.bloomberg.com/opinion/articles/2020-05-03/oil-s-recovery-from-coronavirus-could-take-decades-not-years. [Accessed 3 May.. 2020]

Mohanty S et al (2010) Oil shocks and stock returns: the case of the Central and Eastern European (CEE) oil and gas sectors. Emerg Mark Rev 11(4):358–372

Narayan PK et al (2011) New evidence on oil price and firm returns. J Bank Financ 35(12):3253–3262

Omran MF et al (2010) Heteroscedasticity in stock returns data revisited: volume versus GARCH effects. Appl Financ Econ 10(5):553–560

Ratti A et al (2013) Oil price shocks and volatility in Australian stock returns. Munich Personal RePEc Archive, 49043

Sell C (2020) How the pandemic wiped out oil demand around the world. [online]. Bloomberg. Available at: https://www.bloomberg.com/news/articles/2020-04-09/how-the-pandemic-wiped-out-oil-demand-around-the-world. [Accessed 30 Apr. 2020]

Singhal S et al (2018) Returns and volatility linkages between international crude oil price, metal and other stock indices in India: evidence from VAR-DCC-GARCH models. Resour Policy 50:276–288

Statistics Explained (2020) Energy statistics—an overview.[online]. Available at: https://ec.europa.eu/eurostat/statistics-explained/pdfscache/29046.pdf. [Accessed 25 Apr. 2020]

Tuna G et al (2017) The relationship between oil and stock prices: the case of developing and developed countries. Theoret Appl Econ 24(4):97–108

# The Effect of Initial Public Offerings on Financial Ratios—The Case of NewConnect

**Dominika Kordela**

**Abstract** For young and innovative firms, which have very limited earnings and low credibility, equity may be essential for improving financial soundness and company's development. Initial public offering builds the possibility to access the equity and moreover may has positive promotion effects. The aim of this paper is to assess whether the increase in equity influences the companies' financial condition measured by chosen financial ratios. In order to analyze the financial soundness, widely used accounting measures have been employed as: leverage ratios, performance ratios and liquidity ratio. The literature presents several studies on link between IPO and companies' financial conditions. However, those studies focus on companies listed on main stock exchanges and hence consisted mainly of stable companies with quite high capitalization. In this study, the research covered mainly young companies, with low capitalization and with a little or no experience on capital market, which is the original approach. Presented results allow to conclude that in the studied sample generally the access to the equity did not increase significantly the value of the debt in capital structure. In cases examined, IPO did not improve liquidity and performance of the companies either. In spite of the fact that in majority of studied companies liquidity was on the safe level, performance did not increase. So either the companies did not use properly the chances given by the public market or other factors influenced the financial condition, so further studies are recommended. The study is restricted by certain limitations related to the sample, which consists of companies that submitted IPO in 2007, and they were still listed after 10 years. Aiming to check the financial ratios after 10 years, it was not possible to add to the sample companies entering the alternative market in the following years. Moreover, the companies represent diverse sectors, so they do not have unique characteristics regarding financial condition. That implies further studies focused on chosen sectors. Such studies, however, would have much shorter time range because of relative short history of alternative market NewConnect. So in order to collect bigger sample based on sectors, the shorter study period would be necessary. The findings of this study contribute to the empirical analysis of influence of IPO on main financial ratios in case of small and medium companies entering the alternative stock

---

D. Kordela (✉)
The University of Szczecin, Institute of Economics and Finance, Szczecin, Poland
e-mail: dominika.kordela@usz.edu.pl



G. Karanovic et al. (eds.), *The Changing Financial Landscape*, Contributions to Economics, https://doi.org/10.1007/978-3-030-82778-6_4

markets. Although the subject is widely present in the scientific discussion, there is a little research that focused on companies listed on markets for small and growing companies (multilateral trading facilities, alternative markets).

**Keywords** Corporate finance · Financial performance · Initial public offering

**JEL Classification Codes** D25 · G20 · G30

## 1 Introduction

Access to external financial sources is essential for the development of a company. However, often many entities face difficulties with accessing the external capital including equity. The capital structure is a relevant research problem. The crucial theorem on capital structure was presented by Modigliani and Miller (1958, 1963). According to their first theorem (Modigliani and Miller 1958) based on simplifying assumptions (e.g., no taxes), the company's capital structure does not influence its market value. In further research, Modigliani and Miller (1963) included also the effect of taxes in their work. As a result, according to the second theorem the use of debt in the capital structure benefits from the tax shield and in the end leads to decrease in the weighted average cost of capital (WAAC) and increase in company's value (Błach 2009). The main financial theories indicate various answers to the question: when and why companies use equity? According to Myers (1984), corporate capital structures are the largely unplanned outcomes of individual financing decisions of managers, who follow a financial pecking order—the assumptions and explanations are called "pecking order theory." Companies use internal financing as the first solution; in a situation when internal financing is either no longer accessible or not at the required level, debt is issued; and when it is no longer sensible to issue any more debt, then equity is issued. Theory indicates the following hierarchy of financing sources: companies avoid external financing if they have internal financing available and avoid new equity financing, while they can engage in new debt financing at reasonably low interest rates.

According to the recent hypothesis "market timing hypothesis" (MTH) (Baker and Wurgler 2002), companies in their financial decisions whether to issue equity or debt depend on market timing; hence, market timing has an impact on capital structure. The use of specific market times allows the managers to form the capital structure taking advantage of the lower cost of capital (Vallandro et al. 2015). Baker and Wurgler outcomes suggest that "*firms are more likely to issue equity when their market values or share prices are high, relative to book and past market values, and to repurchase equity when their market values or share prices are low*" (Brendea 2012).

There is no indication whether which theory is the closest to the truth. However, it should be said that the key issue is: *how to access equity*. It is especially crucial for young and innovative firms, which have very limited earnings, low creditability and high operation. It could be observed in Poland in recent decade that the initial public offering (IPO) is gaining popularity among different external financial sources, which offer the access to equity such as venture capital or business angels. The possibility of issuing equity on capital market is easier, cheaper and faster for small and innovative entities, since the multilateral trading facilities (MTF) have been founded. According to Markets in Financial Instruments Directive (Directive 2004/39/EC), MTF is a multilateral system, operated by an investment firm or a market operator, which brings together multiple third-party buying and selling interests in financial instruments—in the system and in accordance with non-discretionary rules—in a way that results in a contract. There can be found new markets in Europe, which are based on this law and which are mostly operated by regular market operators, although investment companies are also allowed to create and organize them. In Poland, a new market called NewConnect was founded as MTF by Warsaw Stock Exchange in 2007. During the past eleven years, 586 companies have gained access to equity on NewConnect.[1]

The aim of this paper is to assess whether the increase in equity influences the companies' financial condition measured by chosen financial ratios of the listed companies. The following hypothesis has been worked out:

H1: The access to the equity increases the creditworthiness and in consequence the value of the debt in capital structure.
H2: IPO improves liquidity and performance of the company in short-, medium- and long-term periods.

The paper presents the results of research carried out among companies listed on the alternative market NewConnect. The research depicts chosen cases and presents an overview of the financial condition of the first issuers on NewConnect. It is to emphasize that companies listed on alternative market differ from companies from main markets, e.g., they have much lower equity value, much lower capitalization, and lower assets value, shorter business history and very often they belong in Poland to SMEs sector. So the research is the first trial to assess the effects on IPO of the financial condition of this specific group of companies.

## 2 Literature Review

An IPO can be understood as the first selling of shares on organized capital market. When a company decides to go public in order to be listed on a stock exchange, it has to carry out initial public offering (IPO). The literature indicated numerous reasons for going public based on both financial and non-financial causes (Gupta and Rust 2016; Gill de Albornoz and Pope 2004). However, it is still significantly important to raise capital for finance investment and growth (Kim and Weisbach 2008; Gill de Albornoz and Pope 2004).

[1] Statistics on www.newconnect.pl, as for 31.08.2018.

The IPO is mainly considered a source of finance accessible and appropriate for large, mature and developed companies. Due to high requirements, complicated procedures and restrict conditions, it is still difficult for young and small entities to enter the main market of stock exchange. Since the appearance of alternative (exchange-regulated) markets, there have been no actual hindrances for companies willing to be listed, and the IPOs have become a real alternative for young and innovative entrepreneurs.

According to Ritter (2013), the creation of exchange-regulated markets for small and innovative companies in Europe was the result of the success of London's exchange-regulated Alternative Investment Market (AIM). The companies on these markets have been exempted from many regulations and requirements that are valid on the main market. However, Ritter indicates that "*heavy-handed regulation has not been the prime deterrent of small-company IPOs.*" This seems not to be the case as far as Poland is concerned, as the rapid development of NewConnect (understood as the increase in number of listed companies and the increase in capitalization) was possible thanks to the lack of minimum equity requirements (Kordela 2013). In fact, as indicated by Gill de Albornoz and Pope (2004), the reasons for the IPO decision can be differentiated based on the country.

Equity is understood as an essential source of finance in case of profit shortfalls, high level of investment in intangible assets and high potential of the growth opportunities (Gatchev et al. 2009). Moreover, in the early stage of its life cycle, a young firm can overcome financial resource scarcity through an IPO. Furthermore, the growth of financial resources achieved thanks to the IPO might increase the possible investment strategies (Schmidt et al. 2006).

According to the findings presented by Gatchev et al. (2009), small, high-growth firms and less profitable companies use more equity to cover their financing needs than large and low-growth firms. This prediction corresponds with their further conclusions stating that companies issue equity to fund investments in intangible assets and advertising campaigns.

In fact, the MTFs, such as Polish NewConnect, have been founded to support the development and growth of innovative and young companies, which mainly generate low profits or loses and invest in intangible and current assets. According to the above-presented statements, access to equity could be seen as a proper solution for small and innovative entities, while MTFs are the right answer to market failure regarding financing of this group of companies.

Unquestionably, using equity does not directly mean applying equity issuance on the stock exchange, as there are other equity sources such as venture capital and business angels. However, issuance on the capital market has positive promotion effects. Moreover, Fama and French (2005), in contrast to Myers (1984), proved that financing with equity should not be adopted as a last resort, and asymmetric information problems are not a crucial determinant of capital structures. The statement above allows identifying the importance of issuing equity as a key financial source. However, going public is often connected with the drop in financial efficiency, as stated by Pastusiak et al. (2016b).

Researchers have studied different aspects connected with the IPO impact. Mikkelson et al. (1997) focused in their research on influence of changes in ownerships after IPO on operating performance of companies. They studied the value of leverage ratio (total liabilities/total assets) and return of assets (using operating income in nominator) over ten years period. The results provided by Mikkelson et al. (1997) indicated that the median value of leverage ratio is the highest one year before submitting an IPO (0.64); a sharp decline (0.40) was observed one year after; whereas five and ten years later, the indicator went up to, respectively, 0.49 and 0.51. On the other hand, the median of return of assets decreased in the all studied periods after offering. Other research conducted by Eckbo and Norli (2005) showed that every three years immediately following the IPO date, listed companies had experienced significantly lower leverage ratios and higher liquidity, in comparison with unlisted firms of comparable size. Moreover, pre-issue profitability is also perceived as a good predictor of aftermarket survival (Peristiani and Hong 2004). An interesting prediction was included in Peristiani and Hong (2004) paper. The researchers believe that the character of the companies that are going public (young, more speculative, highly innovative, active in high-growth technology sector) may lead to their deteriorating financial performance. In fact, when taking into consideration the assumption under which NewConnect was founded (the market for a young, small, innovative company), this may be the case of the companies listed on NewConnect. However, the aim of this paper does not concern comparing the financial standing of listed companies and the companies not present on the market. Nevertheless, when assessing the financial condition of the sample presented in this paper, the conclusions shown by Peristiani and Hong might be taken into consideration.

The influence of IPO on capital structure changes has been investigated as well by Dudley and James (2018), who focused on comparison of a sample of companies with and without preferred stock. It was presented that both groups use a considerable amount of debt in the year before they go public. However, companies without preferred stock had significantly greater leverage than companies that had pre-IPO preferred stock in their capital structure. Essential for this paper is the conclusion that the IPO is associated with a decline in average and median leverage. Five years after the IPO, the median value of the leverage for company without preferred shares was 59% of its pre-IPO level. At the same time, the researchers noticed that companies without pre-IPO preferred stock report a transitory decline in average leverage immediately following the IPO, since these firms issued significant amounts of debt during the two years following the IPO (Dudley and James 2018). Therefore, it may be concluded that the IPO has a positive influence on the ability to issue debt.

As far as Poland is concerned, performance of public companies was analyzed by Pastusiak et al. (2016a), who studied a large number of companies (527) that entered the main stock exchange market of Warsaw Stock Exchange in the years 1991–2012. In this paper, the authors emphasized that profitability ratios increased before the IPO and fell after a certain period of time. However, there are only few studies investigating whether declines in profitability ratios in the IPO were caused by the equity dilution or whether increase in these indicators before the IPO was caused deliberately in order to attract investors and achieve higher market value.

Pastusiak et al. (2016a) studied not only return on equity and return on assets, but also operating and net profit margins, which allowed carrying out broader research. They confirmed that profitability of companies a year before the IPO is higher than one year after it. Furthermore, they concluded that companies improve their accounting data prior to IPO in order to attract potential investors and collect money. They also indicated that companies are not prepared to manage in efficient way the money they collect during IPO, a fact noticeable in financial ratios. It should also be said that the research carried out by Pastusiak et al. (2016a) covered more than twenty years; thus, the IPO took place in different economic circumstances. The analysis provided in this article focuses on companies that entered the market in 2007 and thus had the same macroeconomic surrounding. Another research concerning Polish capital market focused on the relation between the financial performance and efficiency of companies and their ownership structure and size (Pastusiak et al. 2016b). By comparing the average values of return on assets in the group of medium-sized companies, the researchers found out that private companies not listed on the stock exchange operate more profitably than companies that are publicly traded. However, similar results in the case of return on equity cannot be found. In turn, conclusions drawn in the case of large companies are similar to those concerning the group of medium-sized companies. For example, when comparing the average values of return on assets and return on equity, it is visible that private companies not present on stock exchange had higher profitability than companies traded on Warsaw Stock Exchange (Pastusiak et al. 2016b).

The literature review can lead to the conclusions that IPOs enable companies that go public to invest and grow; however, there can be observed a drop in profitability after IPO (Gupta and Rust 2016).

## 3 Research Methods and Characteristic of the Sample

In order to analyze the financial soundness of issuing companies at the year of offering, as well as one, five and ten years following the IPO, widely used accounting measures have been employed.

In order to revise H1, the study focuses on the analysis of the leverage ratios at the end of the year of its issuance, as well as one, five and nine years after it. The literature indicates that a debt increases the returns to shareholders in good times, reduces them in bad times, as well as creates financial leverage. Leverage ratios measure how much financial leverage the company has taken on (Brealey et al. 2009). The information about the leverage ratios might be important when making equity issuing decision. On the one hand, it is believed that highly leveraged firms with investment opportunities should be more likely to go public (Myers 1977). On the other, Gill de Albornoz and Pope (2004) presented many examples of conducted research that indicates either negative correlation between leverage and IPO probability, or no correlation at all.

To examine the effect of the increase in equity value on financial structure, the following ratios were used:

(1) $L1 : \text{Debt to equity}(D/E) = \text{Total debt}/\text{Total equity}$
This ratio indicates the degree of financial leverage being used by the business and includes both short-term and long-term debt. It is also called capital structure ratio. The level of debt to equity ratio is the consequence of both adopted financial strategy and the debt abilities of the company. The value of the ratio higher than 1 implies that the company is a leveraged one, while a ratio less than 1 indicates the company is weighed more toward equity (Pyles 2014). The debt has to be paid off in restricted period; thus, high level of this ratio can be risky in downturn conditions. On the other hand, high level can be the proof that the company has great credibility and the lenders trust it.

(2) $L2 : \text{Debt to assets} = \text{Total debt}/\text{Total assets}$
Another leverage ratio measures the percentage of a company's assets that have been financed with debt (short-term and long-term). The higher the debt-to-total-assets ratio, the greater the financial risk. According to the literature, 0.5 is the optimal value for debt to assets ratio; however, it is difficult to maintain. So it is acceptable to keep the balance between debt and assets by 0.67 (Sierpińska and Jachna 2004). It is believed that the ratio higher than 0.67 indicates excessive credit risk.
The H2 was revised in the study based on profitability ratios and liquidity ratio in the year of IPO, as well as one, five and ten years after IPO:

(3) $P1 : \text{Return on assets}(ROA) = \text{net income}/\text{average total assets} \times 100\%$
It is one of the most important ratios that measures the performance of the company based on all assets. The return on assets ratio measures how efficiently a company can manage its assets to work out net income.

(4) $P2 : \text{Return on equity ratio}(ROE) = \text{net income}/\text{average total equity} \times 100\%$
Another very important performance ratio that focuses on the return from the shareholders' equity. Return on equity is widely use in theory and practice to assess the profitability. A high return on equity indicates that the resources provided by shareholders have been used in an efficient way.

(5) $LQ : \text{Current Ratio} = \text{Current Assets}/\text{Current Liabilities}$

The current ratio is a liquidity ratio that measures a company's ability to convert assets into cash in less than one year in order to—if needed—pay the debts which are to be paid in less than one year. The current ratio considers the current total assets of a company (both liquid and illiquid) relative to that company's current total liabilities. Current ratio of less than one would be a signal for potential problems in corporates' ability to pay short-term liabilities (Pyles 2014). The higher the ratio, the better the company's liquidity position. In the literature, the value 2 or higher is indicated as an appropriate value to prove creditworthiness; however, the value 1.5 is also seen as normal (Tóth et al. 2013). In research conducted on Polish companies, the value from 1.2 to 2 is widely assumed as optimal value (Sierpińska and Jachna 2004; Olszewski 1992), and so was adopted in this paper.

The examined sample consists of all companies that submitted IPO on NewConnect in 2007 and were still listed after 10 years on the alternative market or changed for the main market of Warsaw Stock Exchange.

The sample includes companies that initiated public offering in 2007 under the conditions presented below:

- the company was not taken over, but could have merged,
- the company is not in bankruptcy proceedings.

In 2007, the numbers of IPOs amounted to 24, while after ten years 17 companies out of 24 were still listed on stock exchange. Three companies changed the market to the main one, and 14 were still listed on the NewConnect market (one undergoing bankruptcy proceedings). Thus, the sample comprised 16 companies.

Generally, it can be said that the companies covered by the research represent modern sectors; five come from investment services (ViaGuara/Devoran, WDM/Graviton, Technopark 2/Medcamp, IQ Partners, Blumerang), three belong to IT sector (Digital Avenue, S4E, Makolab), two are active in media sector (Virtual Vision/Euroinvestment, E-muzyka), another two in financial services (Auxilium/UHY ECA, MW Trade), the other companies belong to following sectors building materials (Mera Schody), real estate (Północ Nieruchomości/Aramus), telecommunication (Telestrada), and telecommunications and construction infrastructure (LUG). The data required to carry out the research were taken from the Notoria Online database and in some cases from the information document published before public offering. The data used in the study come from separated financial statement. The values of the above-mentioned ratios were presented at the year of IPO and further their changes in a year, five and ten years after IPO were analyzed. The research was provided in order to find out whether in short, medium and long term the financial condition has improved and whether hypothesis can be verified positively.

## 4 Research Results

To find the answer for a question whether the access to the equity increases the creditworthiness, and in consequence the value of the debt in financial structure, the standard debt ratios were computed. The results for all companies are listed in Table 1.

The growth of both debt ratios in all studied periods is visible only in the case of three companies, whereas when comparing the value of ratios in short term (2008–2007), the debt ratio increased in eight (L1) and three cases (L2). In the medium period, covering 5 years (2007–2012), similar results were obtained as in the case of short-term period: the L1 increased in eight cases, while L2 in seven. In the long term, (comparing 2017–2007), nine companies had higher debt/equity ratio (L1), and in 10 cases, the debt-to-assets ratio (L2) increased. Based on these results, the first hypothesis cannot be verify positively. Firstly, this is due to the fact that too few companies improved the debt ratios (increase does not always mean improvement), and in some cases the improvement is hardly visible. Moreover, in the cases of two companies the value of equity is negative. Particularly worrying is the fact that in many cases the leverage is extremely high. The mean and median computed for

**Table 1** The leverage (debt) ratios in pre-IPO and post-IPO periods

| Company | L1 | | | | L2 | | | |
|---|---|---|---|---|---|---|---|---|
| | 2007 | 2008 | 2012 | 2017 | 2007 | 2008 | 2012 | 2017 |
| Digital Avenue | 0.17 | 0.18 | 0.09 | 0.18 | 0.15 | 0.15 | 0.08 | 0.18 |
| S4E | 8.44 | 8.28 | 6.41 | 7.92 | 0.89 | 0.89 | 0.87 | 0.89 |
| ViaGuara/Devoran | 17.25 | 0.40 | 2.49 | 0.05 | 0.95 | 0.29 | 0.71 | 0.05 |
| Virtual Vision/Euroinvestment | −26.80 | 0.07 | 0.49 | −1.01 | 1.04 | 0.06 | 0.33 | 102.3 |
| WDM/Graviton | 0.14 | 0.02 | 0.02 | −1.04 | 0.12 | 0.02 | 0.02 | 29.27 |
| Mera Schody | 0.34 | 0.36 | 0.77 | 0.65 | 0.26 | 0.26 | 0.44 | 0.40 |
| Auxilium/UHY ECA | 0.05 | 0.07 | 0.10 | 0.04 | 0.05 | 0.07 | 0.09 | 0.04 |
| MW Trade | 0.86 | 0.68 | 6.46 | 4.26 | 0.46 | 0.41 | 0.87 | 0.81 |
| Północ Nieruchomości/Aramus | 0.09 | 0.13 | 1.16 | 1.18 | 0.08 | 0.12 | 0.54 | 0.54 |
| Telestrada | 5.08 | 0.18 | 0.36 | 0.21 | 0.84 | 0.16 | 0.26 | 0.17 |
| Technopark 2/Medcamp | 0.33 | 0.03 | 0.06 | 0.05 | 0.25 | 0.03 | 0.06 | 0.05 |
| LUG | 0.77 | 0.32 | 0.01 | 0.01 | 0.44 | 0.24 | 0.01 | 0.01 |
| IQ Partners | 0.20 | 0.15 | 0.14 | 0.58 | 0.16 | 0.13 | 0.13 | 0.37 |
| Blumerang | 0.17 | 0.17 | 0.60 | 2.20 | 0.15 | 0.15 | 0.38 | 0.69 |
| e-muzyka | 0.35 | 0.47 | 1.40 | 0.92 | 0.26 | 0.32 | 0.58 | 0.48 |
| Makolab | 0.23 | 0.34 | 0.38 | 0.57 | 0.19 | 0.26 | 0.27 | 0.36 |
| **Mean** | **0.48** | **0.74** | **1.31** | **1.05** | **0.39** | **0.22** | **0.35** | **8.54** |
| **Median** | **0.28** | **0.18** | **0.44** | **0.39** | **0.25** | **0.15** | **0.30** | **0.38** |

*Sources* Own calculation

both ratios do not allow drawing common conclusions regarding the improvement of creditworthiness and the value of the debt in capital structure. Nevertheless, based on the leverage ratio, it might be concluded that some companies keep the value of debt on the very low level, a fact that can either be a proof of a conservative financial strategy or not taking advantage of opportunities given by public market. On the other hand, there are few companies with extremely high debt level. However, it must be emphasized that in the study where the separated financial statement was taken into account, the value of ratios could be different (better mean), if the consolidated financial statements were analyzed. However, because many companies from the sample do not form the capital group, separated financial statements were used as a base for assessment for comparison reasons. It is also noticeable that some companies actually have very low values of fixed assets, and a few presented a negative value of equity.

In order to find out whether IPO improves in short-, medium- and long-term periods the financial condition of the company in the next step the performance ratios and liquidity ratio were analyzed.

As given in Table 2, the value of the ratio return of assets was examined. The return of assets in one of the most important performance ratios. The data in Table 2 show

**Table 2** The value of return of assets (ROA) in pre-IPO and post-IPO periods

| Company | ROA [%] | | | |
|---|---|---|---|---|
| | 2007 | 2008 | 2012 | 2017 |
| Digital Avenue | Negative | Negative | Negative | 1.17 |
| S4E | 5.44 | 2.38 | 3.53 | Negative |
| ViaGuara/Devoran | Negative | Negative | Negative | 5.09 |
| Virtual Vision/Euroinvestment | Negative | Negative | Negative | Negative |
| WDM/Graviton | 51.4 | Negative | Negative | Negative |
| Mera Schody | 4.42 | 2.11 | 2.28 | 1.36 |
| Auxilium/UHY ECA | 18.77 | 11.3 | 1.12 | 4.16 |
| MW Trade | 10.59 | 3.35 | 2.53 | 1.49 |
| Północ Nieruchomości/Aramus | 6.9 | Negative | 3.74 | 11.12 |
| Telestrada | 4.95 | 21.11 | 21.67 | 40.97 |
| Technopark 2/Medcamp | 105.71 | 11.48 | 1.54 | 0.07 |
| LUG | 8.52 | Negative | 6.09 | 6.07 |
| IQ Partners | No data | 2.32 | Negative | Negative |
| Blumerang | No data | Negative | 1.24 | Negative |
| e-muzyka | 4.02 | 7.15 | 16.57 | 11.83 |
| Makolab | 10.24 | 15.24 | 14.74 | 8.77 |
| **Mean** | **21.00** | **8.49** | **6.82** | **8.37** |
| **Median** | **9.38** | **7.82** | **3.64** | **5.58** |

*Sources* Own calculations

that only 7 out of 16 companies had a positive ratio in all studied periods, whereas two companies had the negative the ratio return of assets in all four examined years. Only three companies improved their return on assets from the IPO from 2007 to 2017.

The numbers presented in Table 3 reflect that the performance assessed with return on equity is similar to performance assessed on return on assets. This is not surprising as both ratios include the net income in the numerator in equations. If the counter (net income) is negative, then the quotient is negative as well. This is the case of both ratios return on assets and return on equity. Only 8 out of 16 companies had positive performance of return on equity in all four studied periods. Two companies had negative ratio in all periods studied. This shows that accessed equity did not positively influence net profits. Moreover, the increase in value of this ratio is visible only in three cases (assuming that 2007 is a base year), whereas three other companies had a stable positive value of return on equity.

The data in Tables 2 and 3 do not allow concluding that the IPO improves the performance of assessed companies. However, the result can be considered compliant with the results of previous research presented in the literature review. Namely, in

**Table 3** The value of return on equity (ROE) in pre-IPO and post-IPO periods

| Company | ROE [%] | | | |
|---|---|---|---|---|
| | 2007 | 2008 | 2012 | 2017 |
| Digital Avenue | Negative | Negative | Negative | 1.42 |
| S4E | 44.68 | 22.24 | 27.26 | Negative |
| ViaGuara/Devoran | Negative | Negative | Negative | 5.33 |
| Virtual Vision/Euroinvestment | Negative | Negative | Negative | Negative |
| WDM/Graviton | 58.43 | Negative | Negative | Negative |
| Mera Schody | 7.1 | 2.85 | 4.31 | 2.22 |
| Auxilium/UHY ECA | 19.98 | 11.99 | 1.18 | 4.33 |
| MW Trade | 20.72 | 5.91 | 18.44 | 8.85 |
| Północ Nieruchomości/Aramus | 7.68 | Negative | 6.12 | 27.23 |
| Telestrada | 20.2 | 40.05 | 28.21 | 56.2 |
| Technopark 2/Medcamp | 137.52 | 13.46 | 1.62 | 0.07 |
| LUG | 17.39 | Negative | 6.14 | 6.07 |
| IQ Partners | No Data | 2.73 | Negative | Negative |
| Blumerang | No Data | Negative | 1.86 | Negative |
| e-muzyka | 6.11 | 10.2 | 41.29 | 19.63 |
| Makolab | 14.63 | 19.71 | 20.2 | 12.49 |
| **Mean** | **32.22** | **14.35** | **14.24** | **13.08** |
| **Median** | **20.09** | **12.73** | **10.19** | **7.46** |

*Sources* Own calculations

many cases the performance in the year of the IPO (2007) is higher than the value of return on assets and return on equity one year after it (2008).

Talking about the liquidity, the academic literature indicates that the optimal current ratio should be between 1.2 and 2.0. If it is higher than 2.0, the liquidity of the company is very high. When the ratio is below 1.2, the liquidity is low, which might be dangerous for financial stability of the company. A brief look at Table 4 shows that the value of this indicator is very diverse. There are only few companies with the stable value of the current ratio (in bold), with only one having the value of an indicator compliant with the standards during all years taken into account in the research. Most of the studied companies had high liquidity, which is proved by not only separate values of the ratios of particular companies, but also the value of the mean and median of liquidity ratio. However, the value of the mean of current ratio as well as the median of the current ratio (with the exceptions of 2008 when compared with 2007) is decreasing in the studied period.

The comparison of the value of the current ratios in basic year 2007 indicates that only one company had liquidity that was compliant with the theory (1.2–2.0). However, in the year of submitting the IPO, all companies (except three cases) had the value of current ratio on a high level, which meant there were no liquidity

**Table 4** The liquidity in pre-IPO and post-IPO periods (current ratio)

| Company | CR | | | |
|---|---|---|---|---|
| | 2007 | 2008 | 2012 | 2017 |
| Digital Avenue | 0.88 | 0.52 | 0.55 | 4.53 |
| S4E | **1.1** | **1.07** | **1.12** | **1.04** |
| ViaGuara/Devoran | 0.99 | 3.21 | 1.23 | 2.36 |
| Virtual Vision/Euroinvestment | 1.08 | 2.46 | 2.21 | 0.2 |
| WDM/Graviton | 7 | 12.94 | 45.58 | 0.03 |
| Mera Schody | **3.43** | **3.23** | **2.65** | **2.58** |
| Auxilium/UHY ECA | 21.32 | 14.7 | 3.84 | 12.43 |
| MW Trade | **1.93** | **2.26** | **1.14** | **0.85** |
| Północ Nieruchomości/Aramus | 14.46 | 9.39 | 0.44 | 0.75 |
| Telestrada | 1.1 | 4.94 | 3.08 | 2.05 |
| Technopark 2/Medcamp | 3.18 | 18 | 18.43 | 7.78 |
| LUG | 2.23 | 1.72 | 8.9 | 0.78 |
| IQ Partners | 3.58 | 3.9 | 0.91 | 0.01 |
| Blumerang | 64.27 | 9.54 | 2.08 | 1.25 |
| e-muzyka | **3.34** | **1.93** | **1.15** | **1.51** |
| Makolab | 5.58 | 3.79 | 3.31 | 2.61 |
| **Mean** | **10.42** | **7.20** | **7.43** | **3.14** |
| **Median** | **3.34** | **3.79** | **2.21** | **1.51** |

*Sources* own calculations

problems. Moreover, 10 companies had higher value of the current ratio in the year of submitting an IPO, than in the year after stock exchange debut. In 2017, the indicator of three companies reflected the theoretical assumptions. However, in the majority of the studied cases the liquidity is rather too high than too low. This situation can be compliant with the statement presented by Pastusiak et al. (2016a), saying that companies are not prepared to efficiently manage the money they collect during IPO. Half of the companies included in the sample have very high value of the current ratio after 10 years of being public. Therefore, such companies could better manage its current liabilities and assets. Nevertheless, there are also few companies (exactly three) with a very low value of the current ratio after 10 years.

## 5 Conclusions

The conducted research presents an overview on financial condition of entities that entered alternative stock exchange NewConnect in 2007. Results are based on relative limited sample; hence, it is not possible to formulate general conclusions, but still make some relevant remarks. The study to some extent is aimed at filling gap regarding the assessment of influence the IPO on the alternative stock exchange on companies' financial ratios. Results obtained for companies listed on an alternative market are partially compliant with results present in studies covered companies from main markets of stock exchanges (Mikkelson et al. 1997; Pastusiak et al. 2016a).

As far as debt-to-equity ratio is concerned, the mean value recorded in the year of submitting an IPO was lower than the value one year, five years and ten years after it. In general, this increase in the value of the debt in financial structure can be understood as the increase in creditworthiness. However, the median value of debt-to-equity ratio was lower than the mean, which can be seen as a proof that more entities in the sample are conservative ones as far as financial structure is concerned. The mean values of debt to assets ratio in 2007, 2008, 2012 are low—below 0.47, which can be another sign for applying conservative financial strategy, despite general increase in debt in financial structure (as presented by the mean value of debt to equity ratio). Generally, the values of both debt ratios show that the companies included in the sample are characterized by the potential to increase debt in the capital structure. These results and additionally characteristic of the liquidity ratio indicate there is still potential to use leverage in order to increase performance. The analysis of the mean and median values of liquidity ratio shows that entities that entered the NewConnect market could manage the current assets and the current liabilities better. In all studied periods, both median and mean values of liquidity ratio were very high, which presents excess liquidity and influences efficiency in negative way. The weak efficiency is visible in performance ratios. The mean and median of both performance ratios (return on assets and return on equity) were higher in the year of submitting an IPO than in the years following the debut. This conclusion is compliant with the previous research that covered companies listed on main markets of stock exchanges (Mikkelson et al. 1997; Pastusiak et al. 2016a). So the issuance did not improve performance, and ten years of being public company did not result in higher net income in relation to the value of assets and value of equity. Taking into consideration the increase in debt in capital structure, the increase in equity performance would be expected. Observed low and in many cases negative return on equity ratio can be seen as the evidence of inappropriate management. So the question—why companies with no serious liquidity problems and with no exceed leverage are not able to generate higher performance ratio?—would be a good case for further research.

In general, the results allow drawing the following conclusions: the access to equity increased on average the value of debt in financial structure, however, the growth potential in liabilities area can still be observed. Nevertheless, in particular cases, which were included to the sample, extremely high values of leverage ratios can be observed, some even could be called as "irrational high." Moreover, the negative value of equity of some companies should be assessed as a bad sign. It cannot be stated also that IPO improve liquidity and performance of the company. In spite of the fact that in majority of studied cases liquidity was on the safe level (even excess liquidity occurred), performance did not improve. So either the companies did not use properly the chances given by the public market or other factors influenced the financial condition, so further studies are recommended.

## References

### *Book*

Brealey RA, Myers SC, Allen F (2009) Principles of corporate finance, 10th edn. McGraw-Hill-Irwin, New York

Kordela D (2013) NewConnect – rynek giełdowy dla małych i średnich przedsiębiorstw. Systematyka, organizacja, perspektywy rozwoju, CeDeWu, Warszawa

Olszewski D (1992) Podstawy analizy finansowej przedsiębiorstwa, Olympus, Warszawa

Sierpińska M Jachna T (2004) Ocena przedsiębiorstwa według standardów światowych, Wydawnictwo Naukowe PWN, Warszawa

### *Journal*

Baker M, Wurgler J (2002) Market timing and capital structure. J Financ LVIII(1)

Błach J., (2009), Ewolucja teorii struktury kapitału, Finanse: czasopismo Komitetu Nauk o Finansach, PAN, nr 1 (1), Warszawa

Brendea G (2012) Testing the impact of market timing on the Romanian firms' capital structure. Procedia Econ Financ 3

Dudley E, James C (2018) Capita-structure changes around IPOs. Crit Financ Rev 7(1):55–79. https://doi.org/10.1561/104.00000045

Eckbo BE, Norli O (2005) Liquidity risk, leverage, and long-run IPO returns. J Corp Finan 11:1–35

Fama EF, French KR (2005) Financing decisions: Who issues stock? J Financ Econ 76:549–582

Gatchev VA, Spindt PA, Tarhan V (2009) How Do Firms Finance Their Investments? The Relative Importance of Equity Issuance And Debt Contracting Costs. J Corp Finan 15:179–195

Gill de Albornoz B, Pope PF (2004) The determinants of the going public decision: evidence from the U.K, Working Papers. Serie AD, Instituto Valenciano de Investigaciones Económicas

Gupta S Rust J (2016) A simple theory of why and when firms go public, working paper, Department of Economics, Georgetown University. https://www.econ.ku.dk/cce/events/19092016/paper/theory_paper.pdf Accessed 20 Dec 2019

Kim W, Weisbach MS (2008) Motivations for public equity offers: An international perspective. Journal of Financial Economics, Elsevier 87:281–307

Mikkelson WH, Partch MM, Shah K (1997) Ownership and operating performance of companies that go public. J Financ Econ 44:281–307

Modigliani F, Miller MH (1958) The cost of capital, corporation finance and the theory of investment. Am Econ Rev 48(3):261–297

Modigliani F, Miller MH (1963) Corporate income taxes and the cost of capital: a correction. Am Econ Rev 53(3):433–443

Myers S (1977) The determinants of corporate borrowing. J Financ Econ 5:147–175

Myres SC (1984) The capital structure puzzle. J Financ Econ 5(2):147–175

Pastusiak R, Bolek M, Malaczewski M, Kacprzyk M (2016a) Company profitability before and after IPO. Is it a windows dressing or equity dilution effect? Prague Econ Papers 25(01):112–124. https://doi.org/10.18267/j.pep.54.

Pastusiak R, Miszczyńska K, Krzeczewski B (2016b) Does public offering improve company's financial performance? The Example of Poland, Economic Research—Ekonomska Istraživanja 29(1):32–49. https://doi.org/10.1080/1331677X.2016.1152559

Peristiani S, Hong G (2004) Pre-IPO Financial performance and aftermarket survival. Curr issues Econ Financ 10(2)

Pyles MK (2014) Applied corporate finance. Questions, problems and making decisions in the real world. Springer, New York

Ritter JR (2013) Reenergizing the IPO market. In: Baily MN, Herring RJ, Seki Y (eds) Restructuring to Sustain Recovery. Brookings Institution Press, Washington, pp 123–145

Schmidt T, Dowling MJ, Lechner C (2006) The impact of initial public offerings on the external growth strategies of entrepreneurial firms. J Entrepreneurial Financ Bus Ventures 11(2):95–110. Available at: https://digitalcommons.pepperdine.edu/jef/vol11/iss2/6

Tóth M, Čierna Z, Serenčeš P (2013) Benchmark values for liquidity ratios in Slovak Agriculture, Scientiarum Polonorum Actca Oeconomia 12(3)

Vallandro LFJ, Zani J, da Silva CES (2015) IPO market timing and capital structure: evidence from Brazil. Int Bus Res 8(1)

# Comparative Analysis of the Financial Performance of Tourism Companies Located in Central and Eastern Europe

**Laurentiu Droj, Olimpia I. Ban, and Gabriela Droj**

**Abstract** Measuring performance in tourism and hospitality services in general raises issues given the very idiosyncratic nature of tourism. The measurement of performance in tourism and hospitality services, as reflected in the literature, was done from various perspectives: from the perspective of efficiency, from the perspective of labor productivity, from the perspective of measurements in use (industry-specific indices), from the perspective of competitiveness and from the perspective of performance measurement. In this paper, we proposed a composite index to measure the financial performance of the tourism and hospitality services companies that combines the most common financial indicators: ROE, ROA, solvency and ROS. The tourism and hospitality companies covered in this study were selected from a larger database provided by IMIS containing the top 1.000 companies located in 5 Central and Eastern European countries: Croatia, Hungary, Romania, Serbia and Slovenia. These companies were analyzed and clustered based on different criteria: annual turnover, type of activity, location, number of employees, assets, net profit, return on equity, return on investment, solvency, debt analysis, so on. The IMIS database provided complete information regarding all accounting or financial variables over the 5-year period from 2014 to 2018. From the perspective of the composite index, a number of up to 15 companies from each country out of the 5 taken into account (Croatia, Hungary, Romania, Serbia and Slovenia) are analyzed. The selection criterion of the companies was the size of the annual turnover and number of employees. The analysis shows both the differences in financial performance and the specifics of the differences, reflected in the values of the financial indicators, specific for each country. Also, the PERF indicator managed to highlight the decline of financial results in tourism in 2016 which was signaled by the World Travel and Tourism Council caused by the fact that the sector was hurt by economic weakness, Brexit uncertainties and a ramp-up in terrorist attacks.

L. Droj (✉) · O. I. Ban
Faculty of Economic Sciences, University of Oradea, Oradea, Romania

G. Droj
Faculty of Construction, Cadastre and Architecture, University of Oradea, Oradea, Romania



G. Karanovic et al. (eds.), *The Changing Financial Landscape*, Contributions to Economics, https://doi.org/10.1007/978-3-030-82778-6_5

# 1 Approaches to Measuring Performance in Tourism

It is estimated that the issue of firm performance remains one of the most popular concepts in organizational research (Miller 2013).

Compared to the classical quantitative approach to performance, the literature has been supplemented with what is called the alternative approach, which concerns the measurement of performance in qualitative rather than financial terms (Sainaghi et al. 2017).

Measuring performance in tourism in general raises issues given the very idiosyncratic nature of tourism. There is no question of using identical performance practices for all tourism operators.

Sainaghi et al. (2017) conducted a bibliometric analysis of research on tourism performance for 978 articles published between 1996 and 2014. They identified three levels at which performance in tourism is measured: at the company level, at the cluster level and at the destination level.

It is considered that a specific measure of the performance of a tourism company is its close connection with the destination. "Firm performance in the tourism industry depends mainly on two factors: the destination where the company is located (location or destination effect) and the organization's internal resources and characteristics (firm effect)" (Molina-Azorin et al. 2010, p. 22).

Measuring the performance of the destination raises two issues, one related to the definition of the destination (setting geographical boundaries) and another related to the multitude of determinants that can affect the performance of tourism. The Travel and Tourism Competitiveness Index is used which is an index of the ranking of nations but is not a performance index. Measuring performance in tourism, as reflected in the literature (Sainaghi et al. 2017, p. 40), was done from various perspectives: from the perspective of efficiency (data envelopment analysis; stochastic approach; importance–performance analysis), from perspective of competitiveness (importance–performance analysis; competitiveness index; technique for order preference by similarity to ideal solution—TOPSIS; Porter's diamond; competitiveness monitor; travel and tourism competitiveness index); from the perspective of labor productivity (productivity drivers—physical, human capital, information technology, competition; Luenberger productivity indicator), from the perspective of measurements in use (for tourism—average daily rate; rate of occupancy; revenue per available room, occupancy, emetrics; digital footprint, ecological footprint, sustainable performance index) and from the perspective of the performance measurement system (balanced Scorecard, tourism value chain).

The performance literature in tourism has gone beyond financial indices and has taken into account their relationship with indices related to: carbon reduction, green practices, ethics, ecotourism, Internet performance, online consumer reviews, e-commerce success, corporate social responsibility, consumer satisfaction (Inoue and Lee 2011; Goodall 1995; Ham and Lee 2011; Singal 2014; Chi and Gursoy

2009; Denizci and Li 2009; Saeidi et al. 2015). The results reveal that environmental performance affects financial performance in the hotel industry when aggregate environmental performance is used, in the case of some studies (Tan et al. 2017, p. 6).

Evaluating the performance of the tourism company is an interdisciplinary approach: accounting, management, finance, economics, strategy and marketing. There is an intercorrelation between them.

From a managerial perspective, it is considered that the performance at hotel level is an aggregate effort of the different departments, involving the operations in the contact area with the clients but also those outside the contact area (Hsieh and Lin 2010). In this case, the efficiency and effectiveness of the functional departments are pursued, as well as their contribution to the overall performance of the hotel.

Other approaches emphasize the importance of innovation and entrepreneurial effectiveness as predictors of company performance. Lee et al. (2016) highlighted these predictors of restaurant-level performance, showing that they positively influence performance. From a marketing perspective, there is an increase in attention paid to consumer satisfaction seen in direct relation to the company's performance (Denizci and Li 2009; Morgan et al. 2005). A study by Sun and Kim (2013) uses the American Customer Satisfaction Index (ACSI). This index has been recognized as a new type of market-based performance measure for firms, industry, economic sectors and national economies. A critical aspect of ACSI is that it can forecast economic revenues. The basic principle in ACSI is that satisfied customers are economic assets of the company (economic assets). As it is known, economic assets generate future income for the owner of these assets. Thus, with the help of ACSI the financial results of the company can be predicted. This research (Sun and Kim 2013) resulted from the need to assess the relationship between customer satisfaction and a company's financial performance, such as profitability and company value. The study aimed at influencing customer satisfaction on the company's profitability and on the company's value. The company's profitability was assessed by: profit margin (PM), return on assets (ROA) and return on equity (ROE). These three indicators are generally accepted and widely used. ROE is the "true bottom-line measure of performance" says Sun and Kim (2013, p. 71).

There are views (Gursoy and Swanger 2007, p. 224) that show that a positive relationship cannot be established between marketing and financial performance, if sales are treated separately by marketing. From a financial perspective, performance is measured at the corporate level as well as with the specific indicators used in tourism. Traditionally, financial firm performance has been viewed and measured in accounting terms. Chen (2010) used for corporate performance the following indicators: occupancy rate, return on assets, return on equity, stock Return—SRt and a comprehensive score. Six accounting ratios are used to calculate a comprehensive score based on factor analysis: debt–equity ratio, total asset turnover, current ratio, quick ratio, return on assets and return on equity. The comprehensive score thus combines measures of asset management (TAT), profitability (ROA and ROE), short-term solvency or liquidity (CR and QR) and long-term solvency (DE).

Corporate financial performance is evaluated with indicators or combinations of indicators, among which we mention: return on assets—ROA, return on equity—ROE, return on invested capital—ROIC, debt–equity ratio—DE, total asset turnover—TAT, current ratio—CR, quick ratio—QR, etc.

## 2 Case Study of Tourism in Five Countries from Central and Eastern Europe

The countries of Central and Eastern Europe (EEC) are somewhat similar in living the experience of liberation from the communist economy around the same time and with comparative resources. However, "the countries of CEE are not a uniform entity but are diverse in terms of location, topography, climate, history, culture and economic development" (Hughes and Allen 2005, p. 173).

Hall (1998) divides these former socialist states into: more economically advanced and stable states (Hungary, the Czech Republic, Poland and Slovenia) and less developed states (Bulgaria, Albania, the former Yugoslavia, Romania and Croatia) "of the subregion with considerable tourism potential yet still relatively neglected in the literature" (Hall 1998, p. 423).

Tourism plays an important role in the economy of the EEC countries as they are direct competitors in relation to the Western European market. Entering the free market after 1989 meant accepting the challenges of real competition. Some countries did better than others.

"Quite often, the success of tourism is judged on the basis of tourist arrivals, average guest nights spent or gross tourist expenditures" (Jayawardena and Ramajeesingh 2003, p. 178).

Taking a specific indicator of tourism (nights spent by non-residents at tourist accommodation establishments) for 2018, the achievements by the analyzed countries are: Croatia (83.1), Hungary (15.3), Slovenia (11.2), Romania (5.3) and Serbia (1.5) (Graph 1).

According to another tourism-specific indicator (nights spent by residents and non-residents in millions), the hierarchy of the 5 countries analyzed is: Croatia (89.6), Hungary (32.8), Romania (28.5), Slovenia (15.7) and Serbia (9.3) (Table 1).

Also, another index tourism intensity is calculated as nights spent by residents and non-residents at tourist accommodation establishments per inhabitant (Graph 2). Another extremely important element consists in the structural differences of the tourism sector in the five analyzed countries: in Croatia and Romania the number of the micro- and small companies operating in the field of tourism are quite high forcing a high level of distribution of tourists between a large number of tourism companies. In Hungary, the concentration of tourism is highest in Budapest, Balaton and several cities, and therefore, large companies are dominating the market. On the other hand, in Serbia the tourism sector is still developing, as can be seen from the structural organization of the tourism sector.

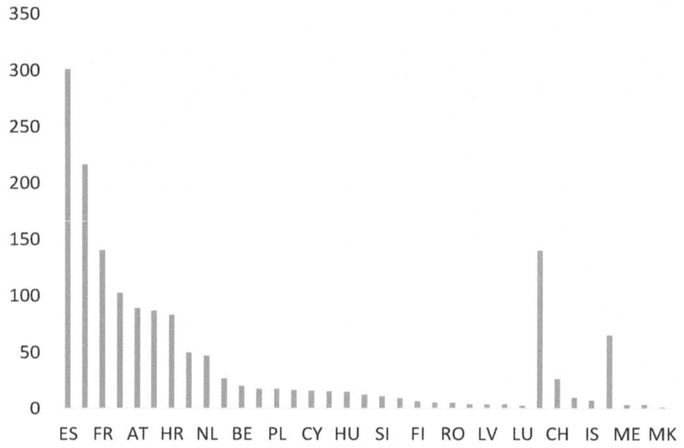


**Graph 1** Nights spent by non-residents at tourist accommodation establishments in 2018 (mil.) Ireland, Slovenia, UK, Switzerland, Norway, Iceland, Montenegro, Serbia and Kosovo[a]: estimated using 2018 monthly data; Turkey: 2016 data
[a] This designation is without prejudice to positions on status and is in line with UNSCR 1244/1999 and the ICJ Opinion on the Kosovo declaration of independence
*Source* Eurostat online data code: tour_occ_ninat, https://ec.europa.eu/eurostat/statistics-explained/index.php/Tourism_statistics accessed 11.05.2020

**Table 1** Nights spent by residents and non-residents (mil.)

| Country | Number of establishments (units) | Number of bed places (thousands) | Nights spent by residents and non-residents (millions) |
|---|---|---|---|
| Croatia | 108,212 | 1116 | 89.6 |
| Hungary | 4587 | 419 | 32.8 |
| Romania | 7720 | 349 | 28.5 |
| Slovenia[a,b] | 3699 | 117 | 15.7[c] |
| Serbia[a] | 3651 | 109 | 9.3[c] |

[a]Nights spent by residents and non-residents estimated using 2018 monthly data
[b]Number of establishments and bed places 2017
[c]Estimated data
*Source* Adapted from Eurostat https://ec.europa.eu/eurostat/statistics-explained/index.php/Tourism_statistics accessed in 11.05.2020

These three indicators for measuring tourism activity for the 5 countries for 2018 show the following situation: Croatia is on the first place on all indicators, Hungary is on the second place on the first two indicators, Serbia is on the last place on all indicators and Romania and Slovenia is competing for 3rd and 4th places.

As can be observed from the analyzed information and also from the IMIS database, there is a structural difference in the tourism sector of the five analyzed countries: Croatia is focused mainly on seaside and attractions tourism with summer

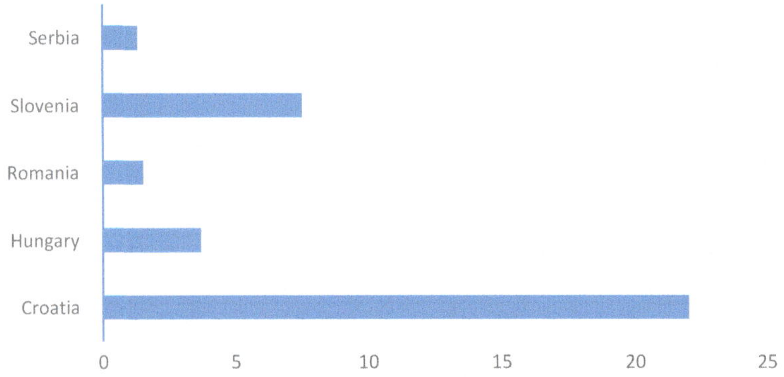


**Graph 2** Tourism intensity for 2018
For Slovenia estimate based on available data; For Serbia 2016 data
*Source* Adapted from https://ec.europa.eu/eurostat/statistics-explained/index.php/Tourism_statistics accessed 11.05.2019

as main season. Hungary benefits from attractions tourism (mainly Budapest) and also from tourism linked with events. Slovenia is recognized mostly for its transit tourism even if in several areas' attraction tourism flourished. The tourism in Romania and Serbia is based mostly on local tourists and concentrated on business tourism in the main cities and attraction tourism in the countryside or an increasing seaside tourism (in Romania).

## 3 Methodology of Research

The tourism and hospitality companies covered in this study were selected from a larger database provided by IMIS containing the top 1.000 companies located in 5 Central and Eastern European countries: Croatia, Hungary, Romania, Serbia and Slovenia. These companies were analyzed and clustered based on different criteria: annual turnover, type of activity, location, number of employees, assets, net profit, return on equity, return on investment, solvency, debt analysis, so on. The IMIS database provided complete information regarding all accounting or financial variables over the 5-year period from 2014 to 2018. The selection of the companies for the case study was performed in different steps: First was applied an algorithm for selection of the companies which are performing in the field of tourism and hospitality services. In the second step of the analysis were eliminated companies with uncomplete financial reporting information. The final step was to eliminate companies which had extreme anomalies in their financial results and which may cause also anomalies in the composite financial indicator proposed to be tested within this paper.

Identification and establishment of a composite indicator proposed to assess the financial performance for private companies is an issue which proved to be interesting for both researchers and professionals from this field of science. As stated in a paper published by Droj and Tara (2018), the first composite indicators were proposed by researchers analyzing the bankruptcy and financial risks such as Beaver (1966) and Altman (1968). Other authors such as Deakin (1972), Ohlson (1980), Gilbert et al. (1990), Altman (1993), Charitou et al. (2004) continued proposing several indicators and analysis methods in the period of 1970 –2004.

Taking into consideration the above-mentioned publications the authors of the current article estimated that research for a composite indicator assessing the financial performance should be developed in several steps:

Step 1—Simple bankruptcy analysis pioneered by Beaver (1966) based on statistical methods,
Step 2—Z-score model proposed by Altman (1968), Altman (1993),
Step 3—Multiple logistic regression models as proposed by Ohlson (1980),
Step 4—Neural networks championed by Charitou et al. 2004),
Step 5—Econometric/Combined models (Tarnoczi and Fenyves 2011; Bedenik et al. 2012).

Most of these studies and other complementary studies (Karanovic and Karanovic 2016) are tackling issues such as solvency and financial performance at the level of companies. The study of financial performance at the level of companies with the goal of creating a composite indicator became important in the last years as one of the most strategic instruments for the financial managers of the companies and also for company owners, investors, bankers or for other professionals.

Taken into consideration the mentioned studies, the authors of this article established several indicators, which can be part of financial performance analysis composite indicator, adapted for tourism and hospitality services companies operating in Central and Eastern Europe. The authors selected several financial early warning indicators, which can be suitable for the proposed model. These are indicators including both solvency (Droj 2012) and financial or economic efficiency indicators (Droj 2015; Fenyves et al. 2018).

Before selecting the indicators, which are considered relevant for the scope of the research, the authors created a correlation analysis matrix including several financial indicators such as solvency, return on assets (ROA), return on equity (ROE) and return on sales (ROS), general liquidity, acid test, total debt ratio, equity multiplier (EM) and price–earnings ratio (PER). The correlation matrix showed a close relationship between several of the considered variables: solvency with the liquidity and acid test, return on assets (ROA) with the equity multiplier, return on equity (ROE) with PER and return on sales (ROS).

Therefore, after performing the Kaiser–Meyer–Olkin test (Jolliffe and Cadima 2016) the main indicators considered relevant for the scope of this research and which were selected for this study were: solvency, return on assets (ROA), return on equity (ROE) and return on Sales (ROS).

With the results of the Kaiser–Meyer–Olkin test as mentioned by the above-mentioned authors and after analyzing several of the proposed models, the authors proposed a test composite indicator PERF which was applied on the selected database within this paper:

$$PERF = 0.35 \cdot SOL + 0.35 \cdot ROE + 0.15 \cdot ROA + 0.15 \cdot ROS \quad (1)$$

Below we will present each of these indicators and their role in assessing the financial performance of the tourism and hospitality companies from the Central and Eastern Europe:

The solvency ratio (SOL) shows the extent to which total debts are covered by total assets and reflects the security enjoyed by creditors, as well as the creditworthiness of the company (Droj 2012). If this indicator has a lower value, the greater the probability that the company will default on its debt obligations. For healthy companies, the indicator exceeds the value of 2.

$$SOL = \frac{\text{Total assets}}{\text{Total debts}} \quad (2)$$

Return on equity (ROE) measures the company's ability to make profit from the usage of its own capital. This rate should register values above the average bank interest rate in order for a business/a company to be considered profitable.

$$ROE = \frac{\text{Net income (After tax)}}{\text{Shareholders Equity}} \cdot 100 \quad (3)$$

The return on assets (ROA) reflects the difference between an economic result: net profit, known in specialized literature as EBIT and the assets used for its achievement and therefore indicates how profitable a company is relative to its total assets. ROA gives a manager, investor or analyst an idea as to how efficient a company's management is at using its assets to generate earnings.

$$ROA = \frac{\text{Net income}}{\text{Total assets}} \cdot 100 \quad (4)$$

The fourth indicator proposed in this study is return on sales (ROS) is a ratio used to evaluate a company's operational efficiency. An increasing ROS indicates that a company is growing more efficiently, while a decreasing ROS could signal impending financial troubles. ROS is very closely related to a firm's operating profit margin.

$$ROS = \frac{\text{Operating Profit}}{\text{Net Sales}} \cdot 100 \quad (5)$$

## 4 Results and Discussion

In order to test the proposed composite indicator, financial information data for the period 2014–2018 were collected from the IMIS database. The information collected was quite generous: annual turnover, type of activity, location, number of employees, assets, net profit, return on equity, return on investment, solvency, debt analysis, so on. Since the study was focused on Central and Eastern Europe, companies from five countries members and non-members of the European Union were selected: Croatia, Hungary, Romania, Serbia and Slovenia. In order to narrow the companies from the database and to obtain the most representative results of the study, the companies were arranged using the annual turnover criteria, and therefore, information from the top 1000 biggest companies was processed.

The selection of the final companies for the case study was performed in different steps: First was applied an algorithm for selection of the companies which are performing in the field of tourism and hospitality services. In the second step of the analysis were eliminated companies with uncomplete financial reporting information. The final step was to eliminate companies which had extreme anomalies in their financial results and which may cause also anomalies in the composite financial indicator proposed to be tested within this paper. Finally, after the selection process, the indicators were calculated based on the average financial results of the 15 most relevant tourism and hospitality companies from each country.

As given in Table 2, the highest value of the average PERF indicator in 2014 was obtained in Hungary with a value of 25.29, followed by Serbia and Romania. The excellent results of the PERF from Hungary in 2014 were based by extremely good levels of average ROE and ROA. However, sometimes an extremely high ROE is often due to a small equity account compared to net income, which indicates risk. The same assessment can be made regarding ROA. The lowest value was reached in Slovenia which had a negative value of PERF, caused by negative values in ROA and ROS. For Croatia, the medium PERF was slightly positive 0.13, caused by negative average of ROE and ROA. As given in Tables 2, 3 and 4, 2014 is the only year in which companies from Croatia and Slovenia register average negative values, except Croatia with negative value of ROE in 2016.

**Table 2** Financial indicators for years 2014–2015

| | 2014 | | | | | 2015 | | | | |
|---|---|---|---|---|---|---|---|---|---|---|
| | ROA | ROE | SOL | ROS | PERF | ROA | ROE | SOL | ROS | PERF |
| Croatia | −0.04 | −3.59 | 1.89 | 4.88 | 0.13 | 2.64 | −2.16 | 10.42 | 0.91 | 3.42 |
| Hungary | 21.40 | 59.17 | 2.23 | 3.96 | 25.29 | 18.60 | 42.08 | 2.18 | 4.64 | 18.98 |
| Serbia | 24.03 | 45.02 | 2.16 | 4.14 | 20.74 | −6.47 | −28.18 | 1.30 | −0.90 | −10.51 |
| Romania | 9.03 | 19.33 | 7.95 | 9.31 | 12.30 | 13.47 | 32.57 | 4.20 | 5.12 | 15.66 |
| Slovenia | −11.29 | 1.49 | 1.04 | −11.29 | −2.50 | 2.93 | 8.44 | 1.61 | 3.89 | 4.54 |

*Source* Own calculations

**Table 3** Financial indicators for years 2016–2017

| | 2016 | | | | | 2017 | | | | |
|---|---|---|---|---|---|---|---|---|---|---|
| | ROA | ROE | SOL | ROS | PERF | ROA | ROE | SOL | ROS | PERF |
| Croatia | 3.46 | −1.44 | 2.13 | 13.84 | 2.84 | 2.53 | 3.81 | 7.42 | 0.81 | 4.43 |
| Hungary | 2.46 | 35.67 | 1.43 | 1.05 | 13.51 | 8.66 | 35.98 | 1.71 | 2.95 | 14.93 |
| Serbia | −11.88 | −1320.05 | 1.03 | −2.40 | −463.8 | 8.97 | 50.91 | 1.32 | 1.98 | 19.92 |
| Romania | 6.14 | 27.15 | 7.42 | 2.20 | 13.35 | 14.23 | 36.04 | 2.14 | 4.63 | 16.19 |
| Slovenia | 3.88 | 10.48 | 1.55 | 2.82 | 5.22 | 4.28 | 12.89 | 1.57 | 2.62 | 6.10 |

*Source* Own calculations

**Table 4** Financial indicators for year 2018

| Year 2018 | ROA | ROE | SOL | ROS | PERF |
|---|---|---|---|---|---|
| Croatia | 4.09 | 8.88 | 9.34 | 0.62 | 7.08 |
| Hungary | 7.67 | 27.36 | 1.91 | 2.83 | 11.82 |
| Serbia | 9.56 | 46.02 | 1.26 | 3.49 | 18.51 |
| Romania | 16.93 | 46.07 | 1.99 | 5.56 | 20.19 |
| Slovenia | 3.40 | 11.58 | 1.22 | 2.16 | 5.31 |

*Source* Own calculations

The situation in 2015 is changing gradually and Serbian companies register negative average of ROA and ROE, and therefore, the PERF indicator is negative (Table 2). The same tendency can be observed in 2016 (Table 3). On the other hand, Slovenian and Croatian companies significantly increase their PERF values based on ROA, ROS and solvency. Hungary still maintains the highest value of average PERF, but the average financial results are declining, especially regarding ROA and ROE. Romania benefits from excellent ROA and ROE and reaches an average value of PERF of 15.66 (Table 2).

The year of 2016 brings an unexpected evolution for the average PERF value, since the composite indicator registers decreasing values in four of the five countries: Croatia, Hungary, Serbia and Romania (Table 3). The only country in which this indicator registers increasing values is Slovenia, which has increasing values of ROA and ROE. An interesting fact is that all the Serbian companies are registering losses and therefore highly negative ROE. During this year, the best average PERF values are recorded by companies from Hungary (13.51) closely followed by Romanian companies (13.35) (Table 3). The decline of financial results in 2016 can be explained by the fact that the sector was being hurt by economic weakness, Brexit uncertainties and a ramp-up in terrorist attacks according to reports of World Travel and Tourism Council.

Meanwhile 2017 brings increases in the value of PERF for each five countries with excellent ROE results. Based on a very high value of average ROE, Serbian companies have the biggest PERF of 19.92 points followed by Romanian companies

**Table 5** Aggregated values of PERF 2014–2018

| | 2014 | 2015 | 2016 | 2017 | 2018 | Δ% |
|---|---|---|---|---|---|---|
| Croatia | 0.13 | 3.42 | 2.84 | 4.43 | 7.08 | 5363.66 |
| Hungary | 25.29 | 18.98 | 13.51 | 14.93 | 11.82 | 46.73 |
| Serbia | 20.74 | −10.51 | −92.76 | 19.92 | 18.51 | 89.23 |
| Romania | 12.30 | 15.66 | 13.35 | 16.19 | 20.19 | 164.20 |
| Slovenia | −2.50 | 4.54 | 5.22 | 6.10 | 5.31 | 312.43 |

*Source* Own calculations

with a PERF of 16.19 points (Table 3). The lowest PERF in 2017 is registered by Croatian companies.

In the final year of our study (2018), the companies from Romania and Croatia register the highest ever PERF score, while Hungarian companies reach the lowest average PERF score: 11.82 based on deteriorating ROE and ROA (Table 4). The highest average PERF score is reached in this year by Romanian companies (20.19) while the lowest PERF score was obtained by Slovenian companies. In case of Romanian companies, these results can be explained by the fiscal measures approved in 2017–2018 in order to support the tourism sector: VAT reduced to 5%, introduction of tourism vouchers, other tax cuts. An interesting aspect is that for the first time, in 2018, the PERF score of Croatian companies surpasses the score of Slovenian companies.

While analyzing the centralized PERF results for the period 2014–2018, Table 5 shows that companies from two countries have an increasing PERF score: Croatia and Romania. In these countries, the PERF score improved significantly in the analyzed period, Romania reaching the highest PERF score in 2017 and 2018. The most stable companies within this analysis were the Slovenian companies for which their PERF score varied in the period 2015–2018 from 4.54 to 6.10 (Graph 3).

As given in Table 5, the companies from Serbia obtained the most inconsistent values of the PERF composite indicator: varying from extremely good positive values in 2014, 2017 and 2018 to negative values in 2015 and 2016. The most surprising year was 2016 when all Serbian companies which were included in the study registered lossless, and therefore, the results of the main financial indicators were negative, especially the PERF score, ROE and ROA.

The country with the highest decrease in the PERF score was Hungary. Hungarian companies registered in 2014 the biggest PERF score from the entire period, but this score declined to 11.82 in 2018. The score from 2018 is still an excellent one since is based on a ROE of 27.36%, and also values of ROA, solvency and ROS are way above the average recommended values. Analyzing the obtained results, we can conclude that an aggregated PERF composite indicator with positive values over 5 can indicate a stable private tourism sector in a certain country.

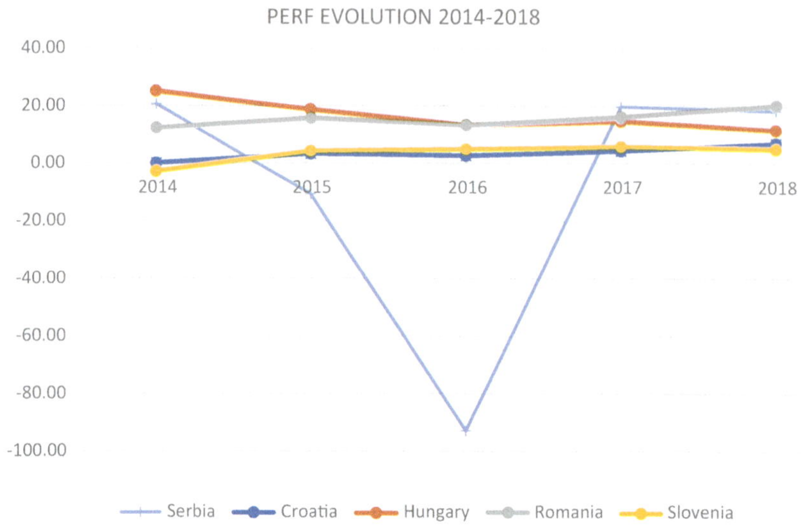


**Graph 3** PERF evolution 2014–2018. *Source* Own calculations

## 5 Conclusion

These results can be also correlated with the structural difference of the tourism sector in the five analyzed countries: In Croatia and Romania, the number of the micro- and small companies operating in the field of tourism is quite high forcing a high level of distribution of tourists between a large number of tourism companies. In Hungary, the concentration of tourism is highest in Budapest, Balaton and several cities, and therefore, large companies are dominating the market. Slovenia is recognized mostly for its transit tourism even if in several areas' attraction tourism flourished. On the other hand, in Serbia the tourism sector is still developing, as can be seen from the structure of the companies performing in the tourism sector where several huge companies seem to influence the entire market.

The measurement of performance in tourism and hospitality services, as reflected in the literature, was taken from various perspectives: from the perspective of efficiency, from the perspective of labor productivity, from the perspective of measurements in use (industry-specific indices), from the perspective of competitiveness and from the perspective of performance measurement. In this paper, we proposed a composite index to measure the financial performance of the tourism and hospitality services companies that combines the most common financial indicators: ROE, ROA, solvency and ROS. The tourism and hospitality companies covered in this study were selected from a larger database provided by IMIS containing the top 1.000 companies located in 5 Central and Eastern European countries: Croatia, Hungary, Romania, Serbia and Slovenia. These companies were analyzed and clustered based on different criteria: annual turnover, type of activity, location, number of employees, assets, net profit, return on equity, return on investment, solvency, debt analysis, so on. The IMIS database provided complete information regarding all accounting or financial variables over the 5-year period from 2014 to 2018. From the perspective of the composite index, up to 15 companies from each country out of the 5 taken into account (Croatia, Hungary, Romania, Serbia and Slovenia) are analyzed. The selection criterion of the companies was the size of the annual turnover and number of employees. The analysis shows both the differences in financial performance and the specifics of the differences, reflected in the values of the financial indicators, specific for each country.

The PERF composite indicator provided an extremely interesting overview of the private tourism sector from all the five private countries analyzed. The private tourism sector from all the five private countries analyzed. The results of PERF composite score showed for Croatia and Romania a developing and increasing private tourism sector with increasing financial performance, caused by fast development of private tourism sector and increase in number of tourism revenues. For Slovenia, the results of PERF showed a stable sector tourism with healthy and stable financial performances for the companies, while the Serbian companies obtained the most inconsistent values of the PERF composite indicator: varying from extremely good positive values in 2014, 2017 and 2018 to negative values in 2015 and 2016. In case of Hungarian tourism and hospitality companies, the PERF indicator showed a deteriorating financial performance in the tourism sector but with very good financial indicators, especially ROE. Also, the PERF indicator managed to highlight the decline of financial results in tourism in 2016 which was signaled by the World Travel and Tourism Council caused by the fact that the sector was hurt by economic weakness, Brexit uncertainties and a ramp-up in terrorist attacks. The PERF composite indicator managed to illustrate the effects of positive national governments policies supporting tourism in Romania and Croatia in 2017 and 2018. This was extremely visible in improving the financial performance of Romanian tourism and hospitality companies in 2017 and 2018 after reduction of VAT to 5%, introduction of tourism vouchers for employees and special tax cuts.

The limitations of the study are brought by the fact that the PERF indicator was tested only over companies from five countries and the limitations given by IMI database. In the future, the authors intend to extend this study by testing the PERF composite indicator over companies from different European countries. In the same time, the authors will further calibrate the indicator in order to include other financial and non-financial variables, as the consumer satisfaction.

## References

Altman EI (1968) Financial ratios, discriminant analysis and the prediction of corporate bankruptcy. J Financ 23(4):589–609

Altman EI (1993) Corporate financial distress and bankruptcy. Wiley, New York

Beaver WH (1966) Financial ratios as predictors of failure. J Account Res 4:71–111

Bedenik NO et al (2012) Early warning system—empirical evidence. TRŽIŠTE 24(2):201–218

Charitou A et al (2004) Predicting corporate failure: empirical evidence for the UK. Eur Account Rev 13(3):465–497
Chen MH (2010) The economy, tourism growth and corporate performance in the Taiwanese hotel industry. Tour Manage 31(5):665–675
Chi CG, Gursoy D (2009) Employee satisfaction, customer satisfaction, and financial performance: an empirical examination. Int J Hosp Manag 28(2):245–253
Chien-Min C et al (2011) The destination competitiveness of Kinmen's tourism industry: exploring the interrelationships between tourist perceptions, service performance, customer satisfaction and sustainable tourism. J Sustain Tour 19(2):247–264. https://doi.org/10.1080/09669582.2010.517315
Deakin EB (1972) A discriminating analysis of predictors of business failure. J Account Res 10(1):167–179
Denizci B, Li X (2009) Linking marketing efforts to financial outcome: an exploratory study in tourism and hospitality contexts. J Hospitality Tourism Res 33(2):211–226
Droj L (2012) Financial Performance Analysis based on the Financial Statements for the Companies Located in the Bihor - Hajdu Bihar Euroregion, Annals of the University of Oradea, Economic Science Oradea, Romania. Series 21(2):464–470
Droj L (2015) Study Regarding the Profitability Indicators for the Romanian Companies Operating in the Tourism and Leisure Services Sector in the Period of 2010–2013. Annals of Faculty of Economics, University of Oradea, Faculty of Economics 24:817–824
Droj L, Tara IG (2018) Early warning indicators—evolution for the medical companies registered at BSE. Ann Faculty of Economics, University of Oradea, Faculty of Economics, vol. 1(2):102–108
Fenyves, V., Bács, Z.,Zéman, Z., Böcskei, E., &Tarnóczi, T., 2018. The role of the notes to the financial statements in corporate decision-making. Corporate Ownership & Control, 15. 138–148. https://doi.org/10.22495/cocv15i4c1p1
Goodall B (1995) Environmental auditing: a tool for assessing the environmental performance of tourism firms. Geogr J 29–37
Gursoy D, Swanger N (2007) Performance-enhancing internal strategic factors and competencies: Impacts on financial success. Int J Hosp Manag 26(1):213–227. https://doi.org/10.1016/j.ijhm.2006.01.004
Hall DR (1998) Tourism development and sustainability issues in Central and South-Eastern Europe. Tour Manage 19(5):423–431
Ham S, Lee S (2011) US restaurant companies' green marketing via company websites: impact on financial performance. Tour Econ 17(5):1055–1069
Hsieh LF, Lin LH (2010) A performance evaluation model for international tourist hotels in Taiwan—an application of the relational network DEA. Int J Hosp Manag 29(1):14–24
Hughes H, Allen D (2005) Cultural tourism in Central and Eastern Europe: the views of 'induced image formation agents.' Tour Manage 26(2):173–183
Inoue Y, Lee S (2011) Effects of different dimensions of corporate social responsibility on corporate financial performance in tourism-related industries. Tour Manage 32(4):790–804
Jayawardena C, Ramajeesingh D (2003) Performance of tourism analysis: a Caribbean perspective. Int J Contemp Hosp Manag 15(3):176–179. https://doi.org/10.1108/09596110310470239
Jolliffe IT, Cadima J (2016) Principal component analysis: a review and recent developments. Philos Trans Seri A, Math, Phys, Eng Sci 374(2065):20150202. https://doi.org/10.1098/rsta.2015.0202)
Karanovic G, Karanovic B (2016) IPOs performance analysis: evidence from emerging markets in the Balkans. Scientific Ann Econ Bus 63(3):381–389. https://doi.org/10.1515/saeb-2016-0129
Lee C et al (2016) Innovation, entrepreneurship, and restaurant performance: a higher-order structural model. Tour Manag 53:215e228
Miller M (2013) Mathematics and statistics for financial risk management, Wiley
Molina-Azorin JF et al (2010) The importance of the firm and destination effects to explain firm performance. Tour Manage 31(1):22–28. https://doi.org/10.1016/j.tourman.2009.02.009
Morgan N, Anderson E, Mittal V (2005) Understanding firms' customer satisfaction information usage. J Mark 69 (July), 131–151

Ohlson JA (1980) Financial ratios and the probabilistic prediction of bankruptcy. J Account Res 18(1):109–131
Saeidi SP et al (2015) How does corporate social responsibility contribute to firm financial performance? The mediating role of competitive advantage, reputation, and customer satisfaction. J Bus Res 68(2):341–350
Sainaghi R et al (2017) Performance measurement in tourism firms: a content analytical meta-approach. Tour Manage 59:36–56
Singal M (2014) The link between firm financial performance and investment in sustainability initiatives. Cornell Hospitality Quarterly 55(1):19–30
Sun KA, Kim DY (2013) Does customer satisfaction increase firm performance? An application of American Customer Satisfaction Index (ACSI). Int J Hosp Manag 35:68–77
Taiwan—An application of the relational network DEA. Int J Hospitality Manag 29(1):14–24
Tan S-H et al (2017) The impact of the dimensions of environmental performance on firm performance in travel and tourism industry. J Environ Manage 203:603–611. https://doi.org/10.1016/j.jenvman.2017.02.029
Tarnoczi T, Fenyves V (2011) Liquidity management and corporate risk. Ann Fac Econ 1:530–536

# The Impact of Renewable Energy Policies and Financial Development on $CO_2$ Emissions and Economic Growth in EU Countries

**Fatbardha Morina, Uğur Ergün, and Chrysanthi Balomenou**

**Abstract** The purpose of this study is to examine the impact of renewable energy policies and financial development on $CO_2$ emissions and economic growth in EU countries. The panel vector autoregression (PVAR) model is employed to investigate the relationship between renewable energy policies, financial development with $CO_2$ emissions, and economic growth during the period of 2000–2017. The results show that renewable policies for solar influence negatively economic growth. However, the polices followed for wind technologies influence positively economic growth. Also, financial development and renewable policies for wind technologies seem to influence $CO_2$ emissions. The results indicate that policymakers should pay attention to the efficiency of policies in renewable energy to increase energy demand from renewable energy sources and to reduce emissions in the environment.

**Keywords** $CO_2$ emissions · Support schemes · Economic growth · Renewable energy · Financial development

**JEL Classification Codes** O44 · Q43 · Q48

## 1 Introduction

The effect of climate change on human health, human life, and the quality of the environment is becoming a great concern. Greenhouse gas (GHG) emission is considered as the main source of climate changes and in order to mitigate environmental degradation, policymakers have taken actions related to the allowed level of emissions. Among sectors that cause a high level of emissions is the energy sector. In 2018, the level of emissions from fuel combustion was accounted for approximately 53% of the EU-27 greenhouse gas emissions, while the contribution to GDP (gross domestic

F. Morina (✉) · U. Ergün · C. Balomenou
Department of Banking and Finance, Epoka University, Tirana, Albania
e-mail: fmorina@epoka.edu.al

C. Balomenou
e-mail: cbalomenou@epoka.edu.al



G. Karanovic et al. (eds.), *The Changing Financial Landscape*, Contributions to Economics, https://doi.org/10.1007/978-3-030-82778-6_6

product) of the industry sector including energy is 18.75%. Since the proportion of energy consumption from fossil energy sources continues to be high compared to the level of renewable energy, it has increased the concerns related to energy for future generation ensuring. Indeed, to cut the greenhouse gas emissions are implemented several environmental strategies that are tightly connected with the promotion of renewable energy technologies to ensure sustainable energy. The use of energy from renewable energy sources is enhanced by the Renewable Energy Directive, known as 2009/28/EC as a respond to climate change challenges and support the achievement of sustainable growth in the EU member states. According to the mentioned directive, the target of 20% of the energy consumption from renewable sources to the total energy of the EU counties should be achieved by 2020. But also, they suggest to the Commission to increase this target to 32% by 2030, which can be reached by individual targets of the member states. Several support schemes in EU member states are implemented to develop renewable energy, and they tend to become a lead in energy security from renewable sources. The level of renewable subsides mainly in wind and solar electricity generation is increased from 25 billion € to 76 billion € between 2008 and 2016, implying a threefold increase (European Commission 2019). Thus, increasing the level of renewable energy production and consumption enhances new technologies that enable employment opportunities and thereby economic growth. Renewable energy production and consumption for EU countries is crucial since these countries are import energy dependency and the development of renewable energy is essential to ensure energy for the future generation. Therefore, the improvement in the renewable energy sector effects not only the energy sector but also is connected with economic growth and impairing environmental degradation. The strong support of renewable energy policies on economic growth is explained by a mix of three externalities such as energy security, air pollution, and knowledge spillover (Maschinen et al. 2010). Policies in the energy sector tend to shift toward renewable energy usage since the energy generated from renewable energy sources is essential for meeting the energy needs with the scope of sustainable energy. Also, the EU's Emission Trading System (ETS) and other climate policies are implemented to combat negative externalities of $CO_2$ emission that contribute to the reduction cost of renewable electricity. Therefore, the policies aim to create economies of scale and further the development of technology through learning by doing that makes renewable electricity more competitive in the long run. However, there is a long debate with controversial findings related to the effect of support schemes on economic growth. Thus, the investigation of the effect of renewable energy polices and financial development on $CO_2$ emission and economic growth for EU countries is crucial since they possess the potential to generate energy by using renewable energy resources. Different from previous studies that have investigated renewable energy consumption and growth nexus, this is the first study that extends the model by including financial development as a macroeconomic factor. Using a panel VAR and impulse response function is examined the relationship between renewable energy policies, financial development, $CO_2$ emissions, and economic growth for 27 EU countries for the period of 2000–2017. The results support the hypothesis that financial development promotes economic growth which is consistent with growth theory. Also, the study provides some evidence in support of the hypothesis that renewable energy promotes economic growth in the case of wind capacity. However, solar capacity has a negative effect on economic growth. Lastly, the financial development for EU countries impairs environmental quality and the EU's renewable energy policies for solar capacity reduce environmental degradation.

Also, policy recommendations are given to promote renewable energy for the reduction in the EU's energy dependency and in meeting targets to combat global warming.

The remaining part of the paper is organized as follows: Sect. 2 describes the literature review on renewable energy policies, financial development nexus economic growth, and $CO_2$ emissions. In Sect. 3, data and methodology of the study is described. Section 4 contains the empirical results and discussion. Finally, the conclusion and policy implications are shown in Sect. 5.

## 2 Literature Review

Several studies in the literature examine the relationship between renewable energy policies, financial development, economic growth, and $CO_2$ emissions in developed and developing countries. The increased attention on renewable energy and rapid development during the last decades has led to various debates on the impact of renewable energy on economic growth and environmental degradation.

*Impact of renewable energy policies on economic growth and $CO_2$emissions*

Global awareness on environmental issues has increased the interest of researchers to study the relationship between renewable energy consumption and economic growth in terms of sustainable energy and environmental pollution. The study by Al-Mulali et al. (2013) in 108 countries during the period of 1980–2009 supports the feedback hypothesis for countries with high-income level, meaning that there is a bidirectional relationship between renewable energy consumption and economic growth. In the same line, Apergis and Payne (2015) argue that for 11 South American countries, there is a bidirectional between renewable consumption, economic growth, and $CO_2$ emissions. An increase in $CO_2$ emissions increases renewable energy consumption, while an increase in renewable energy consumption reduces the $CO_2$ emissions in the short run. However, Apergis and Ozturk (2015) found that in 14 Asian countries spanning the period 1990–2011, there is a unidirectional relationship between growth and emissions. In addition, an increase in the level of income in the early stage of growth causes an increase in the level of environmental degradation and then declines when income per capita achieves at a threshold. Moutinho and Robaina (2016) support the hypothesis of the environmental Kuznets curve (EKC) for an inverse U-shaped relationship between income level and emissions for 20 OECD countries. They found that the main driver of the reduction in carbon emissions in electricity is the share of renewable energy in electricity output. Jaraite et al. (2015)

using the data from 15 EU countries reveal that the relationship between renewable energy policies and economic growth is positive only in the short run, but not in the long run. The support schemes for wind capacity promote economic growth.

In contrast, Silva, Soares, and Pinho (2012) show that renewable energy shares harm economic growth for Denmark, Portugal, and Spain during the period of 1960–2004 and reduce the $CO_2$ emissions. The negative effect of renewable energy can be explained by the period of study in which renewable energy investments were at the early stages and these sources were not so competitive. Although EU countries operate under the same Energy Union, countries differ in terms of political regulation, institutional arrangements, domestic energy sources, and energy policies. To reduce import energy dependency, it is crucial to focus on the development of renewable energy through different strategies and incentives that foster investment in this sector. The contribution to economic growth from renewable energy investment should be significant by generating energy from renewable energy sources and reduce import payment (Can and Korkmaz, 2019).

H1: Renewable energy support schemes in the EU lead to technological development, followed by sustainable growth in the EU countries.
H2: Financial development in the EU leads to technological development, followed by sustainable growth in the EU countries.
*Impact of financial development on economic growth and $CO_2$emissions*

The crucial role of financial development in stimulating economic growth is well accepted by researchers. The development of the financial system contributes to the mobilization of savings, diversifying the risk, allocating the resources, and facilitating the exchange of goods and services (Arestis and Demetriades 1997). But the role of financial development is crucial for the energy sector to foster technological development and to reduce emissions in the environment. As it is stated by Charfeddine et al. (2018), financial support leads to investing in research and technology in terms of reduction in air pollution in order to preserve the environment for the future generation. According to Al-Mulali et al. (2015), financial development increases the level of pollution in the long run. Using the FMOLS estimation method for 23 EU countries during the period 1990–2013, it is shown that financial support from banks to the private sector is invested in non-environmentally friendly projects. Similarly, Hassine and Harrathi (2017) found that there is a significant causality relationship between renewable energy consumption, economic growth, and financial development. The study includes the Gulf Cooperation Council (GCC) countries during the period of 1980–2012 and reveals that financial development has a negative effect on economic growth. Jamel and Maktouf (2017) analyze the nexus between economic growth, financial development, and emission for 40 European countries during the period and conclude that there is no causal relationship between financial development and $CO_2$ emission and bidirectional relationship between financial development and economic growth.

Empirical studies show that there is no consensus among researchers on the nexus between renewable energy, financial development, economic growth, and environmental quality. Everything depends on country characteristics related to energy policies toward renewable energy.

H3: Renewable energy support schemes in the EU lead to a reduction in $CO_2$ emissions.
H4: Financial development in the EU leads to a reduction in $CO_2$ emissions.

## 3 Methodology and Data

### *3.1 Data and Descriptive Statistics*

This study investigates the relationship between renewable energy polices, financial development, economic growth, and $CO_2$ emissions for EU countries for the period of 2000–2017. Annual data are collected from the World Bank Development Indicators (WDI) and US Energy Information Administration (EIA). The model contains seven variables that are: (i) the real GDP per capita (in constant 2010 USD) as a proxy for economic growth, (ii) financial development (FD) measured as a ratio of credit to the private sector over to real GDP, (iii) $CO_2$ emissions per capita that represent environmental degradation measured in thousands of $CO_2$ metric tons, (iv) capital (K) that is calculated as gross capital formation divided by GDP, (v) labor force (L) that indicates the number of persons in millions, and the last two variables that represent renewable energy policies. Renewable energy production capacity of solar (SOL) and wind (WIN) are used as an indicator of renewable energy policies. In European Union countries most of policies relay on solar and wind since they are the leading renewable energy sources. All the data are converted in the logarithmic form to reduce non-normality and to overcome the problem of heteroscedasticity between variables (Sadorsky 2011; Salahuddin et al. 2018).

### *3.2 Panel Unit Root Test*

Before running the panel VAR model, it is required that all variables should be stationary in order to obtain consistent and unbiased results. To choose the right test for stationarity, it needs to test for cross-sectional dependence. The first generation of unit root test suppose the presence of cross-sectional independence and suggest to use Levin et al. (2002) and IPS unit root test for panel data (Im et al. 2003). The second generation of unit root tests overcome the problem of cross-sectional dependence. The test suggested by Pesaran (2007) that constructed a modified version of the IPS test allows for cross-sectional dependence, which is based on cross-sectionally augmented Dickey–Fuller (CADF). The CIPS critical values are

**Table 1** Panel unit root tests results

| Variables | CIPS (2007) | IPS (2003) |
|---|---|---|
| L | −2.076 (0.865) | −0.748 (0.227) |
| D(L) | −3.270***(0.000) | −4.319***(0.000) |
| K | −2.177 (0.720) | −0.060(0.475) |
| D(K) | −2.844*** (0.002) | −7.342***(0.000) |
| FD | 2.333 (0.990) | 2.398(0.991) |
| D(FD) | −2.453**(0.007) | −19.499***(0.000) |
| GDP | −2.200 (0.678) | 0.078 (0.531) |
| D(GDP) | −2.117**(0.027) | −2.534(0.005) |
| CO2 | −1.694(0.996) | 1.824(0.966) |
| D (CO2) | −3.346***(0.000) | −7.455***(0.000) |
| SOL | 9.742(1.000) | −39.081***(0.000) |
| D(SOL) | −5.719*** (0.000) | −39.415***(0.000) |
| WIN | 3.318 (1.000) | 59.738(0.275) |
| D(WIN) | −3.719***(0.000) | 22.982***(0.000) |

*Note* Probability values are reported in parentheses. Panel root test includes intercept and trend. ***and ** denote the significance at 1% and 5% level, respectively. D(.) denotes the first differences

stimulated by Pesaran for different sample sizes. Thus, the panel unit root test in Table 1 shows that all variables become stationary in the first difference.

## 3.3 Model Specification

The panel VAR model proposed recently by Abrigo and Love (2016) is used in this study. This estimation technique is an extension of the traditional VAR model, which considers all the variables in the system as endogenous, with a panel data approach, which allows for unobserved individual heterogeneity. Furthermore, investigating macroeconomic dynamics in practice can yield consistent and efficient estimates through the PVAR approach.

In order to run the PVAR model, the first stage is choosing the optimal lag order in both VAR specification and moment conditions. In Table 2 are shown different selection criteria such as J-statistic test of over-identifying restriction (Hansen 1982), the

**Table 2** The optimal lag and model selection criteria

| lag | CD | J | J pvalue | MBIC | MAIC | MQIC |
|---|---|---|---|---|---|---|
| 1 | 0.93535 | 92.16679 | 0.416895 | -351.936 | -87.8332 | -195.158 |
| 2 | 0.955759 | 32.93811 | 0.810956 | -169.375 | -49.0619 | -97.9541 |

Bayesian information criteria (BIC), Akaike information criteria, and the Hannan–Quinn information criteria (HQIC). The optimal lag to use is the first lag since it provides the lowest values of MBIC, MAIC, and MQIC.

Panel VAR model used country fixed effects to remove unobserved factors that are constant over time. However, the inclusion of country fixed effects may lead to biased estimators since the fixed effects are associated with the regressors. To overcome this problem, it is used forward mean differencing known as Helmert transformation that estimates coefficient using system GMM.

# 4 Empirical Results and Discussion

## *4.1 PVAR Estimation Results*

Results of panel VAR model are given in Table 3. Seven equations are constructed to capture simultaneity between variables. Each dependent variable is regressed not only on its historical realization but also on lagged values of other variables. Table 3, column 1, where the GDP is the dependent variable shows that the first lag of CO2 and financial development positively determines the current level of GDP at the 1% level of significance. The relationship between renewable energy polices and

**Table 3** Results of panel VAR model

| Response to | Response of | | | | | | |
|---|---|---|---|---|---|---|---|
| | GDP | L | K | $CO_2$ | FD | SOL | WIN |
| $GDP_{(t-1)}$ | −0.102 | 0.208*** | −0.832* | 0.362 | 1.356*** | 6.177 | −0.723 |
| | (0.173) | (0.0490) | (0.453) | (0.246) | (0.298) | (5.259) | (1.377) |
| $L_{(t-1)}$ | 0.336 | 0.0621 | -3.071** | -0.418 | 1.737* | 42.34** | 14.65** |
| | (0.233) | (0.0958) | (1.463) | (0.586) | (1.030) | (21.58) | (6.032) |
| $K_{(t-1)}$ | 0.0578 | -0.0164 | 0.129 | -0.171** | -0.202** | 0.113 | 0.501 |
| | (0.0561) | (0.0158) | (0.164) | (0.0667) | (0.103) | (1.688) | (0.433) |
| $CO_{2(t-1)}$ | 0.0865*** | -0.0278*** | 0.289** | -0.239*** | -0.0588 | 0.298 | 0.197 |
| | (0.0332) | (0.00997) | (0.115) | (0.0845) | (0.0706) | (1.783) | (0.476) |
| $FD_{(t-1)}$ | 0.0746*** | 0.0202*** | 0.322*** | 0.313*** | 0.170*** | -3.830*** | -0.448* |
| | (0.0272) | (0.00703) | (0.106) | (0.0462) | (0.0565) | (1.210) | (0.244) |
| $SOL_{(t-1)}$ | -0.00750** | -0.00141 | -0.0202 | -0.00144 | 0.00368 | 0.655*** | 0.0101 |
| | (0.00304) | (0.00116) | (0.0138) | (0.00861) | (0.00832) | (0.180) | (0.0453) |
| $WIN_{(t-1)}$ | 0.00483 | -0.00622* | 0.0110 | 0.0799*** | 0.0285* | -0.0729 | 0.500*** |
| | (0.00760) | (0.00374) | (0.0375) | (0.0222) | (0.0154) | (0.540) | (0.102) |

Standard errors in parentheses
***p < 0.01, **p < 0.05, *p < 0.1

economic growth seems to be negative in case of policies implemented for solar, meaning that the increase in renewable energy capacity from solar through subsidies is not beneficial for economic growth. The findings are consistent with the study by Jaraite et al. (2017) that reveal a negative effect of renewable energy policies toward wind power on economic growth. This can be explained by the fact that the development of renewable energy technologies is in their early stage that do not benefit from international trade. In addition, there is a heterogeneity related to the share of the renewable energy sector in the economy among member countries in EU. However, EU's renewable energy policies related to wind enhance economic growth, and these can be explained by the competitiveness of the wind market.

Labor equation in column 2 shows that the level of GDP per capita of last year has a positive effect on the current level of labor at the 1% level of significance, meaning that increasing the level of GDP fosters the level of employment. The quality of the environment seems to be significant in the level of employment. The relationship between them is negative, meaning that improving the environmental quality leads to higher employment. The results show that indirectly the environmental degradation enhances investment in renewable energy that leads to higher employment. Wind capacity has a negative effect on employment, which can be explained by innovation in the technology that reduces the work force employment.

Capital equation shows that the lagged financial development, $CO_2$ emissions, and wind capacity lagged by one period have a statistically significant effect on capital. The financial development in EU countries is well developed that increases capital accumulation. However, lagged wind capacity has a positive effect on current capital. Wind capacity has a positive effect on financial development in the case of EU countries, which can be explained by the fact that renewable energy requires higher level of capital and to access finance they borrow from banks.

$CO_2$ equation in column 4 shows that capital has a significant negative effect on environmental degradation, which can be explained by the fact that EU countries employee capital in environmentally friendly activities. The impact of renewable energy polices in case of solar capacity reduces the level of emission. This indicates that the development of renewable energy in the EU counties is an effective way to mitigate environmental pollution. An environmentally sustainable path is following by each member country to achieve the target of 20% of renewable energy share in the final energy consumption by the year 2020.

The current financial development is affected positively by lagged financial development, GDP, labor, and wind capacity at 10%, 10%, and 1% level of significance, respectively. The positive relationship between financial development and economic growth is expected from the theory of growth. Also, a bidirectional relationship between economic growth and financial development is evident.

Renewable energy policies in columns 6 and 7 show that the financial development reduces wind and solar capacity, and this can be explained by the fact when the cost of borrowing is higher compared to the revenues that generate from renewable energy. The correlation between labor and EU's renewable energy polices is positive, which shows that the increase in labor force increases wind and solar capacity development.

**Fig. 1** The unit circle results

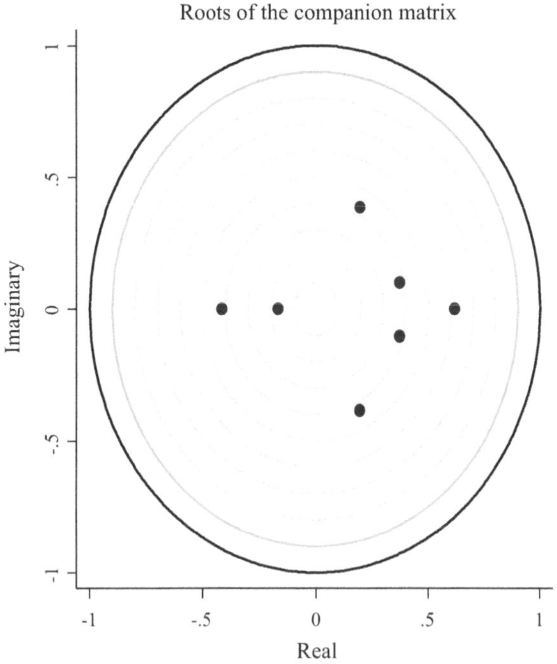


Figure 1 shows the stability condition of the model to support the robustness of the results. It is estimated through computing the modulus of each eigenvalue through PVAR. The VAR model is stable in case that all eigenvalues stay inside the unite circle.

## 5 Conclusion

During the last decades, the importance of renewable energy and consequently polices toward the promotion of renewable energy has attracted a lot of interest both among researchers and policymakers. The utilization of renewable energy sources could be a solution in improving environmental degradation and ensuring energy supply for the future. However, the debate related to renewable energy policies on the promotion of renewable energy remains open. European Union countries operate under the same Energy Union, but every country has its specific related to the energy policies, political regulations meaning that it is affected by the country factors. In this paper, a detail analysis is provided for EU countries in order to examine the effect of EU's renewable energy policies, financial development on economic growth, and $CO_2$ emissions. Panel VAR model estimated by system GMM model is used to provide consistent and unbiased results. The results of this study can be summarized in four important points. First, the support of the hypothesis that financial development promotes economic growth is evident for EU countries and is consistent with growth theory. Second, the results of the study provide some evidence in support of the hypothesis that renewable energy promotes economic growth in the case of wind capacity. However, the solar capacity has a negative effect on economic growth, and this can be explained by the fact that renewable energy companies operate with losses and support from government is fundamental for their development to extend their activity in international trade that leads to higher employment that in turn enhances growth. Third, financial development impairs environmental quality for the EU, and this can be explained by the high level of investments in economic activities that cause high pollution in the environment. Fourth, the EU's renewable energy policies for solar capacity reduce environmental degradation. Also, the nexus between $CO_2$ emission and the labor force shows a negative relationship that is the spillover effect of investing in renewable energy sources. The process of improving the quality of the environment in the region leads to higher employment.

Policy implications for the analysis of the outcome indicate that renewable energy enhances economic growth through sustainable investment in the sector. Thus, the government and policymakers of renewable energy should focus on the effectiveness of these support schemes. EU's renewable energy policies should reduce risk in renewable investments that lead to the job opportunity and in turn economic growth. Also, it is recommended to create subside polices of renewable energy that encourages the energy demand from renewable energy sources, in order to reduce the consumption from conventional energy that reduces the environmental degradation in the long run.

Further research related to the impact of renewable energy policies, financial development on economic growth, and $CO_2$ emission can be done by including other institutional and sociodemographic indicators. Also, other proxies for environmental pollution can be used.

## References

Abrigo MRM, Love I (2016) Estimation of panel vector autoregression in Stata. Stata J 16(3):778–804. https://doi.org/10.1177/1536867x1601600314

Al-Mulali U et al (2013) Examining the bi-directional long run relationship between renewable energy consumption and GDP growth. Renew Sustain Energy Rev. 22:209–222. https://doi.org/10.1016/j.rser.2013.02.005

Al-Mulali U, Ozturk I, Lean HH (2015) The influence of economic growth, urbanization, trade openness, financial development, and renewable energy on pollution in Europe. Nat Haz 79(1):621–644. https://doi.org/10.1007/s11069-015-1865-9

Apergis N, Ozturk I (2015) Testing environmental Kuznets curve hypothesis in Asian countries. Ecolog Ind 52:16–22. https://doi.org/10.1016/j.ecolind.2014.11.026

Apergis N, Payne JE (2015) Renewable energy, output, carbon dioxide emissions, and oil prices: Evidence from South America. Energy Sour Part B 10(3):281–287. https://doi.org/10.1080/15567249.2013.853713

Arestis P, Demetriades P (1997) Financial development and economic growth: assessing the evidence. Econ J 107(442):783–799

Can H, Korkmaz Ö (2019) The relationship between renewable energy consumption and economic growth: The case of Bulgaria. Int J Energy Sect Manage 13(3):573–589. https://doi.org/10.1108/IJESM-11-2017-0005

Charfeddine L, Yousef Al-Malk A, Al Korbi K (2018) Is it possible to improve environmental quality without reducing economic growth: evidence from the Qatar economy. Renew Sustain Energy Rev 82(July 2017):25–39. https://doi.org/10.1016/j.rser.2017.09.001

European Commission (2019) Energy subsidies and government revenues from energy products

Hansen LP (1982) Large sample properties of generalized method of moments. Econometrica: J Econometric Soc 50(4):1029–1054

Hassine MB, Harrathi N (2017) The causal links between economic growth, renewable energy, financial development and foreign trade in gulf cooperation council countries. Int J Energy Economics Policy 7(2):76–85

Im KS, Pesaran MH, Shin Y (2003) Testing for unit roots in heterogeneous panels. J Econometrics 115(1):53–74. https://doi.org/10.1016/S0304-4076(03)00092-7

Jamel L, Maktouf S (2017) The nexus between economic growth, financial development, trade openness, and $CO_2$ emissions in European countries. Cogent Econ Financ. Cogent 5(1):2332–2039. https://doi.org/10.1080/23322039.2017.1341456

Jaraite J, Karimu A, Kazukauskas A (2017) Policy-induced expansion of solar and wind power capacity: economic growth and employment in EU countries. The Energy J 38(5). https://doi.org/10.5547/01956574.38.5.jjar

Levin A, Lin CF, Chu CSJ (2002) Unit root tests in panel data: asymptotic and finite-sample properties. J Econometrics 108(1):1–24. https://doi.org/10.1016/S0304-4076(01)00098-7

Maschinen B et al (2010) Support schemes for renewable electricity in the EU, No. 408. Directorate General Economic and Financial Affairs (DG ECFIN). https://doi.org/10.2765/40994

Moutinho V, Robaina M (2016) Is the share of renewable energy sources determining the CO2 kWh and income relation in electricity generation? Renew Sustain Energy Rev 65:902–914. https://doi.org/10.1016/j.rser.2016.07.007

Pesaran MH (2007) A simple panel unit root test in the presence of cross-section dependence. J Appl Economet 21(22):265–312. https://doi.org/10.1002/jae

Sadorsky P (2011) Financial development and energy consumption in Central and Eastern European frontier economies. Energy Policy 39(2):999–1006. https://doi.org/10.1016/j.enpol.2010.11.034

Salahuddin M et al (2018) The effects of electricity consumption, economic growth, financial development and foreign direct investment on $CO_2$ emissions in Kuwait. Renew Sustain Energy Rev. 81(February):2002–2010. https://doi.org/10.1016/j.rser.2017.06.009

Silva S, Soares I, Pinho C (2012) The impact of renewable energy sources on economic growth and CO2 emissions - a SVAR approach. Eur Res Stud J 15(Special Issue):133–144

# Exemplification of the Implementation of Selected Actions Towards Employees Related to the Concept of Corporate Social Responsibility

**Agnieszka Kwarcińska**

**Abstract** Widely understood responsible management of resources is becoming a common challenge for contemporary organisations. It is based on the inclusion of interests, expectations, needs of various groups of shareholders in conducting its principal activities. In this sense, there functions the concept of corporate social responsibility defined with the acronym CSR. A substantial part of initiatives of CSR is addressed directly to employees most often included in the group of internal stakeholders of each organisation. Their undertaking integrates with the process of human resources management and encompasses various aspects of it. At the same time, the type of activity towards employees in the field of CSR and their intensity is very diverse and depends on many conditions. Based on the analysis of experiences of Polish organisations included in social reports, it is possible to list characteristic actions taken most frequently towards employees. The purpose of the article is both to exemplify the implementation of selected CSR-related actions towards employees in a group of enterprises representing the services sector operating in the West Pomeranian Voivodeship in Poland, as well as to determine the frequency of their undertaking and to analyse the assessment of their significance from the perspective of benefits to organisations.

**Keywords** Corporate social responsibility · Employees · Relations with employees

**JEL Classification Codes** M12 · M14

## 1 Introduction

Social responsibility of business (enterprises) defined in English literature as Corporate Social Responsibility and marked with the abbreviation CSR is interpreted multifariously and defined through the prism of idea, concept, value, business model and even a strategy or part of an organisation's management strategy. In its essence, CSR

A. Kwarcińska (✉)
University of Szczecin, Institute of Management, Department of Human Capital Management, Szczecin, Poland
e-mail: agnieszka.kwarcinska@usz.edu.pl



G. Karanovic et al. (eds.), *The Changing Financial Landscape*, Contributions to Economics, https://doi.org/10.1007/978-3-030-82778-6_7

focuses on the activities of various entities (organisations, enterprises) and integrates primarily basic ethical principles with the assumptions of sustainable development and stakeholder theory. It emphasises the obligation to carry out all activities in compliance with ethical principles, while drawing attention to the identification and minimisation of the negative effects of exploitation of the natural environment and taking into account the rationale of its stakeholder group. This peculiar congruence with the broadly understood environment generates additional value, also intangible, for every organisation. This may be the reason why it is noticeable in business practice that enterprises are increasingly pursuing the assumptions of this concept to conduct their business. This is often done by them with simultaneous unawareness of their strict recognition as the implementation of the principles of corporate social responsibility. This means that entities undertake various types of initiatives, also in relations with their employees, but they are not subordinated to the conscious and deliberate implementation of the CSR concept. Thus, it is also difficult to define them as integrated with the strategic activities of the organisation. They constitute a fragmentary sequence of activities undertaken primarily in areas that will bring potentially the highest and relatively fast profit to the organisation. Nevertheless, even these symptomatic manifestations of accepting responsibility should be assessed positively and treated as the basis for developing an awareness of interdependence.

## 2 Literature Review

The review of current literature indicates the relatively frequent undertaking of the issue of corporate social responsibility. Related topics take into account both theoretical considerations (Dahlsrud 2008; Sheehy 2015; Kwarcińska 2015) and analyses of the pragmatic aspect regarding mainly the engagement of economic entities in the realisation of this concept's assumptions (Wolska 2013; Musiał and Kubacki 2017). Noticeable is also the significant number of publications determining the relationship between the implementation of CSR and competitiveness (Wolak-Tuzimek 2019; Żychlewicz 2014; Paliwoda-Matiolańska 2009; Leśna-Wierszołowicz 2016). Comparatively less often, scientific studies in this research field relate to individual aspects of CSR, as well as to the topic of this article—relations with employees (Kwarcińska 2018; Zieliński 2014). What is also characteristic, among the latter, they most often undertake theoretical and application considerations when referring to analyses taking into account the activities of large organisations (Furmańska-Maruszak and Sudolska 2017; Badura-Mojza 2016). The rationale for choosing such entities is probably on the one hand their relatively more frequent involvement in pursuing CSR activities, including those towards employees, while on the other, the availability of information related to the publication by those entities of the so-called social reports on the implemented initiatives. Since recently, there have been few publications referring to the issues of corporate social responsibility towards employees in the sector of micro, small and large enterprises (Tewari and Pathak 2014; Kaźmierczak 2018).

## 3 Definitions of CSR as a View on Postulated Activities

So far academic literature has formulated numerous diverse definitions for the concept of corporate social responsibility (CSR). Their evolution and the determinants underlined in them create the rules and scenarios for responsible engagement. What is characteristic among them is the fact that some lean more towards stressing ethical, ecological or social aspects, others emphasise interactions with stakeholders, while another part specifies CSR through the prism of benefits with which it is linked, and some accentuate its strategic dimension. An example of a view stressing the ethical aspects may be the conceptualisation by Armstrong (2011), according to which corporate social responsibility means that 'organisations act in an ethical manner when conducting business, considering the social, environmental and economic outcomes of their actions'. Therefore, if entities conduct business in an ethical fashion, and are aware of their consequences in various dimensions and are able to coexist with them, it can be stated that they manage responsibly. If it is mentioned that they manage with the use of resources and in a specific environment, it turns out that the areas of responsibility also include a significant group of stakeholders. The stakeholder aspect was highlighted, among others, in the definition of corporate social responsibility put forward by Szczepańska (2011). According to the definition, CSR is a concept of 'voluntary consideration by enterprises of social and ecological aspects during the realisation of business activities and in contacts with stakeholders'. Similarly, Bartkowiak (2011) centred on indicating the importance of internal and external entities surrounding the organisation; she pointed out that 'social responsibility of enterprises or—from a slightly wider perspective—social responsibility of business is not only about bringing profit to shareholders (owners), but the term applies to the impact of business decisions and all company activities on the whole of entities, dealing with them both inside and outside the organisation'. Thus, she emphasised the sense of the economic existence of enterprises and drew attention to their cooperation with other entities, making them aware of mutual dependencies. Comparatively, Hope (2017) stated that the starting point of the concept of corporate social responsibility 'is a fairly simple statement, namely: the organisation functions as an integral element of society located in nature, and thus affects these environments, whether positively or negatively'. It is worth to add, that of importance is also the impact of the social environment, and internal and external entities on the organisation, and interdependencies imply the need for continuous dialogue and weighing up of interests, or taking into account many-sided rationales.

On the other hand, an attempt to define the concept of corporate social responsibility through the prism of the benefits it can offer was undertaken by Paliwoda-Matiolańska (2012) who defined it as 'an effective process of managing an enterprise which, through responding to the possible to identify expectations of the enterprise's stakeholders, contributes to the growth of its competitiveness, ensuring stability and sustainable development, while shaping favourable conditions for economic and social development, creating both social and economic value'. Therefore, all analytical and cognitive dependencies regarding the impact of CSR on competitiveness, stability and sustainable development in terms of economic and social values remain justified.

When defining CSR, the authors often refer to the strategic importance of this concept and thus emphasise its managerial dimension. According to Klimek (2014), corporate social responsibility is 'a concept thanks to which at the stage of building a strategy companies voluntarily take into account social interests and environmental protection, as well as relations with various groups of stakeholders'. On the other hand, Wolak-Tuzimek (2019) stressed that 'Corporate social responsibility is a new role of the organisation in society, a new vision of partnership and a new way of treating this idea as part of the company's strategy. (…) For an enterprise to function properly on the market, it must include in its strategy such elements as: care for the natural environment, broadly understood employee safety, interests of the local community as well as that of the entire society'. She also marks that the concept of CSR, like the stakeholder theory, is 'managerial in nature, since it determines the relationship between the company and stakeholders and defines means of conducting socially responsible activities for all stakeholders' (Wolak-Tuzimek 2019). It seems that particularly those recently cited definitions of CSR, emphasising its strategic dimension and nature of multi-sided co-dependencies reflect in a more adequate manner its current sense. The organisation's acceptance of this specific moral obligation in the form of responsibility is associated with both the perception of all groups having impact, undertaking correlation analysis and selection of appropriate impact tools, but also, at the most advanced level, directing all its activities by including already at the managerial level specific assumptions about the objectives, plans and means of achieving them. Hence, it is indiscernible to integrate the concept of CSR with the basic business strategy, or either in the form of its superiority or as part of this strategy. According to Rok (2013), specifically two following ways of combination are possible:

- CSR could be a part of the organisation's strategy, then the business strategy defines the limits of social responsibility, which means that in the entity's strategy there exist objectives related to the principles of CSR as well as such which are not associated with it—in such case, there is a conscious withdrawal in a given area from undertaking social responsibility.
- the entity's strategy can be part of CSR, in which case the principles of social responsibility set the boundaries of a possible organisational strategy and the entity undertakes only strategic goals that are not inconsistent with the accepted principles of social responsibility.

Regardless of the approach, it should be emphasised after Armstrong (2011) that 'strategic CSR consists in the fact that the company decides in advance to what extent it will engage in social issues, and then creates a schedule of social responsibility, specifying the challenges that the organisation should deal with and to what extent'. Thus, it can be assumed that if the enterprise recognises the supremacy of the principles of social responsibility, its obligations will systematically cover all areas of management, regardless of the gradation and intensity of involvement. This is defined by each organisation by use of own means. All the more it is not obligatory with a relatively selective approach to the implementation of CSR assumptions. On the other hand, among the areas of corporate social responsibility, issues related to individual stakeholders are most often considered, both internal, such as owners, shareholders, employees, and external, i.e. customers, competitors, suppliers, the local community and the natural environment. In turn, in relation to a specific aspect regarding the employees, significant is also the integration of the CSR strategy with the strategy for managing human resources (Armstrong 2011). As stated by Armstrong (2011), 'it is about creating a work environment in which personal and employment rights are protected, and human resource management policies and practices ensure fair and ethical treatment of employees'. In this scope, organisations apply a diversified set of actions. It is worth mentioning, however, that often, especially in the practice of relatively small market entities, there is significant activity on the side of undertaking initiatives towards employees, with simultaneous unawareness of the affinity of these activities with the concept of CSR, and thus its strategic nature. On the other hand, the driver for taking into account the interests of employees is often the awareness of their significance for the organisation and the related material and intangible benefits.

## 4 Practical Heterogeneity of CSR Initiatives in Relation to Employees and Their Determinants

Normative foundations regarding the areas of activity of organisations in the field of social responsibility have been shaped over the years and constitute a contemporary framework of postulated attitudes. They have been included in several of the most significant acts. Among them, it is worth mentioning primarily the OECD Guidelines for Multinational Enterprises, the Global Compact principles, the ISO 26000 Standard and the SA 8000 Standard. Their content also refers to topics of the responsibility of organisations towards employees. The OECD (2011) Guidelines include a section titled 'Employment and Industrial Relations', in which the following issues are emphasised: respect for the right of employees to establish and join trade unions, contribution to the effective abolition of child labour and to the elimination of forced or compulsory forms of work, being guided by the principle of equal opportunities and equal treatment and not discriminating against own employees, promoting consultation and cooperation between employers and employees, hiring local employees and organising trainings raising professional qualifications. In turn, the Global Compact (http://ungc.org.pl) principles which also refer to labour standards indicate the obligations of: supporting freedom of association and recognising the right to collective negotiations, supporting the elimination of all forms of slavery and forced labour, contributing to the actual abolition of child labour, as well as preventing discrimination in the field of employment. In terms of more detailed implementations, the normative determinants are the ISO 26000 Standard and the SA 8000 Standard, which encompass work practices including, above all, desiderates of accepting responsibility in the field of: employment and industrial relations, working conditions and social protection, social dialogue, occupational health and safety, development and training in the workplace.

Meanwhile, in practice, responsible social initiatives undertaken by organisations towards employees are very diverse (Kwarcińska 2019). They are mainly based upon general guidelines and regard postulated areas and more, but their nature, scope and even intensity are very varied. Their diagnosis was based on the analysis of selected so-called social reports, which take into account information on the non-financial activities of enterprises primarily from the ethical, social and environmental spheres in relation to their own stakeholders. The analysis included several social reports available on the website submitted as part of the 12th edition of the *Social Reports* [http://raportyspoleczne.pl] competition sent by various organisations. At the same time, selected reports were assigned to the following three areas of business activity: construction and real estate—four reports were studied in this field, energy—seven reports and finances—nine reports were viewed (Kwarcińska 2019).

The initiatives towards employees distinguished in the analysis of social reports were conventionally assigned to various aspects of human resources management and the main premises for their selection was cogitated. Perhaps a part of them encompasses external factors, shaping the general conditions for the functioning of enterprises. Among them, it is worth mentioning: globalisation and integration processes, availability of new technologies, situation on the labour market, demography as well as the specificity of requirements of different generations and legal conditions. Other determinants which impact the undertaking of a specific set of initiatives in relation to employees have a nature of internal factors of every organisation and regard, among others: size of entity, number of employees, age structure, gender structure, but also the type and range of operations, the availability of financial resources and the individual needs and expectations of employees and employers.

Regardless of what kind of activities are undertaken by enterprises, it is worth positively assessing each of their contributions to shaping social responsibility. Its manifestation in the form of considering rationales needs and expectation of employees is certainly one of the most significant areas of CSR. It regards a group of fundamental and essential stakeholders of each organisation. Mutual interactions of employers and employees repeatedly decide about the reciprocal respect, engagement, loyalty and shape of cooperation as well as the future of the organisation. This awareness probably induces employers to take a number of diverse initiatives that constitute the carriers of the dual nature of benefits, both for employers and employees.

## 5 Selected CSR Activities in Relation to Employees in the Light of the Results of Primary Research

Analysis of the reports of large entities, constituting a source of information on non-financial data on the organisation's activities, formed the basis for conducting research, the partial results of which are presented in this article. Based on information contained in the social reports of Polish enterprises published at http://raportyspoleczne.pl, activities characteristic of them undertaken towards employees as a group of internal stakeholders were identified. Next, they were contractually assigned to specific aspects of personnel management and were sent in the form of survey questions regarding their implementation to a group of 300 companies from the West Pomeranian Voivodeship in Poland operating in the services sector. At the same time, due to the number of employees the structure of surveyed entities comprised nearly 86% of enterprises hiring from 1 to 9 people, 13% of organisations in which the number of employees was between 10 and 49 people and 1% of companies employing from 50 to 249 people. The aim of the article was to examine the frequency of implementation of selected activities by the surveyed entities and to assess their usefulness from the perspective of the organisation's interest. Questions about specific initiatives were asked; it turns out that companies often take various actions towards their employees, but they are unaware that those could be included in the field of activity for corporate social responsibility. Therefore, the set of initiatives selected from social reports was treated as a reference point for the application of good practices with the possibility of supplementing with other activities undertaken by the surveyed entities in each of the proposed aspects of human resource management.

As already mentioned, based on the analysis of CSR activity towards employees included in the social reports of Polish organisations, examples of actions were selected and used to identify their use in a group of 300 enterprises operating in the West Pomeranian Voivodeship. These entities represented service activities. This article includes a part of results of research conducted in 2019 and concerns initiatives for employees assigned to three aspects of human resource management, including: employment and recruitment planning, induction, employee education and development.

In the first loop, the respondents specified which of the indicated activities are currently being undertaken in their organisation. A set of selected initiatives assigned to aspects of human resource management together with the percentage of enterprises implementing them is presented in Table 1.

Of the selected activities, the surveyed enterprises most often indicated the implementation of initial training, and answers were provided by nearly 80% of respondents. Next, almost 50% of the surveyed entities chose to organise and finance stationary training, e-training and online training for various positions. Thirdly, just over 43% of respondents emphasised support from experienced employees. Such a significant participation in this type of activities should be assessed positively considering the fact that, as a rule, working in new conditions requires special preparation and support of expert colleagues. More surprising is also the significant involvement of the surveyed enterprises in organising and financing various types of training which translates directly into improving skills and raising the qualifications necessary to perform current tasks in the organisation. Hence, entrepreneurs have a relatively quick reflection in work efficiency, and thus an almost immediate return on expenditure incurred for this purpose.

**Table 1** Selected CSR initiatives undertaken towards employees

| Aspects of human resource management | Initiatives | Percentage of enterprises implementing the action |
|---|---|---|
| Employment planning and recruitment | Cooperation with schools and universities | 15.3 |
| | Participation in job fairs | 21.6 |
| | Presence on social media and specialised websites | 31.2 |
| | Employee referral programme | 14.3 |
| | Promoting internal recruitment | 9 |
| Induction | Initial training | 79.4 |
| | Support from experienced employees | 43.2 |
| Employee education and development | Organising and financing stationary training, e-training and online training for various positions | 49.5 |
| | Organising, financing and co-financing foreign language courses | 11.3 |
| | Financing and co-financing studies and post-graduate education | 3 |
| | Career reviews | 4.7 |
| | Managerial programmes | 1.7 |

*Source* Own study based on the results of primary research

Observing the percentage of responses of the surveyed enterprises regarding other activities in the aspect of employee education and development, initially noticeable is their relatively rarer (approx. 11 and 3%) involvement in organising, financing and co-financing foreign language courses as well as financing and co-financing studies and post-graduate education. This clearly indicates a reluctance to take initiatives that require a relatively long implementation time and thus bring later benefits to the organisation. In turn, in a relatively symbolic share of 1.7% of respondents, interest in managerial programmes may be related to the poorly developed organisational structure of the surveyed entities resulting from the low number of employees, and thus the negligible demand for subsequent managers. The issue of undertaking career reviews looks alike. In a low share of 4.7% of respondents, involvement of the surveyed entities in this type of activities may result from the limited opportunities to ensure career development in entities with a small number of employees.

In line with the information about indications regarding engagement of researched enterprises in the aspect of planning employment and recruitment, noticeable is their relatively significant activity in various means of acquiring human resources. At the same time, they most often (31.2%) indicated their presence in social media and specialised internet portals as well as participation in job fairs (21.6%). Relatively fewer organisations were interested in cooperation with schools and universities (15.3%), as well as employee referral programmes (14.3%). Such a proceeding seems justified taking care to see that the study covered entities that do not employ a large number of people and at the same time do not report the need for significant human resources. Their requirements focus more on acquiring individual specialists available here and now.

The next stage of the study consisted in determining by the entrepreneur (owner), on a scale of 1–5, the significance of a particular activity from the point of view of benefits for the organisation. At the same time, a score of 1 meant very low value of the initiative, score 2 insignificant, score 3 medium, score 4 high, and score 5 very high. It should also be emphasised that the assessments were made by organisations that have carried out specific actions in the past three years or are implementing them currently, or plan to pursue them next year. Their declarations are shown in Table 2 as a percentage of indications of a specific degree of importance of activities.

Based on the data presented in Table 2, it should first of all be noted that none of the undertaken actions were assessed by the enterprises as very insignificant in terms of benefits for the organisation. In addition, most of the activities were rated as good and very good which means that the surveyed entities consider them as significant carriers of value for the organisation and possibly for that reason they decide to undertake them. The low level of usefulness at a score of 2 was indicated only by a small group

**Table 2** Percentage of initiative evaluations according to the surveyed enterprises from the perspective of benefits for the organisation

| Initiatives | Score 1 | Score 2 | Score 3 | Score 4 | Score 5 |
|---|---|---|---|---|---|
| Cooperation with schools and universities | – | – | 7.6 | 40.9 | 51.5 |
| Participation in job fairs | – | 1.1 | 11.7 | 43.6 | 43.6 |
| Presence on social media and specialised websites | – | – | 7.6 | 54.3 | 38.1 |
| Employee referral programme | – | 1.7 | 6.7 | 31.7 | 60.0 |
| Promoting internal recruitment | – | – | 13.2 | 44.7 | 42.1 |
| Initial training | – | – | 1.9 | 37.4 | 60.8 |
| Support from experienced employees | – | – | 1.4 | 43.2 | 55.5 |
| Organising and financing stationary training, e-training and online training for various positions | – | 0.6 | 7.1 | 47.1 | 45.3 |
| Organising, financing and co-financing foreign language courses | – | 2.6 | 2.6 | 59.0 | 35.9 |
| Financing and co-financing studies and post-graduate education | – | – | – | 57.1 | 42.9 |
| Career reviews | – | – | – | 73.3 | 26.7 |
| Managerial programmes | – | – | 20.0 | 60.0 | 20.0 |

*Source* Own study based on the results of primary research

of entities in relation to such activities as: participation in job fairs, implementation of the employee referral programmes, organising and financing stationary training, e-training, online training for various positions, organising, financing and co-financing foreign language courses.

## 6 Conclusion

Conscious entities recognise the need for responsible management, i.e. such based on consideration of ethical, social and ecological aspects. Hence, they function on the basis of respecting the basic moral values while maintaining adequate relations with their stakeholders and not neglecting the natural environment. These basic assumptions fall under the realisation of the concept of corporate social responsibility treated as a challenge of contemporary organisations often integrated into the business strategy. It is based on the general principle of respecting all entities with which the company deals in the course of its operations. Among the main internal stakeholders, the most frequent are employees. Employee involvement should be integrated into the process, or the human resource management strategy. First of all, such fusion creates a structured set of specific profiled activities for the relevant groups and/or people at the right time and with adequate intensity.

In Poland, in recent years business practice has seen an increased activity of organisations in the field of undertaking initiatives being part of the implementation of the assumptions of CSR, including those towards employees. Those often take the form of small steps towards changes in human resource management methods or very diverse proposals for specific activities for employees. They arguably serve directly the main beneficiaries—employees, we should not lose sight of the fact that they also contribute to the further development of the organisation. Emphasising the 'over-the-top' interest in their health, safety, career, balance between professional and private life, participation in the life of the organisation, maintaining proper communication, and even the development of personal interests results in greater commitment, efficiency, determination, closer cooperation, and as a consequence, higher work performance and loyalty.

Research carried out on a group of Polish enterprises has allowed to observe which of the activities included in three aspects of human resource management (employment planning and recruitment, work implementation as well as employee education and development) are pursued most often. It turned out that relatively more often companies focus on preparation for work including initial training and support from experienced colleagues, as well as professional development through participation in training. On the other hand, in relation to the methods of acquiring potential employees, the entrepreneurs relatively often chose presence in social media and specialised websites and participation in job fairs. From the perspective of the significance of initiatives realised for the benefit of the organisation, they most often assessed their usefulness at a good and very good level. It should be emphasised that the results of research to a large extent stress the meaning of specific actions for entities which do not hire a large number of people.

Arguably the conducted research is not exhaustive in terms of any possibilities of interaction in the area of relations with employees and should be extended further. Nevertheless, it constitutes a desirable reference point and a contribution to subsequent analyses. For example, it will aid to formulate inquiries into the organisation's involvement in other aspects of human resource management and will become an inspiration to address the issue of assessment of the usefulness of all those activities in terms of benefits for employees. Only at a further stage, the summary of initiatives realised by employers with assessment, expectations and needs of employees would yield a particularly interesting picture.

**Acknowledgements** The project is financed within the framework of the program of the Minister of Science and Higher Education under the name "Regional Excellence Initiative" in the years 2019–2022; project number 001/RID/2018/19; the amount of financing PLN 10,684,000.00.

## References

Armstrong M (2011) Zarządzanie zasobami ludzkimi. Wolters Kluwer Polska Sp. z o.o., Warszawa, pp 157–158

Badura-Mojza A (2016) Działania wobec pracowników w ujęciu zastosowania koncepcji społecznej odpowiedzialności przedsiębiorstwa (CSR) – analiza przypadku. Studia Ekonomiczne. Zeszyty Naukowe Uniwersytetu Ekonomicznego w Katowicach 283:86–98

Bartkowiak G (2011) Społeczna odpowiedzialność biznesu w aspekcie teoretycznym i empirycznym. Difin, Warszawa, pp 15–16

Dahlsrud A (2008) How corporate social responsibility is defined: an analysis of 37 definitions. Corporate Social Responsibility and Environmental Management (15), https://www.researchgate.net/publication/227663040_How_Corporate_Social_Responsibility_Is_Defined_An_Analysis_of_37_Definitions (03.05.2019)

Furmańska-Maruszak A, Sudolska A (2017) Relacje z pracownikami jako obszar wdrażania CSR. Organizacja i Kierowanie 2:253–267

Hope E (2017) Społeczna odpowiedzialność organizacji w zarządzaniu zespołami pracowników, w: Zarządzanie zasobami ludzkimi. Wybrane aspekty, red. Tomczak M, Krawczyk-Bryłka B Dfifin, Warszawa, p 300

https://ungc.org.pl/o-nas/obszary-dzialan/ (03.04.2020).

Kaźmierczak M (2018) Ocena działań na rzecz pracowników w ramach zarządzania społecznie odpowiedzialnego w sektorze MŚP. Zeszyty Naukowe Politechniki Śląskiej, seria: Organizacja i zarządzanie 128:177–189. https://www.polsl.pl/Wydzialy/ROZ/ZN/Documents/z%20128/Ka%C5%BCmierczak.pdf (30.03.2020)

Klimek J (2014) Etyka biznesu. Teoretyczne założenia, praktyka zastosowań. Difin SA, Warszawa, p 270

Kwarcińska A (2015) Corporate Social Responsibility jako zobowiązanie moralne biznesu. Zeszyty Naukowe Uniwersytetu Szczecińskiego (851), Wydawnictwo Naukowe Uniwersytetu Szczecińskiego, Szczecin, pp 157–165. http://www.wzieu.pl/zn/851/ZN_851.pdf (19.04.2020)

Kwarcińska A (2018) Social responsibility of enterprises towards employees. Theoretical and practical aspects. Eur J Serv Manag (28/2, 4/2018), pp 223–230. https://doi.org/10.18276/ejsm.2018.28/2-28

Kwarcińska A (2019) Zróżnicowanie działań wobec pracowników w ramach realizacji koncepcji społecznej odpowiedzialności biznesu na podstawie analizy wybranych raportów społecznych, in: Społeczna odpowiedzialność biznesu – perspektywa zarządzania i ekonomii, red. Mazur-Wierzbicka E, Janczewska D. Studia i Monografie nr 103, Społeczna Akademia Nauk, Łódź-Warszawa, pp 157–165

Leśna-Wierszołowicz E (2016) Społeczna odpowiedzialność biznesu jako element budowania przewagi konkurencyjnej. In: Studia i Prace WNEiZ US (43/1 2016), https://doi.org/10.18276/sip.2016.43/1-05

Musiał M, Kubacki Ł (2017) Społeczna odpowiedzialność biznesu w procesie zarządzania przedsiębiorstwami. Zeszyty Naukowe Politechniki Częstochowskiej Zarządzanie 25:84–93. https://doi.org/10.17512/znpcz.2017.1.2.07

Norma ISO 26000 Społeczna odpowiedzialność. http://www.pkn.pl/sites/default/files/discovering_iso_26000.pdf (19.09.2014)

Norma SA 8000 Społeczna odpowiedzialność, pp. 15–18. https://www.mpit.gov.pl (12.11.2018)

OECD (2011) OECD Guidelines for Multinational Enterprises. OECD Publishing. https://doi.org/10.1787/9789264115415-en

Paliwoda-Matiolańska A (2009) Odpowiedzialność społeczna jako źródło przewagi konkurencyjnej. Prace Naukowe Uniwersytetu Ekonomicznego We Wrocławiu 42:168

Paliwoda-Matiolańska A (2012) Social responsibility in business in theory and practice. Marketing Instytucji Naukowych i Badawczych 223:177. http://minib.pl/en/social-responsibility-in-business-in-theory-and-practice (06.05.2019)

Rok B (2013) Podstawy odpowiedzialności społecznej w zarządzaniu. Wydawnictwo Poltext, Warszawa, pp 141–142

Sheehy B (2015) Defining CSR: problems and solutions. J Bus Ethics 131. https://www.researchgate.net/publication/253236902_Defining_CSR_Problems_and_Solutions (02.05.2019)

Szczepańska K (2011) Zarządzanie jakością. W dążeniu do doskonałości. Wydawnictwo CH Beck, Warszawa, p 177

Tewari R, Pathak T (2014) Sustainable CSR for micro, small and medium enterprises. J Manag Public Policy 6(1), https://doi.org/10.2139/ssrn.2600570

Wolak-Tuzimek A (2019) Społeczna odpowiedzialność przedsiębiorstwa a konkurencyjność przedsiębiorstw. CeDeWu, Warszawa, pp 9–10

Wolska G (2013) Corporate social responsibility in Poland—theory and practice. J Int Stud 6(2):45–53. https://doi.org/10.14254/2071-8330.2013/6-2/4

Zieliński M (2014) Korzyści z wdrożenia koncepcji CSR w zarządzaniu zasobami ludzkimi. Zeszyty Naukowe Politechniki Śląskiej, Seria Organizacja i Zarządzanie 1921:653–663. http://www.woiz.polsl.pl/znwoiz/z74/4_16_Zieli%F1ski_M_po_recenzji.pdf (19.04.2020)

Żychlewicz M (2014) CSR as a tool of building the competitiveness of businesses. Found Manag 6(1). https://doi.org/10.1515/fman-2015-0006.

# Evolvement of the Bank Sector

# Regional Efficiency in European Union Banking Industry—Traditional and DEA Approach

**Anita Peša, Martina Maté, and Marijana Jerić**

**Abstract** Efficient banking system plays an important role in stable economic development. Aware that diminishing of the differences is crucial for even development in EU member countries, the policymakers decided to accelerate the implementation of common banking market with establishment of Banking union. Crucial goal of BU is to reduce financial fragmentation in euro area market, attract EU Member States that are still outside of Monetary Union to join, and lower bank compliance costs to improve overall efficiency of banking systems. The goal of this paper is to present the measurement results of efficiency in the banking sector markets of EU-28 member countries. Two methods were used to examine the efficiency, financial indicator-based approach using ROA and ROE ratios and Data Envelopment Analysis DEA as evaluation model for calculating efficiency scores. Banking systems are classified according to share of total banking assets to national GDP and analysed separately. The DEA results show that the overall efficiency of banking systems in 2018 is lower than in 2017. The best efficiency results are achieved in small banking systems, with amount of total banking assets lower than national GDP, and the reduction of efficiency is showing in the group of large banking systems.

**Keywords** Measure of banking efficiency · EU member states · Financial indicators · Data envelopment analysis

**JEL Classification Codes** C58 · F65 · G21

## 1 Introduction

The banks perform important role in entrepreneurship development and the effective banking sector is prerequisite for economic growth. Access to capital, compliance of requirement and financial assistance to business companies, but also efficient

A. Peša · M. Maté (✉) · M. Jerić
Department of Economics, University of Zadar, Splitska 1, Zadar, Croatia
e-mail: mmate@unizd.hr

 
G. Karanovic et al. (eds.), *The Changing Financial Landscape*, Contributions to Economics, https://doi.org/10.1007/978-3-030-82778-6_8

channelling of deposits and management of investments of clients put banks in key position for successful entrepreneurship growth.

The regional growth in Europe is uneven, regions are on very different growth level. Some regions achieve steady and constant growth, while others are underdeveloped and steadily below average. According to Goecke and Hüther (2016), who tested the convergence of European regions with respect to the variance of GDP per capita over time, found out that the variation shrank after 2000, but increased again in 2015. There are many studies on reasons for these dissimilarities (Papp et al. 2012). One of the reasons for this finding could be that banks perform differently in their financial intermediation function across regions. For example, better access to deposits increases resources that could be channelled into investment. Belke et al. (2015) investigate whether regions which incorporate banks with a higher intermediation quality grow faster in "normal" times and are more resilient in "bad" times. They found out that more profit efficient banks foster growth in their region.

Convergence among regions is one of priorities of European Union, and convergence of banking market has moved far forward. More than ten years after the completion of the last financial crisis, research of impact and consequences, and the level of recovery of the banking sector are still actual. Cost of failures of financial institutions are in focus of interest and a new regulative framework, with the intention to diminish effects of future crises, is in constant progress. The architecture of Banking union should bring better resistance and uniform reactions to future financial crises, and to hope is that this will positively impact on more balanced development of regions.

Our objective is to present the measurement results of efficiency in banking systems in EU-28 using the newest data. The results are obtained by ROA and ROE indicator-based method and Data Envelopment Analyses DEA as evaluation model for calculating efficiency scores of each EU Member country. In the second part, the theoretical framework of previous studies investigating bank efficiency and also the different approaches in selection of input and output variables and achieved results in DEA approach are exposed. In the third part, the methodology of both methods is explained. In the fourth part, the data used in the study are presented and the selected data are defined. Finally, the obtained results are presented in the fifth part, and in the sixth part is the conclusion.

## 2 Theoretical Framework

Measuring the efficiency of banking industry is very common in last years. In general, in the literature there are different ways to classify banking efficiency. Technical efficiency shows the capacity of single unit of inputs to produce the right amount of revenue. Cost efficiency provides information on how close bank's costs are from the best practise bank's costs (Košak et al. 2009). Allocative efficiency reflects the ability of a single unit to use the inputs in optimal proportions, with a given level of prices and production technology (Košišova 2016).

Many earlier studies have used traditional, financial ratio-based approaches combining return on equity ROE and return on asset ROA indicators to compare efficiency of different units (Socol and Danuletiu 2013). Newer studies more often combine this conventional, parametric method with most commonly used non-parametric mathematical programming approach Data Envelopment Analysis DEA. Advantage of DEA model is that it does not use default parameters when determining inputs and outputs and the researches have to formulate the problem in mathematical expression. The model estimates ratio of input and output parameters of efficiency in an implicit way, and the final result is the efficiency of business operations quantification (Ulas and Keskin 2015, 300).

There are many studies combining different variables as inputs and outputs, depending on country characteristics or banking sector development. Tuškan and Stojanović (2014) in their study of measurement of cost efficiency in the European banking industry for the period from 2008 to 2012 compare efficiency results using two approaches, financial indicators and DEA method. They used the profitability approach, comparing expenses as input and income as output. Košišova (2016) analyse cost efficiency in European Union banking systems for the period 2008–2014 using DEA method. In her study, she uses three inputs: total deposits, number of employees and fixed assets. On the output side, she considers two types of outputs, total loans and other earning assets. She found out that the results of DEA analysis, by country, indicated that the average cost efficiency moved from 20.90% in case of Poland to 100% in case of UK, Netherlands, Sweden, Malta, and Luxembourg. In recent study, Belas, Kocisova and Gavurova examine the cost efficiency of banking sectors within the European Union counties during the period 2008–2017 to find out which banking sector specific variables and macroeconomic variables influenced cost efficiency. They compared cost efficiency estimated by the traditional model of Data Envelopment Analysis and new cost efficiency model under different unit prices. They found out that the improvement in cost efficiency during the analysed period can be seen in Austria, Belgium, Bulgaria, Cyprus, Czech Republic, Denmark, Estonia, Finland, Greece, Hungary, Italy, Lithuania, Luxembourg, Latvia, Malta, Netherlands, Poland, Portugal, Romania, Sweden, Slovenia and Slovakia. The decline in new cost efficiency can be seen in Germany, Spain, France, the UK and Ireland. The most significant decrease between the years 2008 and 2017 occurred in Germany, where the new cost efficiency decreased from 86.30 to 41.769% (Belas et al. 2019, 119).

Some recent studies use post-Basel III liquidity ratios including liquidity coverage ratio (LCR), loan-to-deposit (LTD) and financing gap ratio (FGR) for measuring their influence on bank profitability expressed with return on assets (ROA), return on equity (ROE) and earnings before taxes, depreciation and amortization (EBITDA) (Golubeva et al. 2019).

Based on different applications of variables, it is possible to distinguish few approaches in measuring the overall efficiency. Maradin et al. (2018) emphasizes variables that can be used as input and output in evaluating the relative efficiency of banking system. The production approach views banks as a producer of products and services using labour and other resources as inputs and providing deposits, loans and other services. The intermediation approach focuses on intermediary role of banks in collecting deposits and other funds and then landing out as loans and other products. The profitability approach examines the process banks' usage of its inputs in order to produce revenues.

In their study, Balcerzak et al. (2017) analyse the efficiency of banking systems in European Union countries for the period of 2014–2015 also using DEA method, and this paper follows their research related to period of 2016–2018.

The aim is to present the results of less used, profitability approach through profitability indicators for measuring bank efficiency of European banking systems, combined with profitability ratios ROA and ROE, using the newest data for 2016–2018 timeline.

# 3 Research Methodology

## 3.1 Indicator Approach

ROA and ROE are commonly used in financial analyses researching bank performance (Trujillo-Ponce 2013; Kohlscheen et al. 2018). Because they are reported for a certain period of time, it makes them appropriate for comparison with other units. ROA is profitability ratio of net income over total assets. It is calculated as net profit divided by average assets and it shows how well management uses banks assets to earn each unit of profit. Even a relatively low value of ROA of 1–2% may represent substantial revenues and profit for a bank, the commonly accepted efficiency frontier for ROA is at least 1% (Tuškan and Stojanović 2014). ROE measures the rate of returns on the shareholders equity of the company and the efficiency in using every unit of equity for generating profit. It is expressed as profit or loss divided by total equity, and the ratio of 10% is considered satisfactory, although in good times this value grows.

In this, analyse the newest data for 2016–2018 obtained from European Central Bank were used. Banking sectors of 28 European Union countries (UK data were used as it was part of the EU for the period under review) were separated in three groups according to the amount of total assets and the efficiency is analysed for individual groups.

## 3.2 Data Envelopment Analysis (DEA) Approach

Data envelopment analysis (DEA) is the non-parametric mathematical linear programming approach to frontier estimation for measuring relative efficiencies of Decision Making Units (DMUs), when multiple inputs and multiple outputs are present (Cook et al. 2013). In 1978 Charnes A., W. W. Cooper and E. Rhodes developed the original DEA model in a ratio form of outputs/inputs involving the study of school districts in Texas. Although DEA has a strong link to production theory in economics, the tool is also used for benchmarking in operations management, where a set of measures is selected to benchmark the performance of manufacturing and service operations. In the circumstance of benchmarking, the efficient DMUs, as defined by DEA, may not necessarily form a "production frontier", but rather lead to a "best-practice frontier". In general, DEA minimizes "inputs" and maximizes "outputs"; in other words, in input-oriented model, smaller levels of the former and larger levels of the latter represent better performance or efficiency (Cook et al. 2013).

In the DEA methodology, efficiency is defined as a ratio of weighted sum of outputs to a weighted sum of inputs, where the weights structure is calculated by means of mathematical programming and Constant Returns to Scale (CRS) are assumed. Assume there is data on K inputs and M outputs on each of N firms or DMUs—decision making unit. For the $i$th DMU, these are represented by the vectors $x_i$ and $y_i$, respectively. The $K \times N$ input matrix, $X$, and the $M \times N$ output matrix, $Y$, represent the data of all $N$ DMUs. The purpose of DEA is to construct a non-parametric envelopment frontier over the data points such that all observed points lie on or below the production frontier. The best way to introduce DEA is via the ratio form. For each DMU, we would like to obtain a measure of the ratio of all outputs over all inputs, such as $u'y_i/v'x_i$, where u is an $M \times 1$ vector of output weights and $v$ is a $K \times 1$ vector of input weights.

To select optimal weights, the mathematical programming problem is specified by Eqs. 1–3:

$$\max_{u,v}(u'y_i/v'x_i) \tag{1}$$

$$\text{st} \quad u'y_i/v'x_i \leq 1, j \in \tag{2}$$

$$u, v \geq 0 \tag{3}$$

This involves finding values for $u$ and $v$, such that the efficiency measure of the $i$th DMU is maximized, subject to the constraint that all efficiency measures must be less than or equal to one. One problem with this particular ratio formulation is that it has an infinite number of solutions. To avoid this, one can impose the constraint $v'x_i = 1$, which provides:

$$\max_{\mu,v}\left(\mu' y_i\right), \tag{4}$$

$$\text{st} \quad v'x_i = 1, \tag{5}$$

$$u'y_j/v'x_j \leq 0, j = \in, \tag{6}$$

$$\mu, \upsilon \geq 0, \tag{7}$$

where the notation changes from $u$ and $v$ to $\mu$ and $v$ reflects the transformation. This form is known as the *multiplier* form of the linear programming problem. The linear programming problem must be solved N times, once for each DMU in the sample.

Since the DEA method is static method because it does not take into account change over time, and the bank efficiency can be improved, Balcerzak et al. (2017) introduce Malmquist index to measure changes in effectiveness of DMU in time.

Fare et al. (1994) specifies an output-based Malmquist productivity change index as:

$$m_o = (y_{t+1}, x_{t+1}, y_t, x_t) = \left[\frac{d_o^t(x_{t+1}, y_{t+1})}{d_o^t(x_t, y_t)} x \frac{d_o^{t+1}(x_{t+1}, y_{t+1})}{d_o^{t+1}(x_t, y_t)}\right]^{\frac{1}{2}}. \tag{8}$$

This represents the productivity of the production point $(x_{t+1}, y_{t+1})$ relative to the production point $(x_t, y_t)$. A value greater than one will indicate positive Total Factor Productivity (TFP) growth from period $t$ to period $t + 1$. This index is, in fact, the geometric mean of two output-based Malmquist TFP indices.

Balcerzak et al. (2017) in their study on efficiency of EU banking sectors defined that for the all indexes is valid if they are less than one, it means that the position of DMU in the area is worse (wrong decision), if they are equal to one, decisions were neutral, and if greater than one, DMU made good decisions that lead to improvement of status for this DMU.

In this, analyse Malmquist index is also introduced to express the change in efficiency in the observed period with selected input and output variables.

## 4 Data

Selected general data from consolidated financial statements for the EU-28 are shown in Table 1 on annual basis. This data serves primarily to show size-linked relations between EU-28 countries. The sample in this study involves 28 European banking systems and data sets for the period 2016–2018. All input and output data used in the CRS input-orientated DEA analysis models and previously calculated, official accounting indicators analysed by using descriptive statistics methods are taken from the European Central Bank. The calculations were made in *Data Envelopment Analysis (Computer) Program* DATA. For each $j$th DMU (each banking system), there are four inputs ($x_{ij}$; $x \in \mathbb{N}$) used in this model.

Based on earlier research and considering the bank as a mediatory business unit with the profit-generating assets and expenses-generating liabilities, in this paper profitability approach was chosen. Bank liabilities, respectively, total deposits,

**Table 1** Input and output variables in DEA method, 2018

| | Input | | | | Output | |
|---|---|---|---|---|---|---|
| Country | Deposits (in EUR million) | Interest expenses (in EUR million) | Staff/number of employees | HHI | Loans (in EUR million) | Interest income (in EUR million) |
| Belgium | 664,939 | 12,108 | 51,740 | 1218 | 601,842 | 26,514 |
| Germany | 4,857,395 | 59,770 | 564,935 | 245 | 4,981,050 | 91,942 |
| Estonia | 18,020 | 75 | 5317 | 2698 | 24,608 | 631 |
| Ireland | 302,891 | 3004 | 27,940 | 632 | 332,900 | 9428 |
| Greece | 178,114 | 2091 | 39,382 | 2304 | 190,919 | 7909 |
| Spain | 1,843,491 | 37,839 | 179,055 | 1138 | 1,622,581 | 109,249 |
| France | 4,701,364 | 87,751 | 408,941 | 664 | 5,412,610 | 156,497 |
| Italy | 2,623,710 | 13,440 | 274,056 | 579 | 2,388,626 | 48,489 |
| Cyprus | 42,784 | 646 | 8946 | 2378 | 48,545 | 1650 |
| Latvia | 13,991 | 102 | 7345 | 1578 | 18,128 | 554 |
| Lithuania | 24,200 | 66 | 9165 | 2278 | 26,700 | 535 |
| Luxembourg | 455,247 | 8658 | 26,317 | 261 | 470,964 | 14,626 |
| Malta | 23,189 | 835 | 5044 | 1518 | 19,806 | 1752 |
| Netherlands | 1,181,294 | 51,838 | 72,199 | 2178 | 1,383,139 | 85,284 |
| Austria | 543,304 | 7271 | 71,798 | 370 | 565,072 | 19,543 |
| Portugal | 283,121 | 2854 | 50,819 | 1202 | 239,657 | 9146 |
| Slovenia | 31,943 | 124 | 9683 | 1020 | 28,130 | 969 |
| Slovakia | 61,924 | 245 | 19,539 | 1383 | 61,154 | 1903 |
| Finland | 234,683 | 8263 | 20,796 | 2570 | 374,908 | 15,258 |
| Bulgaria | 41,776 | 162 | 29,991 | 939 | 38,367 | 1697 |
| Croatia | 43,118 | 304 | 20,028 | 1554 | 44,320 | 1885 |
| Czech Republic | 166,485 | 1694 | 40,244 | 1069 | 209,573 | 7085 |
| Denmark | 320,447 | 6350 | 41,737 | 1069 | 668,793 | 12,618 |
| Hungary | 82,265 | 927 | 39,434 | 801 | 65,238 | 4282 |
| Poland | 316,487 | 2702 | 166,011 | 683 | 321,229 | 11,563 |
| Romania | 74,863 | 679 | 53,737 | 962 | 65,311 | 3817 |
| Sweden | 509,420 | 9399 | 42,886 | 785 | 831,622 | 19,440 |
| United Kingdom | 3,887,939 | 66,725 | 370,083 | 353 | 4,078,660 | 150,383 |

*Source* Author's from European Central Bank data

together with number of employees, interest expenses and HHI index as a measurement for market structure, are used as input variables. On the other side, total loans and interest income are considered as outputs. Putting this data together, assets are combined with profit from profit and loss account and liabilities with expenses.

Input 1, ($x_{1j}$)—Deposits; the base of banks sources; they are expressed as total liabilities excluding ESCB, total maturity, all currencies combined.
Input 2, ($x_{2j}$)—Interest expenses, cost of deposits, expressed as interest payable on any borrowings;
Input 3, ($x_{3j}$)—Staff/Number of employees; number of employees in all banks of given banking sector;
Input 4, ($x_{4j}$)—Herfindahl–Hirschman Index (HHI) index; ranging from 0 to 10,000 and based on total assets and share of the five largest credit institutions in percentage, measures the concentration of the sector in national level.

and two outputs ($y_{ij}$; $y \in \mathbb{N}$) used in this model (in EUR trillion):

Output 1, ($y_{1j}$)—Loans; expressed as total value of loans, excluding ESCB, invested to population, business sector and other financial institutions
Output 2, ($y_{2j}$)—Interest income; revenue earned by a bank on total loans.

# 5 Results

## *5.1 Indicator Approach Results*

According to European Central Bank data, total assets of banking systems of EU-28 at the end of 2018 were over 43 trillion EUR. In Table 2, total assets of banking systems of EU 28 are presented as a % of GDP, ranked from those with the largest share.

For comparative purposes, banking systems are classified into three categories according to total assets to GDP: over 300%, (8 systems with 23.5 trillion banking assets), from 200 to 300% (7 systems with 17.8 trillion banking assets) and less than 200% (13 systems with 1.9 billion banking assets). Although largest European banking systems by assets are the one of UK, France and Germany, Luxembourg is a banking system with the largest amount of banking assets compared to national GDB, and the Romania is a sector with the least share.

Table 3 presents values of ROA and ROE for EU banking systems, 2016–2018 timeline.

Overall values of ROA and ROE for period 2016–2018, comprising descriptive statistic for all banking systems, and, separately, for sectors classified by value of total assets as a % of GDP are presented in Table 4.

The overall median value for both ROA and ROE for observed years is growing in presented timeline. When separately analysing banking systems, mean value is over the average in all years for a group of countries with the lowest value of banking

**Table 2** Total banking system assets, % of GDP, EU-27 + UK, 2018

| | Bank assets/EUR billion | GDP/ EUR billion | Assets as % of GDP (%) |
|---|---|---|---|
| Luxembourg | 1077.2 | 60.0 | 1795 |
| United Kingdom | 9035.1 | 2420.8 | 373 |
| France | 8810.3 | 2360.6 | 373 |
| Malta | 44.4 | 12.5 | 355 |
| Denmark | 1056.4 | 302.3 | 349 |
| Ireland | 1101.9 | 326.9 | 337 |
| Cyprus | 69.9 | 21.4 | 327 |
| Netherlands | 2321.2 | 773.9 | 300 |
| Sweden | 1284.1 | 470.6 | 273 |
| Finland | 628.5 | 233.6 | 269 |
| Germany | 7776.0 | 3356.4 | 232 |
| Spain | 2645.2 | 1204.2 | 220 |
| Belgium | 1001.9 | 460.1 | 218 |
| Austria | 837.5 | 385.3 | 217 |
| Italy | 3669.3 | 1771.0 | 207 |
| Portugal | 390.7 | 205.1 | 190 |
| Greece | 292.6 | 179.7 | 163 |
| Czech Republic | 258.9 | 210.9 | 123 |
| Croatia | 60.2 | 51.2 | 118 |
| Bulgaria | 57.1 | 56.1 | 102 |
| Estonia | 26.2 | 25.9 | 101 |
| Hungary | 126.0 | 135.9 | 93 |
| Poland | 461.3 | 497.8 | 93 |
| Slovakia | 82.0 | 89.5 | 92 |
| Slovenia | 40.6 | 45.8 | 89 |
| Latvia | 22.8 | 29.1 | 78 |
| Lithuania | 30.0 | 45.4 | 66 |
| Romania | 104.3 | 204.5 | 51 |

*Source* Author's calculation (2020)

assets up to national GDP. ROA and ROE values of the biggest banking systems of France, Germany and UK are far below overall median value for all systems.

Analysing separately the countries, negative value for both ROA and ROE in 2016 are recorded in Greece, Italy, Cyprus and Portugal, but in 2017 and 2018 Italy has recovered, and value of ROA and ROE in these years declined in Germany and Denmark. Generally, better performance of profitability expressed through ROA and

**Table 3** ROA and ROE values, EU-28

| | ROA | | | ROE | | |
|---|---|---|---|---|---|---|
| | 2016 | 2017 | 2018 | 2016 | 2017 | 2018 |
| Belgium | 0.6274 | 0.6652 | 0.6245 | 8.8956 | 8.8104 | 8.2008 |
| Germany | 0.1209 | 0.2062 | 0.1746 | 2.2147 | 2.9159 | 2.4190 |
| Estonia | 1.5456 | 1.3610 | 1.4211 | 11.0998 | 9.1885 | 9.8007 |
| Ireland | 0.8538 | 0.7495 | 0.7219 | 6.3122 | 4.9702 | 4.8579 |
| Greece | −0.8902 | −0.1889 | −0.0575 | −7.5124 | −1.3224 | −0.3606 |
| Spain | 0.3900 | 0.5230 | 0.6120 | 5.0322 | 6.9940 | 8.1947 |
| France | 0.4061 | 0.4216 | 0.4222 | 6.4990 | 6.3937 | 6.4703 |
| Italy | −0.5454 | 0.5853 | 0.4411 | −7.7350 | 7.1430 | 5.7614 |
| Cyprus | −0.3175 | −1.0665 | 0.2641 | 1.7278 | −11.8797 | 7.0670 |
| Latvia | 1.5078 | 0.8843 | 1.2210 | 14.3447 | 7.6068 | 9.2087 |
| Lithuania | 0.9777 | 0.8771 | 1.2432 | 11.8945 | 9.1171 | 12.3134 |
| Luxembourg | 0.5672 | 0.4852 | 0.4323 | 7.4780 | 5.6997 | 5.4729 |
| Malta | 0.8673 | 1.0619 | 0.9335 | 8.0866 | 7.2276 | 5.2114 |
| Netherlands | 0.4225 | 0.5368 | 0.5029 | 7.2892 | 8.7509 | 8.1357 |
| Austria | 0.579 | 0.7647 | 0.7628 | 7.1434 | 8.7191 | 8.6014 |
| Portugal | −0.3235 | −0.0203 | 0.2816 | −5.5281 | −0.8415 | 2.7014 |
| Slovenia | 0.9550 | 1.1142 | 1.2803 | 7.8467 | 9.1101 | 10.6756 |
| Slovakia | 0.8843 | 0.8616 | 0.8375 | 9.8858 | 9.2663 | 9.3001 |
| Finland | 0.5181 | 0.5529 | 0.5383 | 8.6998 | 8.7760 | 8.1190 |
| Bulgaria | 1.4800 | 1.3144 | 1.6138 | 11.3159 | 10.1575 | 11.7784 |
| Croatia | 1.2254 | 0.7975 | 1.1794 | 8.8922 | 5.8701 | 8.8436 |
| Czech Republic | 1.1502 | 1.0907 | 1.1022 | 11.8572 | 13.0185 | 13.2702 |
| Denmark | 0.5807 | 0.6605 | 0.4875 | 9.7174 | 10.8304 | 7.9964 |
| Hungary | 1.2669 | 1.5476 | 1.5968 | 11.7183 | 14.5289 | 14.6852 |
| Poland | 0.8191 | 0.8012 | 0.7608 | 7.4941 | 6.8816 | 7.0062 |
| Romania | 1.1117 | 1.2831 | 1.5322 | 10.6009 | 11.7423 | 13.5757 |
| Sweden | 0.7005 | 0.6869 | 0.7518 | 11.8807 | 10.8653 | 12.2380 |
| United Kingdom | 0.1398 | 0.2869 | 0.3617 | 2.1153 | 4.2975 | 5.5334 |

Source: European Central Bank

ROE indicators were recorded in CEE countries, with all values over the median value.

**Table 4** Indicator approach results of efficiency

| | Mean | St.dev | Min | Max |
|---|---|---|---|---|
| *ROA (overall)* | | | | |
| 2016 | 0.629 | 0.604 | −0.89 | 1.55 |
| 2017 | 0.673 | 0.517 | −0.89 | 1.55 |
| 2018 | 0.787 | 0.451 | −0.06 | 1.61 |
| Assets/GDP over 300% | | | | |
| 2016 | 0.440 | 0.363 | −0.32 | 0.87 |
| 2017 | 0.392 | 0.593 | −1.07 | 1.06 |
| 2018 | 0.516 | 0.200 | 0.26 | 0.93 |
| Assets/GDP 200–300% | | | | |
| 2016 | 0.341 | 0.402 | −0.54 | 0.70 |
| 2017 | 0.569 | 0.167 | 0.20 | 0.76 |
| 2018 | 0.557 | 0.188 | 0.17 | 0.76 |
| Assets/GDP up to 100% | | | | |
| 2016 | 0.787 | 0.692 | −0.89 | 1.48 |
| 2017 | 0.862 | 0.509 | −0.19 | 1.55 |
| 2018 | 1.034 | 0.513 | −0.06 | 1.62 |
| *ROE (overall)* | | | | |
| 2016 | 6.760 | 5.627 | −7.74 | 14.34 |
| 2017 | 6.958 | 5.019 | −11.88 | 14.53 |
| 2018 | 8.109 | 3.471 | −0.36 | 14.69 |
| Assets/GDP over 300% | | | | |
| 2016 | 6.153 | 2.634 | 1.73 | 9.72 |
| 2017 | 4.536 | 6.510 | −11.88 | 10.83 |
| 2018 | 6.343 | 1.193 | 4.86 | 8.14 |
| Assets/GDP 200–300% | | | | |
| 2016 | 5.161 | 5.982 | −7.74 | 11.88 |
| 2017 | 7.746 | 2.303 | 2.91 | 10.86 |
| 2018 | 7.647 | 2.769 | 2.42 | 12.24 |
| Assets/GDP up to 100% | | | | |
| 2016 | 7.807 | 6.379 | −7.51 | 14.34 |
| 2017 | 7.921 | 4.463 | −1.32 | 14.53 |
| 2018 | 9.170 | 4.091 | −0.36 | 14.68 |

*Source* Author's calculation (2020)

## 5.2 DEA Results

The results of output-oriented DEA approach are shown in Table 5. Banking systems whose value of function is equal to 1 are considered efficient, and whose value of function is over 1 are inefficient. In this model, any grow of output variables is considered as a good situation and improvement of banks activity.

**Table 5** Results of efficiency 2018—output-oriented model

| Country | Efficiency | Benchmarks | Outputs | |
|---|---|---|---|---|
| | | | Loans (in EUR million) | Interest income (in EUR millions) |
| Belgium | 1.072 | Spain | 46,645.3 | 2,054.9 |
| Germany | 1.287 | Estonia | 2,007,020.2 | 37,046.3 |
| Estonia | 1.000 | – | 0.0 | 0.0 |
| Ireland | 1.000 | – | 0.0 | 0.0 |
| Greece | 1.019 | Estonia | 3787.1 | 156.9 |
| Spain | 1.000 | – | 0.0 | 0.0 |
| France | 1.148 | Finland | 939,422.8 | 27,161.9 |
| Italy | 1.000 | – | 0.0 | 0.0 |
| Cyprus | 1.171 | Denmark | 9,982.3 | 339.3 |
| Latvia | 1.000 | – | 0.0 | 0.0 |
| Lithuania | 1.000 | – | 0.0 | 0.0 |
| Luxembourg | 1.051 | Finland | 25,392.1 | 788.6 |
| Malta | 1.000 | – | 0.0 | 0.0 |
| Netherlands | 1.000 | – | 0.0 | 0.0 |
| Austria | 1.123 | Spain | 79,204.9 | 2,739.3 |
| Portugal | 1.133 | Denmark | 36,607.6 | 1,397.1 |
| Slovenia | 1.000 | – | 0.0 | 0.0 |
| Slovakia | 1.000 | – | 0.0 | 0.0 |
| Finland | 1.000 | – | 0.0 | 0.0 |
| Bulgaria | 1.000 | – | 0.0 | 0.0 |
| Croatia | 1.000 | – | 0.0 | 0.0 |
| Czech Republic | 1.000 | – | 0.0 | 0.0 |
| Denmark | 1.000 | – | 0.0 | 0.0 |
| Hungary | 1.000 | – | 0.0 | 0.0 |
| Poland | 1.151 | Estonia | 56,933.2 | 2,049.4 |
| Romania | 1.000 | – | 0.0 | 0.0 |
| Sweden | 1.000 | – | 0.0 | 0.0 |
| United Kingdom | 1.112 | Ireland | 516,477.5 | 19,042.9 |

*Source* Author's calculation (2020)

On the other side, in input-oriented model, systems with efficiency lower than 1 are considered ineffective, and reduction in some input variables may result in improvement of banking system efficiency.

As it is shown in the column of efficiency in Table 6, the least efficient system in 2018 was a Germany banking system with the rate of inefficiency of 0,713, the lowest value below 1. As we can make predictions with this model, German system

**Table 6** Results of efficiency 2018—input-oriented model

| Country | Efficiency | Inputs | | | |
|---|---|---|---|---|---|
| | | Deposits (in EUR million) | Interest expenses (in EUR million) | Staff/number of employees | HHI |
| Belgium | 0.928 | 47,828.6 | 870.9 | 3.7 | 0.1 |
| Germany | 0.713 | 1,395,076.1 | 17,166.3 | 162.3 | 70.4 |
| Estonia | 1.000 | 0.0 | 0.0 | 0.0 | 0.0 |
| Ireland | 1.000 | 0.0 | 0.0 | 0.0 | 0.0 |
| Greece | 0.981 | 3464.4 | 40.7 | 0.8 | 0.0 |
| Spain | 1.000 | 0.0 | 0.0 | 0.0 | 0.0 |
| France | 0.852 | 695,300.0 | 12,977.8 | 60.5 | 98.2 |
| Italy | 1.000 | 0.0 | 0.0 | 0.0 | 0.0 |
| Cyprus | 0.829 | 7297.2 | 110.2 | 1.5 | 0.4 |
| Latvia | 1.000 | 0.0 | 0.0 | 0.0 | 0.0 |
| Lithuania | 1.000 | 0.0 | 0.0 | 0.0 | 0.0 |
| Luxembourg | 0.949 | 23,289.1 | 442.9 | 1.3 | 13.4 |
| Malta | 1.000 | 0.0 | 0.0 | 0.0 | 0.0 |
| Netherlands | 1.000 | 0.0 | 0.0 | 0.0 | 0.0 |
| Austria | 0.877 | 66,791.7 | 893.9 | 8.8 | 45.5 |
| Portugal | 0.867 | 37,516.2 | 378.2 | 6.7 | 0.2 |
| Slovenia | 1.000 | 0.0 | 0.0 | 0.0 | 0.0 |
| Slovakia | 1.000 | 0.0 | 0.0 | 0.0 | 0.0 |
| Finland | 1.000 | 0.0 | 0.0 | 0.0 | 0.0 |
| Bulgaria | 1.000 | 0.0 | 0.0 | 0.0 | 0.0 |
| Croatia | 1.000 | 0.0 | 0.0 | 0.0 | 0.0 |
| Czech Republic | 1.000 | 0.0 | 0.0 | 0.0 | 0.0 |
| Denmark | 1.000 | 0.0 | 0.0 | 0.0 | 0.0 |
| Hungary | 1.000 | 0.0 | 0.0 | 0.0 | 0.0 |
| Poland | 0.849 | 47,647.8 | 406.8 | 25.0 | 102.8 |
| Romania | 1.000 | 0.0 | 0.0 | 0.0 | 0.0 |
| Sweden | 1.000 | 0.0 | 0.0 | 0.0 | 0.0 |
| United Kingdom | 0.888 | 436,990.9 | 7,499.7 | 41.6 | 39.7 |

*Source* Author's calculation (2020)

would be considered as effective if the value of loans (volume of lending) increase for 2,007,020 EUR million, and the amount of interest income should increase for 37,046 EUR million, with simultaneous fall for of deposits for 1,395,076 EUR million and fall of interest expenses on these deposits 17,166 EUR million. Low efficiency of German banking system is the subject of analyses in some recent and earlier studies dealing with the reasons for declining income in industry and failure in achieving better efficiency scores (Koch et al. 2019; Detzer et al. 2013). Another important banking system, France, also recorded low level of efficiency with the value of 0.852.

Other ineffective systems in 2018 are Portugal, Cyprus, Greece, Belgium, Poland, UK and Luxembourg.

Introducing the time period of the observed years, as stated earlier, the Malmquist index was used to express the change in efficiency through years. The efficiency results for three years are displayed in Table 7.

The first three columns show the results of efficiency for each country in observed year. Comparing the individual values for countries banking systems, there are 18 efficient and 10 inefficient systems in 2018. Compared to 2017, when the number of efficient systems was 23, the rate of efficiency falls from 82.14 to 64.28%. Analysing separately, the systems that were efficient in 2016 and 2017, such as Germany, Greece, France, Cyprus, Luxembourg, Austria, Poland and United Kingdom in 2018 become inefficient. In previous study of efficiency of European banking sectors (Balcerzak et al. 2017), descending efficiency is confirmed in 2015 in relation to 2014. Results of our study show improvement of efficiency in 2017, but again fall of efficiency in 2018.

Malmquist index in the last column shows the quantified change in effectiveness over time, and, according to Balcerzak et al. (2017), the values over 1 show improvement in effectiveness, values under 1 show decline in efficiency against other DMU. The value of index equal to one show that the impact factors were neutral on banking sector position.

The highest value of Malmquist index is shown for Italy, 1.143 which banking system was shown as efficient in all years, which means that its banking system is in a good position. Interesting is that a Germany, which records the increase of inefficiency, has a value of index over 1 which means the improvement in efficiency.

If look separately for banking system groups, as it is made in the indicator approach, then in the group of large banking system, Germany also recorded the minimal values of both ROA and ROE in 2017 and 2018. From group of large banking systems, also Belgium expressed inefficiency in all years, and France, UK and Luxembourg in 2018. Although showing inefficiency in some of the years, all of these banking systems records values of index around 1 or above.

In the medium size system, Portugal is a sector with the highest values of inefficiency in all years, although the Malmquist index is around 1. Austria recorded inefficiency in 2018, but the index is around 1, Poland recorded increase of inefficiency in all years, but the Malmquist index is of high value, 1.105. Greece is one of 4 countries with index value below 1, which means the increase in inefficiency.

**Table 7** Malmquist index for period 2016–2018

| Country | Efficiency | | | Malmquist index |
|---|---|---|---|---|
| | 2016 | 2017 | 2018 | |
| Belgium | 1.105 | 1.116 | 1.072 | 1.036 |
| Germany | 1.000 | 1.000 | 1.287 | 1.044 |
| Estonia | 1.000 | 1.000 | 1.000 | 0.999 |
| Ireland | 1.006 | 1.000 | 1.000 | 1.069 |
| Greece | 1.000 | 1.000 | 1.019 | 0.994 |
| Spain | 1.000 | 1.000 | 1.000 | 1.015 |
| France | 1.000 | 1.000 | 1.148 | 1.020 |
| Italy | 1.000 | 1.000 | 1.000 | 1.143 |
| Cyprus | 1.000 | 1.000 | 1.171 | 0.888 |
| Latvia | 1.031 | 1.057 | 1.000 | 1.013 |
| Lithuania | 1.162 | 1.088 | 1.000 | 1.131 |
| Luxembourg | 1.000 | 1.000 | 1.051 | 1.022 |
| Malta | 1.003 | 1.000 | 1.000 | 1.049 |
| Netherlands | 1.000 | 1.000 | 1.000 | 1.009 |
| Austria | 1.037 | 1.000 | 1.123 | 1.010 |
| Portugal | 1.220 | 1.226 | 1.133 | 1.072 |
| Slovenia | 1.099 | 1.068 | 1.000 | 1.068 |
| Slovakia | 1.000 | 1.000 | 1.000 | 1.010 |
| Finland | 1.000 | 1.000 | 1.000 | 1.005 |
| Bulgaria | 1.000 | 1.000 | 1.000 | 1.052 |
| Croatia | 1.000 | 1.000 | 1.000 | 0.997 |
| Czech Republic | 1.000 | 1.000 | 1.000 | 1.023 |
| Denmark | 1.000 | 1.000 | 1.000 | 1.025 |
| Hungary | 1.048 | 1.000 | 1.000 | 1.049 |
| Poland | 1.019 | 1.010 | 1.151 | 1.105 |
| Romania | 1.000 | 1.000 | 1.000 | 1.039 |
| Sweden | 1.000 | 1.000 | 1.000 | 1.015 |
| United Kingdom | 1.000 | 1.000 | 1.112 | 1.061 |

*Source* Author's calculation (2020)

Values of Malmquist index lower than 1 are recorded in Estonia, Cyprus, Greece and Croatia. The index values for Estonia and Croatia are slightly below 1, but for the Cyprus index value is 0.888 which means a significant increase in inefficiency. This result is in line with indicator approach results when Cyprus expressed the lowest results in ROA and ROE for all years.

# 6 Conclusion

The aim of this paper was to analyse, perform and compare results of bank efficiency by using two approaches, indicator-based approach using ROA and ROE indicators for each banking sector and DEA profitability approach, both using the latest data. For the purposes of classification, the share of total banking system assets in country's GDP for 2018 was calculated and the sectors were divided in three groups. The results of indicator-based approach show that the overall efficiency in relatively small banking sectors, with share of banking assets less than the amount of GDP, mostly CEE countries, shows the highest values of ROA and ROE, with smallest standard deviation. Large banking sectors with banking assets over 200% of GDP, recorded the lowest values of ROA, lower in 2017 than in 2016, but improving in 2018. Although financial indicators are commonly used for measuring bank efficiency, because of the fact that they are calculated from past results derived from financial statements, they cannot be base for prediction of efficiency results for future periods.

On the other side, using of mathematical DEA approach can contribute to determine which banks are operating on their efficient frontier and those which are not. For the purpose of this paper, banks whose value of function is equal to one are considered efficient, and whose value of function is over one are inefficient in output-oriented model, grow of output variables is considered as a good situation and improvement of banks activity. Malmquist index is introduced in calculation to express the change in efficiency in the observed period. The obtained efficiency results showed the lowest scores for some of the largest banking sectors, such as German, but also France, Portugal, Cyprus, Greece, Belgium, Poland, UK and Luxembourg banking systems.

Although these results can indicate some negative trends in bank efficiency in large EU-28 banking sectors, when Malmquist index is introduced, all of this banking systems record values of index around 1 or above which shows improvement in effectiveness. DEA and Malmquist index results show improvement of efficiency in countries as Italy, Portugal, Spain and France. Decrease in efficiency, compared with other systems, is shown in Croatia, Cyprus and Greece. Although significant indicator for these countries, these results are not significant for overall EU-28 banking systems due to amount of total banking assets of these countries.

Regulatory implementation and enforcement of Banking union supervisory rules will reflect the improvement of additional rules in banking system of individual countries, so this can be a base for new comparative research for individual countries. Another area of research can include other pairs of input and output variables and comparison of results over time.

# References

Balcerzak A et al (2017) Non-parametric approach to measuring the efficiency of banking sectors in European Union Countries. Acta Polytech Hung 14(7):51–70

Belas J et al (2019) Determinants of cost efficiency: evidence from banking sectors in EU Countries. Acta Polytech Hung 16(5):101–123

Belke A et al (2015) Regional bank efficiency and its effect on regional growth in 'normal' and 'bad' times. ROME Discussion Paper Series, No. 15-07, pp 4–25

Cook W et al (2013) Data envelopment analysis: prior to choosing a model. Omega 44(2014):1–4

Detzer D et al (2013) The German financial system. Financialisation, Economy, Society and Sustainable Development, Studies in Financial Systems No. 3

Fare R et al (1994) Productivity growth, technical progress, and efficiency changes in industrialised countries. Am Econ Rev 84:66–83

Goecke H, Hüther M (2016) Regional convergence in Europe. Intereconomics 51(3):165–171. ISSN 1613-964X, Springer, Heidelberg

Golubeva O et al (2019) The impact of liquidity risk on bank profitability: some empirical evidence from the European banks following the introduction of Basel III regulations. J Account Manag Inf Syst 18(4):455–485

Koch P et al (2019) The road to success: perspectives on German banking. McKinsey&Company, May 2019

Kohlscheen E et al (2018) Determinants of Bank Profitability in Emerging Markets. BIS Working paper 686 No. 686

Košak M et al (2009) Bank efficiency differences in the new EU member states. Baltic J Econ 9(2):67–89

Košišova K (2016) Cost efficiency in European banking. In: 19th Applications of mathematics and statistics in economics—AMSE 2016, pp 181–191

Maradin D et al (2018) Performance evaluation of banking sector by using DEA method. In: Conference: economic and social development 35th international scientific conference on economic and social development—"sustainability from an economic and social perspective", Lisbon, Portugal, pp 1–9

Papp IC et al (2012) Regional Differences in the European Union in the past and nowdays. Acta Oeconomica Et Informatica 1(2012):1–5

Socol A, Danuletiu AE (2013) Analysis of the Romanian banks' performance through ROA, ROE and non-performing loans models. Annales Universitatis Apulensis Series Oeconomica 15(2):594–604

Trujillo-Ponce A (2013) What determines the profitability of banks? Evidence from Spain. Account Finan 53(2013):561–586

Tuškan B, Stojanović A (2014) Measurement of cost efficiency in the European banking indistry. Croatian Oper Res Rev 47. CRORR 7 (2016), pp 47–66

Ulas E, Keskin B (2015) Performance evaluation and ranking of Turkish banking ACFA Prague 2015, pp 297–307

# Do Capital Buffers Add to Bank Risk-Taking in South-Eastern Europe? A Look at the Pre-Basel III Period

**Ana Kundid Novokmet**

**Abstract** Based on a dynamic panel data analysis of South-Eastern European (SEE) banks over 10-year period, this paper explores risk-taking implications of changes in capital buffers. Its findings support the capital buffer theory. Firstly, banks increase their asset riskiness within the capital buffers increase and vice versa. Asset riskiness is measured with the risk-weighted assets over total assets and average credit price. However, capital buffers positively impact the risk index (z-score), i.e., reduce banks' overall riskiness. Empirical results confirm appropriateness of restrictive capital regulation as well as recent capital buffers regulation as they add to an overall bank stability and push lower capitalized banks to decrease their risks. In addition, banks' riskiness is also driven with bank size, liquidity, growth, and profitability. Thus, results justify a need for more discretionary approach in prescribing the capital requirements in order to target capital building to those banks which transfer regulatory capital costs to their clients throughout credit availability and affordability. A closer prudential attention should be paid to larger banks due to their increased risk-taking behavior as well as to banks which continuously maintain their capital buffers on minimum. Altogether, a conclusion can be made that commercial banks in the South-Eastern Europe in the post-transitional era do not suffer from a collective moral hazard behavior induced by the restrictive capital regulation, nor their increased risk-taking is without discretionary capital build-up.

**Keywords** Capital requirements · Banking regulation · Risk-taking · Panel data analysis · South-Eastern Europe

**JEL Classification Codes** G21 · G28 · P34

---

A. Kundid Novokmet (✉)
Faculty of Economics, Business and Tourism, University of Split, Cvite Fiskovića 5, Split, Croatia
e-mail: akundid@efst.hr

 
G. Karanovic et al. (eds.), *The Changing Financial Landscape*, Contributions to Economics, https://doi.org/10.1007/978-3-030-82778-6_9

# 1 Introduction

After the occurrence of the financial crisis 2007/2008, the appeals for a more stringent regulation of the financial systems have been made by numerous academicians who were usually overhauled by the prudential authorities with undertaking the urgent and insufficiently debated policy measures. Thus, the years of criticism of certain regulatory instruments are not about to end yet, especially due to a false assumption made by creators of regulatory instruments on regulation being exogenous to market participants, e.g., to the regulated financial institutions. On contrary, "regulation is endogenous" (Slattery and Nellis 2011: 408), and there is the interplay between regulators and regulated companies or so called regulatory struggle phenomenon (Kane 1977). In such a manner, banks' compliance with the capital adequacy standards (Basel Capital Accords) could be nominal or cosmetic, rather than real in order to avoid or decrease the regulatory burden of having expensive recapitalizations, limited credit growth, as well as risk exposure.

The capital adequacy standards have been promoted as the key enhancement of the banking sector safety and soundness for about three decades. Controversies related to its design and (counter) effects turned it into one of the most prominent issues in the banking theory and practice. For instance, the moral hazard theory and the capital buffer theory encompass two opposing views regarding banks' compliance with the capital requirements. The former apostrophizes capital regulation ineffectiveness in limiting banks' risk exposure, and the latter theory finds capital restrictions relevant for the banking stability. Even now rather non-extensive empirical verification of the capital buffer theory (e.g., Stolz 2007; Jokipii and Milne 2011; Zheng et al. 2012; Guidara et al. 2013; Jiang et al. 2020) inspired this research which thus aims to test the capital buffer theory and contribute to an existing debate on the microeconomic effects of holding various levels of capital buffers regarding the risk adjustments. It focuses on the changes in capital buffers, rather than changes in the regulatory capital ratio or equity-to-assets ratio likewise most researches still do (e.g., Ghosh 2014; Šútorová and Teplý 2014). The paper is assumed to be among the first empirical estimations of capital buffers' implications on the banks' risk exposure for South-Eastern European (SEE) economies in the post-transitional era and thus advances the literature on capital buffers and moves forward from the empirical work obtained mainly for developed countries. The key finding is that changes in capital buffers increase bank's asset riskiness, but reduce its overall riskiness. Thus, the restrictive capital requirements regulation seems to serve its purpose. However, attention should be paid to larger banks as they increase their asset riskiness more as well as to banks which maintain their capital buffers on minimum.

The remainder of the paper is organized as follows. Section 2 reviews the survey of literature with a focus on the empirical results for the capital buffer theory. Sects. 3 and 4 discuss the methodology applied, the data, and the results of the empirical analysis, while Sect. 5 concludes the paper.

## 2 A Survey of Literature

There is limited consensus on how do banks adjust their risk posture to changes in capital buffers despite numerous empirical estimations assuming synchronized changes in the risk exposure and capital position according to Shrieves and Dahl's (1992) methodological framework. The obtained results usually uphold the conclusions of either the moral hazard theory or the capital buffer theory. According to the first mentioned theory, banks involve in hazardous actions in order to minimize the regulatory pressures and compliance costs. To be more precise, banks transfer regulatory costs to their clients with the credit price increase as an outcome. According to the asset-substitution hypothesis or expected income effect (e.g., Blum 1999) the risk-taking level will be increased. If the capital requirements restrict banks in their asset growth, under pressure of achieving lower profitability, they might turn to the riskier assets, i.e., a negative selection and moral hazard behavior. Contrary to the moral hazard theory, i.e., the conclusions on the capital adequacy redundancy or counter-efficiency and banks aversion toward the regulatory compliance, the capital buffer theory (Marcus 1984; Milne and Whalley 2001) promotes banks prudent behavior (capital-at-risk effect) as well as the conclusions on their capital being built up and consumed in line with the initial discretionary capital level. Moreover, banks hold the capital surpluses in order to avoid the potential regulatory compliance issues in the future. Furthermore, banks with the higher capital buffers tend to maintain the capital buffers level, while banks with the lower capital buffers tend to build them up.

The capital buffer theory is becoming more popular due to the recent financial crisis, while usual criticism of capital requirements' reform causing a loss in the economic output with sizeable costs and modest benefits is somewhat soften in case of Basel III and prescriptions about the countercyclical capital buffers (see e.g., Angelini et al. 2015). Thus, general impression from the pre-crisis literature on capital regulation being expensive, non-efficient, or even counterproductive as it might spur banks risk-seeking behavior (Benston 2007) is replaced nowadays with attitudes that capital buffers are welcomed and usually regulatory required. Likewise, Arnold et al. (2012: 3131) summarize that it took 20 years and a few false starts to learn three lessons about capital: more capital is good, the amount of capital should be commensurate with the relevant risks, and some capital (e.g., Tier 1 capital) is better than other capital (e.g., Tier 2 capital). This paper empirically tackles the second lesson and questions whether the size of bank capital is relevant for its risk posture and in what way do banks respond to changes in their capital buffers.

Namely, examining the one-side relationship, i.e., the impact of capital on bank risk is more controversial issue than examining their interdependence. According to empirical researches, it is much easier to adjust capital to risk than risk to the capital, as most researches are consistent in the finding that higher risks build-up capital, i.e., there is a positive impact of risk on capital build-up (e.g., Shrieves and Dahl 1992; Rime 2001; Cannata and Quagliariello 2006; Stolz 2007; Matejašák et al. 2009; Jokipii and Milne 2011; Zheng et al. 2012). Likewise, Rime (2001) points out that the adjustment costs in the case of retaining profit and new shares issues are lower in comparison with the adjustment costs of a risk posture modification, while, e.g., Cannata and Quagliariello (2006), Stolz (2007), and Athanasoglou (2011) conclude that banks comply faster to regulatory pressures by adjusting capital compared to risk profile adjustments. Thus, e.g., Camara et al. (2013) examined only the impact of regulatory capital on bank riskiness.

The most of the empirical literature regarding the risk-taking implications of capital buffers shares the same methodological framework, in which the changes in the risk exposure and the bank capitalization are mutually determined. This paper focuses solely on the issue of consequences of capital buffers for risk exposure both in research results and presentation of literature review. According to the pioneer work of Shrieves and Dahl (1992), the changes in bank risk posture ($\Delta\mathrm{RISK}_{j,t}$) are driven by the endogenous, controllable or the discretionary adjustments ($\Delta\mathrm{RISK}^{\mathrm{M}}_{j,t}$) and the exogenous factors ($\widetilde{U}_{j,t}$) or

$$\Delta\mathrm{RISK}_{j,t}=\Delta\mathrm{RISK}^{\mathrm{M}}_{j,t}+\widetilde{U}_{j,t} \tag{1}$$

The discretionary changes in risk ($\Delta\mathrm{RISK}^{\mathrm{M}}_{j,t}$) are determined with a difference between the target ($\mathrm{RISK}^{*}_{j,t}$) and the initial risk ($\mathrm{RISK}_{j,t-1}$), i.e., risk level in the previous period or

$$\Delta\mathrm{RISK}^{\mathrm{M}}_{j,t}=\beta(\mathrm{RISK}^{*}_{j,t}-\mathrm{RISK}_{j,t-1}) \tag{2}$$

Finally, there is equation

$$\Delta\mathrm{RISK}_{j,t}=\beta(\mathrm{RISK}^{*}_{j,t}-\mathrm{RISK}_{j,t-1})+\widetilde{U}_{j,t} \tag{3}$$

where $\beta$ present adjustment speed in risk. Shrieves and Dahl (1992) empirically confirmed that there is a positive impact of changes in the bank equity-to-assets ratio to changes in the bank asset riskiness.

Afterward, Shrieves and Dahl's approach has been replicated many times but with diverse results. Rime (2001), Van Roy (2008), Guidara et al. (2013), and Bougatef and Mgadmi (2016) verified that capital regulation had no effect or had limited impact on bank risk-taking activities. The capital market development and existence of securitization techniques might be an important feature of the (non)flexibility of risk exposure adjustment to the capital adequacy requirements (Rime 2001: 803). Contrary, Bichsel and Blum (2004) calculated that an increase in the capital ratio of 1% results with an increase of 1.2% in the assets risks. However, they reported that an increase in the capital level is irrelevant for the default probability of the bank. Cannata and Quagliariello (2006) obtained different results for banks of different supervisory capital level, and summed up that low-capitalized banks rather build up their capital than carry out assets risk adjustments. Capital buffer theory has been confirmed by Stolz (2007) who reported that banks with low capital buffers practice a simultaneous risk reduction and capital build-up, contrary to banks with high capital buffers which increase their risk when capital increases. However, disparities between different economies and banking sectors surely exist. Thus, Matejašák et al. (2009) obtained diverse results for American and European banks, and found out that European banks are more conservative in their credit risk-taking and do not increase their risk when capital increases, while American banks do exactly the opposite. Later on, Jokipii and Milne (2011) reported that American banks tend to use their capital if they are well-capitalized, and thus, they increase their riskiness, while Šútorová and Teplý (2014) confirmed for European banks the earlier proofs obtained by Matejašák et al. (2009). Šútorová and Teplý (2014) concluded that Basel III will cause a decrease in banks' risky assets, and consequently lead to a drop in bank profitability. Furthermore, Ghosh (2014) evidenced that bank capital increases bank risk index for the different type of banks in the Gulf Cooperation Council (GCC) countries. Results suggest that Islamic banks tend to increase their capital, contrary to conventional banks. Comparison of different concepts of banking is assumed to be a novelty of the research. Rather than investigating solely the effect of bank regulatory capitalization on risk posture, Camara et al. (2013) analyzed the relevance of the regulatory capital structure for the risk-seeking behavior of banks. Their results are consistent with the Basel Committee recommendations that quality of capital, rather than solely the size of capital matters as they proven than banks with the higher subordinated debt are more prone toward risk. In addition, new evidence for the US banking system confirm that holding larger capital buffers discourage risk shifting behavior by banks (Duran and Lozano-Vivas 2014) especially if larger buffer of Tier 1 capital is present (Leung et al. 2015). Finally, the most recent results by Jiang et al. (2020) for Chinese banks again cast serious doubt about the capital buffers impact on downsizing the bank risk, especially for the high-risk banks, as a U-shape connection of bank capital buffers to risk-taking was found. In any case, every attempt to redesign the capital regulation will be of limited scope to banking sector stability if there is a weak institutional and regulatory framework (e.g., for Middle East and North Africa—MENA countries see Bougatef and Mgadmi 2016). Thus, in order to have a fair debate about the capital regulation (in)effectiveness, a knowledge about the contextual characteristics of a research polygon is required.

According to presented surveys, research problem on how do banks react to changes in capital buffers remains partly an empirical issue with modest proof of applicability of the capital buffer theory for the commercial banks' behavior in the SEE countries. Namely, Athanasoglou (2011) already employed 2SLS simultaneous equations models on the data sample composed of commercial banks (70–115 banks) from 7 SEE countries in the period from 2001 to 2009 and confirmed a positive relationship between the capital adequacy and the impaired loans indicator, as well as negative relationship between the equity-to-assets ratio and the impaired loans indicator. A conclusion that the capital level is more adjustable than the assets risk is made once again and the relevance of the regulatory capital structure for the bank risk-taking behavior is indirectly underlined. In addition, some evidence on the cyclicality of capital buffers for SEE area also exists (see e.g., Kundid Novokmet 2015). Therefore, this paper aims to deepen the discussion about the capital buffers implications to risk posture of SEE banks. Cross-country results of the capital and risk linkage for other emerging market economies can be found in e.g., Godlewski (2005), Floquet and Biekpe (2008), Saadaoui (2011), and Bougatef and Mgadmi (2016). The author of this paper would by no means claim that this is a fully comprehensive list of studies, but she believes that the cited studies are among the most relevant. More details about their methodological characteristics are transparent from the appendix (Table 8).

Finally, when compared to the listed references, the added value of this research is recognized in the following aspects: (1) it investigates the validity of the capital buffer theory in practice; (2) it focuses on the panel data of SEE banks in the post-transitional and mainly the pre-crisis period for which there is a research gap considering the research issue; (3) it contains in-depth analysis of capital buffers' implications considering the bank asset riskiness and overall stability; (4) it examines whether the link between capital buffers and bank's risk exposure is sensitive to indicator which proxy a risk; (5) it uses credit price as a new risk variable and defines new regulatory pressure variable; (6) it develops model which takes into consideration a reverse causality problem of some variables by using lagged variables; (7) it serves as empirical confirmation of the appropriateness of the countercyclical and other prudential measures established within the Basel III.

## 3 Empirical Strategy: A Step Forward for South-Eastern European Banks

### *3.1 Data Set and Variables*

The empirical estimation of the capital buffers' effect on the risk exposure of the SEE banks is carried out on the Bankscope/BankFocus (Bureau Van Dijk) annual data set for the active commercial banks in the pre-Basel III period, from 2000 to 2010. Thus, the commercial banks from Slovenia, Croatia, Bosnia and Herzegovina, Serbia, Macedonia, Romania, Bulgaria, Albania, and Greece are encompassed with the analysis, while Montenegro was excluded due to the data unavailability. The distribution of banks by the country criterion varies in the data set according to the availability of variables which build each model. However, banks from Croatia, Romania, Greece, Bulgaria, and Slovenia dominate within the data set. The observed time period is particularly interesting for the empirical analysis as it mostly represents the period of banking sectors' stability. Although the most countries encompassed with this analysis after 2008 recorded impairment of the main macroeconomic indicators, later on, after an increase in the non-performing loans they also faced an increase of the credit price and consequently credit growth slowdown as well as implementation of urgency measures related to enhancing the stability of the observed banking sectors, for instance, increase of the minimum capital requirements, requirements for a more restrictive provisioning policy, more generous deposit insurance schemes, and finally failures of usually small-sized banks. In order to avoid the biased results and thus probable conclusions on the bank capital buffers causing an increase in the credit price and generating riskier behavior by banks, the paper focuses solely on the post-transitional decade of the SEE banking sectors. Therefore, analysis of banks' behavior under capital requirements in the crisis period should be obtained separately, when there would be a sufficient data range for the dynamic panel analysis. Moreover, underestimations of risks and imprudent investment decisions are done in the economic expansion period and focus on the risk implications of certain size of capital buffers in that period could be relevant for the design of future macroprudential policy instruments. Besides Bureau van Dijk's database, some indicators were taken from the other data sources. Thus, the average equity-to-assets ratio for the SEE banking sectors is taken from the World Development Indicators and Global Development Finance database. The minimum levels of the capital adequacy ratios prescribed by the prudential authorities are collected from the official websites of the national central banks as well as from the European Central Bank (ECB). Nevertheless, for countries in which the central banks were not transparent in this matter, the ratios were collected from the Transition Report annual publication in the period from 2000 to 2010 and were compared to the data disclosed in Wisniwski (2005), Barisitz and Gardó (2008), Jokipii and Milne (2008), and Athanasoglou (2011). Finally, recommendations on the capital adequacy ratio increase given by the International Monetary Fund (IMF) for Romania are taken as the minimum ones in 2009 and 2010.

The first difference (Δ—delta) in the bank's risk exposure is set as a dependent variable. Risk exposure is described with three indicators: the ratio of risk-weighted assets to total assets (RWA_A), the risk index or Z-score (ZINDEX), and the average credit price (INCL_L). The risk index is calculated as follows:

$$\text{ZINDEX} = \frac{(\text{CAP} + \text{E(ROA)})}{\sigma \text{ROA}} \tag{4}$$

where CAP is equity-to-assets ratio, E(ROA) stands for average return on assets in a three-year period, while σROA denotes standard deviation of the return on assets in a three-year period. The average credit price (INCL_L) represents total interest income from granted loans over total loans. The most researches (e.g., Shrieves and Dahl 1992; Rime 2001; Cannata and Quagliariello 2006; Stolz 2007; Van Roy 2008; Matejašák et al. 2009; Jokipii and Milne 2011; Camara et al. 2013; Šútorová and Tepl 2014) define risk exposure by focusing on the assets riskiness and thus employ the risk-weighted assets indicator and/or non-performing loans indicator. Although, the bank risk-taking activities are usually proxy with the credit quality, i.e., the ratio of non-performing loans to total loans in similar researches, macroeconomic circumstances likewise unemployment and risk perceptions impact more the credit quality than capital size. Nevertheless, as a result of Makri et al. (2014) evidence that larger capital size adds to credit quality in Eurozone, some estimations of the model in which credit quality variable was set as dependent variable were initially performed, but due to paper size restrictions results for the most relevant risk indicators are furthermore discussed. Namely, some researches (e.g., Jokipii and Milne 2011; Camara et al. 2013; Ghosh 2014) use risk index as a simple proxy of the overall bank stability as it captures both the asset risk and the leverage risk. This study adopts both RWA_A and ZINDEX as risk indicators. In addition, it employs some alternative approximations of bank riskiness likewise the average credit price (INCL_L) and herein acknowledgment that inspiration for using this indicator came from Fonseca et al. (2010) is made. The main assumption is that the credit price reflects the credit risk as well as bank's financing costs.

The main goal of the paper is to examine the impact of the capital buffers on the bank's risk exposure which makes the bank capital buffer another important variable in the model development. In comparison with other researches (e.g., Rime 2001; Cannata and Quagliariello 2006; Stolz 2007; Van Roy 2008; Matejašák et al. 2009; Šútorová and Teplý 2014), the study focuses on the capital buffers (ABBUFF) and not on the regulatory capital ratio for the two main reasons: (1) in order to provide the empirical examination of the capital buffer theory and (2) heterogeneity in the regulators' prescriptions on the minimum capital adequacy ratios among the sample countries and their modification during the observed period. The absolute capital buffer (ABBUFF) represents a surplus in the regulatory capitalization ratio and is calculated as a difference between the bank's capital adequacy ratio and the required regulatory minimum in the capital adequacy ratio. The first differences (deltas) in the risk exposure indicator and absolute capital buffer indicate rapid changes in the risk and capital, respectively.

Taking into consideration empirical background, the next control variables are used in regression models: ROA—return on assets, $(\log A)^2$—squared logarithm value of bank's total assets, GROWL—growth of loans, LLR_L—loan loss reservations to total loans, and LIQ_A—liquid assets to total assets. ROA serves as a profitability indicator and is expected to be in linear relationship with the bank's risk exposure, i.e., an assumption on the existence of the capital market line on the bank market is made. The bank's asset volume is proxy for the bank's size. The study hypothesis is that larger banks especially the ones which are too big to fail will be able to take more risks in their business. Moreover, empirical researches confirm that larger banks in the SEE countries are more profitable (e.g., Athanasoglou et al. 2006), and thus, the bank's size, profitability, and risk-taking are interrelated. In traditional banking, intermediation loans take the largest part of bank assets. As loans volume volatility and credit risk substantially impact the bank risk posture a conclusion can be made about the positive effect of the GROWL variable on the bank riskiness. LLR_L serves to show the bank management reactions with regard to their risk appetites when significant changes in bad debt and consequently loan loans reservations take place. Reducing the asset riskiness and increasing the credit price after an increase in the LLR_L can be considered as a prudent behavior. LIQ_A is expected to be inversely connected to bank's risk posture due to the liquidity and profitability trade-off. All the indicators report annual values. The data were taken in euros.

Finally, in order to examine risk adjustments of banks which are under regulatory pressure for capital regulation compliance, a proxy for the regulatory pressure needs to be established. In the empirical background (e.g., Stolz 2007), dummy variable for the regulatory pressure is usually defined according to the regulatory requirements. If bank's capital adequacy ratio is higher than the regulator's minimum plus a standard deviation of the minimally prescribed capital adequacy ratio, the bank is considered to be a well-capitalized one, otherwise it is characterized as an under-capitalized one. According to that criterion, the most of SEE banks could be perceived as well-capitalized ones. Thus, the study moves forward from defining the dummy variable for regulatory pressure in dependence with a bank's capital adequacy ratio and creates another proxy in relation to the average capitalization level of certain banking sector. To be more precise, if a bank's equity-to-assets ratio is higher than the average value of the corresponding banking sector's equity-to-assets ratio, the bank is perceived to be a well-capitalized one, and in the opposite case, it is low-capitalized one (LOWCA). In addition, the interaction variables are used in order to point out the speed of adjustment in the risk exposure level ($\text{SPEED} = \text{LOWCA} * \text{RISK}_{t-1}$) and in order to indicate the coordination in the changes in the risk levels ($\text{COORDINATION} = \text{LOWCA} * \Delta\text{ABBUFF}$). Stolz's (2007) definition of speed and coordination of risk adjustment were modified by using new regulatory pressure variable—LOWCA.

## 3.2 Methodology and Model Development Issues

The most of reviewed papers on the research problem employ the dynamic panel data methodology (e.g., Stolz 2007; Jokipii and Milne 2011; Camara et al. 2013; Guidara et al. 2013) and so does this one. The problem of autoregressive process which is typical for financial indicators can be solved with the usage of the dynamic panel models as they contain the dependent variable which is being lagged for one or more periods. The dynamic panel model is given with the equation:

$$y_{i,t}=\alpha+\gamma y_{i,t-1}+X'_{i,t}\beta+\varepsilon_{i,t} \quad (5)$$

It is assumed that $\varepsilon_{i,t}$ are IID(0,$\sigma_{\varepsilon}^2$); identically and independently distributed error terms where the dependent variable $y_{i,t}$ is the first difference (delta) of a certain risk indicator, while $y_{i,t\text{-}1}$ stands for a lagged dependent variable, $X'_{i,t}$ is $K \times 1$ matrix of the explanatory variables (K—the total number of the explanatory variables), $\beta=[\beta_1,\beta_2,\ldots,\beta_K]^\tau$ is the vector $K \times 1$ of all the coefficients of the independent variables. Thus, all the $\beta_1,\beta_2,\ldots,\beta_K$ coefficients represent the short-run effects. The basic model which is later upgraded with the regulatory pressure variables (and different types of interaction terms) as well as by using lags of certain independent variables in order to eliminate the problem of endogeneity is as follows:

$$\begin{aligned}\Delta\text{RISK}_{i,t} &= \mu + \gamma \cdot \Delta\text{RISK}_{i,t-1} + \beta_1 \cdot \Delta\text{ABBUFF}_{i,t} + \beta_2\text{ROA}_{i,t} \\ &+ \beta_3 \cdot \left(\text{logA}_{i,t}\right)^2 + \beta_4 \cdot \text{GROWL}_{i,t} + \beta_5 \cdot \text{LLR\_L}_{i,t} \\ &+ \beta_6 \cdot \text{LIQ\_A}_{i,t} + \alpha_\text{i} + \varepsilon_{i,t}, i = 1,\ldots N, t = 1,\ldots T \end{aligned} \quad (6)$$

where $i$ denotes an individual and $t$ denotes time, $\mu$ is an intercept, $\gamma$ is parameter of the lagged dependent variable, $\beta_1$, $\beta_2$, …, $\beta_K$ are the parameters of the exogenous variables, $\alpha_i$ is an individual-specific effect and $\varepsilon_{i,t}$ the error term.

In addition, there are some differences in model development depending on the definition of risk variable. When ΔRWA_A is set out as dependent variable the baseline model is also estimated by treating ΔABBUFF as endogenous variable. Namely, there is mutual determination between the risk-weighted assets and capital buffers as capital buffers are being calculated by taking into consideration the risk-weighted assets which are encompassed by the denominator of the capital adequacy ratio. However, if similar approach is applied to all endogenous variables the number of instruments is several times larger than the number of groups. Besides ΔABBUFF, testing the ΔRWA_A equation with ROA and GROWL as endogenous variables would be correct. Namely, RWA_A impacts ROA as well as ROA impacts the RWA_A in an observed time unit. Furthermore, GROWL determines the value of RWA_A, and at the same time, RWA_A limits loans growth in the observed time unit ceteris paribus. Thus, the study upgrades the baseline model by using lagged values of variables which cannot be treated as endogenous variables due to small number of groups. Although this is a second-best solution, using lagged values of ΔABBUFF, ROA and GROWL helps to avoid the problem of reverse causality with the ΔRWA_A. Thus, the upgraded model in which risk is measured with the risk-weighted assets indicator is defined:

$$\begin{aligned}\Delta \mathrm{RWA\_A}_{i,t} &= \mu + \gamma \cdot \Delta \mathrm{RWA\_A}_{i,t-1} + \beta_1 \cdot \Delta \mathrm{ABBUFF}_{i,t-1} \\ &\quad + \beta_2 \cdot \mathrm{ROA}_{i,t-1} + \beta_3 \cdot \left(\log \mathrm{A}_{i,t}\right)^2 + \beta_4 \cdot \mathrm{GROWL}_{i,t-1} \\ &\quad + \beta_5 \cdot \mathrm{LLR\_L}_{i,t} + \beta_6 \cdot \mathrm{LIQ\_A}_{i,t} + \alpha_i + \varepsilon_{i,t}, i = 1, \ldots N, t = 1, \ldots T\end{aligned} \tag{7}$$

where symbols remain the same as in the aforementioned equation. Regulatory pressure variable and interaction terms are also lagged in the part of LOWCA and ΔABBUFF.

In ΔZINDEX model, ΔABBUFF and ROA are treated as endogenous variables due to the equity-to-assets ratio and average ROA being in the numerator of the ZINDEX. In this case, the number of instruments is still smaller than the number of groups, and thus, there was no need for the solution adopted in the previous case, i.e., lagging the endogenous variables. Namely, more observations were available in comparison with ΔRWA_A model as the compliance to the Basel standards (and calculation of RWA_A) was in its early stage in the SEE countries in the beginning of the observed period. The only variables which were lagged were dummy variable LOWCA and interaction term COORDINATION in order to avoid endogeneity problem and larger number of instruments than groups. SPEED was omitted from the model as it is hard to assume that banks actively manage the risk index, i.e., the use of the speed of risk adjustment variable has no economic justification. Thus, the model in which risk is measured with the risk index—ZINDEX is defined:

$$\Delta \text{ZINDEX}_{i,t} = \mu + \gamma \cdot \Delta \text{ZINDEX}_{i,t-1} + \beta_1 \cdot \Delta \text{ABBUFF}_{i,t} + \beta_2 \cdot \text{ROA}_{i,t} + \beta_3 \cdot (\log \text{A}_{i,t})^2 + \beta_4 \cdot \text{GROWL}_{i,t} + \beta_5 \cdot \text{LLR\_L}_{i,t} + \beta_6 \cdot \text{LIQ\_A}_{i,t} + \alpha_i + \varepsilon_{i,t}, i = 1, \ldots N, t = 1, \ldots T \quad (8)$$

where symbols remain the same as earlier.

The last developed model where changes in the credit price are set out as risk indicator ($\Delta$INCL_L) was also modified following the logic of lagging endogenous variables. It is assumed that $\Delta$ABBUFF, ROA, GROWL and LLR_L need to be lagged as there is a problem of reverse causality with the credit price. Higher bank profitability (ROA) is driven with the higher interest income, while higher average credit price implies potentially lower credit collectability and higher provisioning level (LLR_L) as well as a period of modest credit growth (GROWL). At last, if average credit price stands for riskier assets, it will impact the capital buffer (ABBUFF) and potentially meltdown the surplus in capitalization. Thus, the upgraded model in which risk is measured with the average credit price is defined:

$$\Delta \text{INCL\_L}_{i,t} = \mu + \gamma \cdot \Delta \text{INCL\_L}_{i,t-1} + \beta_1 \cdot \Delta \text{ABBUFF}_{i,t-1} + \beta_2 \cdot \text{ROA}_{i,t-1} + \beta_3 \cdot (\log \text{A}_{i,t})^2 + \beta_4 \cdot \text{GROWL}_{i,t-1} + \beta_5 \cdot \text{LLR\_L}_{i,t-1} + \beta_6 \cdot \text{LIQ\_A}_{i,t} + \alpha_i + \varepsilon_{i,t}, i = 1, \ldots N, t = 1, \ldots T \quad (9)$$

where symbols remain the same as earlier.

The empirical estimation of all presented models which were developed with an aim of answering the question whether an increase in the capital buffer adds to higher risk-taking behavior of SEE's banks was conducted by using the GMM system (Blundell-Bond two-step estimator). The system GMM estimator can improve the performance of the usual Arellano-Bond estimator when the autoregressive parameter is moderately high, and the number of time-series observations is moderately small (Blundell and Bond 1998), but a condition of having the large number of groups should be fulfilled. With more than 80 banks in a data set, Blundell-Bond estimator can be used in order to capture the larger number of observations than it would be the case if the Arellano-Bond estimator was applied. Calculations were made in STATA 12 and Eviews 8. Correlation matrix confirms that at 5% significance level, the most of independent variables are not strongly correlated and thus the multicollinearity problems are overcome (both correlation matrix and descriptive statistics are available upon request).

# 4 Estimations of Developed Models and Discussion of the Results

The two-step estimator and two maximum lags of dependent variables as instruments are used. Sargan test as well as the second-order autocorrelation test prove reliability and quality of estimated models as they exceed 0.10. The first-order autocorrelation can be ignored as it is often being expected.

## *4.1 Results for Equations with Risk-Weighted Assets Indicator as Dependent Variable*

The empirical results of the estimated panel models with ΔRWA_A as risk proxy are given in Tables 1–3. Tables 1 and 2 contain estimations of the baseline model, whereas Table 2 presents estimations with ΔABBUFF as endogenous variable. The main difference between those estimations is found in the statistical significance of profitability (ROA) and regulatory pressure (LOWCA) variable. Both ROA and LOWCA are insignificant in the estimations of the baseline model (Table 1), contrary to estimations of the model with ΔABBUFF as endogenous variable (Table 2). Table 3 contains results of the model adapted with the lagged variables. In comparison with baseline model where ΔABBUFF had negative effect on risk, $\Delta ABBUFF_{t-1}$ has positive effect on risk, while lagged coordination variable ($COORDINATION_{t-1}$) is insignificant (Table 3). Significance and sign of coefficients for the rest of independent variables are pretty much consistent in all models where ΔRWA_A is dependent variable. According to presented results some general conclusions can be made.

Firstly, the lagged dependent variable (ΔRWA_A) has a negative sign which means that the increase in the risk-weighted assets in one year leads to a fall in the risk-weighted assets of the following year and vice versa. Thus, banks which took higher risks in one year will tend to reduce risk-taking activities in the following period in order to comply with the regulatory framework on capital requirements. On the other hand, a slowdown in the credit growth due to macroeconomic circumstances might also serve as an explanation of decrease in the risk-weighted assets ratio instead of bank's management active approach to risk profile which is proxy with that indicator.

Secondly, bank capital buffers (ΔABBUFF) and risk-weighted assets are inversely connected variables, i.e., if there is an increase in the capital buffers, banks will endeavor to reduce their risk-weighted assets. This might lead to a conclusion that regulatory prescriptions on the capital buffer size result in reduction of risk-taking activities of banks. However, the capital buffer size is inherently driven by the risk-weighted assets as the risk-weighted assets are in denominator of the capital adequacy ratio. Thus, an increase in the capital buffer might be induced by an increase in the bank regulatory capital and/or decrease in the risk-weighted assets. A new approach needs to be established.

**Table 1** Panel data estimations of the baseline model with risk-weighted assets indicator as dependent variable

| Explanatory variable | The baseline model | | | |
|---|---|---|---|---|
| $\Delta RWA\_A_{i,t-1}$ | −0.1614[a] (0.0254646) | −0.1594741[a] (0.0260845) | −0.170691[a] (0.0214725) | −0.1631977[a] (0.0246155) |
| $\Delta ABBUFF_{i,t}$ | −0.8781004[a] (0.1648877) | −0.888575[a] (0.1634094) | −0.7989095[a] (0.1580044) | −1.016651[a] (0.1977846) |
| $ROA_{i,t}$ | 0.8471517 (0.8255799) | 0.9307131 (0.8317894) | 0.7506073 (0.792471) | 0.671622 (0.7940511) |
| $(\log A_{i,t})^2$ | 0.0719118[a] (0.0222242) | 0.0713359[a] (0.0247647) | 0.0660785[a] (0.0256158) | 0.0680532[a] (0.0223574) |
| $GROWL_{i,t}$ | 0.066332[a] (0.02205) | 0.0654489[a] (0.023159) | 0.0801152[a] (0.0244382) | 0.080409[a] (0.0235053) |
| $LLR\_L_{i,t}$ | −1.1331[a] (0.4316543) | −1.107037[a] (0.4348315) | −1.232863[a] (0.4150888) | −1.196041[a] (0.4048584) |
| $LIQ\_A_{i,t}$ | −0.3084465[a] (0.0853837) | −0.3186307[a] (0.0844984) | −0.3062659[a] (0.0860281) | −0.2903769[a] (0.0880832) |
| $LOWCA_{i,t}$ | – | −0.0877935 (1.08479) | – | – |
| $SPEED_{i,t}$ | – | – | −0.0514089[a] (0.0178709) | – |
| $COORDINATION_{i,t}$ | – | – | – | 0.472178[c] (0.2605801) |
| $\alpha$ | −6.142334 (4.666274) | −6.008192 (4.88168) | −2.739437 (4.979056) | −5.29022 (4.717359) |
| Number of observations | 201 | 201 | 201 | 201 |
| Number of banks | 82 | 82 | 82 | 82 |
| Sargan test (*p*-value) | 0.2368 | 0.2215 | 0.3692 | 0.1620 |
| First-order autocorrelation (*p*-value) | 0.0477 | 0.0475 | 0.0615 | 0.0733 |
| Second-order autocorrelation (*p*-value) | 0.8376 | 0.8492 | 0.6565 | 0.5961 |

*Source* Bankscope, Author's calculation

[a]Statistically significant at 1% level, [b]statistically significant at 5% level, [c]statistically significant at 10% level

**Table 2** Panel data estimations of the baseline model with risk-weighted assets indicator as dependent variable and difference in absolute capital buffers as endogenous variable

| Explanatory variable | The baseline model with ΔABBUFF as endogenous variable | | | |
|---|---|---|---|---|
| $\Delta RWA\_A_{i,t-1}$ | −0.1946693[a] (0.0035845) | −0.1996378[a] (0.0042264) | −0.2011185[a] (0.002485) | −0.2012149[a] (0.0030537) |
| $\Delta ABBUFF_{i,t}$ | −0.7199497[a] (0.007261) | −0.6842647[a] (0.0249624) | −0.5613715[a] (0.0210927) | −0.4482012[a] (0.0152746) |
| $ROA_{i,t}$ | 0.3593697[a] (0.0682328) | 0.3399485[a] (0.0994299) | −0.0686083 (0.1171299) | −0.0697046 (0.1445341) |
| $(\log A_{i,t})^2$ | 0.0548263[a] (0.0025899) | 0.0578766[a] (0.0033882) | 0.0819504[a] (0.0022468) | 0.0433115[a] (0.0024713) |
| $GROWL_{i,t}$ | 0.0411456[a] (0.0042025) | 0.0497938[a] (0.0041287) | 0.064148[a] (0.0057764) | 0.0648072[a] (0.0069329) |
| $LLR\_L_{i,t}$ | −1.292191[a] (0.0576306) | −1.277283[a] (0.0647428) | −1.445122[a] (0.0581497) | −1.263202[a] (0.0777452) |
| $LIQ\_A_{i,t}$ | −0.2278449[a] (0.0095146) | −0.2199361[a] (0.0144338) | −0.2511758[a] (0.0056656) | −0.2061159[a] (0.0143117) |
| $LOWCA_{i,t}$ | – | −0.7406851[b] (0.335971) | – | – |
| $SPEED_{i,t}$ | – | – | −0.0783868[a] (0.003045) | – |
| $COORDINATION_{i,t}$ | – | – | – | 0.1300485[a] (0.0494672) |
| α | −2.046996[b] (0.8626449) | −2.650491[a] (0.8806738) | −3.833359[a] (0.7544677) | −0.1519104 (0.7011482) |
| Number of observations | 201 | 201 | 201 | 201 |
| Number of banks | 82 | 82 | 82 | 82 |
| Sargan test (*p*-value) | 0.9784 | 0.9655 | 0.8822 | 0.9494 |
| First-order autocorrelation (*p*-value) | 0.0623 | 0.0745 | 0.0725 | 0.0868 |
| Second-order autocorrelation (*p*-value) | 0.5171 | 0.4930 | 0.3601 | 0.3681 |

*Source* Bankscope, Author's calculation
[a]Statistically significant at 1% level, [b]statistically significant at 5% level, [c]statistically significant at 10% level

**Table 3** Panel data estimations of the model with risk-weighted assets indicator as dependent variable and lagged variables

| Explanatory variable | Variables are lagged instead of being treated as endogenous variables | | | |
|---|---|---|---|---|
| $\Delta RWA\_A_{i,t-1}$ | −0.2419543[a] (0.0218819) | −0.2333377[a] (0.0232962) | −0.2214465[a] (0.028927) | −0.2452946[a] (0.0218519) |
| $\Delta ABBUFF_{i,t-1}$ | 0.3007727[a] (0.0944465) | 0.2799655[a] (0.0954675) | 0.2426418[b] (0.1076761) | 0.410232[a] (0.1307878) |
| $ROA_{i,t-1}$ | 1.19298[c] (0.6922064) | 1.241229[b] (0.6189009) | 1.512689[a] (0.6096788) | 1.137777[c] (0.6999715) |
| $(\log A_{i,t})^2$ | 0.0459878[c] (0.0252877) | 0.0692372[b] (0.0330261) | 0.0719948[b] (0.0333454) | 0.0402367 (0.0253128) |
| $GROWL_{i,t-1}$ | 0.0737827[b] (0.0318844) | 0.061906[c] (0.0326463) | 0.0465099 (0.0335349) | 0.0725176[b] (0.0316337) |
| $LLR\_L_{i,t}$ | −1.463518[a] (0.2634925) | −1.549232[a] (0.2786023) | −1.569419[a] (0.3055536) | −1.482631[a] (0.2656) |
| $LIQ\_A_{i,t}$ | −0.2877263[a] (0.0911336) | −0.2463896[a] (0.0889462) | −0.2110579[b] (0.0896261) | −0.2752203[a] (0.0996076) |
| $LOWCA_{i,t-1}$ | – | −2.935529[c] (1.576469) | – | – |
| $SPEED_{i,t-1}$ ($LOWCA_{i,t-1}$· * $RWA\_A_{i,t-1}$) | – | – | −0.0765418[b] (0.0337472) | – |
| $COORDINATION_{i,t-1}$ ($LOWCA_{i,t-1}$ * $\Delta ABBUFF_{i,t-1}$) | – | – | – | −0.3004093 (0.2100387) |
| $\alpha$ | 1.392876 (5.954968) | −2.158936 (6.855086) | −1.795814 (7.036716) | 2.603921 (5.70982) |
| Number of observations | 199 | 199 | 199 | 199 |
| Number of banks | 82 | 82 | 82 | 82 |
| Sargan test (*p*-value) | 0.4195 | 0.4443 | 0.4692 | 0.4333 |
| First-order autocorrelation (*p*-value) | 0.0624 | 0.0456 | 0.0200 | 0.0715 |
| Second-order autocorrelation (*p*-value) | 0.1519 | 0.2124 | 0.2204 | 0.1188 |

*Source* Bankscope, Author's calculation
[a]Statistically significant at 1% level, [b]statistically significant at 5% level, [c]statistically significant at 10% level

This study proposes using lagged explanatory variables, likewise lagged capital buffers ($\Delta ABBUFF_{t-1}$). When lagged capital buffer variable is used as explanatory variable a relationship between capital buffers and risk-weighted assets is linear. Thus, if capital surplus was built up in the previous period, it will be spent out in the next period throughout increased risk-taking activities (risk-weighted assets). In the opposite case, poor capital buffer in the last year reduces abilities for risk-taking in the current year. Altogether, an answer to the question from the paper title might be given, i.e., capital buffers add to risk-taking activities by banks in case when risk is proxy with risk-weighted assets indicator and lagged capital buffers taken into consideration.

Furthermore, the capital buffer theory can be accepted considering banks' risk adjustment behavior. Banks which are under regulatory pressure (LOWCA) or were under regulatory pressure in the previous year ($LOWCA_{t-1}$) decrease their risk-weighted assets by taking into consideration the previous level of risk and do that adjustment somewhat faster than better capitalized banks (SPEED = LOWCA * $RWA\_A_{t-1}$ and $SPEED_{t-1}$). In addition, there is certain evidence that banks which are under regulatory pressure and which increased their capital buffers tend to exploit the surplus by enlarging the volume of risk-weighted assets (COORDINATION = LOWCA * ΔABBUFF). It is evident that capital adequacy regulation is relevant for changing bank's risk posture and that most banks build up their capital in order to "consume" it later on throughout sizeable risk-weighted assets (usually larger credit growth).

The bank profitability proxies with the return on assets (ROA) as well as its lagged value ($ROA_{t-1}$) are positively linked to risk-weighted assets variable. Thus, higher the bank's profitability, higher the risk-taking activities are undertaken and vice versa. However, if lagged ROA is used, more convincing results are obtained, and alternative explanation can be discussed. Usually there is profit persistency in the banking industry and if one of bank's business goals is to maintain or increase their profitability in the following period, without taking more risks (i.e., increasing the risk-weighted assets) in the traditional banking, it will be impossible to do so. In addition, if there is a trend of decreasing profitability, risk perceptions of bank managers will change and more prudent behavior will take place. Throughout an increase in the non-performing loans, loan loss reservations and consequently net charge off of loans reduced profitability indirectly causes a decrease in risk-weighted assets as well as credit growth slowdown. It is confirmed that growth of loans—GROWL (in the previous as well as in the current period) is positively related to risk-weighted assets, while with the first signs of sizeable provisioning (LLR_L) risk-weighted assets will drop. Between bank liquidity (LIQ_A) and asset riskiness, there is a certain trade-off or substitution effect although bank managers need to maintain both asset liquidity as well as bank's functionality in allocating loans. However, an increase in loans and liquid assets is not proportional, especially for larger banks which usually have predisposition for liquidity management by borrowing liquid assets in comparison with small-sized banks who practice liquidity management by asset conversion. Therefore, a negative impact of liquidity to risk-taking changes might be also explained indirectly with the bank size. It is confirmed that larger banks take more risks according to the sign of $(\log A)^2$ variable, while small-sized banks which are expected to be more liquid on the assets size have lower growth opportunities and tend to reduce their risks as they are not too big to fail.

## 4.2 Results for Equations with Risk Index as Dependent Variable

The empirical results of the estimated panel models with ΔZINDEX as risk proxy are given in Tables 4–5. Tables 4 and 5 contain estimations of the baseline model, whereas Table 4 presents estimations with ROA as endogenous variable while Table 5 presents results when both ΔABBUFF and ROA are treated as endogenous variables. Sizeable differences in obtained results are not found. However, there are certain disparities between results obtained when ΔRWA_A is a dependent variable in comparison with ΔZINDEX being set up as a risk proxy. Thus, the signs of estimated coefficients for ΔABBUFF, ROA, LOWCA, and COORDINATION in equations with ΔZINDEX are opposite from the ones obtained in ΔRWA_A models which is reasonable as risk-weighted assets indicator measures only the asset riskiness, while risk index takes into consideration both asset riskiness as well as (re)financing risks. Nevertheless, explanations for the bank size, growth of loans, provisioning indicator, and liquidity ratio are pretty much consistent with the results obtained for ΔRWA_A equations.

Firstly, the lagged dependent variable (ΔZINDEX) has a negative sign which means that growth of risk index in the previous period effects negatively on the risk index in the current period. If bank has higher risk index, it can be perceived to have lower probability of failure. Thus, economic interpretation of this indicator as a risk proxy varies from the explanation for risk-weighted assets indicator. The negative sign of lagged ΔRWA_A variable means that banks with higher asset riskiness tend to reduce it, while an overall bank riskiness (both asset and financing riskiness measured with ΔZINDEX) will decrease only if the risk index was decreasing (and overall riskiness increasing) in the previous period. Thus, if a bank had higher equity to assets financing, high profitability, and low risk-taking and was perceived as stable one, in the following period, probably due to asset growth it will have lower equity indicator as well as return on assets and it will undertake more risks. With decreasing bank profitability and its increasing volatility due to market saturation followed by limited growth opportunities, it is clear why a bank's risk index will drop. Although banks will tend to reduce their asset riskiness (ΔRWA_A), their overall riskiness will enlarge (ΔZINDEX) and vice versa.

Secondly, an increase in the capital buffers (ΔABBUFF) adds to overall banking stability as results reveal a positive sign of ΔABBUFF. Thus, estimated effect of capital buffers on bank's stability is consistent in both cases, i.e., when risk is measured with risk-weighted assets and risk index. Higher capital buffers decrease bank's asset riskiness (ΔRWA_A) as well as its probability of failure (ΔZINDEX).

**Table 4** Panel data estimations of the baseline model with risk index as dependent variable and ROA as endogenous variable

| Explanatory variable | Model with ROA as endogenous variables | | |
|---|---|---|---|
| $\Delta ZINDEX_{i,t-1}$ | −0.0138606[a] (0.0008974) | −0.0146153[a] (0.0011128) | −0.0139127[a] (0.0008966) |
| $ROA_{i,t}$ | −0.9482218[a] (0.1052912) | −0.9325877[a] (0.134819) | −0.7310231[a] (0.1044009) |
| $\Delta ABBUFF_{i,t}$ | 0.8603212[a] (0.0842029) | 0.8613703[a] (0.0845497) | 1.063289[a] (0.098508) |
| $(\log A_{i,t})^2$ | 0.0445392[a] (0.0180896) | 0.0438699[b] (0.0188054) | 0.0239384 (0.0174431) |
| $GROWL_{i,t}$ | 0.0256977[b] (0.0111154) | 0.0306471[a] (0.0123301) | 0.0404983[a] (0.0108882) |
| $LLR\_L_{i,t}$ | −0.6987999[a] (0.0795944) | −0.6701004[a] (0.0801155) | −0.5711782[a] (0.0789222) |
| $LIQ\_A_{i,t}$ | −0.3511362[a] (0.0498992) | −0.3644054[a] (0.0510035) | −0.3519903[a] (0.0450585) |
| $LOWCA_{i,t-1}$ | – | 2.437872[b] (1.244226) | – |
| $COORDINATION_{i,t}$ ($LOWCA_{i,t-1}$ * $\Delta ABBUFF_{i,t}$) | – | – | −0.4233944[a] (0.129975) |
| $\alpha$ | 0.7249827 (4.260943) | −0.3647525 (4.220929) | 3.777921 (3.990984) |
| Number of observations | 383 | 383 | 383 |
| Number of banks | 115 | 115 | 115 |
| Sargan test (*p*-value) | 0.1512 | 0.1484 | 0.1433 |
| First-order autocorrelation (*p*-value) | 0.0112 | 0.0113 | 0.0109 |
| Second-order autocorrelation (*p*-value) | 0.5136 | 0.5163 | 0.5249 |

*Source* Bankscope, Author's calculation
[a]Statistically significant at 1% level, [b]statistically significant at 5% level, [c]statistically significant at 10% level

**Table 5** Panel data estimations of the baseline model with risk index as dependent variable and difference in absolute capital buffers and ROA as endogenous variables

| Explanatory variable | Model with ΔABBUFF and ROA as endogenous variables | | |
|---|---|---|---|
| $\Delta ZINDEX_{i,t-1}$ | −0.016034[a] (0.000183) | −0.0169531[a] (0.0002964) | −0.0171147[a] (0.0001981) |
| $ROA_{i,t}$ | −0.7952782[a] (0.0199522) | −0.7754666[a] (0.0046303) | −0.799481[a] (0.0185981) |
| $\Delta ABBUFF_{i,t}$ | 0.8047659[a] (0.0010644) | 0.6452927[a] (0.0031576) | 1.698581[a] (0.0010017) |
| $(\log A_{i,t})^2$ | 0.149949[a] (0.0030092) | 0.1468489[a] (0.0030695) | 0.0783523[a] (0.0012083) |
| $GROWL_{i,t}$ | 0.0355812[a] (0.0003676) | 0.0238821[a] (0.0008464) | 0.0678843[a] (0.0007055) |
| $LLR\_L_{i,t}$ | −0.3474895[a] (0.0138694) | −0.3814989[a] (0.0081267) | −0.4346527[a] (0.011863) |
| $LIQ\_A_{i,t}$ | −0.2423635[a] (0.0034213) | −0.2560296[a] (0.0024484) | −0.2372566[a] (0.0030081) |
| $LOWCA_{i,t-1}$ | – | 8.027128[a] (0.0238551) | – |
| $COORDINATION_{i,t}$ ($LOWCA_{i,t-1}$ * $\Delta ABBUFF_{i,t}$) | – | – | −1.294054[a] (0.0032453) |
| α | −23.81143[a] (0.7450643) | −26.18105[a] (0.6302377) | −9.549423[a] (0.3832388) |
| Number of observations | 383 | 383 | 383 |
| Number of banks | 115 | 115 | 115 |
| Sargan test (*p*-value) | 0.7806 | 0.6612 | 0.6615 |
| First-order autocorrelation (*p*-value) | 0.0110 | 0.0107 | 0.0105 |
| Second-order autocorrelation (*p*-value) | 0.5228 | 0.5098 | 0.5656 |

*Source* Bankscope, Author's calculation
[a]Statistically significant at 1% level, [b]statistically significant at 5% level, [c]statistically significant at 10% level

In addition, banks which were under regulatory pressure ($LOWCA_{t-1}$) increased their risk index.

However if there is an increase in the capital buffer for the aforementioned banks ($LOWCA_{t-1}$ * ΔABBUFF) they will not manage to lower the overall riskiness by increasing the buffers, but rather by increasing persistency of profitability (σROA). In addition, more profitable banks (ROA) have lower risk index probably due to their low capital base. Namely, in the SEE countries, larger banks are more profitable ones and usually tend to keep their capital buffers on minimum in order to lower the cost of capital. They might not be perceived as the ones under regulatory pressures as they have market position which enables them fast and successful recapitalizations. Thus, larger banks where size is $(\log A)^2$ are more stable and have higher risk index (ΔZINDEX) as their profits are more persistent (σROA).

In addition, banks with higher growth of loans (GROWL) are more stable if stability is proxy with risk index. GROWL is essential for bank profitability, and it should be followed by an increase in the regulatory capital which is mainly composed out of equity financing. Although, fast and sizeable growth of loans precedes banking instability period, according to obtained results a positive impact of GROWL on bank stability is confirmed mainly due to the impact which GROWL variable has on bank profitability and necessity to build up the capital base. Finally, too much liquidity, (LIQ_A) adds to banking instability (ΔZINDEX) as liquid assets are not profitable and do not require regulatory capital increase. Furthermore, small-sized banks which usually have higher asset liquidity are less profitable and riskier in their activities due to poor diversification opportunities and underdevelopment of other risk management practices. The negative impact of loan loss reservations (LLR_L) on bank's stability is logical if the income statement structure as well as the composition of regulatory capital is born in mind.

## *4.3 Results for Equations with Credit Price as Dependent Variable*

The empirical results of the estimated panel models with the credit price (ΔINCL_L) as risk proxy are given in Tables 6–7. Table 6 contains estimations of the baseline model, whereas Table 7 reveals results of the model adapted with the lagged variables. The main difference between estimations of the baseline model (Table 6) and adapted model (Table 7) is found in the level of statistical significance of variables. Thus, in the baseline model, bank size, growth of loans, and provisioning indicator are insignificant, while in the adapted model, they are significant. Furthermore, ΔABBUFF and ROA are mainly insignificant in the adapted model, contrary to the baseline model. In comparison with models with ΔRWA_A and ΔZINDEX, LLR_L and LIQ_A have a positive sign for the first time in models with ΔINCL_L.

The lagged dependent variable (ΔINCL_L) has a positive sign which means that there is a certain persistency in the credit price in the observed time period.

**Table 6** Panel data estimations of the baseline model with credit price as dependent variable

| Explanatory variable | The baseline model | | | |
|---|---|---|---|---|
| $\Delta$INCL_L$_{i,t-1}$ | 0.1669551[a] (0.0261368) | 0.1378378[a] (0.0227571) | 0.1273148[a] (0.0230886) | 0.1614893[a] (0.0252013) |
| $\Delta$AEBUFF$_{i,t}$ | −0.0224802 (0.0239585) | −0.0387151[c] (0.0223327) | −0,047867[b] (0.0217617) | −0.0582953[c] (0.0309918) |
| ROA$_{i,t}$ | 0.1526801[a] (0.0547462) | 0.1379714[b] (0.0596077) | 0.1282414[b] (0.0595486) | 0.1324931[a] (0.0466113) |
| (log A$_{i,t}$)$^2$ | 0.0092004 (0.0067786) | 0.0099013 (0.0063522) | 0.0059385 (0.0060314) | 0.0089999 (0.0064061) |
| GROWL$_{i,t}$ | −0.0045764 (0.0037824) | −0.003534 (0.0037229) | −0.0023488 (0.0028201) | −0.0034075 (0.0043019) |
| LLR_L$_{i,t}$ | −0.0277829 (0.0518541) | −0.0174155 (0.0506551) | −0.0375976 (0.0380285) | −0.0249284 (0.0449501) |
| LIQ_A$_{i,t}$ | 0.0203036[a] (0.0076746) | 0.025222[a] (0.0086745) | 0.0241748[a] (0.0083146) | 0.0234235[a] (0.007738) |
| LOWCA$_{i,t}$ | – | −0.5251997[a] (0.2008645) | – | – |
| SPEED$_{i,t}$ | – | – | −0.1566707[a] (0.0272011) | – |
| COORDINATION$_{i,t}$ | – | – | – | 0.0822322[b] (0.041941) |
| $\alpha$ | −2.675072[c] (1.568772) | −2.80805[b] (1.468548) | −1.511993 (1.41461) | −2.72849[c] (1.480875) |
| Number of observations | 351 | 351 | 351 | 351 |
| Number of banks | 108 | 108 | 108 | 108 |
| Sargan test ($p$-value) | 0.4670 | 0.3546 | 0.5774 | 0.4110 |
| First-order autocorrelation ($p$-value) | 0.0023 | 0.0028 | 0.0025 | 0.0024 |
| Second-order autocorrelation ($p$-value) | 0.1942 | 0.1240 | 0.1203 | 0.1550 |

*Source* Bankscope, Author's calculation
[a]Statistically significant at 1% level, [b]statistically significant at 5% level, [c]statistically significant at 10% level

**Table 7** Panel data estimations of the model with credit price as dependent variable and lagged variables

| Explanatory variable | Variables are lagged instead of being treated as endogenous variables | | | |
|---|---|---|---|---|
| $\Delta INCL\_L_{i,t-1}$ | 0.2674089[a] (0.0383645) | 0.2611939[a] (0.0422821) | 0.2398771[a] (0.0385704) | 0.2582809[a] (0.0407533) |
| $\Delta ABBUFF_{i,t-1}$ | −0.0004053 (0.0252071) | −0.0129406 (0.0242362) | −0.0235483 (0.0213728) | −0.0241692 (0.0272283) |
| $ROA_{i,t-1}$ | 0.0287068 (0.058765) | 0.0488195 (0.0574707) | 0.0322582 (0.0574906) | 0.0047156 (0.0535431) |
| $(\log A_{i,t})^2$ | 0.0165681[a] (0.0043551) | 0.010064[c] (0.0056115) | 0.0073716 (0.0047965) | 0.0140212[a] (0.0046191) |
| $GROWL_{i,t-1}$ | 0.0130515[a] (0.0053243) | 0.009655[b] (0.0047856) | 0.0088281[b] (0.0045357) | 0.0144178[a] (0.0053867) |
| $LLR\_L_{i,t-1}$ | 0.1823163[a] (0.0426679) | 0.1623574[a] (0.042087) | 0.1297671[a] (0.0440618) | 0.1576009[a] (0.0447085) |
| $LIQ\_A_{i,t}$ | 0.0264002[a] (0.0042276) | 0.0299564[a] (0.0055085) | 0.0445228[a] (0.0069918) | 0.0232351[a] (0.0045788) |
| $LOWCA_{i,t}$ | – | −0.369228[a] (0.0903707) | – | – |
| $SPEED_{i,t}$ | – | – | 0.1234114[a] (0.0145905) | – |
| $COORDINATION_{i,t}$ ($LOWCA_{i,t-1} * \Delta ABBUFF_{i,t-1}$) | – | – | – | 0.0574809[c] (0.0315606) |
| $\alpha$ | −5.79946[a] (1.048667) | −4.210769[a] (1.335821) | −3.384145[a] (1.170505) | −5.093627[a] (1.111421) |
| Number of observations | 318 | 318 | 318 | 318 |
| Number of banks | 106 | 106 | 106 | 106 |
| Sargan test (*p*-value) | 0.2863 | 0.2364 | 0.3873 | 0.2431 |
| First-order autocorrelation (*p*-value) | 0.0104 | 0.0106 | 0.0141 | 0.0117 |
| Second-order autocorrelation (*p*-value) | 0.1888 | 0.1627 | 0.1019 | 0.1063 |

*Source* Bankscope, Author's calculation
[a]Statistically significant at 1% level, [b]statistically significant at 5% level, [c]statistically significant at 10% level

Thus, the credit price in one period is going to be driven by the average credit price in the previous period. However, there is no strong evidence that capital buffers influence credit price.

Namely, in the baseline model, there is some evidence on the negative effect of capital buffers on the ΔINCL_L, what might be an evidence of banking rationality in practice due to banks not being willing to expose larger capital base to higher risk-taking and consequently more expensive loans, and will rather reduce their loan granting. Contrary, in the adapted model, the capital buffer variable is insignificant for the credit price. In addition, lower capitalized banks (LOWCA) reduce their loans riskiness and price, by taking into consideration not only their previous price (LOWCA * $INCL\_L_{t-1}$), but also changes in capital (LOWCA * ΔABBUFF). Thus, lower capitalized banks with higher credit price decrease their current credit price more than better capitalized banks, while lower capitalized banks which increased their capital buffers will increase their credit price. A notice should be paid to relation between risk weights of loans and credit price as riskier loans should also bear higher credit price. Lower capitalized banks which enlarged their capital buffers will probably want to use their free capital and increase their risk-weighted assets and average credit price.

According to estimations of the baseline model, banks with larger profitability (ROA) have more expensive loans. However, there is a reverse causality effect, i.e., the credit price impacts bank profitability. This is why, lagged profitability indicator was employed and evidence that bank profitability is irrelevant for the credit price appeared. Larger banks—$(\log A)^2$, banks with higher growth of loans ($GROWL_{t-1}$), larger loan loss reservations ($LLR\_L_{t-1}$), as well as more liquid banks (LIQ_A) will increase the average credit price. If larger banks take more risks as it has been confirmed in the model with ΔRWA_A, then it is clear why they have higher credit price. In addition, banks will be willing to grant their loans (GROWL) more as the interest rate is increasing up to the level of optimum interest rate. If higher provisioning occurs on a substantial level (LLR_L), it might be a consequence of reduced credit collectability and thus increased credit risk premium will enlarge the final credit price. At last, the implicit or opportunity costs of holding more liquid assets (LIQ_A) will also increase the credit price.

To sum up, capital buffer theory is confirmed and conclusion can be made that banks with higher capital buffers tend to exploit them by increasing asset riskiness (ΔRWA_A), although it will not undermine the overall banking stability, but rather improve it (ΔZINDEX). In addition, there is no strong evidence that the cost of holding larger capital buffers will affect the average credit price (ΔINCL_L). Lower capitalized banks will lower their asset riskiness (ΔRWA_A), increase overall banking stability (ΔZINDEX), and reduce their loan riskiness and credit price (ΔINCL_L) especially if there was sizeable level of asset riskiness and credit price in the previous period. Finally, lower capitalized banks which increased their capital buffers in the meanwhile (coordination effect) will endeavor to use their capital surplus by increasing the asset riskiness (ΔRWA_A) and credit price (ΔINCL_L), while increasing the overall riskiness (ΔZINDEX). Thus, the lower capitalized banks probably hold the capital surpluses on minimum and use it simultaneously as they have low refinancing risks, high credit capacity, and can easily approach the financial market. Those banks should not be perceived as banks under regulatory pressures, especially if they are too big to fail. However, more regulatory scrutiny should be given to the latter ones as there is certain evidence that larger banks take more risks in their asset selection. In a similar way, although on a rather conceptual level French et al. (2010: 67–74) concluded their Squam Lake Group report, in which some of the leading financial economists of nowadays were the contributors, demanding the changes in the capital regulation in the direction of the higher capital requirements for the large banks, what later on became a part of the Basel III regime via additional capital requirements for systematically important banks. Requesting additional capital buffers for the largest or systemically important banks seems to be fruitful for dampening their risk-taking, at least for the Euro area in the 2014–2017 period, as was recently demonstrated by Cappelletti et al. (2019).

## 5 Conclusions

No regulatory instrument is perfect, and constant changes in the capital adequacy regulation demonstrate its inability in forcing banks to comply in an expected manner. However, the theoretical and empirical background has moved away from the traditional assumption on the bank moral hazard behavior with a goal of regulatory burden avoidance. It has been noticed that the most banks maintain the capital surpluses or buffers in order to avoid the regulatory pressures and, according to some authors, the market pressures. Thus, the capital buffer theory is in the focus of the recent empirical researches.

This research attempts to fulfill the gap perceived to exist for the SEE banking sectors with a reference to the empirical evaluation of the capital buffer theory, i.e., to the commercial banks' behavior in the presence of the capital requirements. Conclusions of the capital buffer theory are confirmed as banks adjust risk-taking behavior in dependence with their capital buffers. Although capital buffers add to bank's asset riskiness, they reduce its overall riskiness and are irrelevant for an increase in the credit price. Asset riskiness and overall risk index are positively driven with a bank size and growth of loans, and negatively dependable (in the most research results) upon the provisioning and liquidity indicators. Contrary to the numerous studies trying to dispute the capital adequacy concept, this research results support the regulator intentions and efforts to continue with its implementation, especially in direction of prescribing mandatory capital buffers.

For future research, the relevance of regulatory capital structure (quality of capital) for bank's risk exposure is highly recommended to be investigated as well as the impact of capital buffers on bank's net interest margin as the most important segment of profitability in traditional banking sectors. At last, replication of this study is strongly encouraged on the data set beyond the year 2010 and other European countries as well as researching the distinctions in capital buffers' implications to banks' risk-taking behavior in the financial stability and global crisis period.

# 6 Appendix

See Table 8.

**Table 8** Methodological characteristics of presented empirical researches

| References | Research target | Data and methodology |
|---|---|---|
| Shrieves and Dahl (1992) | United States; 1983–1987<br>nearly 1 800 Federal Deposit Insured Corporation (FDIC)-insured independent and holding company affiliated commercial banks with assets in excess of 100 million USD | – Equity-to-assets ratio is used for the bank capital level<br>– Risk-weighted assets to total assets and non-performing loans to total loans serve as the risk indicators<br>– Simultaneous equations model: 2SLS |
| Rime (2001) | Switzerland; 1989–1995<br>154 domestic-owned banks | – Equity-to-assets ratio and capital to risk-weighted assets proxy the bank capital level<br>– Risk-weighted assets to total assets proxy the asset risk<br>– Simultaneous equations model: 3SLS |
| Bichsel and Blum (2004) | Switzerland; 1990–2002<br>19 publicly traded banks | – The bank assets risk is proxy with the volatility per unit of market value of assets, while the bank capital is measured with equity-to-assets ratio and market value of capital<br>– Default probability of bank is measured with the Z—distance to default<br>– Two-stage FGLS regressions |
| Cannata and Quagliariello (2006) | Italy; 1994–2003<br>more than 500 banks | – The ratio of supervisory capital to total assets is used for the bank capital level<br>– Assets risk is measured with the risk-weighted assets to total assets and the ratio of new bad debts to outstanding performing loans<br>– Simultaneous equations model: 3SLS |
| Stolz (2007) | Germany; 1993–2004<br>570 savings banks | – The bank capital is measured with regulatory capital to total assets, and risk is measured with risk-weighted assets to total assets<br>– Simultaneous equations model: 2SLS and 3SLS. Dynamic panel data model: Arellano-Bond and Blundell-Bond GMM estimators |

(continued)

**Table 8** (continued)

| References | Research target | Data and methodology |
|---|---|---|
| Van Roy (2008) | 6 G-10 countries (Canada; France; Italy; Japan; the United Kingdom and the United States); 1988–1995<br>576 commercial banks with assets of more than 100 million USD without bank holding companies—459 banks from the data sample are in the United States | – The bank capital is measured with equity-to-assets ratio and the Tier 1 capital-to-assets ratio<br>– The ratio of risk-weighted assets to total assets is a proxy for the assets risk<br>– Simultaneous equations model: 3SLS |
| Matejašák et al. (2009) | United States and EU-15 countries; 2000–2005<br>1 263 banks (580 banks from the EU-15 and 683 banks from the United States) | – The capital adequacy ratio is used for the bank capital level, and the ratio of risk-weighted assets to total assets measures the assets risk level<br>– Simultaneous equations model: 2SLS and 3SLS |
| Jokipii and Milne (2011) | United States; 1986–2008<br>commercial banks and publicly traded bank holding companies | – The capital buffer is defined as the total capital ratio minus regulatory required minimum<br>– The risk is measured with various ratios: risk index, risk-weighted assets to total assets, non-performing loans to total loans, and commercial and industrial loans over total loans<br>– One- and two-step Blundell-Bond system GMM estimators |
| Camara et al. (2013) | 17 European countries; 1992–2006<br>utmost 1 451 commercial, cooperative, mutual, and savings banks (out of which 677 are Italian, and 226 are French banks) | – The risk level is proxy with four indicators: 1) risk-weighted assets to total assets, 2) non-performing loans to net loans, 3) standard deviation of the return on assets; 4) logarithm value of Z-score<br>– The bank capital is measured with the ratio of total capital-to-total assets, and various dummy variables which indicate the structure of the regulatory capital and the bank capitalization level<br>– Dynamic panel data: Blundell-Bond system GMM estimator; robustness check is done with simultaneous equations model |
| Guidara et al. (2013) | Canada; 1982–2010<br>6 largest banks | – The risk is proxy with several proxies: total equity risk, market idiosyncratic risk, and volatility of asset returns<br>– The capital buffer is measured as an excess in capital over: (1) the minimum leverage ratio cap, (2) minimum regulatory capital requirement, (3) economic capital ratio<br>– Dynamic panel data: two-step SGMM estimator |

(continued)

**Table 8** (continued)

| References | Research target | Data and methodology |
|---|---|---|
| Ghosh (2014) | GCC countries; 1996–2011 around 100 commercial and Islamic banks | – The risk is proxy with logarithm value of Z-score<br>– The bank capital is measured with equity-to-assets ratio<br>– Simultaneous equations model: 3SLS |
| Šútorová and Teplý (2014) | EU-27 countries; 2006–2011 594 banks | – The risk is proxy with risky assets to total assets<br>– The bank capital is measured with common equity, Tier 1 and total regulatory capital to risk-weighted assets<br>– Simultaneous equations model: 2SLS and 3SLS |
| Bougatef and Mgadmi (2016) | MENA countries; 2004–2012 24 banks | – The risk is proxy with loan loss provisions to total assets<br>– The bank capital is measured with equity to total assets<br>– Simultaneous equations model: fixed effects regression method, 2GLS, 3SLS |

*Source* Author's review

# References


Angelini P, Clerc L, Cúrdia V, Gambacorta L, Gerali A, Locarno A, Motto R, Roeger W, van den Heuvel S, Vlček J (2015) Basel III: long-term impact on economic performance and fluctuations. Manch Sch 83(2):217–251

Arnold B, Borio C, Ellis L, Moshirian F (2012) Systemic risk, macroprudential policy frameworks, monitoring financial systems and the evolution of capital adequacy. J Bank Finance 36(12):3125–3132

Athanasoglou PP, Delis MD, Staikouras CK (2006) Determinants of Bank Profitability in the South Eastern European Region, Bank of Greece Working Paper, No. 47

Athanasoglou P (2011) Bank Capital and Risk in the South Eastern European Region, Munich Personal RePEc Archive Paper, No. 32002

Barisitz S, Gardó G (2008) Financial sector development in Serbia: Closing ranks with peers. Focus on European Econ Int 2:94–119

Benston GJ (2007) Basel II and bankers' propensity to take or avoid excessive risk. Atl Econ J 35(4):373–382

Bichsel R, Blum J (2004) The relationship between risk and capital in Swiss Commercial Banks: A panel study. Appl Financial Econ 14(8):591–597

Blum J (1999) Do capital adequacy requirements reduce risks in banking? J Bank Finance 23(5):755–771

Blundell R, Bond S (1998) Initial Conditions and moment restrictions in dynamic panel data models. J Econometrics 87(1):115–143

Bougatef K, Mgadmi N (2016) The impact of prudential regulation on bank capital and risk-taking: The case of MENA countries. Spanish Rev Financial Econ 14(2):51–56

Cappelletti G, Ponte Marques A, Varraso P, Budrys Ž, Peeters J (2019). Impact of Higher Capital Buffers on Banks' Lending and Risk-Taking: Evidence from the Euro Area Experiments, European Central Bank Working Paper Series, No. 2292.
Camara B, Lepetit L, Tarazi A (2013) Ex ante capital position, changes in the different components of regulatory capital and bank risk. Appl Econ 45(34):4831–4856
Cannata F, Quagliariello M (2006) Capital and risk in Italian banks: A simultaneous equation approach. J Bank Regul 7(3/4):283–297
Duran MA, Lozano-Vivas A (2014) Risk shifting in the US banking system: An empirical analysis. J Financ Stab 13:64–74
French KR, Baily MN, Campbell JY, Cochrane JH, Diamond DW, Duffie D, Kashyap AK, Mishkin FS, Rajan RG, Scharfstein DS, Shiller RJ, Shin HS, Slaughter MJ, Stein SC, Stulz RM (2010) The Squam Lake report: Fixing the financial system. Princeton University Press, USA
Floquet K, Biekpe N (2008) The relationship between capital structure and risk in emerging market banks. Banks Bank Systs 3(1):63–74
Fonseca AR, González F, da Silva LP (2010) Cyclical Effects of Bank Capital Buffers with Imperfect Credit Markets: International Evidence, Banco Central do Brasil Working paper, No. 216.
Ghosh S (2014) Risk, capital and financial crisis: Evidence for GCC banks. Borsa Istanbul Rev 14(3):145–157
Godlewski CJ (2005) Bank capital and credit risk taking in emerging market economies. J Bank Regul 6(2):128–145
Guidara A, Lai VS, Soumaré I, Tchana Tchana F (2013) Banks' capital buffer, risk and performance in the Canadian banking system: Impact of business cycles and regulatory changes. J Bank Finance 37(9):3373–3387
Jiang H, Zhang J, Sun C (2020) How does capital buffer Affect bank risk-taking? New evidence from China Using Quantile Regression. China Econ Rev, 60, 101300
Jokipii T, Milne A (2008) The cyclical behaviour of european Bank capital buffers. J Bank Finance 32(8):1440–1451
Jokipii T, Milne A (2011) Bank capital buffer and risk adjustment decisions. J Financ Stab 7(3):165–178
Kane EJ (1977) Good Intentions and unintended evil: The case against selective credit allocation. J Money, Credit, Bank 9(1):55–69
Kundid Novokmet A (2015) Cyclicality of bank capital buffers in South-Eastern Europe: Endogenous and exogenous aspects. Financial Theory and Practice 39(3):139–169
Leung WS, Taylor N, Evans KP (2015) The determinants of bank risks: Evidence from the recent financial Crisis. J Int Finan Markets Inst Money 34:277–293
Makri V, Tsagkanos A, Bellas A (2014) Determinants of non-performing loans: The case of eurozone. Panoeconomicus 61(2):193–206
Marcus AJ (1984) Deregulation and bank financial policy. J Bank Finance 8(4):557–565
Matejašák M, Teplý P, Černohorský J (2009) The Impact of Regulation of Banks in the US and the EU-15 Countries. E+M Ekonomie a Manag 3, 58–68.
Milne A, Whalley EA (2001) Bank Capital Regulation and Incentives for Risk-Taking. Cass Business School Research Paper, December. http://papers.ssrn.com/sol3/papers.cfm?abstract_id=299319
Rime B (2001) Capital requirements and bank behaviour: Empirical evidence for Switzerland. J Bank Finance 25(4):789–805
Saadaoui Z (2011) Risk-based capital standards and bank behaviour in emerging and developed countries. J Bank Regul 12(2):180–191
Shrieves RE, Dahl D (1992) The relationship between risk and capital in commercial banks. J Bank Finance 16(2):439–457
Slattery D, Nellis JG (2011) Rethinking the role of regulation in the aftermath of the global financial crisis: the case of the UK. Panoeconomicus 58(3):407–423
Stolz SM (2007) Bank Capital and Risk-Taking: The Impact of Capital Regulation, Charter Value, and the Business Cycle. Kiel Studies. Springer-Verlag

Šútorová B, Teplý P (2014) EU banks' profitability and risk adjustment decisions under basel III. Ekonomický Časopis 62(7):667–691
Van Roy P (2008) Capital requirements and bank behavior. Int J Cent Bank 4(3):29–60
Wisniwski S (2005) Bankers' perspectives—dynamic banking in a changing market. In: Matthäus-Maier I, von Pischke JD (eds) EU accessio—n—financial sector opportunities and challenges for Southeast Europe. Springer, Germany, pp 131–162
Zheng C, Xu CT, Liang W (2012) The empirical research of banks' capital buffer and risk adjustment decision Making–Evidence from China's banks. China Finance Rev Int 2(2):163–179

# Enterprise Risk Management: What Opportunities for the Banking Sector?

**Grazia Dicuonzo, Francesca Donofrio, Grazia Onorato, and Mario Turco**

**Abstract** Risk management has become increasingly important for companies in all sectors. Many risk management frameworks help firms compete better in the market. One of the most widely used is the Enterprise Risk Management Committee of Sponsoring Organizations (ERM COSO) model, considered a reference for all types of companies. ERM represents a new approach to identify, assess and manage the risks that may interfere with an organisation's operations and objectives. The interest in ERM, supported by its implementation, has increased, following rigorous regulatory requirements and emerging risks. The ERM framework allows managing enterprise risk in a coordinated way and in aggregation across the organisation. The risk management function has evolved into a flexible system, capable of respecting each company's needs. This function is implemented by formulating strategies consistent with a corporation's risk appetite and goals to enable value creation. The ERM framework has improved business results, decreasing the volatility of earnings and stock prices, reducing costs and increasing efficiency, which can enhance firms' performance and value. In this paper, we explore the ERM framework's level of integration in the financial system and investigate the relation between ERM and performance by conducting an explorative empirical analysis on a sample of listed international financial institutions. This contribution has practical implications, offering market participants insights into how ERM can affect financial intermediaries' performance.

---

G. Dicuonzo (✉) · F. Donofrio · G. Onorato
Department of Economics, Management and Business Law, University of Bari Aldo Moro, Largo Abbazia di Santa Scolastica n. 53, 70124 Bari, Italy
e-mail: grazia.dicuonzo@uniba.it

F. Donofrio
e-mail: francesca.donofrio@uniba.it

G. Onorato
e-mail: grazia.onorato@uniba.it

M. Turco
Department of Economic Sciences, University of Salento, Centro Ecotekne Pal. C-S.P. 6 Lecce—Monteroni, 73100 Lecce, LE, Italy
e-mail: mario.turco@unisalento.it



G. Karanovic et al. (eds.), *The Changing Financial Landscape*, Contributions to Economics, https://doi.org/10.1007/978-3-030-82778-6_10

**Keywords** Enterprise risk management · COSO · ERM framework · Banking sector · Performance

**JEL Classification Codes** G21 · G32 · L25

## 1 Introduction

Interest in risk management issues has grown considerably in recent years. In fact, the need for a model to identify, assess and manage risks effectively has become increasingly apparent. For this reason, in 2001, the Committee of Sponsoring Organizations (COSO) launched a study project, in cooperation with PricewaterhouseCoopers, to produce a framework. This model comprises all the different types of risk that could be managed to improve business risk management in organisations.

In 2004, the COSO, in collaboration with PricewaterhouseCoopers, published the enterprise risk management (ERM) framework, which represents the evolution of the previous document (Internal Control—Integrated Framework). This document is aimed at guiding and supporting the management of companies and other entities to improve the management of risks connected with the achievement of corporate objectives, through an integrated model that intends to include all corporate risks (Moeller 2007; Olson and Wu 2008). This model represents a starting point to evaluate the risk management process in individual companies, with the aim of improving it, if the company is already equipped with a risk management system, or a point of reference on which to implement a risk management system.

The COSO framework (COSO 2004) was updated with the 2017 release of "Enterprise Risk Management—Integrating with Strategy and Performance", which highlights the importance of considering risk in both the strategy-setting process and driving performance.

All companies face uncertain events, and the challenge for management is to determine the degree of uncertainty that the company is willing to accept in order to create value for shareholders (Hoyt and Liebenberg 2008).

Uncertainty can represent both a risk and an opportunity and can potentially reduce or increase the company's value. In this regard, ERM is proposed as a reference model that can allow management to effectively manage uncertainties and therefore the consequent risks and opportunities, thus increasing the company's ability to create value. Value is created, preserved or eroded by management's strategic and operational decisions; in this regard, the identification of risks and opportunities and their treatment represent an aspect strictly connected to decision-making processes (Belmont 2004; Lam 2014; Nocco and Stulz 2006).

Value creation can be considered achieved through an effective and efficient use of the resources available to management in the composition of the trade-off between growth and profitability, on the one hand, and risks derived from them, on the other hand (Arena et al. 2010; Beasley et al. 2008; Gordon et al. 2009; Paape and Speklé 2012).

The ERM framework identifies four categories of corporate objectives: strategic objectives, derived directly from the corporate mission; operational objectives, which pertain to the effective and efficient use of resources; reporting objectives, consisting of the reliability of external and internal information; and compliance objectives, that is, following laws and regulations. To identify and evaluate the risks and then proceed with their treatment, it is necessary that the objectives that an organisation intends to achieve be clearly defined in advance and that these be declined and formalised at various levels of the organisational structure.

The implementation of an ERM model therefore allows an improvement of the process of defining and formalising the objectives. By promoting the identification and assessment of risks at various levels of the organisational structure, the ERM model allows the verification of the alignment between the organisation's risk profile and risk appetite (Louisot and Ketcham 2014).

ERM requires the company to consider its overall risk. However, this may require each manager, responsible for a function, division, operating unit or process, to assess the risk relating to the activity that he/she carries out. In other words, the ERM framework allows the management of enterprise risk in a coordinated way and in aggregation across the organisation (Barton et al. 2002; Dickinson 2001; Moeller 2007; Olson and Wu 2008).

In this way, a picture of the risk profile is obtained at various levels of the structure, which allows senior management to determine whether the risk at the company level is in line with the acceptable risk.

Five components contribute to the achievement of all categories of objectives: (1) Governance & Culture, (2) Strategy & Objective-Setting, (3) Performance, (4) Review & Revision and (5) Information, Communication & Reporting. Taken together, these five components define a company's risk management system (Fig. 1).

**Fig. 1** Enterprise risk management framework. *Source* COSO (2017)

ERM can be applied to both the entire company and its individual units. However, it is believed that a widespread application of ERM at various levels of the organisation can bring greater benefits and guarantee more effective risk management at the overall company level. The assessment parameter of the ERM effectiveness is precisely the existence and correct functioning of the five components, which excludes the presence of significant system weaknesses and risks inconsistent with the level of risk deemed acceptable.

In line with the previous considerations, ERM processes could assist management in capturing opportunities, improving information and communication processing, increasing the firm's reputation, accountability and governance and contributing to the enhancement of the firm's planning and performance (Brown et al. 2019). ERM encourages disclosure of risk-related issues at the board level; it aims to deliver organisational benefits by reducing volatility of earnings and equity prices, increasing investment efficiency and creating synergy in the risk management process (Pagach and Warr 2010). All of these improve strategy, effective operations, reduced costs and positive cash flows (Liebenberg and Hoyt 2003). ERM ensures that decision-making is not centralised among top managers but occurs at all organisational levels, ensuring that every business unit evaluates risk as part of its decision-making processes (Nocco and Stulz 2006).

Many researchers and practitioners believe that the organisations where an ERM system is implemented can effectively reduce risk management costs in different departments, due to its holistic and general outlook. When a firm's annual reports show good ERM implementation, it can be stated that the firm is able to manage multiple risks. Thus, ERM implementation could increase shareholders' trust, providing a non-financial information package about invested capital (Liebenberg and Hoyt 2003).

However, financial performance provides information about the company's real profile and evidence of efficient capital management. Therefore, financial performance is an important signal in making investment decisions. ERM implementation will positively influence a firm's value, which is increased by its profitability. Hence, our hypothesis is that a positive relation exists between ERM implementation and a firm's financial performance.

In this paper, we aim to explore the ERM framework's level of integration in the financial system and to investigate the relation between ERM and performance. To achieve these goals, we carry out an explorative analysis on a sample of listed financial institutions. Many studies focus on ERM, while little research explains the relation between ERM and economic performance, especially in the financial sector. Our study aims to fill this gap by offering an empirical analysis in the international context.

We have structured this paper as follows: In Sect. 2, we present the literature review. In Sect. 3, we describe the empirical analysis and the research model. We then discuss the results in Sect. 4. Finally, in Sect. 5, we provide the conclusions, the implications and future research lines.

## 2 Literature Review

Starting in the 1990s, with the succession of economic crises and major corporate failures, corporate managers have sensed the need to strengthen their risk management systems, increasingly moving towards an integrated risk approach. Financial and non-financial institutions have adopted increasingly efficient and appropriate control and management models according to their own risk thresholds. Thus, the interest in ERM has started to grow.

In 2004, the COSO of the Treadway Commission defined ERM as "*a process, effected by an entity's board of directors, management and other personnel, applied in strategy setting and across the enterprise, designed to identify potential events that may affect the entity, and manage risk to be within its risk appetite, to provide reasonable assurance regarding the achievement of entity objectives*" (COSO 2004).

Enterprise risk is the set of all process and functional risks that an organisation must face in the normal course of its business. These risks include strategic, financial, operational and compliance risks, which extend to the whole organisation (Ezeosa 2011). Integrated corporate risk management is the basis of ERM (Tahir and Razali 2011).

ERM is a strategic approach to risk management, aimed to support management in making strategic decisions, on the one hand, and to generate long-term value for businesses, on the other hand (Barton et al. 2002; Beasley et al. 2008; Fadun 2013; Gordon et al. 2009). Integrating and adapting ERM in companies require an important organisational effort, especially for banks under increased regulatory pressure. The focus on the performance and level of implementation of ERM in listed companies, particularly financial ones, is also reflected in the Standard & Poor's rating company's valuation model, as evidenced by its 2007 and 2015 documents, which consider this management scheme a key variable in the risk assessment process (Standard & Poor's 2007,2015).

In recent years, the financial sector has also sensed the need to integrate ERM in the face of a series of external pressures (e.g. requests for reforms from regulators, corporate governance or institutional investors) and internal pressures (e.g. arising from specific commercial conditions and risks of a highly competitive market).

A typical feature of financial institutions is the adoption of third-party risk and consequent development of ad hoc tools. ERM implementation will allow intermediaries to take an advantageous position on the market, resulting in more credibility and facilitating customer loyalty.

Additionally, the financial system is witnessing a strong metamorphosis in the face of technological developments, which are changing the distribution systems and customer expectations. This metamorphosis is associated with new risks, further uncertainties and levels of control. In this context, financial intermediaries must obtain the maximum value from their companies by making good decisions on products and markets, investments, operations, capital and hedging. ERM has the potential to increase corporate value by achieving strategic objectives, boosting growth, increasing yield and improving profit consistency (Hoyt and Liebenberg 2011; Malik et al. 2019; Olayinka et al. 2017; Salaudeen et al. 2018; Silva et al. 2019). For financial intermediaries to achieve these goals, they need to understand the full risk environment where they operate.

On the one hand, it is necessary for financial institutions to analyse the external environment through an examination of the macroeconomic conditions specific to the context in which they operate (e.g. the creation of value for the company in terms of better risk–return organisation and easier market accessibility, as well as better management of reputational and strategic risks) (Martin and Power 2007; Nocco and Stulz 2006). On the other hand, financial institutions must understand the internal environment of the company. They must examine expansion and diversification objectives and programmes, organisational culture, distribution systems, intellectual capital, work processes and technology. Additionally, it is necessary that business decisions come not only from the top manager but from all organisational levels, ensuring a greater frequency of communication about the decisions made and the performance achieved, to evaluate the attainment of set goals (Nocco and Stulz 2006).

For financial intermediaries to manage financial and operational risks efficiently, they must include the set of strategies available to them. They should first understand the financial strategies through an examination of the capital structure, investment strategies, products and services offered. Second, they must understand the operational strategies and therefore pay attention to hiring and training, incentive programmes, internal controls, technology, market strategy and distribution.

Financial institutions must apply this knowledge holistically to manage their financial and operational risks. This framework will enable financial institutions to achieve their integrated risk management goal. In the financial context, ERM occurs when a financial institution undertakes to manage all its risks that represent a financial threat and takes a long time to mitigate the perceived risk and threat (Standard & Poor's 2005).

By combining financial instruments and operational risk modelling tools, financial service managers can in fact achieve their goal of increasing corporate value (Florio and Leoni 2016; Lundqvist and Vilhelmsson 2018; Soliman and Adam 2017). They can do this sensibly for investors, regulators and customers.

## 3 Empirical Analysis

### 3.1 Sample

The analysis focuses on the main European banking groups, designated by the European Banking Authority in December 2018.

First, the universe of global systemically important institutions (G-SIIs) has been chosen because for both systemic and reputation reasons, they are certainly the first subjects called to integrate ERM into their corporate governance systems. The

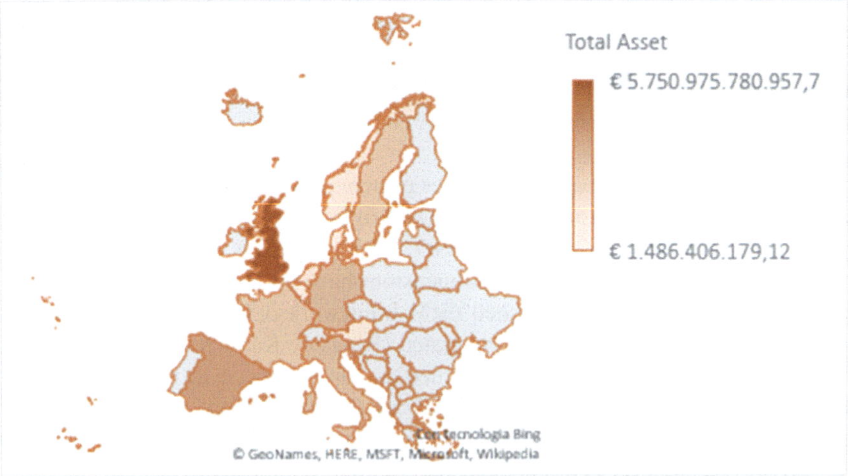


**Fig. 2** Total assets of banks by country (2018). *Source* Authors' illustration using an online map

financial system is undergoing a reform to integrate the lessons learned from the experience of the financial crisis, and in this context, ERM can increase corporate value and generate value for stakeholders.

Second, we have chosen to focus on the G-SIIs because the business models adopted by these banks are rather uniform. If the analysis has also been extended to other international banks or in general, to other financial institutions (O-SIIs), the sample would have been uneven.

Therefore, our sample includes 30 banks. In terms of managed assets in December 2018 (Fig. 2), the UK banks manage overall 37.2% of total assets attributable to the whole sample of examined banks. They are followed by Spanish banks with 17.7% of managed assets, German banks with 11.7% and Italian banks with 10.5%.

To achieve our research goal, a quantitative score (which we have called the bank's ERM index) was constructed to summarise the banks' level of performance in integrating ERM in their systems.

Preliminary analysis focused on the development of a research model consisting of 50 pieces of elementary information. Subsequently, adopting the content analysis approach, all the banks' official documents on corporate governance and risk management (corporate governance report, risk management report if drafted separately, annual report, etc.) were analysed to enhance the elementary items and thus achieve the construction of the final rating.

Our model appears completely innovative, as it combines the approaches actually adopted by the banks, as well as the reference literature.

## 3.2 The Research Model

At the outset, the analysis focused on the elaboration of a research model, composed of 50 pieces of essential information, for the construction of a score, called the bank's ERM index.

The research model is based on a series of items developed by Lundqvist (2014) to build an aggregate measure of ERM. The original Lundqvist list was developed using the ERM COSO framework (COSO 2013; Lundqvist 2014). To answer our research question, Lundqvist's ERM dimensions have been refined, and, based on a careful review of the latest published ERM framework (COSO 2017), some items not included in the list have been integrated (Kingsley Karunaratne 2017; Prewett and Terry 2018). More precisely, our metrics can be traced to the five different components delineated by the ERM framework (COSO 2017).

The first area investigated Governance & Culture, to which 15 metrics belong; the second concerns Strategy & Objective-Setting, composed of 5 indicators; the third consists of Performance, including 19 indicators. The fourth area relates to Review & Revision and includes 6 items. Finally, the last area comprises Information, Communication & Reporting, to which 5 metrics belong.

First, the model investigates the role of the board of directors. In particular, the first area (Kingsley Karunaratne 2017; Prewett and Terry 2018) of investigation—Governance & Culture—examines the board of directors' responsibility for the supervision of the strategy, as well as its governance responsibilities to support management in achieving the strategy and business objectives. In line with the Establishes Operating Structures principle of the ERM framework, our model investigates the organisation's ability to establish operating structures in pursuit of strategic and business objectives (items 9, 13, 14 and 15). The third principle of ERM framework, entitled "Defines Desired Culture", is investigated through the analysis of items 1, 4, 5, 10, 11 and 12.

The organisation's commitment to the fundamental values of the entity (the fourth principle of ERM Framework entitled Demonstrates Commitment to Core Values) is expressed through the bank's propensity to promote training on ethical values for employees (item 2) and/or the alignment of remuneration policies with the interests of managers and shareholders (item 3). Finally, the last principle of the first ERM framework component "Attracts, Develops, and Retains Capable Individuals" ("*The organisation is committed to building human capital in line with the company's strategy and objectives*"), is analysed by examining items 6 and 7.

In line with the second component of the ERM framework, our model investigates the bank's strategy and objective setting. In this context, we analyse the bank's risk profile according to the business model, examining items 11, 12, 13, 52 and 53.

Our third area of investigation, which reflects the third component of the ERM framework, refers to performance. This is certainly the area with the most items (19). This is justified by the fact that this component represents the core of ERM.

After defining the impacts on the risks, the companies must prioritise the risks and report the processes. The risk identification process requires a continuous review that examines emerging and unknown risks. Our model examines the bank's propensity to consider strategic risk events (item 21) or financial events (item 32). Additionally, the model analyses the considerations of compliance events (item 33), economic events (item 36) and reputation events (item 37).

According to principle no. 11 of the ERM framework (Assesses Severity of Risk), the scenario analysis that incorporates quantitative and qualitative analyses allows greater risk mitigation.

This is the risk assessment area and therefore involves the bank's ability to consider the probability that strategic risk events (item 22), compliance events (item 34), technological events (item 35) and reputation events (item 38) influence the company's ability to achieve its goals.

On the one hand, organisations must prioritise their risk responses based on criteria such as adaptability, complexity, speed, persistence, recovery and other variables. On the other hand, management should rely on the business context, the seriousness of the risk and the propensity to risk when deciding whether to accept, transfer, mitigate or avoid the risks (items 29, 30 and 31).

Finally, management and the board of directors must review the interdependencies of the risks derived from integrated business solutions (items 23, 24 and 25).

As part of continuous monitoring (the fourth component), banks should review performance and review appropriateness. All business processes must be monitored for changes that lead to performance gaps (item 40), and the risk assessment team must ensure that the company's business processes are consistently aligned with its risk appetite (items 41 and 45). Furthermore, the undertaking's risk management function must be assessed by an independent entity, that is, by an external auditor (item 42).

Finally, organisations must review and update their ERM regularly, examining the main risk indicators or indicators aimed at emerging risks (item 43) and constantly updating the risk information.

The final area of investigation concerns the fifth component of the ERM framework, entitled Information, Communication & Reporting.

ERM requires internal and external communication to obtain and share information that affects risk appetite and corporate strategies. Information systems must allow more interdepartmental communication to report suspected violations of laws, regulations and other irregularities (item 46). Additionally, risk data should be shared with customers, suppliers and other external partners (items 47 and 49). Finally, ERM requires the board of directors to review the current state of risk and the effectiveness of risk management at least once a year (item 48) and verify the completeness, accuracy and validity of the risk information (item 50).

The scores of the items vary between zero (non-compliance with the items or absence of related information) and 1 (the bank's compliance with essential information) (Gompers et al. 2001; La Porta et al. 1998).

Next, we calculated the cumulative score using the following formulation:

$$\text{Bank's ERM index} = \frac{\text{Number of items disclosed by the bank}}{\text{Total items of the model}}$$

## 4 Results and Discussion

Figure 3 shows the respective ratings for each area of investigation. The first important aspect concerns the extreme homogeneity of the indicated scores, which stand around the average value of 97.8% in 2018.

When examining the first area of investigation, entitled Governance & Culture, the banks show a propensity to integrate the ERM framework into their corporate governance systems. In fact, in 2018, when analysing the average of the items included in the first research area, the result is certainly positive (93.6%).

All the items included in the first survey area have scores close to 100%. The only item with a lower score is item 5, entitled "Formally defined standards for hiring and firing of executive management". In fact, this item shows an average score of 30% since only 9 banks (out of 30) provide information about the standards for hiring and firing of executive management.

Three of the analysed banks do not present a written document describing the board's role, structure, and responsibilities (item 10).

The second area of investigation refers to the internal control framework that focuses on defining a risk assessment that starts with corporate objectives and then implements plans based on the company's risk appetite. In this case, our results also show extreme homogeneity, with the average score of the area equal to 100% (average of items 16–20).

When analysing the third area of investigation (performance), the average score per area is equal to 92.3%. Item 31 has the greatest impact on this result; in fact, only 11 of the examined banks present an alternate risk response to each significant event (36.7%). Additionally, 7 of the examined banks do not present a risk response plan for all significant events identified by the company (item 30). Furthermore, 2 of the examined banks do not consider the impact of technology events (item 35), and 4

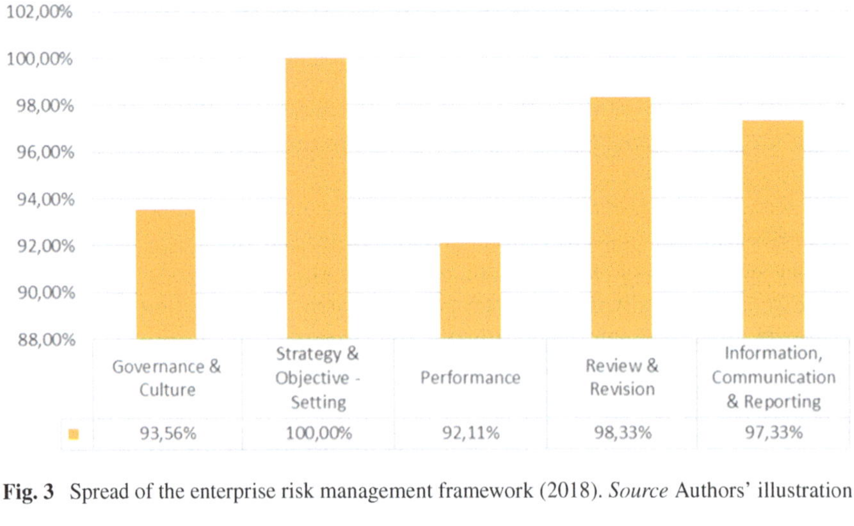


**Fig. 3** Spread of the enterprise risk management framework (2018). *Source* Authors' illustration

banks do not consider the reputation events (item 38). Finally, only one organisation does not assess the severity of a risk (item 39).

To sum up, with the exception of items 26, 28 and 34, which all have a score of 90%, all the other items that make up the third investigation area have a score of 100%.

According to the fourth component of the ERM framework, all banks have reviewed performance and revisions appropriately as part of continuous monitoring. Additionally, all business processes have been monitored for changes that lead to performance gaps or invalidate critical assumptions. All workforce members whose roles include risk management responsibilities ensure that their business processes consistently align with the propensity to risk. Finally, all the examined banks review and update their ERM regularly (the average score in the fourth investigation area is 98.33%).

Finally, the last area of investigation—Information, Communication & Reporting—shows an average score of 97.33%. This means that the examined banks communicate internally and externally to obtain and share information that affects risk appetite and corporate strategies.

An interesting aspect concerns item 46 ("Channels of communication to report suspected breaches of laws, regulations and other improprieties"). In this case, the average score per item is 86.7% as 4 out of 30 banks lack these specific communication channels.

Table 1 shows the respective rating values assigned to all examined banks. The first important aspect concerns the extreme homogeneity of the indicated scores, which are around the average value of 95% in 2018. This result shows the banks' strong convergence towards an integrated risk management model. Three of the examined banks fully comply with the principles of the ERM framework, while the remaining 27 banks are gradually adapting.

Next, by aggregating the information found for each bank, the average final rating by country is expressed in percentage terms (Fig. 4). The positivity of the score is proof of the banks' awareness of the importance of using the ERM framework in their systems.

In 2018, the Italian banks, with an average score of 100%, are particularly inclined to adopt an integrated risk management system. Belgian, French, Spanish, German and Norwegian banks have an average score that varies between 96 and 98%. Dutch, Swedish, Austrian, UK and Danish banks, with an average final score between 90 and 95%, are positioned in the final part of the ranking.

## 5 Conclusion

Banks focus on the ERM framework as an additional lever of innovation and development to better compete in the market in the medium and the long terms. Our work has aimed to explore the ERM framework's level of integration in the European banks' systems. To achieve this goal, we have conducted an explorative analysis on a sample

**Table 1** Banks' ERM index and descriptive variables (2018)

| No | Bank | Score (%) | No | Bank | Score (%) |
|---|---|---|---|---|---|
| 1 | ERSTE group | 94 | 16 | RABO bank | 94 |
| 2 | KBC | 96 | 17 | DNB | 98 |
| 3 | DANSKE bank | 94 | 18 | SANTANDER | 98 |
| 4 | NYKREDIT | 90 | 19 | BBVA | 94 |
| 5 | BNP PARIBAS | 94 | 20 | CAIXA bank | 98 |
| 6 | CREDIT AGRICOLE | 94 | 21 | SABADELL | 94 |
| 7 | BPCE | 96 | 22 | NORDEA | 98 |
| 8 | SOCIETE GENERALE | 98 | 23 | SEB | 94 |
| 9 | COMMERZ bank | 98 | 24 | HANDELSBANKEN | 90 |
| 10 | DEUTSCHE bank | 98 | 25 | SWED bank | 84 |
| 11 | DZ bank | 96 | 26 | BARCLAYS | 92 |
| 12 | LBBW | 100 | 27 | HSBC | 88 |
| 13 | INTESA SANPAOLO | 100 | 28 | LLOYDS | 92 |
| 14 | UNICREDIT | 100 | 29 | RBS | 86 |
| 15 | ABN AMRO | 96 | 30 | STANDARD CHARTERED | 94 |
| Min (%) | 84 | | | | |
| Max (%) | 100 | | | | |
| Average (%) | 94 | | | | |

*Source* Authors' calculations

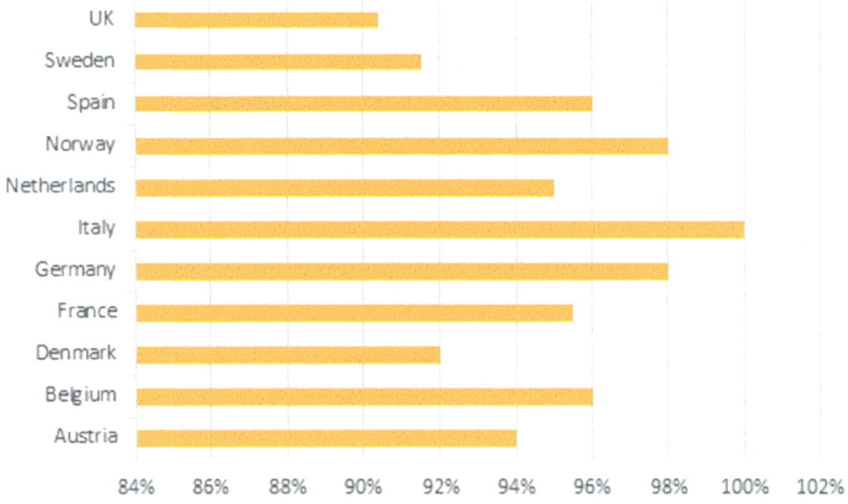


**Fig. 4** Banks' ERM index: geographical trends (percentage values, 2018). *Source* Authors' calculations

of 30 international and listed banks belonging to the G-SII universe in 2018. The analysis focuses on the elaboration of a research model, composed of 50 pieces of essential information, for the construction of a score, called the bank's ERM index.

The growing trend of the score is evidence of the gradual adjustment to the new ERM framework, updated by COSO in 2017, as well as the banks' awareness of the importance of using and spreading an integrated risk management model that is connected to the achievement of corporate objectives and covers all corporate risks.

Our findings have several important implications for both practitioners and scholars. Indeed, the research model assumes two different but complementary functionalities. First, it can be utilised by investors to discern banks that best implement the ERM framework in their systems from banks that seem delayed in this process. From this perspective, the research model represents an analysis tool to understand how and if banks integrate the ERM framework in their corporate and decision-making processes. In this way, investors and practitioners could make their decisions and assessments more consciously. Second, the research model also assumes an important internal functionality because it can be adopted by banks as a diagnostic tool to perform a self-assessment process.

Finally, our study opens up many different future research lines. More specifically, the proposed rating could be used to conduct several econometric studies in order to verify if a greater integration of the ERM framework in the banks' systems can have a positive impact on their economic performance, risk profiles or funding costs.

The empirical approach used in this study may well serve as a basis for further analysis. The study may be replicated across the rest of the financial institutions in European Union countries using a larger dataset; it would permit obtaining more significant results, from a statistical perspective. Regarding the analysed countries, it would be possible to complete the normative framework with the missing provisions.

## References


Arena M, Arnaboldi M, Azzone G (2010) The organizational dynamics of enterprise risk management. Acc Organ Soc 35(7):659–675. https://doi.org/10.1016/j.aos.2010.07.003

Barton TL, Shenkir WG, Walker PL (2002) Making enterprise risk management pay off: how leading companies implement risk management. Financial Times/Prentice Hall PTR., Upper Saddle River, NJ

Beasley M, Pagach D, Warr R (2008) Information conveyed in hiring announcements of senior executives overseeing enterprise-wide risk management processes. J Acc Audit Financ. https://doi.org/10.1177/0148558X0802300303

Belmont DP (2004) Value added risk management in financial institutions: Leveraging Basel II and risk adjusted performance management. Wiley Finance

Brown J, Duane M, Schuermann T (2019) What is enterprise risk management? J Risk Manag Financ Inst 12(4): 311–319(9) (Autumn/Fall 2019)

COSO (2004) Enterprise risk management-integrated framework. Committee of Sponsoring Organizations of the Treadway Commission. https://doi.org/10.1002/9781119201939.app4

COSO (2013) The 2013 COSO framework & SOX compliance. The Committee of Sponsoring Organizations of the Treadway Commission. https://doi.org/10.1111/j.1467-8330.1974.tb00606.x
COSO (2017) Enterprise risk management integrating with strategy and performance. In: The Committee of Sponsoring Organizations of the Treadway Commission (Issue June, p. 16). https://www.coso.org/Documents/2017-COSO-ERM-Integrating-with-Strategy-and-Performance-Executive-Summary.pdf
Dickinson G (2001) Enterprise risk management: Its origins and conceptual foundation. The International Association for the Study of Insurance Economics. Blackwell Publishers, 108 Cowley Road, Oxford OX4 1JF, UK. https://doi.org/10.1111/1468-0440.00121
Ezeosa D (2011) The strategic implications of enterprise risk management: A framework. In: Enterprise risk management symposium, pp. 1–49
Fadun OS (2013) Risk management and risk management failure: Lessons for business enterprises. Int J Acad Res Bus & Soc Sci 3(2):225–239
Florio C, Leoni G (2016) Enterprise risk management and firm performance: The Italian case. Br Account Rev 49(1):56–74. https://doi.org/10.1016/j.bar.2016.08.003
Gompers PA, Ishii JL, Metrick A (2001) Corporate governance and equity prices. Corp GovAnce Corp Financ: Eur Perspect 3:523–556. https://doi.org/10.4324/9780203940136
Gordon LA, Loeb MP, Tseng CY (2009) Enterprise risk management and firm performance: A contingency perspective. J Account Public Policy 28(4):301–327. https://doi.org/10.1016/j.jaccpubpol.2009.06.006
Hoyt RE, Liebenberg AP (2008) The value of enterprise risk management : Evidence from the U.S. Insurance Industry. January, 1–22
Hoyt RE, Liebenberg AP (2011) The value of enterprise risk management. J Risk Insur 78(4):795–822. https://doi.org/10.1111/j.1539-6975.2011.01413.x
Kingsley Karunaratne A (2017) The impact of enterprise risk management on firm performance: Evidence from Sri Lankan banking and finance industry. Int J Bus Manag 13(1):225. https://doi.org/10.5539/ijbm.v13n1p225
La Porta R, Lopez-de-Silanes F, Shleifer A (1998) Law and finance. J Polit Econ 106(6):1113–1155
Lam J (2014) Enterprise risk management: From incentives to controls. John Wiley & Sons, Inc
Liebenberg AP, Hoyt RE (2003) The determinants of enterprise risk management: Evidence From the appointment of chief risk officers. Risk Manag Insur Rev 6(1):37–52. https://doi.org/10.1111/1098-1616.00019
Louisot J-P, Ketcham C (2014) ERM: Enterprise Risk Management KRI: Key Risk Indicator, John Wiley & Sons Inc
Lundqvist SA (2014) An exploratory study of enterprise risk management: Pillars of ERM. J Acc Audit Financ 29(3):393–429. https://doi.org/10.1177/0148558X14535780
Lundqvist SA, Vilhelmsson A (2018) Enterprise risk management and default risk: Evidence from the banking industry. J Risk Insur. https://doi.org/10.1111/jori.12151
Malik MF, Zaman M, Buckby S (2019) Enterprise risk management and firm performance: Role of the risk committee. J Contemp Account Econ 16(1):100178. https://doi.org/10.1016/j.jcae.2019.100178
Martin D, Power M (2007) The end of enterprise risk management. Regulation2point0, August, 1–11
Moeller RR (2007) Coso enterprise risk Management: understanding the new integrated erm framework. Wiley, Hoboken, NJ. https://doi.org/10.1002/9781118269145
Nocco BW, Stulz RM (2006) Enterprise risk management: Theory and practice. J Appl Corp Financ 18(4):8–20. https://doi.org/10.2139/ssrn.921402
Olayinka E, Emoarehi E, Jonah A, Ame, J (2017) Enterprise risk management and financial performance: evidence from emerging market. Int J Manag Account Econ 4(49):937–952
Olson DL, Wu D (2008) New frontiers in enterprise risk management. J Chem Inf Model 53(9). https://doi.org/10.1017/CBO9781107415324.004

Paape L, Speklé RF (2012) The adoption and design of enterprise risk management practices: An empirical study. Eur Account Rev 21(3):533–564. https://doi.org/10.1080/09638180.2012.661937

Pagach DP, Warr RS (2010) The effects of enterprise risk management on firm performance. SSRN Electron J. https://doi.org/10.2139/ssrn.1155218

Prewett K, Terry A (2018) COSO's updated enterprise risk management framework- A quest for depth and clarity. J Corp Account & Financ 29(3):16–23. https://doi.org/10.1002/jcaf.22346

Salaudeen YM, Atoyebi TA, Oyegbile BA (2018) Enterprise risk management and performance of selected listed consumer goods companies in Nigeria. Appl Financ Account 4(1):115. https://doi.org/10.11114/afa.v4i1.2918

Silva JR, da Silva AF, Chan BL (2019) Enterprise risk management and firm value: Evidence from Brazil. Emerg Mark Financ Trade 55(3):687–703. https://doi.org/10.1080/1540496X.2018.1460723

Soliman A, Adam M (2017) Enterprise risk management and firm performance: An integrated model for the banking sector. Banks Bank Syst 12(2):116–123. https://doi.org/10.21511/bbs.12(2).2017.12

Standard & Poor's (2005) Enterprise risk management function in financial institutions. Rating Criteria And Best Practices, November.

Standard & Poor's (2007) A Roadmap For Evaluating Financial Institutions ERM Practices, May, 3

Standard & Poor's (2015) S&P's ERM Framework, May

Tahir IM, Razali AR (2011) The relationship between enterprise risk management (ERM) and firm value: Evidence from Malaysian public listed companies. Int J Econ Manag Sci 1(2):32–41

# Determinants of Bank Profitability in UK on the Eve of the Brexit

**Chris Grose, Aglaia Kanella, Theodoros Kargidis, Mihaela Mocanu, and Theodoros Spyridis**

**Abstract** The paper analyses bank profitability in a sample of UK commercial banks during the period 2007–2018. The models measuring profitability include as dependent variables the Return on Average Assets (ROAA), Return on Average Equity (ROAE) and Net Interest Margin (NIM) while explanatory variables used include a set of internal (bank-specific) and external macroeconomic factors. The results indicate that bank profitability is not only affected by internal-/bank-specific factors, but also affected by macroeconomic indicators. While largely findings corroborate general pertinent literature findings, they provide and up-to-date outlook on bank profitability in the UK on the eve of the Brexit. The findings of the analysis indicate that the size of the banks has a negative role in the profitability due to the existence of economies of scale for the smaller banks and diseconomies for the larger. Additionally, as far as the external macroeconomic factors are concerned, the sign of GDP per capital growth varies and depends on the measurements of profitability. It can be assumed that the macroeconomic factors affects the profitability of the banking sector.

**Keywords** Profitability · Banks · Bank-specific factors · Macroeconomic factors · UK Brexit

**JEL Classification Codes** G20 · G21

C. Grose (✉) · A. Kanella · T. Kargidis
International Hellenic University, Thessaloniki, Greece
e-mail: cgrose@af.ihu.gr

A. Kanella
e-mail: a.kanella@ihu.edu.gr

T. Kargidis
e-mail: kargidis@mkt.teithe.gr

M. Mocanu
Bucharest University of Economic Studies, Bucharest, Romania
e-mail: mihaela.mocanu@cig.ase.ro

T. Spyridis
Independent Authority for Public Revenue, Athens, Greece

 
G. Karanovic et al. (eds.), *The Changing Financial Landscape*, Contributions to Economics, https://doi.org/10.1007/978-3-030-82778-6_11

## 1 Introduction

The banking sector was always deemed to be one of the most vital sectors for the economy in order to be functional. In all economic systems, banks have the leading role in planning and implementing financial policy. During the last decades, it is observed that the banking system constantly has an increased role in each country's economy. Thus, the banks play an important role in the creation of new capital in a country and accordingly enhance the growth process.

There is no doubt that the global financial crisis of 2008 represented a substantial blow to the global economy, leading to wide-ranging and long-lasting consequences. The first phase is clearly represented by the collapse of the US subprime mortgage market, and this was followed by the second stage in which is presented that not only mortgage companies but also investment and universal banks are affected. The third stage was a credit crunch leading to a liquidity crisis, and finally, the subsequent phases were first a commodity price bubble and then the demise of investment banking in the USA as Lehman Brothers filed for bankruptcy protection.

It is well clarified now that the financial institutions bear a tremendous role not only in the performance of the country's economy in which they operate but into the global economy as well. Thus, it is of great importance to investigate further the determinants that affect the performance of banks. The paper focus on the UK commercial banking sector since it is a major financial center in Europe and among the top three banking sectors worldwide after China and the USA, based on tier 1 capital.

There are numerous studies concerning the determinants of bank profitability. Kosmidou et al. (2008) investigate how banks generate their profitability. Profitability strengthens the capital position and places the foundations for future profitability. In order to sustain future growth, projects have to consistently achieve returns greater than the cost of capital. According to Wong et al. (2007) bank performance is driven by leverage, efficiency, earnings and risk-taking. According to the literature, the ROE of banks alone is not an indicator capable of showing which banks are well performing or how sustainable their results will be.

The aim of this paper is to investigate the determinants of bank profitability in the UK and how they have evolved through the period 2007–2018. More specifically, this analysis utilizes the most significant internal (bank-specific) and external determinants. These include capital adequacy, risk management, bank size, liquidity measures and efficiency. Other macroeconomic factors including the long-term interest rates, the gross domestic product per capital growth, and the rate of inflation are also included.

In this context, this paper incorporates the Return on Average Equity (ROAE) and the Return on Average Assets (ROAA) as well as the Net Interest Margin (NIM) in order to evaluate bank profitability. The employed ratios are popular measures by firms' executives. The derivation of the ROAE involves dividing profits after tax or losses to average equity employed. ROAA uses in the denominator average total assets instead. Therefore, the first measures refers to profits made on shareholders' funds while the latter refers to profits attributable to all investors internal and external. Finally, NIM is expressed as the percentage of net interest income over the total earning assets, showing the profitability of the bank's interest-earning business. All metrics use average figures for either equity or assets in an effort to obtain more accurate results, in contradiction to absolute end of year values. The paper employs econometric analysis with the use of balanced panel data in order to determine the profitability and the financial position of banks during the period under investigation.

## 2 Literature Review

The literature on financial performance of banks is extant since it has been a subject of many researchers over the previous years. Early studies about bank profitability include Bourke (1989). The findings on the research of Short (1979) indicate that greater market power has a positive impact on bank's profitability. On the other hand, the study of Bourke (1989) contradicted the results of Short's (1979) aforementioned study, but found a positive relationship between bank's profitability and assets, capital ratios, liquidity ratios and interest rates. These seminal studies are the basis for all the following studies related to the subject of bank's performance.

The studies about bank performance could be easily categorized into two main categories, namely the individual countries analysis and the cross-countries analysis. The first category of studies focuses the analysis on a single country and determines about the profitability and the performance of country's banking sector. On the contrary, the second category performs an analysis on cross-country level, namely investigates the profitability and performance of banking sector in several countries.

The first studies concerning the cross-countries analysis include Short (1979), Bourke (1989) and Molyneux and Thorton (1992). Short (1979) conducted an analysis in sixty banks in Canada, Western Europe and Japan, in order to determine the relationship between the profit rates and concentration in the nationwide banking system of the previous countries. The findings indicate that, the market power has a positive influence in the bank's profit rates and on the contrary the concentration has an insignificant effect in the reduction of profit rates.

Bourke (1989) used a sample of 90 banks, in twelve countries or territories in order to examine the determinants of international bank profitability. The research findings indicate that there is a positive correlation between liquidity risk and bank profitability. During the same period, Molyneux and Thorton (1992) examined the determinants of bank performance throughout eighteen European countries among the years 1986 and 1989. The findings indicate that European banks have a positive relationship between capital adequacy and bank's profitability. Moreover, the same positive correlation found with profitability and interest rates. Furthermore, the study indicates that there is a positive relationship between government ownership and bank profitability, meaning that state-owned banks tent to be more profitable rather than their competitors in the private sector.

Demirgüç-Kunt and Huizinga (1999) examined the determinants of bank profitability and interest margins by employing a sample of 80 countries throughout the years 1988–1995. Their research differentiates from the previous since they incorporate determinants such as tax variables, ownership variables, and financial structure, legal and institutional variables that have never been used in the earlier studies. Their findings suggest that there is a positive relationship between capitalization and profitability, meaning that well-capitalized bank have more equity and as a result less need for external funding. Moreover, Demirgüç-Kunt and Huizinga (1999) stated that foreign banks in developing countries have higher interest margins and higher profitability than the domestic banks. The inverse result is found for foreign banks that operate in industrial countries. Finally, the research indicates that macroeconomic factors, such as GDP, inflation and interest rates, have a positive impact on bank's profitability.

Athanasoglou et al. (2006) conducted a research about bank-specific, industry related and macroeconomic factors, in order to determine about the profitability of the banks in the South Eastern European Region. Their results indicate that the internal factors or bank-specific determinants have a significant impact on profitability in the expected way, with only exception the liquidity, which has a negative relationship. Moreover, concentration is positively related with bank profitability. Finally the research concludes that regarding the macroeconomic factors, inflation has a positive impact on profitability, while the GDP per capital seems to have an insignificant relationship with bank's profitability.

More recently Adelopo et al. (2018) conducted a research on the determinants of bank profitability before, during and after the financial crisis. The sample of the study consisted of 123 commercial banks worldwide, and the period under investigation was 1999–2013. The results of the study show that internal factors affect the profitability the profitability of banks. Moreover, the paper indicates that the banks remain profitable even in the period of financial crisis. With respect to macroeconomic factors, the GDP growth had a positive relationship with bank profitability before and during the financial crisis, but this relationship transformed to insignificant after the financial crisis. Finally, the inflation and profitability have a relationship that changes during the different periods under investigation.

As far as single-country analysis is concerned, the literature investigates profitability determinants on a single-country level. Mamatzakis and Remoundos (2003) performed a study on the determinants of profitability of the commercial banks in Greece during the period 1989–2000. The results show that the loan-to-asset ratio has a positive relationship with profitability, as well as the ratio of equity-to-assets. Moreover, the paper indicates that there is a negative relationship between personnel expenses and bank profitability.

Athanasoglou et al. (2008) performed a research on bank-specific, industry-specific and macroeconomic determinants that affect the profitability of Greek banks in the period 1985–2001. The outcome results argue that operating costs have a negative relationship with profitability which indicates that bank management decisions about costs is of crucial importance. Moreover, credit risk has a negative impact on profitability of the banks. Their work concludes that macroeconomic factors have a positive impact on bank's profitability.

Kosmidou (2008) examined the determinants of bank profitability in Greece during the period of EU financial integration (1990–2002). The findings indicate that well-capitalized banks tend to be more profitable. Moreover, lower cost-to-income ratio points out that there is an efficient expenses management which leads to higher profitability. Size and GDP also have a positive impact on profitability.

Dietrich and Wanzenried (2010) examined the determinants of bank profitability in Switzerland during the time period 1999–2009. The authors divide the sample into pre-crisis period (1999–2006) and crisis period (2007–2009). The results show that efficient banks tend to display higher profitability. Moreover, banks with great dependence on interest income perform lower in accordance to profitability. The same negative impact on profitability is observed with funding costs.

Trujillo-Ponce (2012) conducted a research on the determinants of profitability in Spanish banks during the period 1999–2009. The outcome of the study indicates that deposits and loans are the main determinants of Spanish banks profitability with a significant positive impact. Moreover, well-capitalized banks tend to be more profitable and also the efficiency factor leads to higher profits. In the end, all the external variables under investigation tend to have an impact on profitability.

Lastly, Yao et al. (2018) conducted a research on the profitability determinants of the financial institution in Pakistan. The data consisted of 28 banks, and the period under investigation was 2007–2016. The results indicate that there is an inverse relationship between profitability and bank size. Moreover, the paper reports that factors such as high solvency, financial structure labor, market power, operating costs and economic growth have a positive impact on bank profitability.

Numerous studies have studied the impact of financial crisis on the profitability of banks. Xiao (2009) investigated French banks in the middle of the crisis in order to determine their performance during the period 2006–2008. The findings support that French banks managed to perform considerably well. The reasons underlined behind this performance are the well diversified business cycle, the funding and the geographical position.

Finally, Erfani and Vasigh (2018) performed a research on the profitability of the Islamic banking sector and the impact from the financial crisis. The period under examination was 2006–2013. The findings indicated that Islamic banks remained unaffected from the global financial crisis. Finally, under the period of examination, the outcomes indicated that Islamic banks tend to be more efficient and solvent in comparison with the commercial banks.

## 3 Research Methodology and Data

In this section, we present our research methodology. In accordance with previous studies that examined the determinants of bank's profitability, the analysis we performed includes the use of variables Return on Average Assets (ROAA), Return on Average Equity (ROAE) and Net Interest Margin (NIM). The first one, return on average assets (ROAA) is calculated as net profits after tax divided by average total assets. This measure has a crucial importance in comparing the operating performance of banks, and the use of average value controls for differences that occur in assets during the fiscal year (Kosmidou et al. 2008). In addition, the variable has a fundamental role in comparing operational performance and efficiency because it takes into account returns gained from assets financed by financial institution.

Another measure that is employed is the return on average equity (ROAE), which is defined as net income over the average shareholder's equity. The average value of shareholder's equity is used in order to capture any differences in the equity value during the fiscal year. This financial ratio points out the profitability of a financial institution or corporation by illustrating the percentage of profit that was generated compared shareholders invested money. The final dependent variable used as a measure of profitability is net interest margin (NIM) which is expressed as the percentage of net interest income over the total earnings, showing the profitability of the bank's interest-earning business.

Six bank characteristics are used as internal determinants of performance and more specifically the natural logarithm of bank's total assets (LNSIZE) for measuring the size of the bank and net loans to total assets (LTA) as liquidity ratio. Moreover, as a capital adequacy ratio the equity to total assets (ETA) is used, while the cost-to-income ratio (CIR) is used for evaluating the efficiency of bank's management, and finally loan loss reserves to gross loans (LOSRES), and loan loss provision to net interest revenue (LOSPROV) are used for measuring the credit risk and asset quality.

Analyzing further the previous ratios, starting with the first one, the independent variable of bank's total assets (LNSIZE), this determinant is used in the form of natural logarithm of bank's total assets in order to minimize the scale effect as used in previous studies (Athanasoglou et al. 2006). Bank size as a determinant of profitability is an ambiguous variable. Many studies (e.g., Laeven et al. 2016; Flamini et al. 2009) suggest that there is a positive relationship between bank size and profitability through economies of scale. Those asserting in favor of a positive relationship imply that larger banks operate more efficiently with lower costs than a smaller bank. Moreover, Kosmidou et al. (2008) mentioned that through economies of scope, which result in loan and product diversification, larger banks have access to markets that small banks cannot.

Net loans to total assets (LTA) is a ratio for measuring the liquidity. This ratio indicates how much of the total assets of the bank are tied up in loans. The higher this ratio indicates a bank is loaned up and its liquidity is low. Moreover the higher the ratio, the more risky a bank may be to higher defaults. The next internal determinant of profitability is equity to total assets (ETA) and is considered to be one of the major ratios for measuring capital strength. The ratio of equity to total assets (ETA) is incorporated in the regression model as a proxy for capital adequacy. The next determinant is the cost-to-income ratio (CIR) and is used as a proxy for measure the efficiency of banks. Cost-to-income ratio is important for determining the profitability of a bank.

The final two ratios, loan loss provision to net interest revenue (LOSPROV) and loan loss reserves to gross loans (LOSRES), are measures of credit risk and assets quality. Provision for loan losses and a bank's loan loss reserve signify the amount of funds that management allocates to cover potential losses. In the same notion, the ratio of loan loss reserves to gross loans (LOSRES) is a reserve of losses expressed as a percentage of total loans. It measures the asset quality of the bank and indicates how much of the total portfolio have provided for but not written-off (Kosmidou et al. 2008). A high ratio is an indicator for poor loan quality which as a result implies higher risk.

There are also some external macroeconomic factors that have an impact on bank's profitability. Macroeconomic factors are determinants that are related to economic, industrial and legal environments that are out of a bank's control (Ongore and Kusa 2013). In this study, three macroeconomic factors are included, the gross domestic product per capital growth (GDPPCGR), the inflation rate (INFL) and the long-term interest rate (IR), respectively.

The gross domestic product per capital growth rate is a commonly used macroeconomic determinant. GDP per capital is a metric that breaks down a country's GDP per person. GDP as well as GDP per capital growth rate are indicators of the state of the cycle of economy and is expected to have an impact on the demand for banks loans (Kosmidou et al. 2008). Dermirguc-Kunt and Huizinga (1998) found a positive correlation between bank's profitability and business cycle. Moreover Abreu and Mendes (2002) argued that GDP per capital had a positive impact on bank's profitability. Thus, the expected outcome from this study is a positive correlation among bank's profitability and the macroeconomic factor GDPPCGR.

Another macroeconomic factor that affects bank's profitability is the inflation rate. The inflation rate has a significant impact on interest rates of the bank. The final macroeconomic factor is the long-term interest rate which is used as a proxy for measuring bank's profitability. The interest rate is an important macroeconomic factor which has a positive correlation with country's economic growth. Molyneux and Thorton (1992), as well as Demirgüç-Kunt and Huizinga (1999), found that there is a positive relationship between the interest rate and the performance of the bank due to a favorable economic environment.

In this paper, the data were obtained from two main sources; the first one is the Bankscope Database of Bureau Van Dijk's company, and the second was the official annual reports of certain UK banks as they stated in their Websites. For the macroeconomic factors that are also included in the analysis, the information was collected from the Bank of England and the World Bank database.

In order to form the sample, the banks selected had to meet some conditions in the Bankscope Database, namely: firstly, they had to be active. Secondly they have to be classified as commercial banks in the Bankscope Database. Thirdly, they have to be UK-owned banks, and the forth condition is to have available annual balance sheet and income statements for the period under investigation, which is the years between 2007 and 2018. After the implementation of the aforementioned criteria and some limitations with the available data, the final sample consists of 32 commercial, active UK banks. Also, this yielded to a balanced panel data of 32 commercial banks, constituting of 385 observations.

Descriptive statistics are presented in Table 1 and are expressed in their initial form as percentages and billions of US$ dollars, respectively.

Continuing with the analysis, it is of high importance to perform a correlation analysis in order to acquire the main idea of how the independent variables are correlated with each other and if there is an indication of high correlation that could affect the results. The following table (Table 2) presents the correlation between the independent variables of the sample.

It is observed that the independent variables have a low degree of correlation that is not exceeding the absolute value of 0.30. The highlighted cells present the highest correlation among the variables. The highest correlation is observed between the inflation (INFL) and the interest rates (IR) which is 0.36 as well as among gross domestic product per capital growth (GDPPCGR) and the interest rate which in absolute values is 0.31. Finally, the natural logarithm of bank's assets (LNSIZE) and the equity-to-loans ratio (ETA) shows a negative correlation around 0.30.

Based on the previous studies of the determinants of profitability in banks, we use a similar approach with three dependent variables, namely Return on Average Assets (ROAA), Return on Average Equity (ROAE) and Net Interest Margin (NIM) and nine bank-specific and macroeconomic factors (LNSIZE, LTA, ETA, LOSRES, LOSPROV, CIR, GDPPCGR, INFL and IR) which had already been analyzed in depth earlier. For the performance of the models, panel data analysis appears to be the most suitable.

In order to determine the profitability of UK banks and the impact of internal and external factors, the following regression model is employed:

$$\begin{aligned}\text{ROAA}_{it} &= c + \delta_t + a_1\text{LNSIZE}_{it} + a_2\text{LTA}_{it} + a_3\text{ETA}_{it} + a_4\text{LOSRES}_{it} \\ &\quad + a_5\text{LOSPROV}_{it} + a_6\text{CIR}_{it} + a_7\text{GDPPCGR}_{it} + a_8\text{INFL}_{it} + a_9\text{IR}_{it} + \varepsilon_{it}\end{aligned} \tag{1}$$

$$\begin{aligned}\text{ROAE}_{it} &= c + \delta_t + a_1\text{LNSIZE}_{it} + a_2\text{LTA}_{it} + a_3\text{ETA}_{it} + a_4\text{LOSRES}_{it} \\ &\quad + a_5\text{LOSPROV}_{it} + a_6\text{CIR}_{it} + a_7\text{GDPPCGR}_{it} + a_8\text{INFL}_{it} + a_9\text{IR}_{it} + \varepsilon_{it}\end{aligned} \tag{2}$$

$$\begin{aligned}\text{NIM}_{it} &= c + \delta_t + a_1\text{LNSIZE}_{it} + a_2\text{LTA}_{it} + a_3\text{ETA}_{it} + a_4\text{LOSRES}_{it} \\ &\quad + a_5\text{LOSPROV}_{it} + a_6\text{CIR}_{it} + a_7\text{GDPPCGR}_{it} + a_8\text{INFL}_{it} + a_9\text{IR}_{it} + \varepsilon_{it}\end{aligned} \tag{3}$$

where $i$ denotes the bank and $t$ the year.

In the Appendix, we include further testing for the validity of the employed models. Moving on with the analysis, each of the aforementioned models is tested in order to determine whether it is more suitable to apply fixed or random effects model. In order to decide which the preferred model is, Hausman test is performed in each of the cases. The null hypothesis (Ho) on Hausman test is that the random

**Table 1** Descriptive statistics for the period 2007–2018

| | ROAA | ROAE | NIM | LNSIZE | LTA | ETA | CIR | LOSRES | LOSPROV | GDPPCGR | INFL | IR |
|---|---|---|---|---|---|---|---|---|---|---|---|---|
| Mean | 1.04 | 10.40 | 1.97 | 9.97 | 59.97 | 8.68 | 110.07 | 5.52 | 39.00 | 0.51 | 2.19 | 2.74 |
| Median | 0.46 | 7.19 | 1.69 | 10.07 | 54.02 | 6.46 | 69.71 | 1.64 | 15.24 | 0.99 | 2.19 | 2.48 |
| Maximum | 33.85 | 205.93 | 13.46 | 14.69 | 96.20 | 162.54 | 12,923.24 | 672.01 | 1757.17 | 2.18 | 3.60 | 5.01 |
| Minimum | −9.89 | −222.50 | −0.22 | 3.52 | 0.12 | 0.60 | 4.88 | 0.05 | −578.24 | −4.97 | 0.50 | 1.24 |
| Std. Dev | 3.24 | 31.72 | 1.52 | 2.67 | 21.13 | 12.00 | 657.47 | 34.83 | 127.09 | 1.82 | 0.89 | 1.22 |
| Skewness | 6.07 | 1.10 | 3.49 | −0.35 | −0.31 | 9.10 | 19.35 | 18.36 | 8.15 | −2.21 | −0.44 | 0.48 |
| Kurtosis | 59.28 | 20.79 | 21.51 | 2.53 | 2.46 | 103.37 | 377.63 | 350.95 | 102.57 | 6.97 | 2.53 | 2.00 |
| Jarque–Bera | 53,034.23 | 5141.57 | 6258.19 | 11.29 | 10.88 | 166,501 | 2,269,526.00 | 1,958,639 | 162,869.4 | 564.52 | 15.97 | 30.62 |
| Observations | 384 | 384 | 384 | 384 | 384 | 384 | 384 | 384 | 384 | 384 | 384 | 384 |

**Table 2** Correlation matrix for the independent variables

| | LNSIZE | LTA | ETA | LOSRES | LOSPROV | CIR | GDPPCGR | INFL | ***IR*** |
|---|---|---|---|---|---|---|---|---|---|
| LNSIZE | 1 | | | | | | | | |
| LTA | 0.080235 | 1 | | | | | | | |
| ETA | −0.30855 | −0.24835 | 1 | | | | | | |
| LOSRES | −0.14409 | −0.16183 | 0.062453 | 1 | | | | | |
| LOSPROV | 0.082163 | 0.029886 | −0.04495 | 0.004149 | 1 | | | | |
| CIR | −0.0301 | −0.0878 | 0.016564 | 0.006669 | 0.049406 | 1 | | | |
| GDPPCGR | −0.0175 | 0.005223 | 0.061821 | 0.004941 | −0.10284 | −0.03796 | 1 | | |
| INFL | 0.009171 | −0.04611 | −0.05135 | 0.031469 | 0.144516 | 0.045035 | −0.211 | 1 | |
| IR | 0.008135 | −0.01969 | −0.17258 | −0.02989 | 0.120976 | 0.067968 | −0.31335 | 0.368191 | 1 |

effects model is consistent and efficient, while the alternative hypothesis (Ha) simply indicates that the null is not true and thus fixed effects model is appropriate. If the p value is statistically significant, that is less than 5%, the null hypothesis is rejected and random effects model is not appropriate. In accordance to this hypothesis analysis, the suitable model for its regression is selected.

Furthermore, in order to test the significance of each model (expect for the case of NIM where random effects is the suitable model), the redundant fixed effects–likelihood ratio is performed. The importance of this ratio is to clarify the significance of the use of fixed effects. The results of this test display that the p value is significant in both models and as a consequence the null hypothesis that the cross-sectional effects are redundant is rejected and a pooled sample could not be employed.

Performing an OLS regression with the presence of heteroskedasticity is pretty usual, but there is a high possibility the coefficient estimations to be consistent and unbiased but with biased standard errors. Implementing the technique of robust standard errors, in models, will obtain unbiased standard errors of OLS coefficients. In order to achieve robust models, we conduct the White cross-sectional coefficient covariance method.

Finally, in order to check, for the presence of multicollinearity in the models the Variance Inflation Factor (VIF) has been employed. VIF displays how much the variance of a regression coefficient is inflated because of the existence of multicollinearity. The rule indicates that when VIF is 1, there is no correlation, between 1 and 5 they are moderately correlated, and for cases exceeding 5, there is a highly correlation. In this study, the outcomes indicate that there is not multicollinearity among the explanatory variables.

## 4 Results and Discussion

This section of the paper demonstrates the empirical results of the panel data analysis. Moreover, it explains the outcomes in order to determine the factors that affect the profitability of commercial banks in UK during the period 2007–2018. The tables below illustrate the findings as they are obtained after performing best fitted model for each of the dependent variables.

Table 3 below presents the regression analysis of the first model with dependent variable the Return on Assets (ROAA) and all the other factors as explanatory variables. The appropriate model of estimation for ROAA is the fixed effects model. First of all, it can be observed that R squared which is the percentage of variance explained by the model is high enough, approximately at 57%. Moreover, the F-statistics of 11.27 displays that the regression is statistically significant.

The variable LNSIZE has a significant negative impact on bank's profitability. This negative relationship indicates that larger banks tend to have lower profitability. Furthermore, this finding is in accordance with previous studies which found economies of scale for smaller banks or diseconomies for the larger ones. The ratio of loan loss provisions to net interest revenue (LOSPROV) has a negative correlation

**Table 3** Regression analysis: dependent variable ROAA

| ROAA (FE) | | | |
|---|---|---|---|
| Independent variables | Coefficient | Std. error | *p* value |
| LNSIZE | −0.6204329 | 0.1145578 | 0.000*** |
| LTA | −0.0510808 | 0.0098327 | 0.000*** |
| ETA | 0.0041198 | 0.0098327 | 0.733 |
| LOSRES | 0.0004075 | 0.0036064 | 0.0393** |
| LOSPROV | −0.0031135 | 0.0009876 | 0.006*** |
| CIR | −0.0004496 | 0.0001872 | 0.019*** |
| GDPPCGR | −0.0734935 | 0.0684265 | 0.0399** |
| INFL | 0.0350577 | 0.1450389 | 0.809 |
| IR | 0.4625361 | 0.1102192 | 0.000*** |
| Constant | 8.738548 | 1.338758 | 0.000*** |
| R^2 | 57.45% | | |
| Prob. (F) | 0.0000 | | |
| F-stat | 11.27 | | |

with ROAA. The same negative relationship holds among the loans to asset ratio and the ROAA, which highlights that, there is also a negative impact on profitability from the liquidity risk. Credit risk has a positive correlation with profitability, as it is observed, by the employed ratio of loan loss reserves to gross loans in the analysis. On the other hand, cost-to-income ratio has a significant negative correlation with profitability when the dependent variable of the regression is ROAA. The variable of equity to assets fails to explain the dependent variable.

As for the macroeconomic factors, GDP per capital growth has a negative impact on profitability. The inflation rates show no significant correlation with ROAA. Finally, interest rates variable has a significant positive relationship with bank's profitability, which is an indication of a diversification of the banking products.

The following table (Table 4) has as dependent variable the return on equity (ROAE) and again all the other variables as explained indicators. In line with the previous analysis, the most suitable model for the regression is the fixed effects model. Similarly, with the previous analysis, in this model, the variable of bank's assets (LNSIZE) has a significant negative relationship with the bank profits. From the credit risk side, LOSPROV has again a negative correlation with ROAE and as a result with profitability. Nonetheless, in this model, LOSRES fails to explain the dependent variable. The internal determinant of cost-to-income ratio has again as expected, a negative impact on the banking profitability.

Moving on to the macroeconomic factors, only the interest rate has again a strong and significant positive correlation with the dependent variable of the model (ROAE). Conclusively, GDP per capital growth, as well as the inflation rate, has an insignificant relationship with the performance of banks.

The final m(Table 5) has as dependent variable, the net interest margin (NIM). It can be observed that the variable of LNSIZE, which indicates the bank's size,

**Table 4** Regression analysis: dependent variable ROAE

| ROAE(FE) | | | |
|---|---|---|---|
| Independent variables | Coefficient | Std. error | *p* value |
| LNSIZE | −10.01739 | 2.243778 | 0.000*** |
| LTA | −0.5487636 | 0.1161247 | 0.000*** |
| ETA | −0.416443 | 0.1236612 | 0.737 |
| LOSRES | 0.0158348 | 0.0362713 | 0.663 |
| LOSPROV | −0.0248735 | 0.0099833 | 0.013 |
| CIR | −0.0042474 | 0.0018793 | 0.024 |
| GDPPCGR | −0.9589975 | 0.6846045 | 0.162 |
| INFL | −0.0273896 | 1.450677 | 0.985 |
| IR | 5.133822 | 1.101926 | 0.000*** |
| Constant | 127.5713 | 22.13668 | 0.000*** |
| R^2 | 53.00% | | |
| Prob. (F) | 0.0000 | | |
| F-stat | 11.27 | | |

**Table 5** Regression analysis: dependent variable NIM

| NIM (RE) | | | |
|---|---|---|---|
| Independent variables | Coefficient | Std. error | *p* value |
| LNSIZE | −0.09753 | 0.076888 | 0.052** |
| LTA | 0.028777 | 0.003996 | 0.0000 |
| ETA | 0.001823 | 0.005935 | 0.7589 |
| LOSRES | −0.0005832 | 0.000856 | 0.496** |
| LOSPROV | −0.0003256 | 0.000164 | 0.0485*** |
| CIR | 0.0000386 | 0.0000186 | 0.0383*** |
| GDPPCGR | 0.0153298 | 0.006304 | 0.0155** |
| INFL | −0.1187067 | 0.036735 | 0.0013** |
| IR | −0.0695401 | 0.028965 | 0.0168** |
| Constant | 1.860977 | 0.773828 | 0.0167*** |
| R^2 | 24.23% | | |
| Prob. (F) | 0.0000 | | |
| F-stat | 13.29 | | |

has again negative relationship with the banking performance. In contrast to the previous models, loans to assets ratio shows a positive correlation with NIM which indicates better banking performance. Additionally, LOSRES and ETA have an insignificant impact on the performance of the banks. The bank-specific ratio of cost-to-income has a positive relationship with NIM, which means that efficiency in expenses management has an impact on banking performance.

As for the macroeconomic factors of the model, in this case, GDP per capital growth has a significant positive impact on profitability. This relationship confirms the hypothesis that there is positive linkage between the growth and the financial sector. On the other hand, the inflation and the interest rate have a negative correlation with the NIM and as a result with the performance of banks.

## 5 Conclusion

This paper examined the determinants of bank profitability in the years 2007–2018. For this reason, a set of internal (bank-specific) and external, macroeconomics factors are employed. The measures of the profitability are ROAA, ROAE and NIM, in accordance with the existing literature. It can be deduced that the results of the paper are in line with those expected, as well as with the prior literature review on the topic of the bank performance and profitability.

The findings of the analysis indicate that the size of the banks has a negative role in the profitability due to the existence of economies of scale for the smaller banks and diseconomies for the larger ones. With respect to liquidity, the impact is not clear and depends on the measure of profitability. More precisely, liquidity is negatively associated with ROAA and ROAE and positively with NIM. On the contrary, credit risk and especially LOSRES have a positive correlation with ROAA and ROAE, but as for the NIM, the relationship is inverse. In addition, the variable of credit risk which is employed in this model holds a negative impact with all the measurements of profitability. The efficiency indicator cost-to-income has negative relationship with ROAA and ROAE, which displays the importance of the cost efficiency management in the UK's banking sector. In the case of NIM, the relationship is positive but slightly insignificant. Additionally, as for the external macroeconomic factors, the sign of GDP per capital growth varies and depends on the measurements of profitability.

The derived results could prove useful in the formation of strategic policies on the part of financial institutions and regulators. Bank profitability matters for financial stability. Profits are the first line of defence against losses from credit impairment. Retained earnings are an important source of capital, enabling banks to build strong buffers to absorb additional losses. Those buffers ensure that banks are able to provide financial services to households and businesses, even in the face of adverse developments, thereby smoothing rather than amplifying the impact of negative shocks on the real economy. Therefore, the UK banking system on the eve of the Brexit appears to be lying on solid ground. Banking authorities can ensure the smooth transformation of the local banking system in one where institutions are less dependent on business with the European Union countries.

The present paper does not lack limitations. Data unavailability reduced the sample. At the same time, the study investigates profitability determinants on the eve of the Brexit. In this respect, we cannot claim that we have any clear clue of the actual impact of either the looming ahead Brexit or the event itself currently experienced.

Further research on the subject could incorporate industry-specific variables such as concentration ratio and banks' ownership or variables related to quality measures of banks such as managerial skills. Moreover, an expansion on the time span could enhance the validity of the results and capture the more significant events of the past. Similarly, a research could incorporate an investigation on the impact of the Brexit, the recent UK's decision to leave the European Union, and how this is affecting and will affect further the banking system. This further line of research will enable scholars to see how EU membership affects the profitability of the banking sector and how this in turn could prove a deterrent in sustainable economic growth.

# Appendix

See Tables 6, 7, 8, 9, 10.

**Table 6** Hausman test ROAA

| Hausman test | | |
|---|---|---|
| Test summary | Chi sq. statistics | Prob. |
| Cross-sectional random | 0.0011 | 27.65 |

**Table 7** Hausman test NIM

| Hausman test | | |
|---|---|---|
| Test summary | Chi sq. statistics | Prob. |
| Cross-sectional random | 8.11 | 0.5228 |

**Table 8** Redundant fixed effects tests ROAA

| Redundant fixed effects tests | | | |
|---|---|---|---|
| Test cross-sectional fixed effects | | | |
| Effects test | Statistics | d.f | Prob. |
| Cross-sectional F | 9.417371 | −31.343 | 0.0000 |
| Cross-sectional $\chi^2$ | 236.466322 | 31 | 0.0000 |

**Table 9** Redundant fixed effects tests ROAE

| Redundant fixed effects tests | | | |
|---|---|---|---|
| Test cross-sectional fixed effects | | | |
| Effects test | Statistics | d.f | Prob. |
| Cross-sectional F | 8.541177 | −31.343 | 0.0000 |
| Cross-sectional $\chi^2$ | 219.677464 | 31 | 0.0000 |

**Table 10** Variance inflator factor

| Variable | VIF |
|---|---|
| IR | 1.29 |
| ETA | 1.21 |
| INFL | 1.19 |
| LNSIZE | 1.14 |
| GDPPCGR | 1.13 |
| LTA | 1.11 |
| LOSRES | 1.05 |
| LOSPROV | 1.04 |
| CIR | 1.02 |

# References


Abreu M, Mendes V (2002) Commercial bank interest margins and profitability: evidence from E.U countries. Porto Working paper series

Adelopo I, Lloydking R, Tauringana V (2018) Determinants of bank profitability before, during, and after the financial crisis. Int J Manag Financ 14(4):378–398

Athanasoglou P, Brissimis S, Delis M (2008) Bank-specific, industry-specific and macroeconomic determinants of bank profitability. J Int Finan Markets Inst Money 18(2):121–136

Athanasoglou P, Delis M, Staikouras C (2006) Determinants of bank profitability in the South Eastern European region. Working Papers 47, Bank of Greece

Bourke P (1989) Concentration and other determinants of bank profitability in Europe, North America and Australia. J Bank Finance 13(1):65–79

Demirgüç-Kunt A, Huizinga H (1999) Determinants of commercial bank interest margins and profitability: Some international evidence. World Bank Econ Rev 13(2):379–408

Dietrich A, Wanzenried G (2010) Determinants of bank profitability before and during the crisis: Evidence from Switzerland. J Int Finan Markets Inst Money 21(3):307–327

Erfani G, Vasigh B (2018) The impact of the global financial crisis on profitability of the banking industry: A comparative analysis. Economies 6(4):66

Flamini V, Schumacher L, McDonald C (2009) The determinants of commercial bank profitability in sub-Saharan Africa. IMF Working Papers 9(15): 1

Kosmidou K (2008) The determinants of banks' profits in Greece during the period of EU financial integration. Manag Financ 34(3):146–159

Kosmidou K, Tanna S, Pasiouras F (2008) Determinants of profitability of domestic UK commercial banks: panel evidence from the period 1995–2002. Economics finance and accounting applied research working paper series no. RP08-4. Coventry University, Coventry

Laeven L, Ratnovski L, Tong H (2016) Bank size, capital, and systemic risk: Some international evidence. J Bank Finance 69:S25–S34

Mamatzakis EC, Remoundos PC (2003) Determinants of Greek commercial banks profitability 1989–2000. Spoudai 53(1):84–94

Molyneux P, Thorton J (1992) The determinants of European bank profitability. J Bank Finance 16(6):1173–1178

Ongore OV, Kusa BG (2013) Determinants of Financial performance of commercial banks in Kenya. Int J Econ Financ Issues 3(1):237–252

Short BK (1979) The relation between commercial bank profit rates and banking concentration in Canada, Western Europe, and Japan. J Bank Finance 3(3):209–219

Trujillo-Ponce A (2012) What determines the profitability of banks? Evidence from Spain. Account & Financ 53(2):561–586

Wong J, Fong T, Wong E, Choi K (2007) Determinants of the performance of banks in Hong Kong. Hong Kong Monetary Authority Working Paper 06/2007

Xiao Y (2009) French banks amid the global financial crisis. No. 09/201. International Monetary Fund

Yao H, Haris M, Tariq G (2018) Profitability determinants of financial institutions: Evidence from banks in Pakistan. Int J Financ Stud 6(2):53

# Efficiency and Productivity of Islamic Banking Industry by Using DEA Method: A Literature Review

**Dario Maradin, Stella Suljić Nikolaj, and Bojana Olgić Draženović**

**Abstract** Efficient and smooth performance of the banking sector is very important for the functioning of the financial system of an economy as it affects economic stability and growth. Along with conventional banking systems, Islamic banks are playing an increasingly important role and have become an essential part of the financial structure of many Muslim and non-Muslim countries. Accordingly, efficiency and productivity measurement of Islamic banks has a great importance in scientific research. Based on the literature review, this paper analyzes two concepts of performance evaluation—efficiency and productivity of Islamic banking sector using Data Envelopment Analysis method. As a nonparametric scientific method, DEA together with Malmquist total factor productivity index has become one of the most widely used methods to evaluate the relative efficiency and productivity of various financial institutions, including Islamic banks. The purpose of this paper is to present the most important studies on performance management of banking sector in Islamic countries. We have conducted a comprehensive literature review on the methodology and studies on measuring bank performance with emphasis on DEA method. The results of the efficiency and productivity assessment of the Islamic banking sector show a range of inputs and outputs used in DEA models, their relative efficiency results and productivity changes. This paper provides the basis for further empirical research of the relative efficiency or productivity growth of the Islamic banking sector.

**Keywords** Efficiency measurement · Islamic banks · DEA method

**JEL Classification Codes** G21 · C61 · D24

D. Maradin (✉) · S. Suljić Nikolaj · B. Olgić Draženović
Faculty of Economics and Business, University of Rijeka, Ivana Filipovića 4, Rijeka, Croatia
e-mail: dario.maradin@efri.hr

S. Suljić Nikolaj
e-mail: stella.suljic.nikolaj@efri.hr

B. Olgić Draženović
e-mail: bojana.olgic.drazenovic@efri.hr

 
G. Karanovic et al. (eds.), *The Changing Financial Landscape*, Contributions to Economics, https://doi.org/10.1007/978-3-030-82778-6_12

# 1 Introduction

Efficient and smooth performance of the banking sector is very important for the functioning of the financial system of an economy as it affects improvement in the level of profitability, better prices and quality of services to consumers, larger volumes of funds intermediated and ultimately economic stability and growth. As a measure of banking performance, the evaluation of efficiency and productivity has been intensively carried out in different countries, for both the conventional and Islamic banking systems, especially during the period associated with financial crises. Most studies on banking performance focused on the conventional banking system and paid little attention to Islamic banks, which are an essential part of the financial structure in many Muslim and non-Muslim countries.

The Islamic banking system can be defined as a banking system whose principles underlying its operations and activities are based on Islamic or Syariah principles. Despite its humble beginnings, the Islamic banking system today has become more competitive compared to the conventional banking system, although the size of a typical Islamic bank is much smaller than that of a conventional bank. Given the rapid development of the Islamic banking sector, it is expected that the performance of Islamic banks has become the focus of all stakeholders of Islamic banks, i.e., managers, policy makers, regulators, etc. (Kamarudin et al. 2019).

Therefore, the purpose of this paper is to present the most important studies on performance management of banking sector in Islamic countries. We conducted a comprehensive literature review on the methodology and studies on measuring bank performance with emphasis on the DEA method. The results obtained from the efficiency and productivity evaluation of the Islamic banking sector show a number of inputs and outputs used in DEA models, mostly applied by the intermediation approach, and their relative efficiency results and productivity changes.

# 2 Methodology and Approaches in Evaluation of Islamic Banking Sector

The performance evaluation of the Islamic banking sector is mainly conducted in terms of efficiency or productivity as well as stability, asset quality, business model or orientation, etc. The term efficiency refers to the efficient use of available resources. Applied to the banking sector, this term shows how banks efficiently use the inputs they possess to maximize their potential outputs (Mansour and El Moussawi 2020). The relative efficiency of banks or their productivity improvements can be considered very important for the normal functioning of the financial system. Moreover, efficiency can usually have a great impact on the banking stability. It is also becoming increasingly clear that efficiency is an important factor in terms of market power and risk. Different levels of efficiency can affect banks' capital, leverage and risk decisions. Theoretically, it is known that increased competition should increase the efficiency of firms or banks (Kasman and Carvallo 2014).

Two concepts of efficiency are distinguished in the literature (Farrell 1957): technical efficiency (which is related to productive efficiency) and allocative (or cost) efficiency. Efficiency can refer to a specific/fixed level of outputs given a minimum level of inputs or to maximizing outputs given an existing level of inputs. Efficiency can be assumed to be input or output oriented. While efficiency refers to the operation of business units with the current level of technological development, productivity implies a change in technology over time. In economic literature, Total Factor Productivity (TFP) refers to growth in output that cannot be explained by changes in the quantity of inputs. A change in TFP may be the result of an improvement in efficiency or technology. TFP is measured by productivity indices or productivity indicators. The Malmquist TFP index is the most commonly used measure of productivity change (Casu et al. 2004).

In addition, there are two main approaches to measuring banking efficiency: a parametric approach and a nonparametric approach. The parametric approach, such as Stochastic Frontier Analysis (SFA), is concerned with the specification and econometric estimation of a statistical or parametric function, while the nonparametric method provides a linear boundary by enveloping the experimental data points, known as Data Envelopment Analysis—DEA (Yudistira 2004). The original DEA model as originally presented by Charnes et al. (1978)—CCR model measures relative efficiency assuming constant returns to scale, which was later extended with the BCC model (Banker et al. 1984) to allow for variable returns to scale. DEA method avoids distributional assumptions by using linear programming techniques to estimate frontiers connecting the input/output requirements of the efficient units. In this method, there is no random error, i.e., all variances that cannot be attributed to inputs or outputs are considered inefficiencies. In contrast to the nonparametric approach DEA, the parametric SFA method, attributed to Aigner et al. (1977) and Meeusen and van den Broeck (1977), takes into account deviations from the frontier (error term) that do not fully capture the inefficiency problem, but are also caused by capturing aspects of statistical noise, measurement errors or lucky factors (Miah and Uddin 2017; Zuhroh et al. 2015).

DEA is an interdisciplinary scientific methodology used in finance, such as the efficiency assessment of the conventional banking sector (Maradin et al. 2018) or the measurement of banking productivity (Maradin et al. 2019) in European countries. DEA methodology can also be used to study the efficiency of various sectors, such as non-depository financial institutions, i.e., pension funds (Olgić Draženović et al. 2019), insurance companies, investment funds and universities, schools, health care facilities, the energy sector, shopping facilities, municipal service providers, business units in forestry, etc.

In selecting inputs and outputs of banks, there are three available approaches to capture the nature of banking business. First, the production approach pioneered by Benston (1965) considers banks as producers of products and services, using labor and other resources as inputs and providing deposits, loans and other services (in terms of value or number of transactions) as outputs. In contrast, Sealey and Lindley

(1977) proposed an intermediation approach that examines the bank's ability in transforming deposits into loans and advances. The intermediation approach examines the intermediary role of banks to investigate the efficiency of banks in collecting deposits and other funds from customers (inputs) and then lending out money in various forms of loans, mortgages, and other assets (i.e., investments). The intermediation approach examines how much progress or regress a bank has made in the increasingly difficult environment by producing profit from its inputs (Azad et al. 2017). Finally, the profitability approach examines the process by which banks use their inputs (expenses) to produce revenues.

As can be seen in the following sections of this paper, most studies on the efficiency of Islamic banks DEA have used the intermediation approach.

## 3 Characteristics of Islamic Banking

With the emergence of Islamic banks in the 1960s, Western economists were skeptical about the profit-making and ultimate viability of these banks, given the fundamental feature of the prohibition of interest (Riba') under Islamic religious law (Shari'a). Nevertheless, Islamic finance, led by Islamic banks, has grown steadily. "Islamic banking is the largest sector in the Islamic finance industry, contributing to 70% or $1.760 billion of the industry's assets" (Global Islamic Finance Market Growth, Trends and Forecast (2018–2024) 2019). Apart from Islamic banking, Islamic finance includes various aspects: Islamic insurance - Takaful, Islamic bonds—Sukuk, Islamic funds—Shariah Capital Market. According to 2018 data, there were 520 Islamic banks (301 full-fledged Islamic banks and 219 Islamic windows), in 72 countries of the world (not only in Muslim countries) (Islamic Finance Development Report 2019). Precisely because of the aforementioned growth of Islamic banks, conventional banks are increasingly trying to offer Islamic financial products without the presence of Islamic banks, which is referred to as Islamic windows (Cerović et al. 2017).

Apart from the already prominent business without the presence of interest, Islamic banking is recognizable and risk-averse in terms of the customer. Theoretically, a unique feature of Islamic banking is the profit and loss sharing (PLS) paradigm (mudarabah) (Chong and Liu 2009), according to which Islamic banking is considered more socially responsible than conventional banking. It is based on joint venture arrangements (musyarakah) between the banks and the customers where profit and loss sharing is present (direct participation in venture capital—equity financing). Due to the fact that the bank's income does not depend on fixed interest rates but on the success of the customer's business, it can be said that Islamic banking has introduced the concept of venture banking (Khan and Bhatti 2008). Moreover, Islamic banks are more conservative in their operations (due to many prohibitions in accordance with Islamic religious law) than conventional banks (US and EU) whose growth is mostly based on secondary securities and derivatives, which ultimately leads to increased risk taking (Suljić Nikolaj et al. 2019). Despite the fact that Islamic banking differs from conventional banking mainly due to the absence of interest, it should be noted that they receive fees and commissions for their transactions.

The peculiarity of Islamic banking is present in terms of supervision and regulation. There are two supervisory bodies in the world that are responsible for Islamic banking: The Bahrain-based Accounting and Auditing Organization for Islamic Financial Institutions (AAOIFI) and the Malaysian Islamic Financial Services Board (IFSB) (Ullah et al. 2018). Both of them are responsible for promoting Shariah-based business through collaboration with global institutions such as the World Bank and International Monetary Fund (IMF). Compared to conventional banks, the problem of regulating Islamic banks is that the standards of a single institution are not mandatory in all countries where Islamic banks operate (with the exception of Bahrain and United Arab Emirates). Therefore, in most countries, the operations of Islamic banks are based on the rules of national central banks. Thus, Islamic banks have to adapt to a dual regulatory framework: the rules of a country in which they operate together with conventional banks and the fundamental law of Islam—Shariah. In view of the above, Islamic banks need the legal, corporate and regulatory framework that is consistent with their business principles, institutional and cultural environment.

## 4 Empirical Review of the Efficiency and Productivity of Islamic Banking Sector

This section presents the most significant studies that deal with the analysis of the efficiency and productivity of the Islamic banking sector. In the first part, the measurement of productivity of Islamic banks is analyzed by only a few studies, while the focus is on the efficiency performance of Islamic banks themselves. Comparative studies between the efficiency evaluation of Islamic banks and conventional banks are conducted in the second part of this section.

### *4.1 Measuring Efficiency and Productivity of Islamic Banks*

Mansour and El Moussawi (2020) analyze the evolution of productive efficiency of 139 banks and the factors related to their overall productivity in 12 Arab countries over the period 2000–2014. Using the production approach and the intermediation approach, the inputs are fixed assets, total interest expenses and personnel costs, and the outputs are total earning assets, total customer deposits and impaired loans (for the price variables, total assets and total non-interest expenses are calculated). The results obtained using the DEA method reveal that the technical, allocative and cost inefficiencies of Arab banks are 13%, 21% and 30%, respectively. Moreover, the productivity of the factors of production measured by the Malmquist and Luenberger indices improved by about 2.44% and 1.79%, respectively. The main factors explaining the productivity improvements are bank size, profitability, equity ratio and economic growth rate, while bank risk ratio is associated with the deterioration of productivity.

Kamarudin et al. (2019) examine the revenue, cost and profit efficiency of 17 Malaysian domestic and foreign Islamic banks over the period 2006–2015 using the DEA method and, in the second stage of analysis using a pooled (OLS) and panel regression (GSL) analysis framework to examine the potential determinants of revenue efficiency of Islamic banks. Two inputs of deposits and labor, two input prices of deposits and labor, two outputs of loans and income (investment), and two output prices of loans and investment were chosen as variables in the DEA model. The results indicate that the level of revenue efficiency of Malaysian domestic Islamic banks is lower compared to their foreign Islamic bank counterparts. Bank market power, liquidity and management quality have a significant impact on improving the earnings efficiency of Malaysian domestic Islamic banks.

Bahrini (2017) measures and analyzes the overall technical efficiency (and its components, namely pure technical efficiency and scale efficiency) of 33 Islamic banks operating in the Middle East and North Africa (MENA) region over the period 2007–2012 using the bootstrap approach of Simar and Wilson DEA (1998). The intermediation approach is assumed with three input variables: staff costs, fixed assets and total deposits, and two output variables: total loans (which include Murabaha and deferred sales, ijara (leasing and hire purchase), Mudarabah (profit sharing) and Musharakah (partnership)) and other earning assets (which include investment in business, securities, land and real estate). The main results show that pure technical inefficiency instead of scale inefficiency was the main source of overall technical inefficiency. Moreover, the Islamic banks of Gulf Cooperation Council (GCC) had stable efficiency scores during the global financial crisis (2007–2008) and in the initial post-crisis period (2009–2010).

Kamarudin et al (2017) examine different types of efficiency, i.e., technical efficiency, decomposition of pure technical efficiency and scale efficiency of 29 Islamic banks from Malaysia, Indonesia and Brunei over the period of 2006–2014 by applying the method DEA along with the parametric (t test) and nonparametric (Mann–Whitney [Wilcoxon] and Kruskall–Wallis) tests. In the empirical study, total deposits, labor and capital are selected as input variables, while loans and investments are selected as output variables. The results indicate that the banks of Malaysian Islamic have higher efficiency levels than banks in Indonesia and Brunei for all three efficiency measures.

Ahmad et al. (2010) investigate the relative efficiency (i.e., technical, pure technical, and scale efficiency) of 77 Islamic banks in the world covering 25 countries over the period 2003–2009 (yielding 270 bank-year observations) using the DEA method. Empirical research is based on three inputs: deposits, labor cost and fixed assets, and three outputs: total loans, income and other earning assets. The empirical results indicate that pure technical efficiency outweighs scale efficiency in the Islamic banking sector, suggesting that Islamic banks were fully operationally efficient in exploiting their resources. Banks from the high-income countries were leading by dominating the efficiency frontier the most during the study period.

Hassan (2005) employs a stochastic frontier approach to compute cost and profit efficiency of a panel of 43 Islamic banks from 21 countries (238 DMUs) for each year over the period 1995–2001. In addition, a nonparametric DEA method is used to calculate the overall, technical, pure technical, allocative and scale efficiency of selected Islamic banks along with Malmquist TFP indices. By applying the intermediation approach, the input variables used in this study are labor cost as labor, cots on premises and fixed assets as capital, and total deposits (demand deposits and time deposits) and non-deposit funds as consumer and short-term funding. The output variables are total credit, other profit earning assets (short-term investments, equity and other investments, and public sector securities), and off-balance sheet activities. Some of the results show that all efficiency measures are highly correlated with ROA and ROE, suggesting that these efficiency measures can be used simultaneously with conventional accounting ratios in determining Islamic bank performance of Islamic banks. While technical inefficiency is caused by management and is correctable, allocative inefficiency is caused by regulation and cannot be controlled by management.

Yudistira (2004) calculates the technical, pure technical and scale efficiency of 18 Islamic banks from 12 countries over the period 1997–2000 using the method DEA. In specifying the input–output variables of the model, the intermediation approach is chosen because it is consistent with the principle of the Islamic financial system. Therefore, the input variables are personnel costs, fixed assets and total deposits, and the output variables are total loans, other income and liquid assets. The results of overall efficiency indicate that inefficiency is low for the 18 Islamic banks at just over 10 percent, which is quite low compared to many conventional banks. Moreover, there are diseconomies of scale for small- to medium-sized Islamic banks, suggesting that mergers and acquisitions should be encouraged. Publicly listed Islamic banks are less efficient than their unlisted counterparts.

Moreover, there are some studies in the literature by previous authors that analyze the efficiency and productivity of Islamic banks: Mezzi (2018) on a sample of Islamic banks in the MENA region and Southeast Asia, Aghimien et al. (2016) on a sample of 43 banks in the GCC region over the period 2007–2011, Belanès et al. (2015) on a sample of 30 Islamic banks in the GCC region over the period 2005–2011, Havidz and Setiawan (2015) on a sample of 4 Indonesian Islamic banks over the period 2008–2014, El Moussawi and Obeid (2011) on a sample of 23 Islamic banks in the GCC region over the period 2005–2008, Mostafa (2011) on a sample of the 100 largest Islamic banks using cross-sectional data for the year 2009, Sufian and Akbar Noor Mohamad Noor (2009) on a sample of Islamic banking sector in 16 MENA and Asian countries over the period 2001–2006, Saad and El Moussawi (2008) on a sample of 11 Arab banking sectors over the period 1994–2004 using DEA method and Malmquist productivity index.

### 4.2 Measuring Efficiency of Islamic and Conventional Banks

Wanke et al. (2019) examine the impact of exogenous variables such as bank type (Islamic (26.83%) vs. conventional (73.17%) banks), origin (local vs. foreign banks), and ownership (public vs private banks) on various accounting and financial indicators, taking into account the underlying cultural and regulatory barriers in 15 MENA countries, which are the endogenous variables. The efficiency scores of 738 DMUs (82 banks) on profit, balance sheet and financial indicators were analyzed over the period 2006–2014 using a Dynamic Network DEA model. The empirical analysis is based on five inputs (net loans, total earning assets, non-earning assets, loan loss provisions and expenses), three intermediate or link variables (net interest margin, equity and total assets), three outputs (net interest margin, equity and income) and on three transfers (gross loans, total assets and income). The effects of endogenous and exogenous contextual variables on three efficiency substructures are further tested using a stochastic nonlinear model solved by differential evolution combining bootstrapped simplex, Tobit, beta and Simar and Wilson (2007) truncated regression results. The results show that bank type, origin and ownership have differential effects on efficiency levels in terms of income statement, balance sheet and financial health indicators, although the effects of culture and regulatory barriers at the country level seem to predominate.

Sakti and Mohamad (2018) assess how 11 Indonesian Islamic banks differ from 37 conventional banks in terms of their business model, asset quality, stability, and efficiency (overall technical efficiency, pure technical efficiency, and scale efficiency) over the period 2008–2012 by applying t-test, z-score, and DEA. Three inputs (total deposits, staff cost and fixed assets) and two outputs (loans and non-interest income) are used to examine the efficiency scores of banks. The results of DEA indicate that Islamic banks are relatively more efficient than conventional banks as evidenced by their higher overall efficiency and technical efficiency. Moreover, Islamic banks appear to have better asset quality and be more stable than their conventional counterparts.

Azad et al. (2017) examine the efficiency of 16 Islamic and 27 conventional Malaysian banks (which constitute the entire banking sector in the country) over the period of 2009–2013 with a balanced panel of 215 observations by adopting a two-stage DEA method. In the first stage, a meta-frontier technology is used to account for bank heterogeneity - bank type (Islamic vs. conventional banks) and bank ownership (local vs. foreign banks). In the second stage, a double bootstrap regression as presented by Simar and Wilson (2007) is used to estimate the determinants of efficiency in Malaysian banks. For each approach, different variables are used in the model, i.e., for the production approach, the variables used are interest expense, salary expense, operating expense (as inputs) and interest income and net income (as outputs); for the profitability approach, the variables used are total capital, salary expense, interest expense (as inputs) and total deposits and total loans (as outputs); for the intermediation approach, the variables used are total capital, total deposits, salary expense (as inputs) and total loans (as outputs). This study shows that Islamic banks performed better than others. The frontier results show that local Islamic banks have moved toward group technology and foreign Islamic banks have taken the lead in country frontier technology. The double bootstrap regression results confirm that bank ownership, type of bank and GDP have a significant impact on bank efficiency.

Batir et al. (2017) investigate the technical, allocative and cost efficiency of 4 participating (Islamic) banks and 27 conventional banks (3 state-owned, 11 privately-owned and 13 foreign banks) in Turkey over the period 2005–2013 using an input-oriented DEA model with intermediation approach. In addition, a Tobit regression analysis is used to determine the factors affecting efficiency. The DEA analysis is based on three inputs (personnel expenses, fixed assets, total deposits), two outputs (total long-term and short-term loans, total guarantees, commitments and financial derivatives as off-balance sheet items) and corresponding input prices. The results of DEA show that the average participation bank efficiency is higher than the average conventional bank efficiency each year. Looking at the Tobit regression analysis, findings reveal that cost and credit quality have a significant negative relationship with the efficiency of conventional banks, while they have a significant positive relationship with the efficiency of participation banks. While total loans have significant positive relationship, external variables have significant negative relationship with efficiency of both types of banks.

Shawtari et al. (2015) examine the practices of discretionary loan/loan loss provisions (DLLP) and their relationship with efficiency between Islamic and conventional banks in Yemen. A two-stage approach is conducted on a sample of all 16 banks, 4 of which are Islamic banks, with unbalanced data over the period 1996–2011 (221 observations). Efficiency scores are estimated using Data Envelopment Windows Analysis. The results show that both banking models use discretion over LLP to control their earnings for different factors. Contrary to the authors' expectations, Islamic banks also resort to earnings management, similar to conventional banks, ignoring their ethical identity prescribed in Shari'ah law. The overall results show that Islamic banks have lower DLLP compared to conventional banks, except for foreign banks which have significantly lower DLLP compared to Islamic banks.

Yilmaz and Güneş (2015) study and analyze the efficiency of 4 (Islamic) participation banks (PBs) and 28 (conventional) deposit banks (DBs) over the period 2007–2013 in Turkey using DEA in terms of technical, pure technical and scale efficiencies. By using an intermediation approach, the input vector contains two inputs: total deposits and capital, while the output vector contains three outputs: total loan, income and investments. The results indicate that PBs have a mean technical efficiency of 84.5 percent, indicating a mean input waste of 15.5 percent, and for DBs the mean technical efficiency score is 81.6 percent. Scale inefficiency dominates pure technical inefficiency in determining the overall technical efficiency of PBs during the observed period, while the reverse is true for DBs.

In addition to the nonparametric DEA methodology, which is the most well-known for performance evaluation, the parametric SFA method is also very popular in the analysis of efficiency evaluation of the banking sector. Nevertheless, few studies on efficiency measurement of Islamic and conventional banks using SFA method are presented in this research.

Miah and Uddin (2017) examine the differences between 28 Islamic and 48 conventional banks in GCC countries (KSA, UAE, Kuwait, Qatar, Bahrain and Oman) over the period 2005–2014 in terms of business orientation, financial stability and cost efficiency. By using the intermediary approach, loans and securities are chosen as outputs, while labor and capital costs are used as inputs to determine the cost efficiency of banks. The methodology used is accounting ratios, SFA and ordinary least square regression technique. The results show that conventional banks are more efficient in cost management than their Islamic counterparts. However, Islamic banks are more sound in terms of short-term solvency, but no such difference exists in terms of long-term stability. The results also suggest that highly capitalized banks are more stable but cost inefficient, which proves that highly capitalized banks have failed to take advantage of the leverage effect.

Zuhroh et al. (2015) estimate the cost efficiency (which is decomposed into technical efficiency and allocative efficiency) of 3 Islamic and 19 conventional banks in Indonesia over the period from 2004 to 2010 using the stochastic cost frontier approach and analyze the impact of managerial competence and structural variables on cost efficiency. The data included in the analysis are total assets, loans, fixed assets, third party funds, equity, total cost, depreciation value, interest cost (profit sharing) and personnel cost. The results showed that Islamic banks are superior in achieving technical efficiency, but the average cost efficiency is much lower than conventional banks. The cost inefficiency of Islamic banks comes from allocative inefficiency.

Moreover, additional studies of measuring efficiency of Islamic and conventional banks can be found in the literature: Erfani and Vasigh (2018) on a sample of 8 Islamic and 11 conventional banks worldwide during 2006–2013, Shawtari et al. (2018) on a sample of 4 Islamic and 12 conventional banks in Yemen during 1996–2011, Cerović et al. (2017) on a sample of Islamic and conventional banks before, during and after the 2007–2008 financial crisis, Kamarudin et al. (2016) on a sample of 27 Islamic and 47 conventional banks in GCC countries over the period 2007–2011, Johnes et al. (2014) on a sample of 45 Islamic and 207 conventional banks in 18 countries over the period 2004–2009, Ismail et al. (2013) on a sample of selected Islamic and conventional commercial banks in Malaysia over the period 2006–2009, Hassan et al. (2009) on a sample of 22 Islamic and 18 conventional banks in 11 organizations of Islamic Conference countries over the period 1990–2005.

## 5 Conclusion

Determining the efficiency and productivity of the banking system is increasingly present in scientific research due to the great importance of banks in the overall financial system. The evaluation of efficiency and smooth performance of conventional banks is still predominant, but in line with the growth of Islamic banks, their specific characteristics and way of doing business, the number of studies on Islamic banking is increasing. A large proportion of published studies focus on efficiency and productivity measurement of Islamic banks and efficiency comparison between Islamic and conventional banks. Islamic banks are specific because their activities are harmonized with religious law (Shariah) which prohibits certain forms of business (interest, profit, speculative risk transactions) that are an integral part of the business of conventional banks. The specificity of Islamic banking is reflected in its regulation and supervision, which is not unique as in conventional banking. Despite the existence of two supervisory bodies of Islamic finance: AAOIFI and IFSB, Islamic banks in most countries are not required to adjust their standards. Therefore, Islamic banks usually have to adapt the requirements of the central banks of the countries in which they operate (which apply to conventional banks), while respecting the basic principles of Shariah. Therefore, there is a need for specific and uniform regulation and supervision of Islamic banks based on the characteristics of their operations.

The empirical part of this study aims to make an important contribution to regulators or policy makers, Islamic banking itself, investors and existing knowledge on the operational performance of the Islamic banking sector. The paper analyzes two concepts of performance evaluation of Islamic banking sector using Data Envelopment Analysis as a methodology that is widely accepted in evaluating homogeneous entities in comparison with each other. According to the literature analyzed, the conclusion is that there are a number of inputs and outputs used in DEA models that are mostly applied through the intermediation approach. This paper provides the basis for further empirical research on the relative efficiency or productivity growth of the Islamic banking sector.

**Acknowledgements** This work has been fully supported by the University of Rijeka under the project number uniri-drustv-18-61 and project number uniri-mladi-drustv-20-13.

## References

Aghimien PA et al (2016) Efficiency of Gulf Cooperation Council Banks: Empirical evidence using data envelopment analysis. Rev Int Bus Strat 26(1):118–136

Ahmad NHB et al (2010) Measuring Islamic banks efficiency: the case of world Islamic banking sectors. J Islam Bank Financ 27(4):251–277

Aigner D et al (1977) Formulation and estimation of stochastic frontier production function models. J Econ 6(1):21–37

Azad AK et al (2017) Bank efficiency in Malaysia: a use of malmquist meta-frontier analysis. Eurasian Bus Rev, Springer; Eurasia Bus Econ Soc 7(2):287–311

Bahrini R (2017) Efficiency analysis of Islamic banks in the Middle East and North Africa region: A bootstrap DEA approach. Int J Financ Stud 5(1):1–13

Banker RD et al (1984) The use of categorical variables in data envelopment analysis. Manage Sci 30:1078–1092

Batir TE et al (2017) Determinants of bank efficiency in Turkey: Participation banks versus conventional banks. Borsa Istanbul Rev 17(2):86–96

Belanès A et al (2015) What can we learn about Islamic banks efficiency under the subprime crisis? Evidence from GCC Region. Pac Basin Financ J 33:81–92

Benston GJ (1965) Branch banking and economies of scale. J Financ 20(2):312–331

Casu B et al (2004) Productivity change in European banking: A comparison of parametric and non-parametric approaches. J Bank Finance 28(10):2521–2540
Cerović Lj et al (2017) Comparative analysis of conventional and Islamic banking: Importance of market regulation. Ekonomska misao i praksa [Econ Thought Pract] 26(1):241–263
Charnes A et al (1978) Measuring the efficiency of decision making units. Eur J Oper Res 2(6):429–444
Chong BS, Liu MH (2009) Islamic banking: Interest-free or interest-based? Pac Basin Financ J 17(1):125–144
El Moussawi C, Obeid H (2011) Evaluating the productive efficiency of Islamic banking in GCC: A non-parametric approach. Int Manag Rev 7(1):10–21
Erfani GR, Vasigh B (2018) The impact of the global financial crisis on profitability of the banking industry: A comparative analysis. Economies 6(4):1–13
Farrell MJ (1957) The measurement of productive efficiency. J Roy Stat Soc 120(3):253–290
Global Islamic Finance Market Growth, Trends, and Forecast 2018–2024 (2019) Mordor intelligence
Hassan MK (2005) The cost, profit and X-efficiency of Islamic banks. Economic Research Forum, 12th Annual Conference. Cairo, Egypt, 1–22
Hassan T et al (2009) Efficiency of conventional versus Islamic banks: evidence from the Middle East. Int J Islam Middle East Financ Manag 2(1):46–65
Havidz SAH, Setiawan C (2015) Bank efficiency and non-performing financing (NPF) in the Indonesian Islamic banks. Asian J Econ Model 3(3):61–79
Islamic Finance Development Report (2019) Available at: https://icd-ps.org/uploads/files/IFDI%202019%20DEF%20digital1574605094_7214.pdf
Ismail F et al (2013) Efficiency of Islamic and conventional banks in Malaysia. J Financ Report Account 11(1):92–107
Johnes J et al (2014) A comparison of performance of Islamic and conventional banks 2004–2009. J Econ Behav Organ 103:93–107
Kamarudin F et al (2016) Does country governance foster revenue efficiency of Islamic and conventional banks in GCC countries? EuroMed J Bus 11(2):181–211
Kamarudin F et al (2017) Assessing the domestic and foreign Islamic banks efficiency: Insights from selected Southeast Asian countries. Future Business J 3(1):33–46
Kamarudin F et al (2019) Bank efficiency in Malaysia a DEA approach. J CentL Bank Theory Pract 8(1):133–162
Kasman A, Carvallo O (2014) Financial stability, competition and efficiency in Latin American and Caribbean banking. J Appl Econ 17(2):301–324
Khan MM, Bhatti MI (2008) Islamic banking and finance: On its way to globalization. Manag Financ 34(10):708–725
Mansour R, El Moussawi C (2020) Efficiency, technical progress and productivity of Arab banks: A non-parametric approach. Q Rev Econ Finance 75:191–208
Maradin D et al (2018) Performance evaluation of banking sector by using DEA method. In: Proceedings of Economic and Social Development, 35th International Scientific Conference on Economic and Social Development—Sustainability from an Economic and Social Perspective. Lisbon, Portugal, 684–690
Maradin D et al (2019) The productivity of European banking sector: A review of the post-2000 literature. UTMS J Econ 10(2):249–257
Meeusen W, van den Broeck J (1977) Efficiency estimation from Cobb-Douglas production functions with composed error. Int Econ Rev 18(2):435–444
Mezzi N (2018) Efficiency of Islamic banks and role of governance: Empirical evidence. Manag Financ 44(5):590–603
Miah MD, Uddin H (2017) Efficiency and stability: A comparative study between islamic and conventional banks in GCC countries. Future Business J 3(2):172–185
Mostafa MM (2011) Modeling Islamic banks' efficiency: a non-parametric frontier approach. Int J Islam Middle East Financ Manag 4(1):7–29

Olgić Draženović B et al (2019) The efficiency of mandatory pension funds: Case of Croatia. South East Eur J Econ Bus 14(2):82–94
Saad W, El Moussawi C (2008) Efficiency and productivity growth of the Arab commercial banking sector: A non-parametric approach. J Dev Econ Policies 10(1):6–36
Sakti MRP, Mohamad A (2018) Efficiency, stability and asset quality of Islamic vis-à-vis conventional banks: Evidence from Indonesia. J Islam Account Bus Res 9(3):378–400
Sealey CW, Lindley JT (1977) Inputs, outputs, and a theory of production and cost at depository financial institutions. J Financ 32(4):1251–1266
Simar L, Wilson PW (1998) Sensitivity analysis of efficiency scores: How to bootstrap in nonparametric frontier models. Manage Sci 44(1):49–61
Simar L, Wilson PW (2007) Estimation and inference in two-stage, semi-parametric models of production processes. Journal of Econometrics 136(1):31–64
Shawtari FA et al (2015) The impact of efficiency on discretionary loans/finance loss provision: A comparative study of Islamic and conventional banks. Borsa Istanbul Rev 15(4):272–282
Shawtari FA et al (2018) Decomposition of efficiency using DEA window analysis: A comparative evidence from Islamic and conventional banks. Benchmarking: Int J 25(6):1681–1705
Sufian F, Noor ANM (2009) The determinants of Islamic banks' efficiency changes: Empirical evidence from the MENA and Asian banking sectors. Int J Islam Middle East Financ Manag 2(2):120–138
Suljić Nikolaj S et al (2019) European deposit insurance systems in the time of crisis. In: Proceedings of 8th International Scientific Conference on Economic and Social Development—"Managerial Issues in Modern Business", Warsaw, Poland, 350–361
Ullah MH et al (2018) Comparative compliance status of AAOIFI and IFSB standards: An empirical evidence from Islami Bank Bangladesh Limited. J Islam Account Bus Res 9(4):607–628
Wanke P et al (2019) A dynamic network DEA model for accounting and financial indicators: A case of efficiency in MENA banking. Int Rev Econ Financ 61:52–68
Yilmaz A, Güneş N (2015) Efficiency comparison of participation and conventional banking sectors in Turkey between 2007–2013. Procedia Soc Behav Sci 195:383–392
Yudistira D (2004) Efficiency in Islamic banking: An empirical analysis of eighteen banks. Islam Econ Stud 12(1):1–19
Zuhroh I et al (2015) Cost efficiency of Islamic banks in Indonesia—A stochastic frontier analysis. Procedia Soc Behav Sci 211:1122–1131

# Online vs Offline Banking

**Zoe Papadopoulou, Stavros Valsamidis, Ioannis Petasakis, and Athanasios Mandilas**

**Abstract** Banking industry has undergone radical changes and improvements in the last few years because of digitalization, but there is little evidence for the borderline between online and offline banking regarding the customers. The habits of customers and the new competitive environment are forcing banks to address their digitalisation process as a matter of urgency if they are not to be left behind in a market which finds itself in the full throes of transformation. The customers want the banks to understand their unstated needs as well as their likes. Increasingly, banks offer simultaneously both offline and online services, but some customers still seem to prefer using offline services rather than online ones. The survey aims at identifying the factors that affect the customers to use online banking than offline banking. The objectives are to measure the factors which affect the use online banking versus offline banking. This will provide valuable information to banks so that could improve online banking services and develop new products and programs. The study carries out the analysis by collecting quantitative data through structured questionnaires from 200 bank customers. The overall evaluation discloses the findings for the transference channel from offline to online banking with habits and preferences of customers in Greek banks. The contribution of the study is the valuable information for banks so that improve online banking services and develop new products and programs.

**Keywords** Online banking · Offline banking · Customers · Questionnaire

**JEL Classification Codes** G21 · L86

Z. Papadopoulou · S. Valsamidis (✉) · I. Petasakis · A. Mandilas
Department of Accounting and Finance, International Hellenic University, Campus of Kavala, Agios Loukas, 65404 Kavala, Greece
e-mail: svalsam@teiemt.gr

A. Mandilas
e-mail: smand@teiemt.gr



G. Karanovic et al. (eds.), *The Changing Financial Landscape*, Contributions to Economics, https://doi.org/10.1007/978-3-030-82778-6_13

# 1 Introduction

The integration of digital technologies into business processes has become increasingly imperative for contemporary organizations seeking to survive and attain competitive advantages in a digital economy (Bharadwaj 2000). The increasing use of mobile phones and the use of the Internet have changed many industries, including banking (Gupta 2013). Banking industry has undergone radical changes and improvements in the last few years because of digitization. The competitive environment between banks and customer habits pushes banks to evolve their services and understand their customers' needs and preferences. This is because by nature of online services creates rise to a lack of trust and uncertainty about the use of online banking among some customers as there is no direct physical contact between buyer and seller. This spatial distance means that customers cannot use the physical cues, such as observing the salespeople or the physical office/store space, to judge trustworthiness (Reichheld and Schefter 2000).

Each and every day, new technologies and devices are providing various customer touch points (Shivakumar and Sethii 2019). The access to a computer screen is an everyday common habit, and also nowadays smartphones give a numerous abilities to the users through applications. Each bank has its own app which provides a big variety of services and moreover, and the level of security provides is very high (Khan et al. 2016). All these technological developments have changed the traditional banking industry which is being replaced by new models and practices that changed the customers' experience (Evdokimova et al. 2019). This is a challenge that all the banks should take into account because the customers' experience is valuable. To fully capitalize on that opportunity, they will need to enhance and innovate products that deliver the just-in-time and just-in-case experiences customers crave (Brodsky and Oakes 2017).

Some of the most well-known services are Internet banking, telephone banking and electronic retailing (Yousafzai and Yani-de-Soriano 2012). Online banking services can be defined as the provision of information or services by a bank to its customers via the computer, cellular phone or other Internet-oriented devices (Daniel 1999). This evolution has increased customers' expectations, availability of customers' service and competitive pricing (Hough and Chan 2018). Hew et al. (2015) suggested that user friendly applications would attract customers to operate them.

One of the most prominent effects of the Internet's continuing expansion and development is that the companies and customers acquire more ways of communicating with one another, leading to profound impact on the banking industry (Ganguli and Roy 2011). Customers no longer need to abide by the bank's opening hours or spend time waiting in phone queues in order to get into contact with their bank advisors (Larsson and Viitaoja 2017). A large-scale study revealed that modern bank customers of today desire freedom in where to conduct their business, while also requiring a deeper personal relationship with their bank advisors (Skan et al. 2015). The results indicate that the banks need to garner a better understanding of their customers. The respondents perceive the customers to seek simple and swift solutions who will turn to whatever actor who can best supply such a service. The respondents would indeed often reiterate that a deep and loyal relationship with the customer could only be generated through providing good service and availability. However, the respondents also claimed that the banks aspired to make the customers more autonomous and independent in order to reduce their need of keeping frequent contact with the banks (Larsson and Viitaoja 2017).

Of course, even though banks are adapting to customer requirements, there are some customers still seem to prefer using offline banking services rather than online banking. According to Suh and Han (2002), Rexha et al. (2003) and Lichtenstein and Williamson (2006), bank managers faced by uncertainty and/or scepticism. So, in order to grow online banking they need to bridge the trust gap in order to become a more viable medium of service delivery. Trust is an important factor that plays a key role in the use of the online banking service (Yap et al. 2009; Kang et al. 2011). The trust in an offline bank influences key factors in an online bank environment (Lee et al. 2007).

The aim of this survey is to identify the factors that affect the customers to use online banking than offline banking. The objectives are to measure the factors which affect the use online banking versus offline banking. This will provide valuable information to banks so that could improve online banking services and develop new products and programs.

## 2 Literature Review

Many surveys have focused on digitizing the banking industry and its impact on bank customers and employees.

More specifically, for customers, Ramaswami et al. (2000) suggest that for both offline and online transactions, there are two factors that influence purchase of online financial products. These are previous indications that the customer is 'gaining' on the offline channel and using the online channel for information search. This means that customer online behaviour is often determined by previous indications on the offline channel, which corresponds to the mental model on the online channel. Thus, if the customers are satisfied with an offline product, they are likely to favour that product on the online channels as well. The research by Ramaswami et al. (2000) shows that if there is trust in the offline vendor from the customer, then there will be a positive customer attitude towards online products; Gefen et al. (2003) show that trust in an e-commerce vendor leads to the customer's intention to purchase from that vendor. Therefore, the research by Lee et al. (2007) investigating the researches of Ramaswami et al. (2000) and Gefen et al. (2003) concluded that, similarly, trust on the offline banking should positively influence the extent of the intended use of the bank's online system. Yousafzai et al. (2005) find that top online banks, ranked in terms of their perceived trustworthiness attributes (i.e. ability, integrity, and benevolence), were present in the marketplace with the same brand name. This implies that an offline presence may influence online trust (Yousafzai et al. 2005; Kuan and Bock 2007).

The results of Boateng et al. (2016) research showed that trust is closely related to customers' intentions to adopt online banking. This means that trust plays an important role in its use. It is one of the central elements of social environment, as evidenced by both the researches of Aboobucker and Bao (2018) and Boateng et al. (2016). This reduces the uncertainty between individuals in the respective social environment they belong to, and encourages customers to use online banking rather than offline banking. Jarvenpaa et al. (2000) showed that customer trust leads to purchase intentions, while the research of Liu et al. (2005) found that what Jarvenpaa et al. (2000) showed is also true in online banking.

AbuShanab and Pearson (2007) used also three variables in their research: performance expectancy, effort expectancy and social influence. Using these variables for their research showed that customers with high-performance expectancy were more likely to use Internet banking. However, this variable was influenced by age, which was an important factor in this relation because younger customers could accept technology more easily than older people. This was also the conclusion of Serener's survey (2016), which in addition to age has used other variables such as income and education, where it has emerged that people with higher income or higher education are more likely to adopt online banking services. While AbuShanab and Pearson (2007) using expectation effort demonstrated that the relation with gender, age, and experience was not important because the convenience of a system weakens with experience, while customers are more concerned about safety and utility. Finally, consumers with high social influence were intent on using online banking services.

On the other hand, Julien and Tsoni (2013) conducted a comparative quantitative research on banking services, where the bank's financial advisers and consumers were asked to answer a number of the same questions about customer perceptions of quality bank services. The results of the research showed significant discrepancies of perception between bank customers and frontline employees (financial advisors). Julien and Tsoni's (2013) findings show also that employees find it difficult to put themselves in the customer's shoes, and understand the customer experience they have. The key features of service quality are less strict because frontline employees do not want to blame themselves for any poor performance. The development of multi-channel distribution strategies has negatively affected time allocation of frontline employees (Karatepe and Aga 2016). Bank customers are increasingly contacting financial advisers through various channels of communication (e.g. email, Internet, mobile, face-to-face), with the expectation that they will be more and more readily available.

Another research was conducted by Yoon and Barker Steege (2013) for the acceptance factors of online banking customers. They came to a positive conclusion that the research model can help bank managers and generally the banking system to discover motivating factors and prospective barriers to using online banking services, so that they can improve their banking systems, for the purpose of attracting customers.

Takieddine and Sun (2015) also conducted an investigation in 33 European countries (Austria, Belgium, Bulgaria, Croatia, Cyprus, Czech Republic, Denmark,

Estonia, Finland, France, Germany, Greece, Hungary, Iceland, Luxembourg, The Netherlands, Norway, Poland, Portugal, Romania, Serbia, Slovakia, Slovenia, Spain, Sweden, and Turkey) to answer the research question why different countries exhibit different levels of online banking adoption. They proposed an online banking diffusion model that examined the impact of economic, technological and cultural factors on online banking diffusion. Their results indicate that the effects of socio-economic and technology-related factors on online banking diffusion are fully mediated by Internet access. Surveys conducted by Koufaris and Hampton-Sosa (2004), Hampton-Sosa and Koufaris (2005), Casaló et al. (2007) and Vatanasombut et al. (2008) have categorized four factors in the banking sector using online banking services, which are perceived security, perceived usefulness, perceived privacy and perceived ease of use. The authors of these study point out that these factors influence trust of online banking services.

Yap et al. (2009) argued that traditional service quality builds customer trust in the online banking service. The size and reputation of the bank were found to provide structural assurance to the customer but not in the absence of traditional service quality. Web site features that give customers confidence are significant situation normality cues.

Finally, the 'usability' or the effort required to use the computers of the digital banking website, as defined by Casaló et al. (2007) can directly affect customer confidence. Moreover, the same research notes that trust in digital transformation has a direct and positive relation with the potential of the bank. The better the reputation of the bank, the more reliable the reputation of its digital services will be. Thus, according Casaló et al. (2007) and Mukherjee and Nath (2003), it was found that an important factor directly related to both online and offline banking services is the reputation of the bank's physical store. Therefore, reputation is a key factor in customer confidence in using digital banking services.

## 3 Methodology

The present study investigates the attitudes of customers to offline services versus online ones. More specifically, it identifies the factors that influence the attitude of customers towards the services offered by online banking and measure these factors which affect the use of online banking versus offline banking. The results of this survey will answer how the demographic characteristics of customers are related with their online banking behaviour. Therefore, the data for the present research were collected by individual bank customers from all over Greece. A sample of 200 bank customers completed questionnaires about the banking services offered by the new digital era. The survey was conducted in the last quarter of 2019. The questionnaire consists of five sections. More specifically, the first section includes demographic data of each respondent, concerning gender, age, education, profession, marital status and income. In the second section, there is a question that focuses on whether the respondent uses online banking services, which determines whether they will continue in the third and fourth sections, or whether the respondent will have to go straight to the fifth. The question is multiple choice. In the third section, there are three questions that explore which services they use, how often, from which device are connected to implement these transactions, as well as their bank preference. All questions in this section are multiple choice. In the fourth section, there are three questions related to the satisfaction of the respondents with the online services offered by their bank, and their thoughts on their use in the near future. The two questions in this section are multiple choice, and one demands short answer. Finally, in the fifth section there are three questions that investigate the reasons that respondents do not choose to use e-services, and their perceptions on this issue.

The non-probabilistic sampling was used, which means that each customer will have the same chance of participating in the research. Therefore, the stratified sampling method is adopted, where due to time constraints, the number of 200 individuals is determined, as a satisfactory sample to provide representative results. This method is based on the techniques of simple/random sampling and systematic sampling.

The research was conducted through the process of providing, completing and collecting the questionnaire by the participants. The questionnaire was completed online through a google docs form, as the link was sent through popular social media. When the questionnaire was distributed to the respondent, it became clear that it was a collection of statistical data related to the elaboration of a survey. The sample includes people regardless of gender, age, marital status, income, educational level and profession, with the aim of collecting a more reliable sample, which in turn led to more impartial research.

For the statistical analysis were adopted descriptive statistics and non-parametric Pearson Chi-Square independency test. The IBM SPSS Statistics version 25 was used.

## 4 Results

The participants involved in this research were people who carried out bank transactions either online or offline. More specifically, they were asked if they use the services of online banking in Greece. Table 1 summarizes the social and demographic characteristics of the participants, while Table 2 summarizes customer data for the use of online banking.

From the Table 2, it was observed that 51.5% (103 people) intends that in the future they will not change the frequency of banking transactions, while only 23% (46 people) argue that they wish to increase their use in the near future. The reasons they avoid using online banking are mainly the fear for the security of transactions, the low familiarity with technology and the fear of making a mistake when individuals do online banking on their own.

In addition, the largest percentage of respondents, as shown in Table 2, does not rule out that in the future they may use some of the online banking methods, as they

**Table 1** Socio-demographic data

| Gender | Percent |
|---|---|
| Male | 43.0 |
| Female | 56.0 |
| Did not answer | 1.0 |
| *Age* | *Percent* |
| Under 25 years old | 28.5 |
| 26–34 years old | 13.5 |
| 35–44 years old | 15.5 |
| 45–54 years old | 22.0 |
| >= 55 years old | 19.5 |
| Did not answer | 1.0 |
| *Marital status* | *Percent* |
| Unmarried | 37.5 |
| Married/cohabitation agreement | 45.5 |
| Divorced | 9.5 |
| Separated | 1.5 |
| Widowed | 5.0 |
| Did not answer | 1.0 |
| *Educational level* | *Percent* |
| Basic education | 7.0 |
| Secondary education | 14.0 |
| Post-high school education | 16.0 |
| Tertiary education | 44.0 |
| Master/PhD | 18.0 |
| Did not answer | 1.0 |
| *Main occupation* | *Percent* |
| Public employee | 21.5 |
| Private employee | 32.5 |
| Freelance | 11.0 |
| Unemployed | 9.0 |
| Student | 13.5 |
| Retired | 10.0 |
| Other | 1.5 |
| Did not answer | 1.0 |
| *Annual family income* | *Percent* |
| <= 6000 € | 18.5 |
| 6001–12,000 € | 20.0 |
| 12,001–24,000 € | 40.5 |

(continued)

**Table 1** (continued)

| Gender | Percent |
|---|---|
| 24,001–48,000 € | 17.5 |
| > 48,001 € | 2.5 |
| Did not answer | 1.0 |

believe that it is now necessary for easier money transfer, although they do not have the appropriate equipment or they do not know how to implement them.

In the present study, in order to investigate whether demographic characteristics are associated with the use of online banking services, the Pearson X2 statistical method was performed.

In Table 3, by choosing 5% as a level of significant, it is observed that gender and marital status do not affect whether respondents choose to use the bank's online services, but on the contrary, age, educational level and main occupation are associated with their use. However, how often they do online banking does not seem to be affected by gender, educational level and main occupation, but is affected by marital status and age.

The results of Table 3 are described in detail below. All of the following Pearson Chi-square test applications look at whether the test conditions are met; otherwise, any problem is explicitly mentioned.

A key question was whether the use of online banking services differs between men and women. Table 4 shows that approximately the same percentages of men and women use online banking services (75.6% of men and 79.5% of women in the sample). The value for the Pearson Chi-square test with 1 degree of freedom was 0.424 and a corresponding $p$ value = 0.515. Thus, the null hypothesis is accepted according to which $H_0$: *that there is no statistically significant dependence between the use of online banking services and gender.*

Table 5 shows that the percentages of those who use online banking services differ between the age groups. More specifically, while in all age groups under the age of 55 the percentages of use of online banking services range between 82 and 89%, in the participants over the age of 55 the corresponding percentage is limited to only 51%. The value for Pearson Chi-square test with 4 degrees of freedom is 20.464 and a corresponding $p$ value < 0.001. Thus, the alternative hypothesis is accepted according to which $H_1$: *There is statistically significant dependence between the use of online services in relation to the age group. That means the differences observed above are statistically significant.*

Table 6 shows that the percentages of those who use online banking services differ between the educational levels. More specifically, while in all levels of education the percentages of use of online banking services range between 72 and 91%, in the participants of the research with basic education the corresponding percentage is limited to only 43%. The value of Pearson Chi-Square test with 4 degrees of freedom is 17.020 and a corresponding $p$ value = 0.002. Thus, the alternative hypothesis is accepted according to which $H_1$: *there are statistically significant dependence*

**Table 2** Use of online banking

| Are you currently using online banking services | Percent |
|---|---|
| Yes | 77.0 |
| No | 22.0 |
| Did not answer | 1.0 |
| *What online banking services do you use?* | *Percent* |
| Payment of bills | 74.7 |
| Transfer money between accounts | 51.9 |
| Redemption of awards | 9.7 |
| Travel services | 22.7 |
| Account transactions | 59.1 |
| Credit/debit cards | 44.8 |
| Remaining control | 58.4 |
| Personal control | 39.0 |
| *How often do you use online banking?* | *Percent* |
| More than once a week | 25.0 |
| Once a week | 19.5 |
| Twice a week | 18.0 |
| Once a month | 9.5 |
| Other | 5.0 |
| Did not answer | 23.0 |
| *What devices do you use for your online banking transactions?* | *Percent* |
| Computer | 59.1 |
| Laptop | 41.6 |
| Mobile phone | 64.9 |
| Ipad or tablet | 20.8 |
| *Which bank do you prefer for online transactions?* | *Percent* |
| Alphabank | 13.0 |
| National Bank | 18.0 |
| Eurobank | 15.0 |
| Piraeus Bank | 30.5 |
| Other | 0.5 |
| Did not answer | 23.0 |
| *Are you planning or believing that in the coming months to?* | *Percent* |
| Increase the use of online banking services | 23.0 |
| Continue to use at the same level of banking services | 51.5 |
| Reduce of online transactions | 2.5 |
| Did not answer | 23.0 |

(continued)

**Table 2** (continued)

| Are you currently using online banking services | Percent |
|---|---|
| *Reasons for non-adoption of online services* | *Percent* |
| Incomplete information about web-banking services | 33.3 |
| Fear for the security of transactions | 59.5 |
| Little familiarity with technology | 45.2 |
| It is considered a complicated process | 16.7 |
| Better service—information in the bank's store | 19.0 |
| High cost | 11.9 |
| Fear of the possibility of error if you make bank transactions yourself via online banking | 35.7 |
| *How likely do you think it is that you will start using some of the online banking methods in the near future?* | *Percent* |
| Extremely likely | 4.5 |
| Somewhat probable | 3.5 |
| Neither possible nor unlikely | 6.0 |
| Somewhat unlikely | 3.6 |
| Extremely unlikely | 4.5 |
| Did not answer | 78.0 |

**Table 3** Demographic characteristics use of online services

| Correlation | Statistical control | p value |
|---|---|---|
| Use of online services * gender | Pearson $X^2$ | 0.315 |
| Use of online services * age | Pearson $X^2$ | 0.002 |
| Use of online services * marital status | Pearson $X^2$ | 0.074 |
| Use of online services * Educational level | Pearson $X^2$ | 0.002 |
| Use of online services * main profession | Pearson $X^2$ | 0.000 |
| Use of online services * annual income | Pearson $X^2$ | 0.301 |

*between the use of online services in relation to the educational level. That means the differences observed above are statistically significant.*

Table 7 shows that the percentages of those who use online banking services differ between the categories of the profession. More specifically, while in all categories of profession the percentages of use of online banking services range between 85 and 90%, the exception is the unemployed/other with a corresponding percentage of 62% and as might be expected, retirees with only 35%. The value for Pearson Chi-square test with 5 degrees of freedom is 29.971 and a corresponding value $p < 0.001$.

**Table 4** Use of online banking services and gender

| | | | Are you currently using online banking services? | | Total |
|---|---|---|---|---|---|
| | | | Yes | No | |
| Gender | Male | Frequency | 65 | 21 | 86 |
| | | % within gender | 75.6 | 24.4 | 100.0 |
| | Female | Frequency | 89 | 23 | 112 |
| | | % within gender | 79.5 | 20.5 | 100.0 |
| Total | | Frequency | 154 | 44 | 198 |
| | | % within gender | 77,8 | 22.2 | 100.0 |

**Table 5** Use of online banking services and age group

| | | | Are you currently using online banking services? | | Total |
|---|---|---|---|---|---|
| | | | Yes | No | |
| Age | Under 25 years old | Frequency | 47 | 10 | 57 |
| | | % within age | 82.5 | 17.5 | 100.0 |
| | 26–34 years old | Frequency | 24 | 3 | 27 |
| | | % within age | 88.9 | 11.1 | 100.0 |
| | 35–44 years old | Frequency | 27 | 4 | 31 |
| | | % within Age | 87.1 | 12.9 | 100.0 |
| | 45–54 years old | Frequency | 36 | 8 | 44 |
| | | % within age | 81.8 | 18.2 | 100.0 |
| | > = 55 years old | Frequency | 20 | 19 | 39 |
| | | % within age | 51.3 | 48.7 | 100.0 |
| Total | | Frequency | 154 | 44 | 198 |
| | | % within age | 77.8 | 22.2 | 100.0 |

It follows that the alternative hypothesis is accepted according to which $H_1$: *there is statistically significant dependence between its use of online services and professions*. Thus, the above differences are statistically significant.

Table 8 shows that the percentages of those who use online banking services range from 67 to 85% between the categories of annual family income. The value for Pearson Chi-square with 4 degrees of freedom is 4.872 and a corresponding value $p = 0.301$. Therefore, the null hypothesis is accepted according to which $H_0$: *there are no statistically significant dependence between the use of online services based on annual income* and the conclusion is that the differences observed above are not statistically significant, i.e. the annual income does not statistically significantly affect the use of online banking services.

The summary of the key findings is portrayed in Table 9.

**Table 6** Use of online banking services and educational level

| | | | Are you currently using online banking services? | | Total |
|---|---|---|---|---|---|
| | | | Yes | No | |
| Educational level | Basic education | Frequency | 6 | 8 | 14 |
| | | % within educational level | 42.9 | 57.1 | 100.0 |
| | Secondary education | Frequency | 24 | 4 | 28 |
| | | % within educational level | 85.7 | 14.3 | 100.0 |
| | Post-high school education | Frequency | 27 | 5 | 32 |
| | | % within educational level | 84.4 | 15.6 | 100.0 |
| | Tertiary education | Frequency | 64 | 24 | 88 |
| | | % within educational level | 72.7 | 27.3 | 100.0 |
| | Master/PhD | Frequency | 33 | 3 | 36 |
| | | % within educational level | 91.7 | 8.3 | 100.0 |
| Total | | Frequency | 154 | 44 | 198 |
| | | % within educational level | 77.8 | 22.2 | 100.0 |

## 5 Discussion and Conclusions

The survey identified the factors that affect the customers to use online banking than offline banking.

The banking industry has been affected by the evolution of technology and generally by the digital transformation that has taken place year after year and continues to evolve. The daily and 24-h use of online banking services has significantly improved and simplified banking procedures and allows customers to have unlimited access to their account, although there are customers who do not use online banking applications and resort to offline banking services.

Based on the findings of the present study, online banking can be considered to be very fast and reliable, with more and more people adopting the services it offers. The non-use of the Internet to conduct transactions can be a limiting factor for the bank's customer to deal with fast transactions, and further, customers reported that online banking offers significant processing speed that could not be compared to offline banking transactions. In terms of accessibility, it was concluded that bank customers knew what accessibility meant and the most accessible digital platform was mobile banking, with the feeling that online banking could be used on a moderate scale. In addition, having the ability to make bank transactions at anytime and anywhere could be interpreted as accessibility. The use of technology was the main obstacle to

**Table 7** Use of online banking services and main profession

| | | | Are you currently using online banking services? | | Total |
|---|---|---|---|---|---|
| | | | Yes | No | |
| Main occupation | Public employee | Frequency | 36 | 7 | 43 |
| | | % within main profession | 83.7 | 16.3 | 100.0 |
| | Private employee | Frequency | 55 | 10 | 65 |
| | | % within main profession | 84.6 | 15.4 | 100.0 |
| | Freelance | Frequency | 20 | 2 | 22 |
| | | % within main profession | 90.9 | 9.1 | 100.0 |
| | Unemployed/other | Frequency | 13 | 8 | 21 |
| | | % within main profession | 61.9 | 38.1 | 100.0 |
| | Student | Frequency | 23 | 4 | 27 |
| | | % within main profession | 85.2 | 14.8 | 100.0 |
| | Retired | Frequency | 7 | 13 | 20 |
| | | % within main profession | 35.0 | 65.0 | 100.0 |
| Total | | Frequency | 154 | 44 | 198 |
| | | % within main profession | 77.8 | 22.2 | 100.0 |

accessibility, as technology changed very quickly, without bank customers adopting the necessary skills to deal with this new phenomenon or having the right equipment. In terms of adaptability, mobile phones were the most customizable digital channel due to the personal information it offers to the bank's customers. Furthermore, the customers' daily transactions concluded that the adaptability to the data channels of digital banking was very high, as shown by the daily number of transactions and the frequency with which customers used online banking. Finally, in terms of the availability of digital channels, the research concludes that online banking channels are affordable. Customers will trade using any other channel that is fast, accessible and easily customizable.

Based on the findings presented, the following actions are suggested:

- In order to speed up online banking processes, banks need to invest more in reliable systems to reduce the number of failed transactions and trading errors in ATMs, Mobile banking and POS. Banks will need to further automate most services, such as loan recovery, loan disbursement and the introduction of queue management systems.

**Table 8** Use of online banking services and annual income

| | | | Are you currently using online banking services? | | Total |
|---|---|---|---|---|---|
| | | | Yes | No | |
| Annual family income (last year) | <= 6000€ | Frequency | 27 | 10 | 37 |
| | | % within annual family income (last year) | 73.0 | 27.0 | 100.0 |
| | 6001–12,000€ | Frequency | 27 | 13 | 40 |
| | | % within annual family income (last year) | 67.5 | 32.5 | 100.0 |
| | 12,001–24,000 | Frequency | 66 | 15 | 81 |
| | | % within annual family income (last year) | 81.5 | 18.5 | 100.0 |
| | 24,001–48,000€ | Frequency | 30 | 5 | 35 |
| | | % within annual family income (last year) | 85.7 | 14.3 | 100.0 |
| | >= 48,000€ | Frequency | 4 | 1 | 5 |
| | | % within annual family income (last year) | 80.0 | 20.0 | 100.0 |
| Total | | Frequency | 154 | 44 | 198 |
| | | % within annual family income (last year) | 77.8 | 22.2 | 100.0 |

**Table 9** Key findings

| Finding |
|---|
| Almost 80% are currently using online banking services |
| More than 70% use online banking services at least once per week |
| Age and marital status affect the use of online services |
| Gender, educational level, main profession and annual income do not affect the use of online services |
| The main reasons for avoiding using online banking are the fear for the security of transactions, the low familiarity with technology and the fear of making a mistake when individuals do online banking on their own |
| The main reason for using online banking is the easy money transfer |

- Banks must submit an application that can be used to enhance online banking, which will be considered secure and private in order to enhance the functions, availability and accessibility of digital banking.
- There is a further need to facilitate skills in new technologies so that they can embrace technology. Through a collaborative business with educational organizations, skills in this area can be influenced by banks that teach individuals and collaborate in the changing world of banking technology.
- Customer satisfaction surveys need to be conducted to determine how customers are adapting to technology. Appropriate techniques should be designed based on what customers want, and not what is convenient for banks.
- Therefore, the banks should increase the security and confidence of customers in relation to their online services, so that a relationship of trust can be achieved with online banking, which is considered almost common sense in offline banking.

Despite the sufficient sample, there are limitations since from the beginning the research focused on a specific number of respondents and a specific short period of data collection. Also, for faster and easier concentration of the results, the questionnaires were completed online and in this way the non-users of the technologies may not have been given the necessary attention and opportunity to give their own answers, which would have the opportunity if the questionnaires were given with different way. In addition, the survey analyses only the results of the answers given by users of online and non-banking services and not entrepreneurs as well as employees. Also, from the presented findings it is clear that access to digital banking takes place taking into account only those individuals who are of course considered appropriate in society. A study is needed to determine the impact of accessibility to online banking among people with disabilities. These are some of the limitations that could in the future be a source of concern and inspiration for a more complete and expanded picture of this research.

However, several bank customers believe that contact with the banking staff of a bank is necessary and more effective because customers do not feel safe using the bank's online services, as identified in research by Suh and Han (2002), Rexha et al. (2003), Lichtenstein and Williamson (2006), Aboobucker and Bao (2018) and Boateng et al. (2016).

The contribution of the study is the valuable information for banks so that improve online banking services and develop new products and programs. The originality derives from the updated identified factors that influence the attitude of customers towards the services offered by online banking versus offline banking. The replicability of the results in regional or world level could generalize the approach for the policy makers regarding the online banking. Only further research and discussion can determine whether our findings can be generalized to other industries that offer online services.

In conclusion, it would be appropriate to mention that online banking transactions have entered people's lives dynamically and will continue to evolve. It is worth noting that the ethical issues that may arise are observed in this primary investigation, preserving the anonymity of their results and protecting the personal data of bank customers. However, this research is a small part of the issue it is developing, because in the future there will be improvements as well as further development.

As future work, it would be interesting to compare those who use only online banking and those who use only offline banking; it might shed further light on the reasons behind the adoption of online banking. A cross-sectional study and future research should adopt a longitudinal approach in order to generalize the results. A longitudinal study would be helpful in other offline/online domains or in other cultures.

## References

Aboobucker I, Bao Y (2018) What obstruct customer acceptance of internet banking? Security and privacy, risk, trust and website usability and the role of moderators. J High Technol Manag Res 29(1):109–123

AbuShanab E, Pearson, JM (2007) Internet banking in Jordan. The unified theory of acceptance and use of technology (UTAUT) perspective. J Syst Inf Technol 9(1):78–97

Bharadwaj AS (2000) A resource-based perspective on information technology capability and firm performance: an empirical investigation. MIS Q 169–196

Boateng H, Adam DR, Okoe AF, Anning-Dorson T (2016) Assessing the determinants of internet banking adoption intentions: A social cognitive theory perspective. Comput Hum Behav 65:468–478

Brodsky L, Oakes L (2017) Data sharing and open banking. McKinsey & Company

Casaló LV, Flavián C, Guinalíu M (2007) The role of security, privacy, usability and reputation in the development of online banking. Online Inf Rev 31(5):583–603

Daniel E (1999) Provision of electronic banking in the UK and the Republic of Ireland. Int J Bank Mark 17(2):72–82

Evdokimova Y, Shinkareva O, Bondarenko A (2019) Digital banks: development trends. In: 2nd International scientific conference on new industrialization: global, national, regional dimension (SICNI 2018). Atlantis Press

Ganguli S, Roy SK (2011) Generic technology-based service quality dimensions in banking: Impact on customer satisfaction and loyalty. Int J Bank Mark 29(2):168–189

Gefen D, Karahanna E, Straub DW (2003) Inexperience and experience with online stores: The importance of TAM and trust. IEEE Trans Eng Manage 50(3):307–321

Gupta S (2013) The mobile banking and payment revolution. Eur Fin Rev 2(36):215–254

Hampton-Sosa W, Koufaris M (2005) The effect of web site perceptions on initial trust in the owner company. Int J Electron Commer 10(1):55–81

Hew JJ, Lee VH, Ooi KB, Wei J (2015) What catalyses mobile apps usage intention: An empirical analysis. Ind Manag Data Syst 115(7):1269–1291

Hough J, Chan K (2018) Factors influencing the acceptance of digital banking international association for management of technology

Jarvenpaa SL, Tractinsky N, Vitale M (2000) Consumer trust in an Internet store. Inf Technol Manage 1(1–2):45–71

Julien A, Tsoni C (2013) Front-line employee versus customer perceptions of quality attributes. Qual Manag J 20(2):48–59

Kang I, Lee KC, Kim SM, Lee J (2011) The effect of trust transference in multi-banking channels; offline, online and mobile. Int J Mobile Commun 9(2):103–123

Karatepe OM, Aga M (2016) The effects of organization mission fulfilment and perceived organizational support on job performance: The mediating role of work engagement. Int J Bank Mark 34(3):368–387

Khan I, Rahman Z, Fatma M (2016) The role of customer brand engagement and brand expe-rience in online banking. Int J Bank Mark 34(7):1025–1041
Koufaris M, Hampton-Sosa W (2004) The development of initial trust in an online company by new customer. Inf & Manag 41(3):377–397
Kuan HH, Bock GW (2007) Trust transference in brick and click retailers: an investigation of the before-online-visit phase. Inf Manag 44(2):175–187
Larsson A, Viitaoja Y (2017) Building customer loyalty in digital banking: a study of bank staff's perspectives on the challenges of digital CRM and loyalty. Int J Bank Mark
Lee KC, Kang I, McKnight DH (2007) Transfer from offline trust to key online perceptions: An empirical study. IEEE Trans Eng Manage 54(4):729–741
Lichtenstein S, Williamson K (2006) Understanding consumer adoption of internet banking: an interpretive study in the Australian banking context. J Electron Commer Res 7(2):50–66
Liu C, Marchewka JT, Lu J, Yu CS (2005) Beyond concern—A privacy-trust-behavioral intention model of electronic commerce. Inf & Manag 42(2):289–304
Mukherjee A, Nath P (2003) A model of trust in online relationship banking. Int J Bank Mark 21(1):5–15
Ramaswami SN, Strader TJ, Brett K (2000) Determinants of on- line channel use for purchasing financial products. Int Journal Electron Commer 5(2):95–118
Reichheld FF, Schefter P (2000) E-loyalty: your secret weapon on the web. Harv Bus Rev 78(4):105–113
Rexha N, Kingshott RPJ, Aw ASS (2003) The impact of the relational plan on adoption of electronic banking. J Serv Mark 17(1):53–65
Serener B (2016) Statistical analysis of internet banking usage with logistic regression. Procedia Comput Sci 102:648–653
Shivakumar SK, Sethii S (2019) Transforming legacy banking applications to banking experience platforms. In: Building digital experience platforms. Apress, Berkeley, CA, pp 261–295
Skan J, Dickerson J, Masood S (2015) The future of fintech and banking: digitally disrupted or reimagined. Accenture, London
Suh B, Han I (2002) Effect of trust on customer acceptance of Internet banking. Electron Commer Res Appl 1(3):247–263
Takieddine S, Sun J (2015) Internet banking diffusion: A country-level analysis. Electron Commer Res Appl 14(5):361–371
Vatanasombut B, Igbaria M, Stylianou AC, Rodgers W (2008) Information systems continuance intention of web-based applications customers: the case of online banking. Inf & Manag 45(7):419–428
Yap K, Wong DH, Bak LR (2009). Building trust in e-banking: Where is the line between online and offline Banking?
Yoon HS, Steege LMB (2013) Development of a quantitative model of the impact of customers' personality and perceptions on Internet banking use. Comput Hum Behav 29(3):1133–1141
Yousafzai S, Pallister JG, Foxall GR (2005) Strategies for building and communicating trust in electronic banking: a field experiment. Psychol Mark 22(2):181–201
Yousafzai S, Yani-de-Soriano M (2012) Understanding customer-specific factors underpin-ning internet banking adoption. Int J Bank Mark

# The Profitability of the Central and Eastern European Banking Systems in Correlation with the Macroeconomic Environment

**Radulescu Magdalena, Belascu Lucian, and Dita Sandra Maria**

**Abstract** The macroeconomic situation is correlated with the performance of the banking sector, and the last financial and economic crisis clearly demonstrated that. That is why we have considered the external factors of the banking sectors in this research. Our analysis covers the post-crisis period when the macroeconomic environment became more stable to stress how it impacted on the banking profitability in the CEE area. By analyzing the trends of the banking profitability ratios and the developments of some important macroeconomic factors, we can see if they can be correlated or not for 11 CEE countries. We have found that a low unemployment rate and low interest rate bonds yields are associated with the increase of the banking profitability ratios in the CEE region. A low taxation level supports net interest margin (NIM). An increase of the GDP per capita and high concentration level of the banking systems are associated with a decrease of NIM, but are associated with the increase of ROE. The high inflation rates and large public deficits in some CEE countries significantly supported the increase of the banking profitability ratios in this region, but that cannot represent a solution in the long-run for the banking managers in the CEE countries.

**Keywords** Banking profitability ratios · Macroeconomic environment · CEE countries

**JEL Classification Codes** E44 · G21

R. Magdalena (✉)
University of Pitesti, Str. Targu din Vale, No.1, Pitesti, Romania
e-mail: magdalena.radulescu@upit.ro; magdalena.radulescu@ulbsibiu.ro

R. Magdalena · B. Lucian · D. S. Maria
Lucian Blaga University of Sibiu, Calea Dumbrăvii 17, Sibiu, Romania
e-mail: lucian.belascu@ulbsibiu.ro

 
G. Karanovic et al. (eds.), *The Changing Financial Landscape*, Contributions to Economics, https://doi.org/10.1007/978-3-030-82778-6_14

# 1 Introduction

Economic theory and studies are not only the result of objective intellectual curiosity about social and economic phenomena but also the product of an intense need to reconstruct a system (Krstić 2012).

In the past decades, most countries in Central and Eastern Europe (CEE) have adopted structural reforms in view of increasing the size, stability, and efficiency of financial systems. The banking systems in CEE, which had largely eschewed sub-prime loans and more exotic credit products, had been able to side-step the problems that befell their Western counterparts during the crisis. Previous studies have shown that the CEE banking sectors performed better than other developed European sectors during the crisis, due to their sound capitalization, high profitability and a stable macroeconomic environment before the crisis (Căpraru and Ihnatov 2014).

In Kosmidou, Tanna and Pasinouras (2005) and Demirgüç-Kunt and Huizinga (1999), the authors have used ROA and net interest margin as best ratios for reflecting banking profitability. In CEE region, the share of the interest revenues and interest costs is higher than in other European developed banking sectors, but due to regulatory changes within European Union some banks tend to take on less interest products on their balance sheet (Goddard et al. 2007) and they have argued that using NIM for assessing bank's profitability could lead to distorted results.

According to Krakah and Ameyaw (2010) or Rivard and Thomas (1997), ROA is an appropriate measure of bank profitability, because ROA cannot be distorted by high equity multiplier.

Comparing to ROE, the use of ROA takes into account the risks derived from the leverage and is the key bank profitability ratio (Athanasoglou et al. 2008). A possible limitation of ROA is the existence of the off-balance-sheet assets (not considered for ROA estimation), which represent an important source of profit for European banks.

The macroeconomic situation and performance is inter-correlated with the state and performance of the banking sector, and the last financial and economic crisis clearly demonstrated that. That is why we have considered the external factors of the banking sectors in this research. Our analysis covers the post-crisis period when the macroeconomic environment became more stable to stress how it impacted on the banking profitability in the CEE area.

Besides the internal specific factors of the banking activity, it is interesting to study how macroeconomic environment impacts on the banking profitability. Last financial crisis from 2007 has emphasized a great differences in the impact of the macroeconomic environment on the banking sectors. Staikouras and Wood (2004) studied the impact of internal and external factors on performance for a sample of 685 European banks from 13 countries, (1994–1998). The results show that the profitability of European banks is not only influenced by management decision factors, but also by changes in the external macroeconomic environment.

## 2 Literature Review

In the paper of Onofrei et al. (2018), where the authors studied 96 banks belonging to seven countries of the CEE region using a panel analysis, it was shown that the factors who have a significant influence on banking profitability in this region are the GDP/ capita, the domestic non-governmental credit, the size of banks, the cost income ratio, and provisions for non-performing loans.

The study showed a negative correlation between the increasing inflation and the banks' profitability during the analyzed time period.

A negative significant correlation was found between product diversification and market concentration (Herfindhal-Hirschman index), but banks' profitability is positively correlated with a growing economy (Korytowski 2018). The study aims to find out how the fluctuation of the internal and external factors impact the profitability of 4179 European commercial banks between 2011 and 2015.

Sufian (2009) studies the influencing factors on commercial banks' profitability in Malaysia between 2000 and 2004. The paper shows that a higher level for credit risk and for loan concentration are associated with lower profitability. At the same time, a high level of capitalization, a high level of income from non-interest sources, and higher operational expenses are associated with higher profitability. As far as the impact of the macroeconomic environment on banks profitability is concerned, the increase of the GDP/capita is negatively correlated with profitability, while an increase in inflation is positively correlated.

Mirzaei et al. (2013) empirical study shows the impact that market structure, bank specific characteristics, financial structure, and macroeconomic environment have on profitability by studying 1929 banks from 40 European emergent countries between 1998 and 2008. Less competitive market conditions are correlated with a higher level of profitability in emergent systems, whereas bank operating in advanced economies need a larger market share to achieve that.

Dietrich and Wanzenried (2014) study the determinants of banking profitability using a large sample of over 10,000 banks from 118 countries between 1998 and 2012. There are significant differences regarding profitability and its determinants between banks.

Martinho et al. (2017) study a sample of 110 European banks in the EU-15 countries and discovered a positive correlation between real GDP growth and bank profitability (ROA) due to the procyclicality of impairments. European banks benefit from higher references rates. Borio et al. (2017) discovered a negative correlation between interest rates, the slope of the yield curve, and bank profitability, while GDP growth has no significant impact.

Alper and Anbar (2011) study the internal and macroeconomic factors of profitability in Turkey using a panel data set between 2002 and 2010. The authors use the return on assets (ROA) and the return on equity (ROE) as indicators of a bank's profitability. The only macroeconomic variable to have a positive correlation on banking profitability was the real interest rate.

Naceur (2003) shows that banking profitability and the net interest margin are positively impacted by stock market development, but negatively influenced by inflation and growth rates by studying Tunisian banks between 1983 and 2000.

Dietrich and Wanzenried (2009) show that the most important determinants within the Swiss banking sector are GDP growth, which is positively correlated with bank's profitability, and the effective tax and market concentration rate, both being strongly negatively correlated with profitability.

Bashir (2000) shows that there is a positive correlation between the macroeconomic environment and bank profitability, between stock market development and profitability, but that taxation has a negative impact within the Islamic banking sector.

Athanasoglou et al. (2006) have studied the correlation of a select set of determinants on bank profitability in the SEE region between 1998 and 2002. The research shows that market concentration has a positive impact on profitability. Inflation has a strong effect on banks' profits, while GDP/capita does not have a significant impact on them.

Sayilgan and Yildirim (2009) use monthly data for a sample of Turkish banks for 2002 and 2007 to analyze the relationship between ROA and ROE. There is a negative correlation between profitability and inflation, while between profitability and the industrial production index and the budget balance, there is a positive relationship. Kaya (2002) discovered that profitability (measured by ROA and ROE) of the Turkish banking system is positively correlated with the public budget deficit. Olson and Zoubi (2011) found that bank size, market concentration, and GDP growth positively impact the banking profitability.

Pan and Pan (2014) study the Chinese banking sector and show that economic growth, inflation, interest rates, and money supply growth have a positive impact on bank profitability, while total market capitalization of stock has a negative one. The strongest correlation between the above macroeconomic factors is the one between profitability and money supply growth.

Hasanov et al. (2018) find that bank profitability in Azerbaijan is negatively impacted by the depreciation of the national currency, while being positively impacted by the economic cycle, bank size, and inflationist expectations.

Robert Clair (2004) studied the banking system in Singapore and determined that the exchange rate, interest rate, unemployment rate, and aggregated demand influence the stability and performance of the local banks. The author also showed that the fluctuations of the macroeconomic development generate two-third of the changes in banking profitability.

Abreu and Mendes (2002) found that both ROA and ROE are negatively correlated with inflation and unemployment rate.

Jiang et al. (2003) studied the Hong-Kong banking sector between 1992 and 2002 and found that ROA is positively impacted by real GDP growth rate, inflation, and real interest rate.

Demirgüç-Kunt and Huizinga (1998), show that ROA is positively correlated with GDP per capita, inflation, real interest rate, capital adequacy, and foreign ownership by studying the banking systems of 80 countries between 1988 and 1995. The research shows that in developing countries, domestic banks are less profitable than foreign ones. This finding is also confirmed by the study of Athanasoglou et al. (2006) where they analyzed seven countries in the Central and Southern Europe region between 1998 and 2002. Their research included the index that reflects the bank reform progress, characteristic to developing countries, and discovered that it is strongly negatively correlated with both profitability ratios (ROA and ROE).

Both Brissimis et al. (2008) and Fang et al. (2011) determined that regulation implementation, credit expansion, and sound macroeconomic policies had a positive influence on banking profitability.

Andries et al. (2016) elaborated a panel analysis for the CEE banking sector between 2004 and 2013 showing a weak correlation between bank ownership and profitability; however, foreign banks were able to better withstand the effects of the last economic crisis. Both the inflation rate and exchange rate fluctuations have a negative impact on bank profitability, but only inflation is statistically relevant. According to the research, ROA is positively and significantly influenced by the GDP growth rate, bank size, and bank reform index.

Atasoy (2007) studies the Turkish banking system between 1990 and 2005. This research finds that the inflation rate is positively correlated with bank profitability, while the concentration rate has a negative impact on ROA.

The paper of Havrylchyk and Jurzyk (2006) compared the domestic and foreign banks in terms of banking profitability and its determinants in 10 countries of the CEE region between 1990 and 2005. They found that the macroeconomic conditions of host countries have a reduced effect on the profitability of foreign banks, while domestic banks have a higher level of profitability on markets that are more concentrated.

Beckmann (2007) studied 16 Western-European countries and showed that there is no significant influence between bank profits and the concentration of national banking systems, while the business cycle has a pro-cyclical impact on profitability.

Trujillo-Ponce (2013) determined that bank profits are influenced by inflation, interest rate, economic style, and market concentration.

## 3 Correlation Between the Macroeconomic Environment Variables and Banking Profitability Ratios for CEE Banking Sectors

An important research would be represented by an analysis of the relation between the trend of the profitability ratios of the banking systems (ROA, ROE, and NIM) in the CEE region and the developments of some important determinants of the macroeconomic environment in these countries after the last financial and economic crisis (we analyzed in this paper 11 CEE countries namely Bulgaria, Croatia, Czech Republic, Estonia, Hungary, Latvia, Lithuania, Poland, Romania, Slovak Republic and Slovenia, all of them being EU countries and 6 of them being also in the euro-area). Analyzing the trends of those three banking profitability ratios and the developments of some important macroeconomic factors, we can see if they can be correlated or not in this CEE region where the banking systems perform better in terms of profitability against the other EU banking systems.

In the CEE countries with the highest share of the GDP per capita of the average EU GDP per capita (Czech Republic, Estonia, Lithuania and Slovenia), ROA fluctuates between 1.2 and 1.5% with the highest level in Estonia which is the most concentrated banking market in the CEE region and ROE ranges between around 10–13%. The most stable and high ROE ratios are displayed in Lithuania and Czech Republic, while Slovenia faced a recovery in this area after large negative ROE ratios after the crisis. Estonia faced an important drop of ROE in 2018. NIM decreased in those four CEE countries. In the CEE countries with the lowest share of the GDP per capita of the average EU GDP per capita (Bulgaria, Croatia, Romania), ROA ranges between small negative levels and maximum 15% (except in Romania in 2018). In 2014 and 2015, these CEE countries displayed losses and negative ROA and ROE levels. The lowest banking profitability ratios are displayed by Croatia, and the highest levels of the profitability ratios are displayed by Romania among these last three CEE countries with the lowest GDP per capita. So, in the CEE countries with the highest GDP per capita, the banking profitability ratios display the highest levels, while in the CEE countries with the lowest GDP per capita, the banking profitability ratios are the lower if we consider ROE, while NIM is high (except Romania where the banking profitability ratios increased but GDP per capita also largely increased during 2013–2018) (see Table 1 and Tables 10, 11, 12). We stress mixed effects of GDP per capita developments on ROA. So, ROE is positively correlated with GDP per capita in the CEE region. These results are in line with the findings of Korytowski (2018) and Onofrei et al. (2018) that analyzed this relation both during the crisis, but also in the

**Table.1** GDP/capita (% of total EU28 GDP/capita)

| | 2013 | 2014 | 2015 | 2016 | 2017 | 2018 |
|---|---|---|---|---|---|---|
| Bulgaria | 45.4 | 46.7 | 47.3 | 48.8 | 49.7 | 50.8 |
| Croatia | 59.6 | 58.7 | 59.3 | 60.7 | 61.8 | 62.9 |
| Czech Republic | 83.5 | 85.8 | 86.9 | 87.5 | 89.2 | 90.5 |
| Estonia | 75.5 | 77.4 | 76 | 76.2 | 78.4 | 81.6 |
| Hungary | 67 | 68.1 | 68.8 | 67.5 | 68.4 | 70.7 |
| Latvia | 62.1 | 63.4 | 64.1 | 64.4 | 66 | 68.9 |
| Lithuania | 73 | 74.9 | 74.4 | 75.4 | 78.3 | 80.2 |
| Poland | 66.8 | 67.3 | 68.4 | 68.2 | 69 | 70.3 |
| Romania | 54.2 | 54.8 | 55.8 | 59.3 | 63.2 | 65.6 |
| Slovak Republic | 76.5 | 77.1 | 77.2 | 72.3 | 71.6 | 73.1 |
| Slovenia | 82 | 82.1 | 81.6 | 82.4 | 84.9 | 86.9 |

*Source* Global financial report database, World Bank and Eurostat database 2013–2018

**Table 2** Unemployment rate (% of active population)

| | 2013 | 2014 | 2015 | 2016 | 2017 | 2018 |
|---|---|---|---|---|---|---|
| Bulgaria | 13 | 11.4 | 9.2 | 7.6 | 6.2 | 5.2 |
| Croatia | 17.4 | 17.2 | 16.1 | 13.4 | 11 | 8.4 |
| Czech Republic | 7 | 6.1 | 5.1 | 4 | 2.9 | 2.2 |
| Estonia | 8.6 | 7.4 | 6.2 | 6.8 | 5.8 | 5.4 |
| Hungary | 10.2 | 7.7 | 6.8 | 5.1 | 4.2 | 3.7 |
| Latvia | 11.9 | 10.8 | 9.9 | 9.6 | 8.7 | 7.4 |
| Lithuania | 11.8 | 10.7 | 9.1 | 7.9 | 7.1 | 6.2 |
| Poland | 10.3 | 9 | 7.5 | 6.2 | 4.9 | 3.9 |
| Romania | 7.1 | 6.8 | 6.8 | 5.9 | 4.9 | 4.2 |
| Slovak Republic | 14.2 | 13.2 | 11.5 | 9.7 | 8.1 | 6.5 |
| Slovenia | 10.1 | 9.7 | 9 | 8 | 6.6 | 5.1 |

*Source* Global financial report database, World Bank and Eurostat database 2013–2018

post-crisis period. The same relation was found by Dietrich and Wanzenried (2009), Andries et al. (2016), or Pan and Pan (2014). NIM is negatively correlated with GDP per capita for CEE countries. This negative relation was also found by Naceur (2003). ROA fluctuates a lot in the area, no matter of the GDP per capita developments. These results are in line with the findings of Athanasoglou et al. (2006).

Czech Republic displays the lowest unemployment rate, while in Croatia the unemployment rate is the highest among the CEE analyzed countries. The Czech Republic displays high and stable banking profitability ratios after the crisis, while Croatia displays the lowest banking profitability ratios among the CEE countries (see Table 2 and Tables 10, 11, 12). These ratios are negatively correlated in the CEE region. This is in line with the findings of Abreu and Mendes (2002).

The CEE countries with the lowest interest rate bond yields (the Baltic countries, Slovak Republic, and Slovenia) display high profitability ratios of their banking systems (except ROA in Slovak Republic and Latvia which is quite low, but in these two countries NIM is higher than in Lithuania, Slovenia, or Estonia). In Poland, where the long-term interest rate bond yields are high, the banking profitability ratios are low and decreased in the analyzed period. Romania displays the highest levels of the interest rate bond yields, but the banking profitability ratios are also high, especially ROE and NIM. The negative correlation between interest rate bond yields and the banking profitability ratios is not validated for Romania (see Table 3 and Tables 10, 11, 12). Some researchers suggest that banks perform better in low interest rate environments. When the interest rates are low, banks focus on consultancy services and trading activities to generate non-interest income such as fees and commissions (Borio et al. 2017). Romania is an exception because its banking system relies much more on the interest income than on fee income. A negative relation between the banking profitability ratios and interest rate bond yields can be explained by the impact of low interest rate bond yields on GDP per capita or unemployment rate.

**Table 3** Long-term interest rate bond yields (%)

| | 2013 | 2014 | 2015 | 2016 | 2017 | 2018 |
|---|---|---|---|---|---|---|
| Bulgaria | 3.47 | 3.35 | 2.5 | 2.27 | 1.6 | 0.9 |
| Croatia | 4.68 | 4.05 | 3.55 | 3.49 | 2.77 | 2.17 |
| Czech Republic | 2,11 | 1.58 | 0.58 | 0.43 | 0.98 | 1.98 |
| Estonia | 0.8 | 0.3 | 0.2 | 0.1 | – | – |
| Hungary | 5.92 | 4.81 | 3.43 | 3.77 | 2.62 | 2.18 |
| Latvia | 3.34 | 2.51 | 0.96 | 0.53 | 0.83 | 0.9 |
| Lithuania | 3.83 | 2.79 | 1.38 | 0.9 | 0.31 | 0.31 |
| Poland | 4.03 | 3.52 | 2.7 | 3.04 | 3.42 | 3.2 |
| Romania | 5.41 | 4.5 | 3.47 | 3.32 | 3.96 | 4.7 |
| Slovak Republic | 3.19 | 2.07 | 0.9 | 0.54 | 0.92 | 0.9 |
| Slovenia | 5.81 | 3.27 | 1.71 | 1.15 | 0.96 | 0.93 |

*Source* Global financial report database, World Bank and Eurostat database 2013–2018

Large public deficits (in Romania and Hungary) are associated with an increase of the banking profitability ratios in these two countries (positive correlation), but also with losses for the banking systems and this fact is also demonstrated by the cases of Bulgaria or Slovenia during 2013–2014. The case of Croatia is an exception in the CEE region where high public deficits were not associated with banking system losses during 2013–2016. Improving the public deficit situation seems to impact more on ROA than on ROE, while NIM is not largely affected in the CEE region by an improvement of the public deficit (except in Estonia where the worsening of the public deficits was associated with a decrease of the banking profitability ratios) (see Table 4 and Tables 10, 11, 12). A positive relation between the public deficits and the banking profitability ratios was also found by Kaya (2002).

In Slovak Republic, Estonia, Lithuania, and Czech Republic with the highest level of taxation and contribution rate of profit, ROA is low among the analyzed countries (in Estonia and Lithuania NIM is also low). In the Baltic countries, we can stress that NIM is low among the analyzed CEE countries because of very low levels of the interest rate (except Latvia) which means that they are relying most of fee income in their banking systems, while ROE is ranging between 10 and 12%. The CEE countries with a low level of taxation (Bulgaria and Croatia), ROA is also low, but ROE and NIM are high. ROA and ROE are not affected much by the level of taxation, but NIM is. NIM and the level of taxation are negatively correlated in the CEE countries (see Table 5 and Tables 10, 11, 12). This result is in line with the findings of Dietrich and Wanzenried (2009) or Bashir (2000).

Estonia, Latvia, and Slovak Republic display the highest level of the domestic credit granted to the private sector (as share of GDP), but ROE is negatively correlated with the domestic credit granted. NIM is also negatively correlated, except in Leton banking system which rely more on banking interest income. Romania and Hungary display the lowest level of the domestic credit granted to the private sector (as share of

**Table 4** Public deficit (% of GDP)

| | 2013 | 2014 | 2015 | 2016 | 2017 | 2018 |
|---|---|---|---|---|---|---|
| Bulgaria | −0.4 | −5.4 | −1.7 | 0.1 | 1.1 | 1.8 |
| Croatia | −5.3 | −5.3 | −3.3 | −1.1 | 0.8 | 0.3 |
| Czech Republic | −1.2 | −2.1 | −0.6 | 0.7 | 1.6 | 1.1 |
| Estonia | 0.2 | 0.7 | 0.1 | −0.5 | −0.8 | −0.6 |
| Hungary | −2.5 | −2.8 | −2 | −1.8 | −2.4 | −2.3 |
| Latvia | −1.2 | −1.4 | −1.4 | 0.1 | −0.5 | −0.7 |
| Lithuania | −2.6 | −0.6 | −0.3 | 0.2 | 0.5 | 0.6 |
| Poland | −4.2 | −3.6 | −2.6 | −2.4 | −1.5 | −0.2 |
| Romania | −2.1 | −1.2 | −0.6 | −2.6 | −2.6 | −3 |
| Slovak Republic | −2.9 | −3.1 | −2.7 | −2.5 | −1 | −1.1 |
| Slovenia | −2.9 | −3.1 | −2.7 | −2.5 | −1 | −1.1 |

*Source* Global financial report database, World Bank and Eurostat database 2013–2018

**Table 5** Total tax and contribution rate (% of profit)

| | 2013 | 2014 | 2015 | 2016 | 2017 | 2018 |
|---|---|---|---|---|---|---|
| Bulgaria | 27 | 27 | 27 | 27 | 27.1 | 27.7 |
| Croatia | 19.3 | 18.4 | 20 | 20.9 | 20.6 | 20.5 |
| Czech Republic | 45.6 | 46.5 | 46.5 | 46.1 | 46.1 | 46.1 |
| Estonia | 49.6 | 49.2 | 49.2 | 48.5 | 48.5 | 48.5 |
| Hungary | 49.2 | 47.9 | 48.2 | 46.3 | 46.4 | 40.3 |
| Latvia | 35 | 35 | 35.9 | 35.9 | 35.9 | 36 |
| Lithuania | 49.2 | 42.4 | 42.6 | 42.6 | 42.7 | 42.6 |
| Poland | 40.1 | 40.1 | 40.3 | 40.4 | 40.5 | 40.7 |
| Romania | 43.2 | 43.2 | 42 | 40 | 40 | 40 |
| Slovak Republic | 48.7 | 49.4 | 50.4 | 50.1 | 50.1 | 49.7 |
| Slovenia | 31.4 | 31 | 31 | 31 | 31 | 31 |

*Source* Global financial report database, World Bank and Eurostat database 2013–2018

GDP), but all the three banking profitability ratios are high for those two countries. So, the correlation is negatively between the banking profitability ratios and the domestic credit granted by banks for most of the CEE countries, but this relation depends on the share of the interest income in the total banking income for the CEE banking systems. Most of these CEE banking systems increased the share of non-interest income of their total banking income (see Table 6 and Tables 10, 11, 12).

A real appreciation of the local currency determined an increase of ROE in Hungary, but a decrease of ROE in Poland. NIM and ROA increased at large appreciations (negative relation) in Poland and Hungary. Large depreciations determined an increase of ROE and ROA (positive relation) in Romania, while NIM fluctuated

**Table 6** Domestic credit to private sector (% of GDP)

| | 2013 | 2014 | 2015 | 2016 | 2017 | 2018 |
|---|---|---|---|---|---|---|
| Bulgaria | 66.5 | 59.5 | 55.4 | 52.7 | 50.6 | 51.3 |
| Croatia | 69.6 | 68 | 64.4 | 60.2 | 57.2 | 55.7 |
| Czech Republic | 51.1 | 49.8 | 49.8 | 51.3 | 51.5 | 52.1 |
| Estonia | 69 | 66.8 | 68.4 | 69.9 | 64.2 | 61.7 |
| Hungary | 46.1 | 42.7 | 35.3 | 33.7 | 32.8 | 32.9 |
| Latvia | 47.9 | 49.7 | 52.7 | 57.1 | 60.2 | 61.8 |
| Lithuania | 43 | 40.8 | 41.5 | 42.6 | 40.9 | 40.6 |
| Poland | 51 | 52.3 | 53.6 | 54.4 | 52.5 | 52.7 |
| Romania | 33.9 | 31.1 | 29.9 | 28 | 26.4 | 25.9 |
| Slovak Republic | 47.8 | 49.7 | 52.7 | 57 | 60.2 | 61.8 |
| Slovenia | 65.3 | 54.5 | 49.8 | 46.7 | 45 | 43.4 |

*Source* Global financial report database, World Bank and Eurostat database 2013–2018

a lot in the analyzed period. So, the results of real exchange rate fluctuations are mixed for the CEE banking sectors, but large fluctuations of the real exchange rate are associated with large fluctuations of the banking profitability ratios (see Table 7 and Tables 10, 11, 12).

Romania, Hungary, and Estonia display a high inflation rate. For Romania and Hungary, a high inflation was associated with high banking profitability ratios, while for Estonia, this correlation is negative. Croatia displays the lowest inflation rate in the region which is positively correlated with ROA and ROE and negatively correlated with NIM that increased (see Table 8 and Tables 10, 11, 12). The positive correlation

**Table 7** Real exchange rate fluctuations (index 2010 = 100)

| | 2013 | 2014 | 2015 | 2016 | 2017 | 2018 |
|---|---|---|---|---|---|---|
| Bulgaria | 99.4 | 97.2 | 95.4 | 95 | 95 | 96 |
| Croatia | 96.9 | 95.8 | 95 | 96.1 | 96.9 | 97.5 |
| Czech Republic | 97.5 | 91.6 | 91.8 | 94.2 | 97.7 | 100.7 |
| Estonia | 104.4 | 104.8 | 104.4 | 106.1 | 108.6 | 111.5 |
| Hungary | 96.8 | 92.5 | 91.3 | 92.1 | 93.7 | 91.8 |
| Latvia | 99.9 | 99.9 | 99.3 | 100.5 | 101.9 | 103.1 |
| Lithuania | 101.2 | 100.6 | 98.9 | 100.9 | 103.2 | 104.4 |
| Poland | 96.3 | 96.1 | 94.3 | 91 | 93.7 | 93.2 |
| Romania | 100.6 | 100.8 | 99.4 | 98.2 | 96.3 | 96.8 |
| Slovak Republic | 102.6 | 102.2 | 100.8 | 101.3 | 101.2 | 102.1 |
| Slovenia | 100.1 | 100 | 98.5 | 98.9 | 98.9 | 99.2 |

*Source* Global financial report database, World Bank and Eurostat database 2013–2018

**Table 8** Harmonized index of consumer price (% annual change, 2010 = 100)

| | 2013 | 2014 | 2015 | 2016 | 2017 | 2018 |
|---|---|---|---|---|---|---|
| Bulgaria | 108.9 | 106.7 | 106.6 | 105.7 | 107.9 | 110.7 |
| Croatia | 108.1 | 107.8 | 107.3 | 106.1 | 107.3 | 108.9 |
| Czech Republic | 106.7 | 107.1 | 107.4 | 108.2 | 110.8 | 113.1 |
| Estonia | 112.1 | 112 | 111.4 | 111.6 | 115.4 | 119.3 |
| Hungary | 111.7 | 111.4 | 111.3 | 111.8 | 114.4 | 117.6 |
| Latvia | 106.7 | 107.3 | 107.5 | 107.7 | 110.8 | 113.6 |
| Lithuania | 108.4 | 108.5 | 107.6 | 108.6 | 112.6 | 115.4 |
| Poland | 109 | 109 | 108.1 | 107.4 | 109.6 | 111.5 |
| Romania | 113.6 | 114.8 | 114.2 | 112.4 | 113.9 | 119.1 |
| Slovak Republic | 109.1 | 109 | 108.7 | 108.1 | 109.6 | 111.4 |
| Slovenia | 106.3 | 106.5 | 105.9 | 105.8 | 107.4 | 110 |

*Source* Global financial report database, World Bank and Eurostat database 2013–2018

between inflation rate and banking profitability is also confirmed by Sufian (2009), Pan and Pan (2014) or Athanasoglou et al. (2006), and a negative impact of inflation rate on NIM was also confirmed by Naceur (2003).

Estonia and Lithuania display the most concentrated banking markets in the CEE region. NIM is low for those two countries (negative relation), ROE in Lithuania is high, and ROA is high in Estonia. Poland is a less concentrated banking market. In Poland, ROA and ROE are low, but NIM is high. So, concentration of the banking market is negatively correlated with NIM, but ROA is not affected by the concentration. ROE tend to decrease if the banking market is not concentrated (positive relation), but it is not a valid rule for all CEE countries (see Table 9 and Tables 10, 11, 12). The negative correlation between the concentration level of the banking systems and the banking profitability ratios was also demonstrated by Sufian (2009), Atasoy (2007) or Mirzaei et al. (2013).

Estonia, Hungary, Czech Republic, and Romania display the highest ROA in the CEE region, while Bulgaria, Croatia, Slovenia, and Poland rank on the last positions with low ROA ratios (Table 10).

Estonia, Hungary, Czech Republic, and Romania display the highest ROE in the CEE region, while Bulgaria, Croatia, Slovenia, and Poland rank on the last positions with low ROE ratios (Table 11). ROE trend is similar to ROE for CEE region. Large fluctuations of ROA and ROE can be observed in Slovenia, for ROA in Bulgaria, too, those two countries displaying low profitability ratios on average and smaller fluctuations can be observed also in Hungary and Romania, those last two countries displaying high profitability ratios.

Bulgaria, Croatia, Romania, and Hungary display high NIM rates. High NIM rates can also be noticed in Estonia, but NIM largely fluctuated in this country during the analyzed period. Lithuania, Czech Republic, and Slovenia display low NIM rates (Table 12). Slovenia displays low ROA, ROE, and NIM rates, while in Bulgaria and

**Table 9** Banking market concentration (three top banks assets % of total banking sector assets)

| | 2013 | 2014 | 2015 | 2016 | 2017 |
|---|---|---|---|---|---|
| Bulgaria | 43.9 | 49.6 | 56.7 | 55.9 | 49.8 |
| Croatia | 58.8 | 59 | 67.6 | 60.3 | 65.2 |
| Czech Republic | 60.6 | 59.4 | 60.3 | 60 | 60.2 |
| Estonia | 93.4 | 93.1 | 92.2 | 75.1 | 93.2 |
| Hungary | 52 | 52.5 | 78.7 | 66.5 | 58.8 |
| Latvia | 50.7 | 48.6 | 85.7 | 52.5 | 49.1 |
| Lithuania | 81.6 | 80.3 | 91.3 | 87.9 | 88.6 |
| Poland | 37.9 | 39.4 | 41.9 | 40.2 | 42.1 |
| Romania | 53.7 | 53.4 | 65.6 | 59.3 | 61.1 |
| Slovak Republic | 72.2 | 71.9 | 73.1 | 74.6 | 78.1 |
| Slovenia | 51.4 | 52.5 | 56.2 | 59.7 | 61.6 |

*Source* Global financial report database, World Bank and Eurostat database 2013–2017

**Table 10** Return on assets ROA (%)

| | 2013 | 2014 | 2015 | 2016 | 2017 | 2018 |
|---|---|---|---|---|---|---|
| Bulgaria | 0.4 | −5.9 | 0.5 | 1.2 | 1.4 | 1.2 |
| Croatia | 0.1 | 0.3 | −0.5 | 1.3 | 0.76 | 1.6 |
| Czech Republic | 1.4 | 1.2 | 1.3 | 1.4 | 1.4 | 1.2 |
| Estonia | 2.9 | 1.9 | 3.3 | 0.2 | 2.7 | 1.5 |
| Hungary | −0.4 | −1.9 | 0.3 | 1.9 | 2 | 2.2 |
| Latvia | 0.4 | 0.8 | 0.7 | 1.7 | 0.7 | 1.5 |
| Lithuania | 1.4 | 0.9 | 1 | 1.2 | 1 | 1.2 |
| Poland | 1 | 1 | 0.8 | 0.9 | 0.9 | 1.3 |
| Romania | −0.1 | −1.9 | 1.3 | 1.2 | 1.5 | 2.1 |
| Slovak Republic | 0.9 | 0.8 | 0.9 | 1.2 | 1 | 1.6 |
| Slovenia | −10.4 | −0.2 | 0.3 | 1 | 1 | 1.4 |

*Source* Global financial report database, World Bank and Eurostat database 2013–2018

Croatia, ROA and ROE are low, but NIM is high. Contrary, in Czech Republic, ROA and ROE are high, and NIM is low. Romania, Hungary, and Estonia (Estonia presents some large fluctuations of NIM) display high ROA, ROE, and NIM rates.

Concluding our analysis, GDP per capita is positively correlated with ROE (in line with the findings of Andrieș et al., 2016; Korytowski 2018; Olson and Zoubi 2011; Dietrich and Wanzenried 2009; Pan and Pan 2014; Jiang et al. 2003), but negatively correlated with NIM, as Sufian (2009) and Naceur (2003) demonstrated in their studies. For ROA, the results are mixed in the CEE area. Unemployment rate is negatively correlated with all the banking profitability ratios. These results are in line with the findings of Abreu and Mendes (2002) who found a negative

**Table 11** Return on equity ROE (%)

| | 2013 | 2014 | 2015 | 2016 | 2017 | 2018 |
|---|---|---|---|---|---|---|
| Bulgaria | 3.3 | −5 | 4.4 | 9.5 | 11.1 | 11.9 |
| Croatia | 1.2 | 3.1 | −3.4 | 9.6 | 5.4 | 8.8 |
| Czech Republic | 13.8 | 12 | 12.2 | 13.7 | 15.1 | 13.5 |
| Estonia | 18.4 | 11.4 | 20.3 | 16 | 17.2 | 9.8 |
| Hungary | −4 | −17.3 | 3.5 | 15 | 17.5 | 14.6 |
| Latvia | 9.2 | 9.1 | 8.3 | 16.4 | 7.4 | 9.2 |
| Lithuania | 12.7 | 7.75 | 8.2 | 10.4 | 10.2 | 12.3 |
| Poland | 9.7 | 9.5 | 7.5 | 8.6 | 8.8 | 7 |
| Romania | −1.6 | −18.4 | 12.6 | 11.3 | 13.7 | 13.6 |
| Slovak Republic | 8.7 | 8.1 | 8.6 | 11.9 | 10.4 | 9.3 |
| Slovenia | −117.6 | −2.4 | 3 | 7.6 | 11.3 | 10.7 |

*Source* Global financial report database, World Bank and Eurostat database 2013–2018

**Table 12** Net interest margin NIM (%)

| | 2013 | 2014 | 2015 | 2016 | 2017 | 2018 |
|---|---|---|---|---|---|---|
| Bulgaria | 3.3 | 3.4 | 3.4 | 3.8 | 4.2 | 3.8 |
| Croatia | 3.2 | 2.9 | 2.8 | 3.4 | 3.9 | 3.4 |
| Czech Republic | 2.6 | 2.4 | 2.3 | 2.2 | 2.4 | 2.2 |
| Estonia | 3.6 | 2.7 | 2.4 | 1.2 | 4.2 | 1.2 |
| Hungary | 3.4 | 3.3 | 2.4 | 3.2 | 4.5 | 3.2 |
| Latvia | 2.3 | 2 | 1.2 | 2.5 | 2.5 | 2.5 |
| Lithuania | 1.7 | 1.7 | 1.5 | 1.8 | 2 | 1.8 |
| Poland | 2.9 | 2.6 | 2.3 | 2.5 | 3.2 | 2.6 |
| Romania | 4 | 3.5 | 3.2 | 3.6 | 3.6 | 3.6 |
| Slovak Republic | 3.4 | 3.3 | 3 | 2.8 | 3 | 2.8 |
| Slovenia | 1.8 | 2.3 | 2.2 | 2 | 2.7 | 2 |

*Source* Global financial report database, World Bank and Eurostat database 2013–2018

relation, too. There is a negative correlation between long-term interest bond yields and the banking profitability ratios (except in Romania). This is in line with the findings of Borio et al. (2017). Large public deficits are positively correlated with the banking profitability ratios (ROA especially), except in Estonia. These results are in line with the findings of Sayilgan and Yildirim (2009) or Kaya (2002). NIM is not affected by the public deficit in the CEE area, but it is negatively affected by the level of taxation and contribution rate of profits. The negative correlation between taxation and profitability rates was also demonstrated by Dietrich and Wanzenried (2009) or by Bashir (2000). ROA and ROE are not affected by the level of taxation. The domestic credit granted to the private sector is negatively correlated with ROE

**Table 13** Banking profitability ratios correlation with macroeconomic indicators (based on their developments) in the CEE region

| | ROA | ROE | NIM |
|---|---|---|---|
| GDP/capita | Mixed results | Positive correlation | Negative correlation |
| Unemployment rate | Negative correlation | Negative correlation | Negative correlation |
| Long-term bond interest rate yields | Negative correlation[a] | Negative correlation[a] | Negative correlation[a] |
| Public deficit of GDP | Strong positive correlation[b] | Positive correlation[b] | Weak correlation |
| Total tax contribution rate | Weak correlation | Weak correlation | Negative correlation |
| Domestic credit to private sector | Weak correlation | Negative correlation | Negative correlation |
| Real exchange rate fluctuations (2010 = 100) | Mixed results | Mixed results | Mixed results |
| HICP (2010 = 100) | Positive correlation[b] | Positive correlation[b] | Positive correlation[c] |
| Banking market concentration rate | Mixed results | Positive correlation | Negative correlation |

*Source* Authors' results based on the analysis of the developments of the variables presented above. [a]except for Romania, [b]except for Estonia, [c]except for Estonia and Croatia.

and NIM, ROA being less affected by this indicator. The results of real exchange rate fluctuations are mixed for the CEE banking sectors. Inflation rate is positively correlated with ROA and ROE (except for Estonia). These results are in line with the findings of Sufian (2009), Hasanov et al. (2018), Atasoy (2007), Jiang et al. (2003) or Pan and Pan (2014) that demonstrated a positive correlation between inflation and profitability rates. For NIM, the positive correlation with inflation is valid with the exception of Estonia and Croatia. ROE displays a positive correlation with the concentration degree of the banking system (as in the study of Athanasoglou et al. (2008) and Olson and Zoubi (2011), while NIM displays a negative correlation with this indicator. The negative correlation was also demonstrated by Korytowski (2018), Dietrich and Wanzenried (2009), Atasoy (2007), Havrylchyk and Jurzyk (2006), and Mirzaei et al. (2013). For ROA, the results are mixed for the CEE countries (Table 13).

## 4 Conclusions

For high ROE levels, GDP per capita, inflation, public deficits, and the concentration degree of the banking sector should be high. Unemployment rate, long-term interest rate bond yields, and domestic credit granted to the private sector should be low for ROE to increase. Level of taxation shows mixed results for ROE trend in the CEE region. The factors impacting on ROE display effects both on banking profits and banking capitalization that is why their impact on ROE is very different.

GDP per capita, unemployment rate, level of taxation, long-term interest rate bond yields, concentration degree of the banking sector, and the domestic credit granted to the private sector are negatively correlated with NIM in the CEE countries. A high inflation rate determines an increase of NIM, while the public deficits and real exchange rate fluctuations display mixed results for NIM development.

For ROA, high inflation rate and large public deficits determine an increase of this banking profitability ratio, while high unemployment rate and long-term interest rate bond yields determine a decrease of ROA. GDP per capita, concentration degree of the banking sector, taxation level, domestic credit, and real exchange rate fluctuations display mixed results for ROA.

In the CEE countries with banking systems that faced losses (Romania, Bulgaria, Croatia, Slovenia, Hungary) at the beginning of the analyzed period (2013–2015), we can stress an appreciation of their national currencies (especially in Romania and Hungary that faced great losses during 2013–2014 in their banking systems), a low share of the domestic credit for private sector of GDP, large public deficits and a low concentration degree of their banking systems and a high inflation that made the macroeconomic environment unpredictable, although the inflation rate supported rather high banking profitability ratios in the CEE area most of the analyzed period.

In the light of the Basel III requirements for a solid capitalization, ROE is expected to decrease in the near future all over the world. To support a ROE increase, CEE countries should aim a more rapid growth of their GDP per capita, a higher concentration level of their banking systems, low real exchange rate fluctuations, low interest rate bond yields, and a low unemployment rate. A high inflation rate and some large public deficits cannot represent a solution for increasing ROE. Low unemployment rate and low interest rate bond yields also support the increase of NIM and ROA in the CEE region. A low taxation level also supports the increase of NIM in those banking systems. A more rapid growth of the GDP per capita and a higher concentration level of the banking systems will decrease NIM.

The sound capitalization of the CEE banking sectors represented the key for their resilience during the 2007–2008 financial crisis. Achieving goals such as a low unemployment rate, low fluctuations of the exchange rate, and low interest rate bond yields also support the convergence process for the CEE countries that target accession to the eurozone, not only increase the profitability rates of the banking sectors in this CEE area. The good performance over time of the Baltic banking sectors proved that a sound economic growth and a concentrated banking market supports the profitabiliy of the banking systems. The last crisis supported the concentration process on the banking markets in the CEE area, because there were some important mergers and acquisitions on this market during the 2008 crisis and right after that crisis. The economic growth relaunched starting with 2014, but the pandemic stopped the rapid economic growth rates and unemployment increased again in the whole Europe. However, the banking sectors can benefit from the increasing inflation rates and increasing public deficits lately in the governments' attempts to support the economy. However, there was a sharp drop of the banking credit as a result of the pandemic and very difficult times can be seen in the near future for the economic activity and or the banking sectors in the whole world. Investors became resilient and very prudent in this context, and they need a stable macroeconomic context. The interest rate bond yields have also started to increase currently.

A direction of a future research would be represented by a LS panel analysis to stress which of these macroeconomic factors are the most important for the banking profitability ratios in the CEE region. This is the main limitation of this study, namely the lack of an empiric panel analysis for the CEE banking sectors to underline better the impact of the macroeconomic variables on the banking profitability ratios in the CEE region.

## References


Abreu M, Mendes V (2002) Commercial Bank interest margins and profitability: Evidence for some E.U. countries. University of Porto Working Paper Series, No. 122

Alper B, Anbar A (2011) Bank specific and macroeconomic determinants of commercial bank profitability: Empirical evidence from Turkey. Bus Econ Res J 2(2):139–152

Andrieş AM, Căpraru B, Fl I-M, Ihnatov I (2016) The impact of international financial crisis on Bank performance in Eastern and Central European countries. EuroEconomica 35(1):111–126

Atasoy H (2007) Expenditure-income analysis in Turkish banking sector and determinants of profitability. Un Published Dissertations of Senior Specialists. Central Bank of Turkey, Ankara

Athanasoglou P, Brissimis SN, Delis M (2008) Bank-specific, industry-specific and macroeconomic determinants of bank profitability. J Int Finan Markets Inst Money 18(2):121–136

Athanasoglou PP, Delis MD, Staikouras CK (2006) Determinants of bank profitability in the South Eastern European region. Munich Personal RePEc Archive

Bashir A (2000). Assessing the performance of Islamic banks: some evidence from the Middle-East. Paper Presented at the ERF 8th Meeting in Jordan

Beckmann R (2007) Profitability of Western European banking systems: Panel evidence on structural and cyclical determinants. Deutsche Bundesbank, Discussion Paper Series 2: Banking and Financial Studies, no. 17

Borio C, Gambacorta L, Hofmann B (2017) The influence of monetary policy on bank profitability. Int Financ 20(1):48–63

Brissimis SN, Delis MD, Papanikolaou NI (2008) Exploring the nexus between banking sector reform and performance: evidence from newly acceded EU countries. Bank of Greece, Working Paper 73

Căpraru B, Ihnatov I (2014) Banks' profitability in selected central and Eastern European countries. Procedia Econ Financ 16:587–591

Clair R (2004) Macroeconomic determinants of banking financial performance and resilience in Singapore. MAS Staff Paper no.38

Demirgüç-Kunt A, Huizinga H (1998) Determinants of commercial bank interest margins and profitability. Policy Research Working Paper 1900

Demirgüç-Kunt A, Huizinga H (1999) Determinants of commercial bank interest margins and profitability: Some international evidence. WB Policy Research Working Paper No. 1900, Washington, DC, World Bank

Dietrich A, Wanzenried G (2014) The determinants of commercial banking profitability in low-, middle-, and high-income countries. Q Rev Econ Finance 54(3):337–354

Dietrich A, Wanzenried G (2009) What determines the profitability of commercial banks? New evidence from Switzerland. In: 12th Conference of the Swiss Society for Financial Market Researches, Geneva
Fang Y, Hasan I, Marton K (2011) Bank efficiency in transition economies: recent evidence from South-Eastern Europe. Bank of Finland Research, Discution Papers 5
Goddard J, Molyneux P, Wilson JOS, Tavakoli M (2007) European banking: An overview. J Bank Finance 31(7):1911–1935
Hasanov F, Bayramli N, Al-Musehel N (2018) Bank-specific and macroeconomic determinants of bank profitability: Evidence from an oil-dependent economy, Int J Financ Stud 6(78):1–21
Havrylchyk O, Jurzyk E (2006) Profitability of foreign and domestic banks in Central and Eastern Europe: does the mode of entry matter? LICOS Centre for Transition Economics, Discussion Paper 166
Jiang G, Law E, Sze A (2003) The Profitability of the Banking Sector in Hong Kong. Hong Kong Monetary Authority Quarterly Bulletin, September 2003
Kaya TY (2002) Determinants of profitability in Turkish banking sector. Turkish Banking Regulation and Supervision Agency, No 1
Korytowski M (2018) Banks' profitability determinants in post-crisis European Union. IJFBS 7(1):1–12
Kosmidou K, Tanna S, Pasinouras F (2005) Determinants of profitability of domestic UK commercial banks: panel evidence from the period 1995–2002. In: 37th Annual Conference of the Money, Macro and Finance Research Group, 1–3 Sept 2005, Rethymno, Crete
Krakah AK, Ameyaw A (2010) Determinants of bank's profitability in Ghana. Working paper: Blekinge Tekniska Högskola. Available at http://www.camessays.com/upload/doc/Thesis%20bank.pdf
Krstić M (2012) The role of rules in the evolution of the market system: Hayek's concept of evolutionary epistemology. Econ Ann 57(194):123–140
Martinho R, Oliveira J, Oliveira V (2017) Bank profitability and macroeconomic factors. Financial Stability Factors, Bank of Portugal. Available online at https://www.bportugal.pt/sites/default/files/anexos/papers/paper_5_en.pdf
Mirzaei A, Moore T, Liu G (2013) Does market structure matter on banks' profitability and stability? Emerging vs. advanced economies. J Bank Financ 37(8):2920–2937
Naceur SB (2003) The determinants of the Tunisian banking industry profitability: Panel evidence. Universite Libre de Tunis Working Papers
Olson D, Zoubi TA (2011) Efficiency and bank profitability in MENA countries. Emerg Mark Rev 12:94–110
Onofrei M, Bostan I, Roman A, Firtescu BN (2018) The determinants of commercial bank profitability in CEE countries. RomIan Stat Rev 2:33–46
Pan Q, Pan M (2014) The impact of macro factors on the profitability of China's commercial banks in the decade after WTO accession. Open J Soc Sci 2:64–69
Rivard RJ, Thomas CR (1997) The effect of interstate banking on large bank holding company profitability and risk. J Econ Bus 49(1):61–76
Sayilgan G, Yildirim O (2009) Determinants of profitability in Turkish banking sector: 2002–2007. Int Res J Financ Econ 28:207–213
Staikouras CK, Wood GE (2004) The determinants of European bank profitability. International Business and Economics Research Journal 3(6):57–68
Sufian F (2009) Factors influencing bank profitability in a developing economy: Empirical evidence from Malaysia. Glob Bus Rev 10(9):225–241
Trujillo-Ponce A (2013) What determines the profitability of banks? Evidence from Spain. Account Financ 53(2):561–586

The manufacturer's authorised representative in the EU is Springer
Nature Customer Service Centre GmbH, Europaplatz 3, 69115 Heidelberg,
Germany. If you have any concerns regarding our products, please
contact ProductSafety@springernature.com

Printed and bound by CPI Group (UK) Ltd, Croydon, CR0 4YY
30/09/2026
02225687-0001